2/00

THE ENCYCLOPEDIA OF 20TH CENTURY CONFLICT

SEA WARFARE

THE ENCYCLOPEDIA OF 20TH CENTURY CONFLICT

SEA WARFARE

PAUL KEMP

ARMS AND
ARMOUR

Arms and Armour
An Imprint of the Cassell Group
Wellington House, 125 Strand,
London WC2R 0BB

First published 1998

British Library Cataloguing-in-Publication
Data: a catalogue record for this book is
available from the British Library

ISBN 1-85409-221-9

Distributed in the USA by Sterling
Publishing Co. Inc., 387 Park Avenue South,
New York, NY 10016-8810.

Designed and edited by DAG Publications
Ltd. Designed by David Gibbons; edited by
Michael Boxall; layout by Anthony A. Evans;
printed and bound in Great Britain by
The Bath Press, Bath.

CONTENTS

INTRODUCTION

Naval warfare in the twentieth century has been more destructive than at any other time in history. In the days of sail there were tremendous sea battles involving hundreds of ships but few ships were actually sunk. This was not because wooden ships were able to absorb more punishment and stay afloat if seriously damaged, rather because there was no effective weapon that could sink a ship. The technological revolution in naval warfare which dominated the latter half of the nineteenth century provided such weapons in abundance. A century elapsed between Nelson's victory at Trafalgar in October 1805 and the equally significant Japanese victory at the Battle of Tsushima in May 1905. Yet at Trafalgar only one enemy ship was sunk and seventeen were taken; at Tsushima twenty-nine out of the thirty-eight Russian ships engaged were sunk. The nature of naval warfare had changed for ever.

Another feature of the twentieth century has been the rise and fall in the naval power and influence of a number of countries. At the beginning of the century the Royal Navy was unchallenged. Not only was it the largest single fleet but it possessed a world-wide network of bases and superb telegraphic communications. During this century new navies have come into being, either through the birth of new nations, such as Germany, Israel and Italy, or through the revitalisation of empires, such as Austria-Hungary and Japan. Other navies have expanded as nations, notably the United States and the Soviet Union, have realised the value of seapower. Two of the older navies which in their day had held tremendous influence, those of Spain and the Netherlands, have declined to the point where they no longer influence world events outside their own territorial waters. Some navies, such as those of Austria-Hungary and Yugoslavia, have disappeared altogether as a result of political change. Others, such as that of Iraq, have been completely wiped out in conflict. At the time of writing China, a country of unfulfilled potential, is on the brink of becoming a super-power in her own right.

1905-14 Navalism Triumphant

The nine years which elapsed between the Battle of Tsushima and the outbreak of the First World War witnessed an unparalleled period of naval expansion and development. The pace was set by the Royal Navy, which in 1906 produced HMS *Dreadnought*, a new type of capital ship which rendered all her predecessors obsolete by a combination of large-calibre guns, armour protection and great speed. Other countries, notably Italy and the United States, were working towards a *Dreadnought*-type design, but the extraordinary dynamism of Admiral Fisher, allied to Britain's industrial base, enabled the ship to be produced within twelve months. The naval race which was to be a prime factor in the instability of European diplomatic relations was on. Germany, France, Italy, Austria-Hungary, the United States, Japan and Spain all rushed to produce their own *Dreadnought*-type designs. Possession of such a ship was the outward symbol of great-power status and no nation aspiring to such a position could afford to be without one. The main naval race between Britain and Germany in the North Sea produced similar rivalries in the Adriatic between Italy and Austria-Hungary, in the Aegean between Greece and the Ottoman Empire and in South America, where Brazil, Chile and Argentina all sought to acquire this new status symbol.

The development of the *Dreadnought*-type was rapid. In an eight-year period average tonnages rose by 50% from some 21,000 tons to 31,000 tons. Gun

Above: Commander E. O. Bickford at the periscope in HMS *Salmon*. British submarines were unique in that the attack periscope and tactical instruments were located in the main body of the control room and not in a separate conning tower. (RNSM)

calibres increased from 12in to 15in and ever more powerful engines maintained the top speed of these behemoths at around 24kts. Improvements in the nascent science of fire control extended the probability of scoring hits on a moving target at ranges out to the visible horizon. But there were signs by the summer of 1914 that the sheer cost of the naval race might bring about its termination. The responsibilities of government had extended into the fields of economic intervention and social welfare, and even in Britain, where the Royal Navy was regarded as nothing less than a temporal manifestation of divine will, there was no longer a blank cheque for naval expenditure. Moreover, there were fears about the vulnerability of the battle fleet (into which vast national resources had been sunk) in the face of the threat posed by the submarine and the mine. There arose the concept of 'Flotilla Defence', whereby massed flotillas of torpedo boats and submarines could effectively contain the enemy fleet while preserving one's own battle fleet. Certainly the British Government was seriously considering switching funds voted for capital ship construction towards destroyer and submarine programmes instead before the declaration of the First World War put an end to such thinking

Capital ship development tended to overshadow equally significant progress in other areas. The small and extremely hazardous submersibles which had entered the order of battle of the world's navies from the early days of the century had matured into ocean-going vessels of some sophistication. There were also those who prophesied that the first hesitant experiments with naval aviation promised much for the future.

Above all, the period 1905–14 was a period of intense public involvement in naval affairs: never before or since has the average citizen had such a knowledge of or interest in the subject. This situation was encouraged by the popular press, which presented the capital ship as the sum of all the industrial and scientific developments of the age. Public interest was also fanned by pressure groups such as the Navy League in Britain and the *Flottenverein* in Germany. The latter in particular was a phenomenally effective and successful organisation, funded by the German steel industry, which had

a membership of over 240,000 at the turn of the century.

The First World War saw all this new technology put to the test. Attempts to integrate submarines and aircraft into the main body of the battle fleet were not always successful, and of the various new developments in naval warfare only the submarine exceeded the claims made for it by its advocates. The projected clash between the two fleets in the North Sea (Jutland, 31 May 1916) did not result in a decisive victory for either side. So much money and material had been poured into the battle fleets that to risk them was thought to be imprudent – hence they remained behind their net and boom defences while the burden of war fell on smaller forces. The failure to win a significant victory with their battle fleet and the pressures exerted by the British blockade led the Germans to use their submarines in an offensive against British merchant shipping. This came as close as anything did during the First World War to bringing Britain to the point of surrender. The introduction of the convoy system (although 'reintroduction' might be a more appropriate term) saved the day, although refusal to do so earlier represented a major failing on the part of the British war leadership. It did, however, illustrate the fact that although technology has advanced and changed naval warfare out of all recognition, the classical tenets of sea power remain the same. Convoy was as relevant in 1917 as when King John set out with his fleet for France in 1213.

The inter-war period was a period of stagnation. Naval construction was limited by a series of disarmament treaties (Washington in 1922 and London in 1930 and 1936) which imposed quantitative and qualitative limits on the size and number of warships which could be constructed. As a result reduced fleets were the norm and there was little technical progress. If there was one exception it was in the development of naval aviation, with the United States and particularly Japan taking the lead. Britain was also a major player in this field although divided control of and lack of funding for the Fleet Air Arm meant that progress was not as fast as the British would have liked. Britain faced the additional problem of having to protect a large and far-flung empire with totally inadequate resources. This problem was exacerbated by Britain's major ally in the Far East, Japan, being transformed into a potential enemy by the ending of the Anglo-Japanese alliance, a partnership which had served both parties well.

The Second World War saw some very intense naval fighting, with aircraft exerting an ever greater influence on naval operations. The aircraft carrier matured into a major capital ship in her own right on account of the potential of her air group for reconnaissance, strike and air defence duties. By the end of the Second World War carrier aircraft could deliver the same salvo (in terms of weight of explosive) as a light cruiser, and this capability was enhanced by the aircraft being able to deliver it over a much greater distance. In the Pacific, aircraft carriers enjoyed the capability of using air power to strike or protect the fleet without having to recourse to airfields ashore. The same theatre witnessed a new phenomenon – sea battles (Midway and the Philippine Sea) fought between carrier aircraft where the opposing ships did not sight one another. In the Atlantic a trade protection campaign was fought by Allied convoys against German U-boats from the very first day of the war until the last.

The development of electronics was another significant aspect of naval warfare during the Second World War. The First World War had seen electronics used for radio communication, interception of radio traffic and the development of underwater detection apparatus. For reasons of economy these advances had not been taken very much further down the road in the 1919–38 period, but the spur of another world war provided the impetus for massive advances. The development of radar permitted the detection of targets beyond the limits of visual detection and the control of aircraft and guns at ranges and under weather conditions previously unheard of. Other electronic developments transformed the primitive pre-war asdic into a precise submarine detection device and improved the means of interception and exploitation of enemy wireless traffic. Another electronic battle, though fought far from the sea, was the skilled application of mathematics to crack enemy codes using sophisticated electronic calculating machines.

The defeat of Nazi Germany in Europe and a successful campaign against Japan through the Pacific islands required that the Allies develop a capability to land and maintain troops on a hostile shore. This led to the development of a whole new fleet of ships and floating vehicles for amphibious warfare. The sheer distances involved in operations, particularly in the Pacific, required ships that were capable of keeping a fleet at sea for months on end without recourse to a shore base and fully supplied with every conceivable commodity, from fuel and ammunition to the latest Hollywood movie and the all-important mail. The development of techniques for replenishing a fleet at sea restored true strategic mobility – a feature which had been absent since the days of the Revolutionary and Napoleonic Wars. In the final analysis the Allies won the Second World War because of their command of the sea and their ability to land their ground forces at a place and time of their choosing to retake the territory of their enemies. In all cases this ability was sustained by sea power.

Sea power had reached unprecedented levels of capability during the Second World War, capable of being projected on, over and under the water with considerable effect. The combination of naval with air power was extremely potent, combining speed and flexibility with the proviso that aircraft carriers could adapt to handling the larger and faster aircraft demanded by the planners. The battleship, which had been the *ne plus ultra* of naval warfare, was banished to the role of fire-support ship or anti-aircraft defence ship for a carrier group. Smaller ships had had to deal with the threats posed by aircraft and submarines and had adapted to this multi-threat environment rather well.

The explosion of the two atomic bombs over Hiroshima and Nagasaki appeared to alter all forms of warfare for ever. The proponents of air power argued that political influence could now be exerted by a fleet of nuclear-capable bombers and that there was no longer a role for large-scale naval forces. These arguments enjoyed a certain limited validity. Surface ships, amphibious fleets and port facilities were vulnerable to a nuclear strike. However, these arguments were tackled resolutely by naval planners, with the result that there was still a significant role for sea power. To begin with, any nuclear role, though devastating, would not result in total world

Above: The 'Jolly Roger' of the British submarine *Unseen* on her return from the Mediterranean. The symbols on the flag refer to six successful gun actions, eleven ships sunk by torpedo and two Axis submarines sunk. The dagger refers to one special operation successfully carried outwhile the train and oil refinery symbols refer to successful shore bombardments. (Author)

destruction because of the limited number of warheads available and the rather crude methods of delivery – dropping a bomb from an aircraft remained the only method of delivering a nuclear weapon for some time. Following a limited nuclear exchange there might well follow a 'broken-backed' form of warfare in which naval assets would be highly significant. Secondly, it was realised that it would be possible to deploy nuclear weapons at sea (thus eliminating the vulnerability of an airfield to a pre-

emptive strike), giving aircraft carriers and submarines a new, strategic role.

The other feature of the post-1945 period was the rapid collapse of the wartime Anglo-Soviet-American alliance into two ideological camps, a period which lasted until 1989 and which is known as the Cold War. The massive predominance of the USSR in land warfare was to a certain extent balanced by NATO's control over the North and Eastern Atlantic, from where strikes could be launched on the USSR. The

Korean War (1950–53) showed that the next war would be by no means a devastating nuclear exchange. Sea power during this conflict was low key but important. It enabled MacArthur to deliver his knock-out blow at Inchon in September 1950 and it allowed supplies to be maintained, coastal bombardments to be carried out by warships and the projection of power to inland targets by means of carrier-based aircraft. This was a pattern of operations that would be repeated off Vietnam fifteen years later. It was only in the field of mine warfare that the communists made any advances.

Technical developments during this period centred on the aircraft carrier and the submarine. The introduction of jet-powered aircraft finally placed carrier aircraft on a performance par with land-based aircraft. German submarine technology was exploited by the British and Americans in the introduction of streamlined, high-speed diesel-electric submarines. However these boats were still constrained by the need to surface or snorkel to charge their batteries. It was not until the introduction of the nuclear submarine with its almost limitless qualities of speed and endurance that the true submarine was created. The nuclear-powered fleet submarine, with its armament of cruise missiles, homing torpedoes and mines and almost limitless qualities of speed and endurance, has supplanted the aircraft carrier as the new capital ship. Other developments in the field of guided weapons have greatly increased the range at which engagements can be fought.

The nuclear submarine and the 'super carrier' represent one end of the spectrum of naval development but there was still a significant role for smaller, less technologically sophisticated craft. The Indonesian Confrontation in the early 1960s showed ships of frigate size and below playing a very important role in maintaining Malaysian territorial integrity. Indeed, financial constraints meant that small warships were all that most countries could afford. However, the development of sophisticated guided weapons such as the Exocet missile gave these ships a much greater punch than their size would suggest.

The Cold War ended in 1989–90 and its forty-year existence represented a high point in naval development, certainly in terms of the massive resources which both the Americans and the Soviets poured into their navies. Despite the end of the Cold War, the world remains a very unquiet place. The discipline imposed on international relations by the superpower rivalry had led to the outbreak of many nasty little wars which threaten the economic interests of the West and thereby threaten to embroil Western forces. A review of these areas (listed in no particular order) does not make for optimistic reading.

The Aegean

Greece and Turkey are not comfortable bedfellows despite their joint membership of the NATO alliance, which has failed to put the lid on centuries of enmity. The Cyprus question remains a perennial thorn in relations between the two countries following the Turkish invasion of 1974 and the declaration of an autonomous state in the north of the island. An additional ingredient to an already volatile brew is the Greeks' threat to increase their territorial waters in the Aegean from a six-mile to a twelve-mile zone. This would have the effect of turning much of the Aegean Sea into a Greek lake and is, not surprisingly, unacceptable to Turkey. In return, the Turkish Government, never shy to threaten or use force in furtherance of its aims, has threatened to annex Greek islands off the Turkish coast. Both countries are engaged in as much expansion of their fleets as budgets will allow, while both have benefited from the 'cascading down' of ex-US Navy vessels and weaponry since the end of the Cold War. The situation remains extremely volatile.

The South Atlantic

Although Britain and Argentina have come to a *modus vivendi* (full diplomatic relations were reestablished in 1990) following the 1982 Falklands War, there is no guarantee that the situation will remain thus. The Argentine military *Junta* which launched the war has been replaced by a democratically elected government. Alas, democratic governments do not have a record of particular longevity in South America, and should the military ever return to power in Buenos Aires then the 'Malvinas question', which remains an issue of extraordinary potency in Argentina, would be the perfect stick with which to whip up popular sentiment while distracting attention from less palatable issues on the home front. Argentina has never renounced her claim to sovereignty over the islands and has even refused to allow the bodies of her war dead which lie buried on the Falklands to be repatriated. The presence of the Argentine dead gives Argentina a potential future *casus belli* on the issue. The possible presence of massive oil and gas deposits around the Falklands as well as the economic importance of the fishing industry in the area only serve to focus attention on this part of the world. Moreover, the commitment to maintain a high-profile naval presence around the islands is yet one more burden placed on the Royal Navy.

The Persian Gulf

At the upper end of the Persian Gulf the situation is fairly calm. Although Saddam Hussein has managed to remain in power, his naval forces were wiped out in the 1991 Gulf War when the Iraqi Navy ceased to exist as an operational force. There is no domestic shipbuilding base and UN sanctions make it an unlikely prospect that Saddam will be able to replace his losses by buying abroad. The naval rearmament being vigorously pursued by Iraq's Gulf neighbours will be able to keep him in check for some time. However, at the southern end of the Gulf the Iranian Government remains implacably hostile to the West and is now acquiring modern Soviet built 'Kilo' class SSKs. This represents a dangerous boost in weapons proliferation in an area of fundamental economic importance to the West. Iran is also embarking on a substantial midget submarine building programme using both an indigenous design and a version imported from North Korea. The purposes for which such craft are intended are not clear, but since Iran has been castigated as a supporter of international terrorism they are presumably intended for the landing of special forces to subvert pro-Western governments and stir up Muslim fundamentalism. Para-naval Iranian forces (operated by the Revolutionary Guards) in the Straits of Hormuz have not abandoned their piratical activities against commercial shipping, which include the extraction of 'tolls' at gunpoint. Iran has successfully surmounted the West's arms embargo by acquiring missiles, mines and ordnance from Russia, China and North Korea.

Despite being given a comprehensive drubbing by the US Navy in 1987 and in 1988, the Iranian Navy retains a substantial missile and minelaying capability and, given the unstable nature of the Iranian Government, has the capability to do anything.

The Korean peninsula

The Korean peninsula remains the scene for the last conflict arising from the Cold War. The Democratic Peoples' Republic of (North) Korea (DPRK) and the Republic of (South) Korea (RoK) have never achieved any relationship other than mutual hostility. During the Cold War both sides were backed by their superpower supporters and this was reflected in the development of their respective navies. The DPRK is the last unreconstituted communist regime left in the world and has carried out an unremitting hit-and-run campaign against the RoK since the end of the Korean War which shows no sign of abating. The order of battle of the DPRK Navy reflects its mission: submarines for offensive action against RoK vessels, the seaborne reinforcement in time of crisis, minelaying; small surface ships for coast defence and an array of assault craft (midget submarines, SDVs and fast motor boats) for special operations. Like Iran, North Korea is a sponsor of international terrorism and an exporter of midget submarines to her like-minded allies, Iran and Libya. Although economic collapse may have put a brake on Pyongyang's ambitions, the DPRK remains a dangerous and uncertain player in world events.

The People's Republic of China

The simultaneous collapse of the Soviet Union in the Far East and the rapid economic growth resulting from deregulation has enabled the Peoples' Republic of China to lay claim to the title of regional superpower. The end of the threat posed by the Soviet Union in the Far East has allowed the Chinese Government to focus its attentions on other, wider, areas of concern. The question of Taiwan ('the sacred mission of reunification', to quote official Chinese Government policy) remains of perpetual interest to the old men in Beijing. The question of the Spratly Islands ('living space' in 1990s Beijing terminology) and their potentially massive mineral reserves is also of considerable interest. The Chinese Government seems bent on a resolution of these questions in their favour despite the fact that a forced solution to one or both questions would bring them into conflict, directly or indirectly, with Russia, India, North Korea, South Korea (it would be no mean feat for China to make an enemy of both Koreas at the same time), Malaysia, the Philippines, Taiwan, Vietnam, Brunei, Japan, the United Kingdom and the United States. In March 1996 the Chinese attempted to influence the outcome of elections in Taiwan by a display of military and naval might. However, the prompt dispatch of two USN carrier battle groups into the Taiwan Strait demonstrated to the Chinese the limitations of the current fleet. The lesson has not been lost: China is engaged on a considerable naval expansion programme, and more muscle-flexing by Beijing can be expected.

The Future

Predicting that there is no future role for navies or maritime trade has been a fashionable intellectual exercise for the past fifty years. However, the truth is exactly the opposite. The world economy depends on trade, the bulk of which moves by sea since air transport is limited to passengers and high value/low volume freight. Another factor is the growing exploitation of undersea natural resources. Thus two of the fundamental generators of a requirement for naval forces remain intact. The security of maritime trade and the protection of a nation's undersea natural resources require maritime forces. Human nature has always produced a tendency for some individuals to seek advantage by unscrupulous means. Piracy in the Far East is on the increase, as is the incidence of drug-smuggling by sea. On a larger scale, the invasion of territory by governments who thought they could get away with the act without sanction or remedial action have occurred, for example in the Falklands in 1982 and in Kuwait in 1990.

Sea power played a central role in the resolution of both these conflicts. In 1982 the Royal Navy exploited its sophisticated submarine fleet to eliminate a major unit of the Argentine Navy and then to blockade the rest of its ships in harbour. Britain could then use the South Atlantic to launch an amphibious assault on the islands which resulted in their liberation. Where the Royal Navy was deficient,

particularly in the lack of any AEW, the Argentines exacted similar penalties using their very capable air forces to sink four British warships and a valuable stores ship and damage many others The role of sea power in the liberation of Kuwait was less high-profile but nonetheless important. The massive military build-up in Saudi Arabia was only possible by the movement of men and equipment by sea. The threat of an amphibious landing tied down thousands of Iraqi troops, while an effective mine countermeasures capability largely negated extensive Iraqi mining of the northern waters of the Persian Gulf. Lastly, carrier air power augmented the already considerable Coalition air forces with strikes against targets deep in Iraq, strikes that were complemented by cruise missiles fired from ships and submarines.

The Gulf War showed that sea power is indivisible from geography or economics or from other aspects of military power. There is nothing very new in this statement. Nelson was perfectly aware that the Royal Navy alone could not defeat Napoleon, but the twentieth century has provided pertinent examples of this. Technology is likely to play a major role in naval warfare. The increasing cost of warships means that there are likely to be fewer of them and there will be more reliance on electronic systems, including stealth technology, for defence and protection against attack. The underwater war – always the most effective and efficient method of sinking ships – will hardly go away. The export of diesel-electric submarines is one of the few aspects of naval construction to have increased since 1945 and the continued development of midget submarines for surveillance and sabotage is a cause for concern.

One trend which has become apparent in post-Cold War operations has been the importance placed on naval, land and air units operating together under a joint command structure. This requires great forbearance on those involved to bury their loyalty to their own service in favour of the common good, and whether it works or not will be tested over the coming decades. Another trend is that operations in support of maritime economic assets, oil and gas deposits, fishing grounds etc., will continue to be important. Piracy, too, is a problem which requires suppression. Thus there will always be a need for relatively unsophisticated naval forces to tackle these important tasks at the lower end of the scale.

It would be remarkable, and the first such period in the history of man, if the twenty-first century were to proceed without a conflict of medium or high intensity. There is thus considerable uncertainty about the challenges faced by sea power from the year 2000. What can be said with confidence is that there will be a role – and a significant one – for sea power in the year 2000 and beyond.

Acknowledgements

There are three main sections to this Encyclopedia. The first is a year-by-year chronology of naval events from 1900 to 1998. Then comes an 'A to Z', which seeks to explain, as simply as possible, the events, battles, hardware and terminology used by navies in this turbulent century. Finally there are biographies of personalities, prominent and not so prominent, who have shaped naval events this century. It should be borne in mind that this volume is one of a trilogy. Similar volumes produced by other authors exist on land and air warfare.

I must thank all those who supplied information and photographs for the book. Writing an encyclopedia has been a fascinating if fraught project which I would never have dreamed of attempting, so I must also thank Rod Dymott of Arms & Armour Press for giving me the chance to so.

Paul Kemp
Maidstone

Above: A US Coast Guard Cotter approaches to refuel from a Norwegian tanker in mid Atlantic in 1944. the development of under replensihment techniques during the Second World War made a significant difference to the conduct of naval operations. (USN)

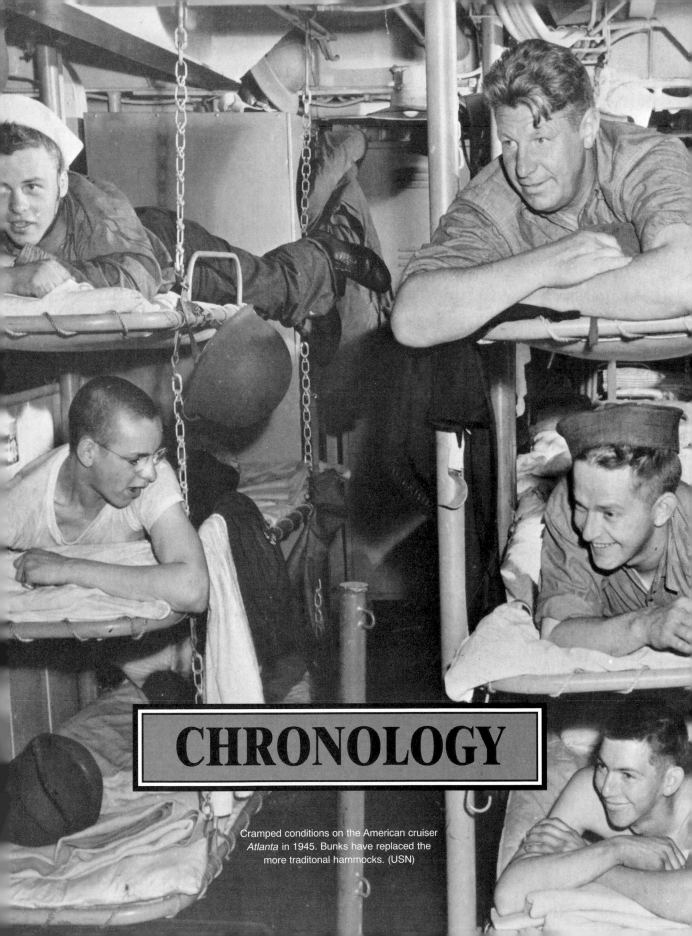

CHRONOLOGY

Cramped conditions on the American cruiser *Atlanta* in 1945. Bunks have replaced the more traditonal hammocks. (USN)

1900

5 January. The United States dispatches two cruisers to Nicaragua in order to protect US interests and US nationals in the fighting between Nicaragua and Costa Rica.

11 April. The US Navy Department formally purchases the submarine *Holland* from the J. P. Holland Boat Company for $150,000. In 1947 Navy Secretary James V Forrestal will declare 11 April to be Submarine Day.

12 June. The Second German Naval Law is passed (the first was in 1897).

1901

2 October. Launch of the Royal Navy's first submarine, *Holland 1*, at Barrow. Britain becomes the third nation to acquire a submarine.

28 October. Launch of the cruiser HMS *King Alfred* at Barrow. Press reporting of the event describes the ship as the world's fastest cruiser.

7 November. French naval forces occupy the island of Mytilene in the eastern Mediterranean, forcing Turkey to pay compensation for losses suffered by French interests in 1896.

1902

30 September. In Great Britain, the Cunard company agrees to place all its vessels at the disposal of the Admiralty in the event of a war in return for an annual subsidy.

19 October. Britain announces that all small naval bases in China will be closed and all repair facilities concentrated at Hong Kong.

9 December. British and German warships bombard Caracas and seize the Venezuelan Navy to force the Venezuelan Government to pay compensation for losses suffered in the 1899 *coup d'état*. Following the bombardment a blockade is imposed, which will be lifted on 13 February 1903, and the dispute will be settled on 22 February 1904. In the Far East, the signing of the Anglo-Japanese Naval Treaty guarantees Japanese protection of British possessions in that region.

1903

11 January. Considerable alarm is caused by (untrue) press reports that a Russian torpedo boat has made a secret transit of the Bosporous and Dardanelles.

22 January. The United States and Colombia sign the Panama Canal Treaty and fix a six-mile US zone on both sides of the canal.

6 March. The British Government announces the construction of a major naval base at Rosyth on the south side of the Firth of Forth.

Above: HM *Submarine No. 1* on the crane at Barrow in 1901. Compare this photograph with that of the SSBN HMS *Victorious* (page 254) as an indication of how far submarine development has come this century. (Author)

6 May. Italian and Austrian warships are dispatched to Macedonia to assist the Turks in quelling a local uprising. The *Entente Cordial* between Britain and France is agreed. With Japan guarding Britain's interests in the Far East and France no longer a threat in the Mediterranean, Germany is now left as Britain's main naval rival.

1904

10 February. A Japanese attack on Port Arthur starts the Russo-Japanese War.

13 April. The Russian battleship *Petropavolovsk* is lost in the Far East.

14 August. The Battle of the Japan Sea takes place. In Britain, the creation of Home Fleet marks a concentration of naval forces in home waters.

15 October. Russia's Baltic Fleet is dispatched to the Far East to offset losses suffered in the war against Japan.

1905

2 January. The Russian garrison at Port Arthur surrenders.

27/28 May. The Battle of Tsushima sees a crushing victory by the Imperial Japanese Navy over the Russian Fleet.

27 June. The Russian Black Sea Fleet mutinies.

1906

10 February. HMS *Dreadnought*, the first 'all big gun' capital ship, is launched. She will be adjudged completed in December of the same year when she undergoes her first basin trial.

19 May. In Germany, the First Naval amendment to the 1900 Second Naval Law is passed. This provides for five armoured cruisers plus forty-eight torpedo boats. It will be followed on 26 May by the passing of the regular budget which allocates funds for the construction of two capital ships together with funds for the widening of the Kiel Canal and improvements to dockyards.

15 November. The launch takes place of the Japanese Navy's first dreadnought battleship, *Satsuma*, at Kure Navy Yard.

5 December. In Russia, the trial of Admiral Niebogatov, the Russian naval commander in the Far East, begins.

1907

Sixteen American warships – the 'Great White Fleet' – begin a round-the-world cruise. The cruise will be completed in 1909, and although the voyage is dogged by mishap and scandal it is striking proof that the United States is capable of projecting naval power into the Far East and beyond.

The Anglo-French *Entente Cordial* is extended by the admission of Russia.

15 June. The second international conference takes place in The Hague (*see* Hague Convention for details).

11 December. British shipbuilders express concern to the government about the growing size and competence of the Japanese shipbuilding industry.

1908

7 March. The battleship *Nassau*, Germany's answer to HMS *Dreadnought*, is launched.

27 March. The Second Naval Amendment Act, which will rapidly accelerate German naval construction by authorising the ordering of four capital ships per year for the next four years, is passed. The passing of this legislation initiates the 'We want eight and we won't wait!' naval scare in Britain.

11 July. The United States' first dreadnought battleship, the USS *South Carolina*, is launched.

1909

The Declaration of London institutes the concept of naval establishments formed by the dominion governments of Australia, Canada and New Zealand.

14 November. The US Government announces the construction of a major base in the Pacific at Pearl Harbor on the island of Oahu.

1910

20 August. The first Italian dreadnought battleship, *Dante Alighieri*, is launched at Castellammare.

1 September. The first French dreadnought battleship, *Courbet*, is launched at Brest.

1911

January. In the United States, Eugene Ely lands a Curtiss biplane on a 120ft platform on the fantail of the USS *Pennsylvania*.

24 June. The first Austrian dreadnought battleship, *Viribus Unitis*, is launched at the STT Yard at Trieste.

27 June. The first Russian dreadnought battleship, *Sevastopol*, is launched at the Baltic Yard in St Petersburg.

1 July. The German gunboat

Panther is sent to Agadir following the French decision to intervene in the Moroccan civil war, thus precipitating a diplomatic crisis which, given the overheated state of European relations as a result of the naval race, could lead to war.

29 September. Italy declares war on Turkey for the possession of Tripolitania. *See* Italo-Turkish War.

5 November. The end of the Italo-Turkish War sees Italy take all of Turkey's North African possessions.

1912

10 January. An aircraft flown by Lt C. R. Samson RN, makes the first flight from the deck of a ship, the battleship HMS *Africa*, anchored at Sheerness.

5 February. The first Spanish dreadnought battleship, *España*, is launched at Ferrol. All the major naval powers now have dreadnought-type battleships in commission or under construction.

9 May. The first flight of an aircraft from a ship under way is made by Lt R. Gregory RN from the battleship HMS *Hibernia*.

21 May. Germany passes the Third Naval Amendment Act, which provides for three additional battleships and two light cruisers. The passing of this legislation means that that there is no hope of achieving any sort of naval *rapprochement* with Britain. War is inevitable: it only needs the appropriate incident.

17 October. In the eastern Mediterranean, the first Balkan War breaks out involving Italy,

Bulgaria, Montenegro and Serbia against Turkey. *See* Balkan War.

9 December. The first submarine attack takes place when the Greek submarine *Delfin* fires a torpedo at the Turkish cruiser *Medjidieh* in the eastern Mediterranean.

1913

30 May. The Balkan War ends: Greece has succeeded in taking all of Turkey's Aegean island possessions.

June. A secret naval agreement is concluded by Germany, Austria-Hungary and Italy (renewing an earlier agreement made in 1900) providing for a joint command and co-ordination of the operations of their naval forces in the Mediterranean in the event of war.

1914

June. Archduke Franz Ferdinand of Austria is assassinated at Sarajevo. The assassination provides the impetus for a general outbreak of hostilities in Europe as the various alliance systems trigger first the mobilisation of forces and then declarations of war.

July. A test mobilisation of the British Home Fleet takes place. Following the assassination of Archduke Franz Ferdinand, orders are issued on 26 July which keep the operational ships of the First Fleet – shortly to be renamed the Grand Fleet – together and on 27 July reserve units are reactivated.

28 July. The first shots of the First World War are fired when monitors of the Austro-Hungarian Danube flotilla bombard Serbian positions around Belgrade.

29 July. The Grand Fleet makes a

secret transit of the Strait of Dover, all ships darkened and steaming without lights, from Portland to the new base at Scapa Flow in the Orkney Islands. Thus British naval preparations for war are complete before the commencement of hostilities.

31 July. The German High Seas Fleet moves from the Baltic, where it had been concentrated against Russia, to the North Sea.

3 August. The German battlecruiser *Goeben* and cruiser *Breslau* bombard Phillipeville and Bône respectively in French North Africa. French coastal batteries return fire.

4 August. Britain declares war on Germany following the invasion of Belgium.

5 August. First blood goes to the Royal Navy with the sinking of the German minelayer *Königen Luise* in the North Sea. In the Mediterranean, *Goeben* and *Breslau* arrive at Messina.

9 August. *U15* is sunk by HMS *Birmingham* in the North Sea; this is the first sinking of a U-boat.

11 August. *Goeben* and *Breslau* reach the safety of the Dardanelles.

13 August. British naval forces bombard Dar-es-Salaam in German East Africa.

17 August. The Austrian light cruiser *Zenta* is sunk by the French Fleet at the entrance to the Adriatic. The destroyer *Ulan* escapes. This is followed on 24 August by a bom-bardment of the Austrian base of Cattaro by the French fleet.

27 August. The German cruiser *Magdeburg* is lost in the Baltic. Her ciphers are salvaged by the Russians and sent to Britain.

28 August. The Battle of the Heligoland Bight takes place.

30 August. The Japanese Navy, supported by the British battle-ship *Triumph* and destroyer *Usk*, land troops on the Shantung peninsula to lay siege to the German colony at Tsingtao.

5 September. HMS *Pathfinder* is sunk by *U21* in the North Sea. She is the first British warship to be sunk by a U-boat.

10 September. The German cruis-er *Emden* operates in the Bay of Bengal, causing considerable dis-ruption to British shipping. On 22 September *Emden* bombards the oil terminal at Madras, causing panic in the city.

21 September. By means of Orders in Council the British Government unilaterally enlarges the lists of Absolute and Conditional Contraband by adding many of the commodities which had previously been declared Free. The effect of these measures is to tighten the blockade on Germany.

22 September. The German sub-marine *U9* sinks the British cruis-ers *Hogue*, *Aboukir* and *Cressy* in less than two hours. In the Pacific, the German cruisers *Scharnhorst* and *Gneisenau* of the East Asia

Above: HMS *Hogue*. One of three British cruisers sunk on 22 September 1914 by the German submarine *U9*. (Author)

Squadron bombard Papeete in French Tahiti.

2 October. The British cruiser HMS *Cumberland* captures nine German merchant ships in the Cameroon River in West Africa.

3 October. The British Government announces the laying of a large defensive minefield in the North Sea.

7 October. Japan occupies the Marshall Islands.

17 October. The German destroyers *S.115*, *S.117*, *S.118* and *S.119*, on a minelaying operation in the Thames estuary, are intercepted off Texel by the cruiser HMS *Undaunted* and four destroyers. All four German ships are sunk. In the Far East, the German torpedo boat *S.90* breaks out of Tsingtao, sinks the Japanese cruiser *Takaschio.* and then is abandoned on the coast of China.

18 October. British naval forces support the Belgian Army in the Battle of the Yser River.

20 October. The British merchant ship *Glitra* is sunk by *U17*. This is the first sinking of a British merchant ship by a U-boat.

28 October. The German cruiser *Emden* attacks the harbour at Penang and sinks the Russian cruiser *Zemchung* and French destroyer *Mousquet*.

29 October. The Turkish Fleet, bolstered by *Goeben* and *Breslau*, bombard the Russian ports of Odessa and Novorossisk. The Russian gunboat *Donetz* is sunk at Odessa and the minelayer *Prut* off Sevastopol, and six Russian merchant ships are sunk or captured. The British Government further extends the lists of Absolute and Conditional Contraband.

1 November. The Battle of Coronel takes place in the South Pacific.

2 November. The British Government announces that from 5 November the entire North Sea will be a War Zone.

3 November. Ships of the German High Seas Fleet bombard the port of Yarmouth on the East Coast of England.

9 November. The German cruiser *Emden* is sunk at Direction Island by the Australian cruiser HMAS *Sydney*. Some of *Emden*'s ship's company, under the Executive Officer, escape on the schooner *Ayesha* and after myriad adventures reach Constantinople.

8 December. The Battle of the Falkland Islands.

Above: A British pre-dreadnought battleship providing fire support for British and dominion forces on the Galipolli peninsula in 1915.

13 December. The British submarine *B.11* (Lt Norman Holbrook RN) passes up the Dardanelles and sinks the old Turkish battleship *Messudieh.*

16 December. Hartlepool, Scarborough and Whitby are bombarded by ships of the High Seas Fleet.

25 December. RNAS aircraft attack German Zeppelin sheds at Cuxhaven. This is the first attack by shipborne aircraft on land targets.

1915

24 January. The Battle of the Dogger Bank takes place in the North Sea.

4 February. The German Government announces that the waters around the British Isles are to be regarded as a War Zone in which all ships, regardless of status and nationality, will be at risk. The War Zone will be effective from 18 February. This announcement marks the commencement of the first campaign of unrestricted submarine warfare.

23 February. The British Government announces that the entrance to the North Channel is closed to all shipping except for a small channel to the south of Rathlin island.

5 March. British naval forces begin a bombardment of the town of Smyrna to prevent the port being used as a submarine base by the Germans. At the same time the British also attempt (unsuccessfully) to suborn the loyalty of the Vali of Smyrna. The attack is called off on 15 March.

14 March. The German light cruiser *Dresden,* sole survivor of the German East Asia Squadron, is scuttled at Juan Fernandez Island after being found there by the British cruisers *Kent* and *Glasgow.*

18 March. Anglo-French naval forces attempt to force a passage of the Dardanelles and into the Sea of Marmara (and thereby threaten Constantinople). Gunfire from mobile shore batteries, whose fire cannot be suppressed by the battleships, prevents the minesweepers from clearing a way through the minefields. The Allied warships also run into a field of twenty mines laid by the Turkish minelayer *Nousret* parallel to the shore in Eren Keui Bay in the Dardanelles, with disastrous results. The British battleships

Above: A wrecked Italian train on the Adriatic coastline near Sennigailia. The train was destroyed by the Austrian battleship *Zrinyi* in the naval bombardment on 24 May 1915 which marked Italy's entry into the war. (Author)

Irresistible and *Ocean* and the French *Bouvet* are sunk and the battlecruiser *Inflexible* damaged. The failure of this operation leads to plans for a landing to be made on the Gallipoli peninsula.

28 March. The Russian Black Sea Fleet bombards Turkish forts at the northern end of the Bosporus. The operation is repeated on 25 April.

25 April. The Royal Navy supports the landings by British and Dominion troops at Cape Helles and Anzac Cove on the Gallipoli peninsula.

27 April. The French cruiser *Léon Gambetta* is sunk by the Austrian submarine *U5*. The sinking forces the French to withdraw all their heavy units from the Adriatic.

7 May. The Cunard liner *Lusitania*

is sunk by the German submarine *U20* while returning from the United States.

24 May. Austria declares war on Italy. Units of the Austrian fleet bombard towns on Italy's Adriatic coast.

25 May. The British battleship HMS *Triumph* is torpedoed by the German submarine *U21* (*Kapitän-leutnant* Otto Hersing) in the

Dardanelles. Two days later Hersing torpedoes and sinks the battleship HMS *Majestic*. The loss of two battleships in three days causes the British command to withdraw all capital ships from bombardment duties in support of the Army on the Gallipoli peninsula.

6 July. The British monitors *Severn* and *Mersey* begin the bombardment of the German cruiser *Königsberg*, which has taken refuge up the Rufiji river in German East Africa. Their gunnery is directed by RNAS aircraft. Although the monitors fire 633 rounds of 6in shell, only three hits are scored on *Königsberg*. A second bombardment is carried out on 11 July which results in *Königsberg*'s destruction.

7 July. The Italian cruiser *Amalfi* is torpedoed by the German sub-marine *UB14* in the Adriatic. Although Germany is not yet at war with Italy, the German U-boat flies Austrian colours and has been entered into the Austrian Navy List for administrative convenience. Coming so soon after the bombardment of the Adriatic coast, the loss of *Amalfi* causes a political crisis which results in the resignation of the Minister of Marine, Vice-Admiral Leone Viale, on 28 August.

18 July. The Italian cruiser *Giuseppe Garibaldi* is torpedoed by the Austrian submarine *U4* in the Adriatic.

19 August. *U24* torpedoes and sinks the liner *Arabic* in the Atlantic. Among the casualties are a number of US citizens. Following pressure from the US Government and from moderate elements within the German Government, restrictions are placed on U-boat operations which effectively end the first unrestricted warfare campaign as from 18 September.

27 September. The Italian battleship *Benedetto Brin* blows up while at anchor in Brindisi harbour as a result of Austrian sabotage. The casualties number 595, of which 456 are killed.

5 October. The first Anglo-French forces land in Salonika.

7 November. The Italian liner *Ancona* is torpedoed by the German submarine *U38* (*Kapitänleutnant* Max Valentiner) in the Mediterranean.

20 December. The evacuation of the beach-heads at Anzac Cove and Suvla Bay in the Dardanelles is completed. British forces are now concentrated at Cape Helles.

29 December. The French submarine *Monge* is rammed and sunk

Above: The Italian cruiser *Giuseppe Garibaldi* sinking on 18 July 1915 after being torpedoed by the Austrian *U4*. (Dott.Achille Rastelli)

Above: A German *UC1* class submarine minelayer in 1915. These small submarines caused havoc with their minelaying activities in the waters around the Thames Estuary and East Coast. (Author)

by the Austrian cruiser *Helgoland* in the Adriatic.

1916

6 February. In the Adriatic, a raid on the sea route between Brindisi and Durazzo by the Austrian cruiser *Helgoland* and six torpedo boats is frustrated when they were engaged by HMS *Weymouth* and the French destroyer *Bouclier*. In the confusion two of the Austrian TBs collide and the raid is abandoned.

8 January. The final evacuation of

British and Commonwealth forces from Cape Helles in the Dardanelles is completed.

4 March. The German Government announces the commencement of the second campaign of unrestricted submarine warfare against Britain.

24 March. The cross-Channel steamer *Sussex* is torpedoed by *UB29* in the English Channel. Among the casualties are a number of Americans. Diplomatic pressure from Washington causes the campaign to be abandoned

25 March. RNAS seaplanes bomb German targets in Sylt and Schleswig-Holstein.

24 April. Orders are issued to U-boats to cease unrestricted submarine warfare and operate in accordance with the Prize Rules.

24/25 April. Units of the German High Seas Fleet bombard Lowestoft on the East Coast of England. The German battlecruiser *Seydlitz* is mined and the British light cruiser *Conquest* is hit by five 12in shells and badly damaged.

31 May. The Battle of Jutland takes place in the North Sea.

5 June. The cruiser HMS *Hampshire*, carrying Lord Kitchener and his staff to Russia, is mined off the Orkney Islands.

2 August. The Italian dreadnought *Leonardo da Vinci* explodes at Brindisi with great loss of life.

19 August. The last sortie by the German High Seas Fleet takes place in the North Sea. The German battleship *Westfalen* is torpedoed by the British submarine *E.23* and the British lose the

Above: A near miss along the starboard side of the Austrian cruiser *Kaiser Karl VI*, during operations against Montenegrin positions on Mount Lovcen in January 1916. Mount Lovcen overlooked the Austrian base at Cattaro and the port was not fully secure until the Montenegrins were driven from the mountain in January/February 1916.
(Kriegsarchiv, Vienna)

Above: The successful German submaine *U35* returns to Cattaro after a successful cruise in the Mediterranean in 1916. (Author)

cruisers *Nottingham* and *Falmouth*. However, neither Jellicoe nor Scheer is prepared to risk an engagement and both sides retire.

2 November. In the North Sea, four British destroyers rescue the Dutch merchant ship *Oldenbarnevelt*, which has been taken by a force of German destroyers.

Elsewhere the Russian Black Sea Fleet bombards the port of Costanza, and again on 4 November. In the Aegean the White Star liner *Britannic*, which had been requisitioned as a hospital ship, is mined while outward-bound for Mudros. At 85,000 tons she is the largest single British merchant ship loss of the First World War.

4 November. The Norwegian Government protests to the German Government about the activities of German U-boats which are transiting Norwegian territorial waters.

29 November. In Britain, Admiral

Sir John Jellicoe becomes First Sea Lord and Admiral Sir David Beatty becomes CinC Grand Fleet.

8 December. The German *U38* (*Kapitänleutnant* Max Valentiner) bombards Funchal Roads on the island of Madeira and sinks three merchant ships. To save fuel Valentiner had a (neutral) Norwegian merchant ship tow his submarine to the island.

22/23 December. Six Austrian *Huszar* class destroyers raid the Otranto Barrage. Only one drifter is damaged but in the darkness two of the Anglo-French-Italian formations at sea to protect the Barrage collide and four destroyers are damaged.

1917

3 January. The British Government asserts the right of merchant ships to defend themselves when attacked.

4 January. The Russian battleship *Peresviet* is mined off Port Said by mines laid by *U73*.

9 January. The German Government takes the decision to commence unrestricted submarine warfare for a third time on 1 February.

22 January. The British are warned through radio intelligence of the transfer of the 6th Flotilla (eleven destroyers) from the Heligoland Bight to Zeebrugge and deploy the Harwich Force (six cruisers and eighteen destroyers) to intercept them. In a confused night action the German *V.69* is damaged (but manages to seek safety in Ijmuiden) and the remainder of the German ships escape.

31 January. The German Govern-ment announces that, following several repeated allegations that British hospital ships in the English Channel are carrying munitions, such vessels in the Channel will no longer be accord-ed protected status by German naval forces.

4 February. The crews of nine German merchant vessels which have been interned in Manila in the Philippines since the outbreak of war wreck their ships when they suspect that the vessels are to be seized by the US administration.

25 February. German destroyers based at Zeebrugge make a three-pronged attack on the Dover Barrage. The raid is unsuccessful and all three groups turn back when engaged by the British patrols. However the German destroyers do shell the North Foreland wireless station near Ramsgate, killing three civilians. In the Western Approaches, the Cunard liner *Laconia* is torpedoed by *U50* north-west of the Fastnet. Among the twelve casualties are four Americans.

February. Shipping losses for February total 520,412 tons.

17 March. Sixteen German destroyers raid the Dover Barrage and attack shipping anchored in The Downs. In the fighting the destroyer HMS *Paragon* is sunk and HMS *Llewellyn* damaged. One steamer at anchor outside the Downs is sunk and Ramsgate and Broad-stairs are shelled.

March. Shipping losses for March total 564,497 tons

April. Shipping losses for April total 860,334 tons. The German campaign of unrestricted subma-rine war is an astonishing success with an Exchange Rate of 167.

6 April. The Wilson administra-tion in the United States declares war on Germany as a direct result of the unrestricted submarine warfare campaign.

20/21 April. Twelve German destroyers bombard Dover and Calais before being engaged by HMS *Swift* and *Broke*. *Swift* torpe-does *G.85* and *Broke* rams *G.42*. While the two latter ships are locked together their crews fight a hand-to-hand action reminiscent of an earlier age.

10 May. The first Atlantic convoy of sixteen ships leaves Gibraltar for the UK. The convoy arrives in The Downs on 22 May without loss.

15 May. In the Adriatic, three Austrian cruisers raid the Otranto Barrage and sink fourteen drifters and damage four. Despite the deployment of sizeable Anglo-French-Italian forces in a favourable position between the Austrians and their base, the three Austrian cruisers escape and the cruiser HMS *Dartmouth* is dam-aged by a torpedo.

24 May. The first transatlantic convoy of twelve ships leaves Hampton Roads in the USA for the UK.

May. Shipping losses for May total 616,316 tons.

27 June. In the Atlantic, the hos-pital ship *Llandovery Castle* is tor-pedoed and sunk by *U86*; 234 of the survivors are drowned or killed by the U-boat's crew.

July. Shipping losses for July total 555,514 tons.

21 August. In the North Sea, a Sopwith Pup aircraft flown by Lt B. A. Smart RNAS is flown off from

Above: A meeting between *U35* and a small UC type submarine minelayer in the Mediterranean, 1917. (USN)

the cruiser HMS *Yarmouth* and shoots down the German Zeppelin *L.23*. This is the first combat success for an aircraft launched from a warship.

August. Shipping losses for August total 472,372 tons

September. Shipping losses for September total 353,602 tons

5 October. In the Adriatic, the crew of the Austrian torpedo boat *TB.11* are persuaded to lock up their officers and take the boat into internment in Italy.

9 October. Disturbances break out in the High Seas Fleet at Kiel but are suppressed.

17 October. In the North Sea, the German minelaying cruisers *Brummer* and *Bremse* attack a UK-bound Scandinavian convoy. The destroyers HMS *Mary Rose* and *Strongbow* are sunk, together with nine of the twelve merchant ships.

October. Shipping losses for October total 466,542 tons

November. Shipping losses for November total 302,599 tons

4 December. The Allied Naval Council is created in Paris to co-ordinate naval strategy.

5 December. German destroyers attack another Scandinavian convoy and sink all five merchant ships, four trawlers and the destroyer HMS *Partridge*.

9 December. The old Austrian coast defence battleship *Wien* is sunk at Trieste by an Italian MAS boat commanded by Lt Luigi Rizzo.

26 December. In Britain, the First Sea Lord, Admiral Sir John Jellicoe, is dismissed by the Government and replaced by Admiral Sir Rosslyn Wemyss.

December. Shipping losses for December total 411,766 tons.

1918

20 January. *Goeben* and *Breslau* make a dramatic sortie from the Dardanelles. The British monitors *Lord Raglan* and *M.28* are sunk off the island of Imbros but *Breslau* strays into a British minefield and sinks after striking five mines. *Goeben* is also mined but manages to reach the safety of the Dardanelles.

30 January. Following the Brazilian declaration of war against Germany (26 October 1917), the Brazilian Navy sends a squadron consisting of two cruisers, four destroyers and an auxiliary to European waters. However, mechanical problems with the ships and an outbreak of fever among their crews at Freetown delay their arrival at Gibraltar until the last days of the war, by which time the question of their employment will be academic.

January. Shipping losses for January total 295,630 tons.

1 February. A mutiny inspired by Croat nationalist and Bolshevik agitators breaks out in some units of the Austrian Navy based at Cattaro in the Adriatic. The crews of the light cruisers, destroyers and U-boats (who had seen the most fighting) remain loyal. The mutiny is eventually suppressed after shore-based artillery fires on the ships and over 800 sailors are landed to face court martial. Four

will be sentenced to death and shot.

14/15 February. German destroyers raid the Dover Barrage and sink one trawler and seven drifters and damage a paddle steamer, a trawler and five drifters.

February. Shipping losses for February total 335,202 tons.

3 March. In the North Sea, US naval forces commence the laying of the first two sections of the Northern Barrage.

21 March. Nine German destroyers and six torpedo boats raid the Dover Barrage but are repulsed, losing two of their number. However, in the confusion of a night engagement the French destroyer *Capitaine Mehl* torpedoes and damages HMS *Botha*. On the same night HMS *Terror* conducts a bombardment of Ostend. Although the German destroyers carry out a half-hearted bombardment of La Panne on 9 April, this operation marks the last German attempt to attack the Dover Barrage forces.

22 March. The Dutch Government is informed by Britain that all Dutch-flag shipping in Allied ports is to be seized.

March. Shipping losses for March total 368,746 tons.

1 April. The amalgamation takes place of the Royal Naval Air Service and Royal Flying Corps into the Royal Air Force.

3 April. Seven British submarines, some of which have operated in the Baltic since 1915, are blown up at Helsingfors to prevent their falling into Bolshevik hands.

22/23 April. The raid on Zeebrugge takes place.

April. Shipping losses for April total 300,069 tons.

10 May. A raid on Ostend takes place.

May. Shipping losses for May total 296,558 tons.

3 June. In the North Sea, US naval forces begin the laying of the third and final section of the Northern Barrage.

9 June. In the Adriatic, the Austrian Navy launches a raid on the Otranto Barrage in which for the first time the four *Tegetthoff* class dreadnoughts are to be employed. On the morning of 10 June the Italian *MAS.15* torpedoes and sinks the battleship *Szent István*.

June. Shipping losses for June amount to 268,505 tons.

19 July. The cruiser USS *San Diego* is lost off Long Island to a mine laid by *U156*. Although only six of her crew are killed, she is the US Navy's largest single loss during the First World War.

July. Shipping losses for July total 280,820 tons.

11 August. An operation by six British CMBs to attack German minesweepers at the mouth of the River Ems goes disastrously wrong when, owing the lack of wind, the supporting aircraft are unable to take off. The CMBs are engaged by up to thirteen German aircraft. Although they succeed in shooting down one Brandenburg W.29, three of their number are sunk and the remainder are so badly damaged that they are forced to seek shelter and internment in Holland. The episode is a striking example of the new dimension in naval warfare provided by aircraft.

August. Shipping losses for August total 310,180 tons.

7 September. In Britain, the Admiralty publishes a list of 151 German U-boat commanders who either have been killed or are prisoners of war.

September. Shipping losses for September total 171,972 tons.

2 October. In the Adriatic, British and Italian naval forces bombard the port of Durazzo on the Dalmatian coast. One Austrian steamer is burnt out and sunk and two others are damaged. However, the two Austrian warships in the port escape and the British cruiser HMS *Weymouth* has her stern blown off by the Austrian *U31*. This is the last naval action in which units of the *KuK Kriegsmarine* participate.

17 October. The Austrian Government announces that, as part of a series of decisions to put some distance between Vienna and Berlin, its submarines will no longer be operating outside the Adriatic.

31 October. The *KuK Kriegsmarine* is formally dissolved by Imperial decree. Ships in the Adriatic are handed over to the representatives of the new SHS (Slavs, Hrats and Slovenes – a convention which would eventually emerge as Yugoslavia) Government in the Adriatic. Ships on the Danube are handed over to the Hungarian Government. The following morning the battleship *Viribus Unitis* is sunk at Pola by a two-man Italian human torpedo.

October. Shipping losses for October total 116,237 tons.

3 November. Amid the disintegra-tion of the Austrian Empire the Italian destroyer *Audace* enters the former Austrian port of Trieste. On 4 November the Italians, evidently acting to a well-prepared plan, occupy Fiume and Zara on the Dalmatian coast and on the 5th they occupy the port of Pola. In the Baltic, the German High Seas Fleet mutinies at Kiel.

9 November. The battleship HMS *Britannia* is torpedoed off Cape Trafalgar by *UB50*. She is the last British battleship lost during the First World War.

11 November. An Armistice is signed at Compiègne ending hostilities. Germany and Austria are required to surrender the majority of their fleets for internment while negotiations for a peace treaty are in force.

13 November. An Anglo-French fleet passes up the Dardanelles to the city of Constantinople.

15 November. The German cruiser *Königsberg* arrives in the Firth of Forth carrying a German delegation headed by Rear-Admiral Meurer, who are to dis-cuss implementation of the terms of the Armistice. On 19 November the first U-boats arrive at Harwich for internment: by 1 December 114 U-boats have been interned.

November. Shipping losses for November total 10,233 tons.

21 November. *Der Tag*: the bulk of the German High Seas Fleet – nine battleships, five battlecruisers, seven light cruisers and forty-nine destroyers – arrives at Rosyth. After verification that the ships have been disarmed, they will be sent north to Scapa Flow for internment. At 11.00 that day Admiral Beatty makes the general signal 'The German ensign will be hauled down at sunset today, Thursday, and will not be hoisted again without permission.' The war is over.

1919

22 March. Two British motor launches, *ML.210* and *ML.228*, are seized by Red Guards in Budapest. They are returned, after being comprehensively looted, on 24 March.

Above: An American built Motor Launch in British service in 1918. These small but very seaworthy craft fulfilled a multitude of roles: port defence, anti-submarine duties, convoy escort, despatch vessel and many others. (USN)

Above: A replica of the British 18in naval gun- the largest employed in British naval service is towed up the River Thames during the 1919 Victory Celebrations. (Author)

23 March. In the Adriatic, the Italians stage a 'surrender' ceremony of the former Austrian ships named in the 1918 Armistice. Since no Austrian personnel are available, the ships are steamed to Venice with Italian crews.

16 April. An 'interim' German Navy (*Vorläufige Reichsmarine*) is established.

17 June. British CMBs sink the Russian cruiser *Oleg* at Kronstadt.

21 June. The warships of the former German High Seas fleet interned at Scapa Flow are scuttled by their crews in order to prevent the ships being parcelled out amongst the Allies.

18 August. The old Russian armoured cruiser *Pamiat Azova* is

sunk at Kronstadt by the British *CMB.74*.

1920

13 March. Former German naval personnel in a *Freikorps* unit entitled *Brigade Erhardt* join a revolt in Berlin against the provisions of the Versailles Treaty. The revolt is suppressed and there are counter-riots at Kiel and Wilhelmshaven.

Above: Surrender. A whaler from the British destroyer HMS *Forester* pulls past the abandoned Austrian battleship *Erzherzhog Franz Ferdinand* at Pola in February 1919. (Author)

1921

16 January. The trial begins at Leipzig of two officers of *U86* for the massacre of 234 survivors from the hospital ship *Llandovery Castle* on 27 June 1917.

21 July. In the United States, General 'Billy' Mitchell sinks the ex-German battleship *Ostfriesland* with six 2,000lb bombs during anti-shipping trials.

31 October. The ex-Emperor Karl of Austria-Hungary and the Empress Zita are taken into exile in the British gunboat HMS *Glowworm* following the failure of his second bid to regain the Hungarian throne.

13 December. The Washington Treaty, which places quantitative and qualitative limits on capital ship, aircraft carrier and cruiser construction, is concluded. Britain, America and (reluctantly) Japan agree to be bound by a 5:5:3 ratio.

1922

14 August. The Royal Navy evacuate the defeated Chinese President Sun-Yat-Sen from Canton and removed him to the safety of Shanghai.

1923

9 September. Seven US Navy destroyers are wrecked off Santa Barbara. Casualties amount to twenty-three killed.

October. German sailors from the cruiser *Hamburg* are landed to quell communist inspired riots in the city of the same name.

6 December. British, French, American, Japanese, Italian, and Portuguese warships arrive at Canton to protect the foreign-administered Customs House from being taken over by the Chinese. They remain in the port until April 1924 when the Chinese government offers Guarantees about the safety of the premises.

1924

30 September. The Allied Control Commissions, which have been overseeing the dismantling of Germany's naval forces and infrastructure in accordance with the terms of the Treaty of Versailles, are dissolved.

1925

7 January. The launch takes place of the (significantly named) cruiser *Emden*, the first warship to be built in Germany since the end of the First World War.

17 March. The British Government announces its intention to construct a major naval base at Singapore.

1926

3 May. In the British General Strike in support of the miners, ships and submarines of the Royal Navy supply electricity to keep vital industries and services running in port areas.

2 September. An Italian agreement with the Yemen allows Italy to dominate both coasts of the Red Sea.

1927

February. British, French, Italian and US warships gather at Shanghai and land forces to protect the city's International Settlement during fighting in the Chinese Civil War.

24 March. British and US warships carry out a retaliatory bombardment of Nanking following the murder of British and US citizens.

9 July. Talks in Geneva aimed at the further limitation of naval armaments break up in disagreement. A few more weeks of desultory negotiations cause the complete collapse of the enterprise in August.

1929

Britain and China sign an agreement whereby the latter will receive technical help and assistance from the Royal Navy in order to build up the Chinese Navy.

1930

31 January. British, French, Italian, Japanese and United States delegates assemble in London at a Conference aimed at the further limitation of naval armaments. On 21 March the French leave the talks, followed by the Italians on 3 April; the latter will not be bound by any settlement not including the French. On 21 April Britain, the USA and Japan sign a three-power treaty.

1931

13 September. Disturbances occur in the British Home Fleet at Invergordon when news breaks that the men of the Navy are going to face severe pay cuts as a result of Government economies brought about by the international financial crisis. The men return to their duties and the Fleet is dispersed after the Government rescinds the worst of the cuts and agrees to consider cases of hardship.

1932

28 January. Fierce fighting breaks out in Shanghai after the Japanese land armed sailors to retaliate for the burning of a Japanese-owned factory. The sailors are repulsed by Chinese troops and Japan pours more forces into the city in order to save face. The dispute is eventually settled by the personal diplomacy of Admiral Sir Howard Kelly, the British Commander-in-Chief. It is Britain's last moment of influence as an individual great power in the Far East.

1934

2 October. India. The Royal Indian Navy is formally established.

1935

16 March. The German Government announces that it no longer considers itself bound by the various disarmament clauses of the Versailles Treaty.

18 June. The Anglo-German Naval Agreement is concluded, allowing the Germans to build up to 35% of the strength of the Royal Navy.

October. The Royal Navy is put on a war footing in the Mediterranean as the League of Nations imposes sanctions on Italy.

1936

15 January. In the naval disarmament talks in London to draw up a replacement treaty for the 1922 Washington and 1930 London Naval Treaties – both of which expire at the end of 1936 – it proves impossible to find a formula acceptable to the Japanese, who walk out. On 25 March Britain, the US and France sign an agreement which the USSR also ratifies on 1 October. This provides for further reductions in naval armaments, but without the participation of Japan the naval disarmament framework is no longer valid.

17 July. The Spanish Civil War breaks out. Poor co-ordination among the ratings ensures that the Nationalist elements seize control of the dockyards at Ferrol and Vigo. Naval forces loyal to Government implement a blockade of the Strait of Gibraltar in order to prevent Nationalist reinforcements being sent from Spanish North Africa.

9 September. A conference in London agrees a policy of 'non-intervention' in the Spanish Civil War. Naval patrols are to be established to prevent either side importing arms from a third country.

29 September. The Spanish Nationalist cruisers *Canarias* and *Cervera* sink the destroyer *Ferrandiz* and damage *Gravina* during operations to clear the Strait of Gibraltar, thus allowing General Franco to transport 8,000 troops from Spanish North Africa.

1937

31 May. The German pocket battleship *Deutschland* bombards Almeria in Spain in retaliation for an attack on the ship by Republican aircraft. The British Air Ministry restores control of the Fleet Air Arm to the Admiralty.

August. The Italian submarine *Iride*, which is operating covertly in support of the Spanish Nationalist forces, attacks, but misses, the British destroyer *Havock.* The destroyer's counter-attack is equally unsuccessful.

10–14 September. In France, a conference at Nyon agrees to establish anti-piracy patrols in the Mediterranean to combat the activities of rogue submarines attached to the Nationalist cause in the Spanish Civil War.

November. Spanish Nationalist forces begin a complete naval blockade of the Spanish coast.

1938

5/6 March. The Battle of Cape Palos takes place, in which the cruiser *Balaere* is sunk.

April. The British Government vol-

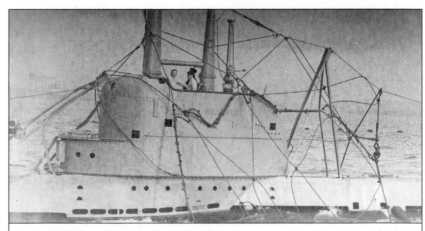

Above: HMS *Seawolf* festooned in netting after abortive attempts to breach an anti submarine net in trials in February 1938. Boom Defence is now largely a forgotten art. (Author)

untarily gives up its rights to the three 'Treaty ports' at Berehaven, Lough Swilly and Queenstown in Ireland.

September. The Royal Navy is mobilised during the crisis over the Sudetenland.

1939

14 February. The launch of the 35,000-ton battleship *Bismarck* takes place.

28 March. The Spanish Civil War ends in a complete victory for the Nationalist forces.

28 April. The German Government announces the unilateral abrogation of the Anglo-German Naval Agreement.

21 August. In view of the growing international crisis over Poland, the German Navy makes preparatory dispositions of surface ships and U-boats. The 'pocket battleship' *Admiral Graf Spee* makes a quiet departure from Germany for the South Atlantic on 21st and her sister ship *Deutschland* heads for the North Atlantic on the 28th.

Between the 19th and the 21st fourteen U-boats take up their positions around the British Isles as a precautionary move.

30 August. The Polish government takes the view that their small navy (four modern destroyers and five submarines) could have no real bearing on the fighting if Germany invaded, and take the decision to send the destroyers and one submarine to Britain. The other four submarines are dispatched to waiting positions in the western Baltic.

Above: A shocked survivor from the liner *Athenia* brought ashore in Eire, 3 September 1939 – a foretaste of the grim scenes that would be repeated – world-wide for the next five years.

31 August. Royal Navy reservists are 'called up' and the Fleet is placed on a war footing. The first steps are taken to institute the convoy system for merchant shipping and on 2 September the first convoy leaves from Gibraltar for Cape Town.

1 September. Germany invades Poland.

3 September. First the British (at 1100) and then the French (at 1700) declare war on Germany. Winston Churchill is appointed First Lord of the Admiralty, an office he relinquished in 1915. German warships begin a bombardment of Polish defences at Hela and Westerplatte in the Gulf of Danzig. The Polish destroyer *Wicher* and minelayer *Gryf* are sunk by air attack. The Polish garrison at Hela lasts out until 1 October before capitulating. In the Atlantic, the German submarine *U30* torpedoes and sinks the liner *Athenia*.

17 September. IIMS *Courageous* is torpedoed and sunk in the Western Approaches. She is the first British warship to be sunk in the Second World War.

9 October. The US-flag merchant ship *City of Flint* is captured by the pocket battleship *Deutschland* in the Atlantic. The ship is taken to Murmansk and then to Germany. But on 6 November the pocket battle is recalled to Germany and she returns via the Denmark Strait.

13/14 October. The battleship HMS *Royal Oak* is sunk at her moorings in Scapa Flow by the German submarine *U47* (*Kapitänleutnant* Günther Prien).

14 October. The Polish submarine *Orzel* arrives at Rosyth after an epic voyage from the Baltic.

November. The *Luftwaffe* begins a minelaying campaign in British waters using the new magnetic mine. This campaign results in the loss of the destroyer *Blanche* on the 13th (mined while escorting HMS *Adventure*, which has been damaged by a mine a few hours previously) and the destroyer *Gipsy* on the 21st. Submarine-laid mines also badly damage the new cruiser *Belfast* on 10 December.

8 November. Winston Churchill announces in the House of Commons that the Germans have claimed several times to have sunk the aircraft carrier *Ark Royal.*

21 November. For the first time a German magnetic mine is successfully recovered (off Shoeburyness) and defused.

23 November. The British armed merchant cruiser HMS *Rawalpindi* is sunk south of Iceland by the German battlecruisers *Scharnhorst* and *Gneisenau*

13 December. The Battle of the River Plate takes place. The pocket battleship *Admiral Graf Spee* is damaged by the gunfire of the cruisers HMS *Exeter, Ajax* and *Achilles* and takes refuge in Montevideo. After protracted diplomatic manoeuvrings *Admiral Graf Spee* is scuttled on 17 December.

Above: The German pocket battleship *Admiral Graf Spee* manoeuvres in Montevideo Roads on 17 December 1939, shortly before she was scuttled by her crew. The tender alongside is the *Tacoma* which would take the crew into internment in Argentina.

Above: The British destroyer HMS *Walker*, a V/W class destroyer built in 1918. Destroyers had to shoulder much of the escort work in both world wars, a task for which they were basically unsuited since they lacked the endurance required for convoy operations. (Author)

1940

21 January. The cruiser HMS *Gloucester* stops the Japanese liner *Asama Maru* off the Japanese island of Honshu and removes twenty-one German nationals. Following Japanese protests, the Germans are returned and Britain is forced to apologise.

10 February. HM Ships *Salve* and *Servitor* demonstrate the first successful 'sweeping' of a magnetic mine using an electrically charged loop of cable towed behind the vessel.

16 February. The destroyer HMS *Cossack* enters Jössingfjord (inside Norwegian territorial waters) to rescue some 299 British merchant seamen imprisoned on board the German tanker *Altmark*. The seamen were from the nine ships captured by *Admiral Graf Spee* during her commerce-raiding cruise in the South Atlantic.

23 February. Two German destroyers, *Leberecht Maas* and *Max*

Above: The German tanker *Altmark* heads into Jössingford in February 1940 while being shadowed by a British destroyer. Onboard were some 299 British seamen, freed on 16 February by HMS *Cossack*. (Author)

Schultz, are sunk in the North Sea. While proceeding down the safe channel in a German minefield, the destroyers are mistakenly attacked by a German aircraft, and in evading this attack the destroyers stray into a line of British mines laid to foul the swept channel.

7 March. The new British liner *Queen Elizabeth* arrives in New York, having made a secret voyage across the Atlantic.

8/9 April. The Germans launch a seaborne invasion of Norway. Coincidentally the British Home Fleet is also at sea, one part covering a minelaying operation and the main part cruising off Bergen to await developments. On 8 April the destroyer *Glowworm* is sunk by *Admiral Hipper* (which sustains severe damage in return). On 9 April the German cruiser *Blücher* and torpedo boat *Albatros* are sunk in Oslofjord by Norwegian coastal defences. However, at Narvik on 9 April the Norwegian warships *Eidsvold* and *Norge* are sunk. On the same day the Germans sink the torpedo boats *Aegir* at Stavanger and *Tor* at Frederikstad. German air attacks on the Home Fleet result in the loss of the destroyer *Gurkha* on 9 April, but on the same day the submarine HMS *Truant* sinks the cruiser *Karlsruhe*.

10 April. The first Battle of Narvik. On the same day Blackburn Skua dive-bombers of 800 and 803 Naval Air Squadrons fly from bases in the Orkney Islands to Bergen to attack the German cruiser *Königsberg* with 500lb bombs; the ship becomes the first major warship to be sunk by air attack in wartime.

13 April. The second Battle of Narvik.

10 May. The German invasion of the Low Countries places fresh strains on the Allied navies since the Norwegian campaign is still at a critical phase. Between 10 and 15 May German aircraft sink the Dutch warships *Van Galen* at Rotterdam, *Friso* at Ijsselmeer, *Johan Maurits van Nassau* at Callantsoog, *Brinio* at Ijsselmeer, *Tjerk Hiddes* and *Gerard Callenburgh* at Rotterdam and HMS *Valentine* at Terneuzen.

26 May. The decision is taken to evacuate the British Expeditionary Force by sea from the French port of Dunkirk. Operations last until 4 June, by which time more than 335,000 British, French and Belgian troops and civilians have been evacuated. An armada of 720 ships of all descriptions is employed; 71 are lost, including six British and three French destroyers, and many other ships are so badly damaged (seven on 29 May) that they are out of action for months.

June. The fall of France and the Low Countries results in the evacuation of Norway by British and French forces. Some 27,000 troops and Norwegian civilians (including the Norwegian royal family) are evacuated by sea almost without loss.

8 June. The British aircraft carrier HMS *Glorious*, evacuating seventeen RAF fighters from Norway, and her two escort destroyers, *Ardent* and *Acasta*, are sunk by *Scharnhorst* and *Gneisenau*. The destroyers manage to score one torpedo hit on *Gneisenau*.

10 June. Italy declares war on Britain and France, with hostilities starting on the 11th.

17 June. The British troopship *Lancastria* is sunk by German aircraft at St Nazaire with the loss of more than 2,500 of the British and French troops on board and also of refugees.

22 June. The French Government concludes an armistice with Germany, and a second armistice with Italy on the 24th. All resistance by French forces ceases by the 25th.

2 July. The British merchant ship *Arandora Star* is sunk by *U47* in the Atlantic.

3 July. Following the failure of efforts to persuade the French naval commander at Oran either to join the British or to send his ships into internment, British warships open fire on the French Fleet. The French battleship *Bretagne* blows up and *Dunkerque* is badly damaged. However, the battleship *Strasbourg* and six destroyers escape to Toulon. On the same day all French warships in British ports are boarded and seized by Royal Navy personnel. At Portsmouth three British personnel and a French seaman die in scuffles on board the submarine *Surcouf*.

5 July. Between 5 and 20 July the eighteen Swordfish aircraft of 813 and 824 NAS embarked in HMS *Eagle* carry out a series of highly successful operations against the Italian Navy in the Mediterranean. On 5 July they sink the Italian destroyer *Zeffiro* at Tobruk and damage the destroyer *Euro* as well as sinking a merchant ship and damaging another. On 10 July they sink the destroyer *Leone*

Pancaldo at Augusta, and on 20 July they sink the destroyers *Nembo* and *Ostro* in Tobruk Roads.

7 July. At Alexandria, the French naval commander, Admiral Godfoy, agrees that the ships of his squadron will be partially disarmed and go into internment.

9 July. The Battle of Calabria takes place in the Mediterranean.

19 July. The Italian cruiser *Bartolomeo Colleoni* is badly damaged by the Australian cruiser *Sydney* north-west of Crete and is finished off by the destroyers *Hyperion*, *Ilex*, *Hero* and *Hasty*. In the United States, Congress approves an additional $4bn of naval expenditure demanded by President Roosevelt in order to maintain a balanced fleet in both the Atlantic and the Pacific.

24 July. Britain and the United States conclude the 'Destroyers for Bases' agreement.

15 August. The Greek cruiser *Helle* is torpedoed in error by the Italian submarine *Delfino* while at anchor off Tenos in Crete. Greece is not at war and the cruiser's company are celebrating the Feast of the Assumption at the time of the attack. There are very heavy casualties.

21 August. Four Swordfish aircraft from 824 NAS attack the Italian submarine *Iride* in the Gulf of Bomba. *Iride* is fitted to carry the SLC human torpedo and was preparing for an attack on Alexandria.

30 August. The five ships of the British 20th Destroyer Flotilla, the Royal Navy's only offensive surface minelaying force, run into a German minefield while on a minelaying operation off Vlieland. The German field had been laid but hours beforehand. HMS *Esk* sinks almost immediately and HMS *Ivanhoe* is damaged and is later scuttled by HMS *Kelvin*. On the same night HMS *Express* is mined north of Terschelling but is towed stern-first to the Humber and repaired.

Above: Two miserable Polish seamen on lookout duty in the winter of 1940 in the destroyer ORP *Piarun*. (Author)

Above: Wrecked shipping in the harbour at Bardia, North Africa, after an attack by the tiny British river gunboat HMS *Aphis* on the night of 16/17 December 1940. (Author)

18 September. The British liner *City of Benares*, en route for Canada with child evacuees, is torpedoed and sunk by *U48*.

22 September. The Italian destroyer *Palestro* is sunk by HM Submarine *Osiris* off Durazzo in the Mediterranean.

11/12 October. Italian naval forces attempt to intercept an eastbound convoy from Malta but the Italian destroyers and torpedo boats run into the convoy's covering screen which includes the cruisers *York* and *Ajax*, the latter being the first radar-equipped ship to join the Mediterranean Fleet. The Italian destroyer *Artiglieri* is crippled by *Ajax*'s gunfire; taken in tow by *Camicia Nera*, she is later abandoned and surrendered to HMS *York*. *Ajax*

also sinks the torpedo boats *Ariel* and *Airone*.

3 November. In a double sinking in the Atlantic, the German submarine *U99* (*Kapitänleutnant* Otto Kretschmer, q.v.) sinks the armed merchant cruisers *Laurentic* and *Patroclus* in less than ninety minutes.

5 November. The British armed merchant cruiser *Jervis Bay* is sunk by the pocket battleship *Admiral Scheer* during her defence of the Atlantic convoy HX.84.

8 November. The US-flag merchant vessel *City of Rayville* becomes the first US maritime casualty of the war when she is mined in the Bass Strait.

9 November. The French sloop *Bougainville* is sunk off Libreville in West Africa by the Free French

sloop *Savorgnan de Brazza* – a very sad encounter between two ships of the same class manned by fellow-countrymen.

11/12 November. British Swordfish aircraft from the carrier HMS *Illustrious* attack the Italian naval base at Taranto

1941

2 January. The British warships *Terror*, *Aphis* and *Ladybird* (all veterans of the Great War) carry out a successful bombardment of Italian positions at Bardia in North Africa.

10 January. The *Luftwaffe* makes its first appearance in the Mediterranean with a devastating dive-bombing attack on the British aircraft carrier HMS *Illustrious*.

17 January. The Thai Navy is vir-

Above: The French cruiser *Duquesne* and the destroyer *Le Fortun* interned at Alexandria in 1941. (Author)

tually annihilated by a small but efficient Vichy French squadron in the Battle of Koh-Chang in the Gulf of Siam.

9 February. The British battlecruiser *Renown* and battleship *Malaya*, supported by Swordfish aircraft from the carrier *Ark Royal*, carry out a bombardment of the Italian port and industrial centre of Genoa.

March. The German submarine *U47*, commanded by *Kapitänleutnant* Günther Prien, is missing in the Atlantic following an attack on convoy OB.293, possibly on the night of 7/8 March.

17 March. During a series of engagements around convoy HX. 112 in the Atlantic, the German submarine *U100* (*Kapitänleutnant*

Above: The British monitor HMS *Terror*. Her sole armament was the massive twin 15in gun turret. *Terror* did sterling work in the Dover Patrol in the First World War and off the North African coast in the Second World War before being sunk on 23rd February 1941. (Author)

Above: The destroyer HMS *Vanoc* passes an outward bound convoy in March 1941. (USN)

Joachim Schepke, is rammed and sunk by HMS *Vanoc*. Shortly afterwards *U99* (*Kapitänleutnant* Otto Kretschmer, q.v.) is detected by HMS *Walker*, depth-charged to the surface and sunk. The loss of three such experienced U-boat commanders in less than three weeks represents a severe blow for the *Kriegsmarine*.

26 March. The British cruiser HMS *York* is sunk at Suda Bay in Crete by MTM explosive motor boats of the Italian *Decima Mas*.

28/29 March. The Battle of Matapan takes place in the Mediterranean.

30 March. US Coast Guard officers seize twenty-seven Italian-flag merchant vessels in various US ports after reports are received that crews of five of the ships are starting to sabotage their ships.

3 April. The Italian destroyers *Nazario Sauro*, *Daniele Manin* and *Cesare Battisti* sortie from Massawa to attack British shipping in the Gulf of Suez. They are attacked by Swordfish aircraft of 813 and 824 NAS and all three ships are sunk.

5 April. The German battlecruiser *Gneisenau* is damaged in an attack by RAF Beaufort aircraft while lying at Brest.

10 April. The destroyer USS *Niblack* engages a German U-boat in the Atlantic, thus creating the first clash between US and German armed forces.

16 April. The British destroyers *Jervis*, *Janus*, *Mohawk* and *Nubian* intercept an Italian convoy of five merchant vessels heading for North Africa escorted by the destroyers *Tarigo*, *Baleno* and

Lampo. In return for the loss of *Mohawk* (which is torpedoed by *Tarigo* and later has to be scuttled), seven of the eight Italian ships are sunk.

20 April. As the Germans invade Greece, the *Luftwaffe* begins an air offensive against units of the Greek Navy which are concentrated in the Gulf of Athens: on the 20th the destroyer *Psara* is sunk, on the 22nd the destroyers *Thyella*, *Ydra* and *Leon* are sunk, on the 23rd the battleships *Kilkis* and *Lemnos* are sunk and on the 27th the destroyer *Vasilevs Georgios 1* is captured in a floating dock at Salamis. Also on the 27th the British destroyers *Diamond* and *Wryneck* are sunk south of Nauplia. Both ships have just rescued 700 troops from the Dutch liner *Slamat* but only fifty

Above: The British U class submarine, HMS *Ursula*. Originally designed as unarmed training submarines, the small U class did sterling work in the Mediterranean and in Home Waters. (Author)

publications. This success complements another when the German weather ship *München* is captured on 7 May by HMS *Somali*.

12 May. The British gunboat *Ladybird* is sunk at Tobruk in an air raid.

18 May. The German battleship *Bismarck*, accompanied by the cruiser *Prinz Eugen*, leaves Gotenhafen (Gdynia) for a commerce-raiding cruise in the Atlantic. On 24 May she is intercepted by the British battleship HMS *Prince of Wales* and battle-cruiser HMS *Hood* and sinks the latter after a brief engagement. However, on 27 May, after attacks by Swordfish aircraft from HMS *Victorious* and HMS *Ark Royal*, she was found by the battleships HMS *Rodney* and *King George V* and sunk. Only 110 officers and men are saved.

21 May. The German invasion of Crete results in the seaborne evacuation of British and Commonwealth troops on the island. In carrying out this task the Royal Navy vessels involved are exposed to the full ferocity of the *Luftwaffe* and losses are heavy. Between 21 May and 1 June three cruisers are sunk, together with six destroyers; additionally, two battleships, an aircraft carrier, five cruisers and four destroyers are damaged.

22 June. Germany invades the USSR. While supporting the Red Army the Navy loses seven destroyers and two minesweepers up to the end of July.

24 August. The Iranian sloops *Babr* and *Palang* are sunk in the Persian Gulf by HMAS *Yarra* and HMS *Shoreham* respectively during the joint Anglo-Soviet occupa-

survivors are found from the combined complements and passengers of all three vessels.

8 May. The German HSK cruiser *Pinguin* is sunk in the Indian Ocean by HMS *Cornwall*. *Pinguin* blows up after the engagement, with the loss of all 292 of her crew

and 155 British PoWs on board.

9 May. The German submarine *U110* is captured by HMS *Bulldog* during a series of engagements around Atlantic convoy OB.318. A boarding party goes aboard *U110* and recovers an Enigma cipher machine and a number of secret

tion of Iran. The remainder of the Iranian Navy surrenders *en masse*.

24 August. During the evacuation of Reval in the Baltic, Soviet naval forces run into minefields laid by the Finns off Cape Juminda. On the 24th three destroyers are lost off Cape Juminda and on the 28th another three destroyers and two torpedo boats are sunk in the same area. Also on the 28th, two Soviet destroyers are mined in the Gulf of Riga.

4 September. The destroyer USS *Greer* is unsuccessfully attacked in the Atlantic by *U652*; in return, *Greer* carries out an equally unsuccessful depth-charge attack. As a result of this incident, on 11 September President Roosevelt orders the US Navy to adopt a 'shoot first' policy in the Atlantic against German U-boats.

20 September. Italian *Decima Mas* human torpodoes damage one and sink two merchant ships within the confines of the Bay of Gibraltar.

17 October. In the Atlantic, the destroyer USS *Kearny*, which is escorting convoy SC.48, is torpedoed and damaged by *U568*.

31 October. The American destroyer USS *Reuben James* is torpedoed and sunk in the Atlantic by *U526* with the loss of 115 lives. She is the first US warship to be sunk during the Second World War.

4 November. A convoy of five Vichy-flag merchant ships, escorted by the sloop *D'Iberville*, is intercepted by British and South African naval forces in the South Atlantic. The merchant ships are carrying tin and rubber from Indo-China to France (and thence Germany) and are taken into Cape Town after their crews unsuccessfully try to scuttle them.

9 November. An Italian convoy heading for Tripoli is intercepted by the cruisers HMS *Aurora* and *Penelope* with the destroyers *Lance* and *Lively*. Two tankers and five cargo ships are sunk by gunfire and torpedo while the Italian destroyer *Fulmine* is sunk and *Euro* and *Maestrale* are damaged. The destroyer *Libeccio* returns to pick up survivors, is torpedoed by HMS *Upholder* and later sinks while under tow.

13 November. The aircraft carrier HMS *Ark Royal* is torpedoed by *U81*. After damage control fails to save the ship she rolls over and sinks at 06.13 on the 14th with the loss of one life. Good damage control might have saved the 'Ark' but such facilities were not available within the ship. The sinking of *Ark Royal* begins a period of unrelieved disaster for the Royal Navy.

19 November. The Australian cruiser *Sydney* is sunk with the loss of all hands in an action with the German raider *Kormoran* off Western Australia. The latter is damaged and set on fire by Sydney's gunfire. The fire spreads out of control and *Kormoran* is abandoned; 315 of her crew survive.

22 November. The cruiser HMS *Devonshire* makes no mistakes when she sinks the HSK ship *Atlantis* north-west of Ascension island.

25 November. The battleship HMS *Barham* is sunk by *U331* in the Mediterranean. The U-boat manages to penetrate the destroyer screen and torpedo the battleship with the loss of 862 of her crew.

7 December. Japanese carrier-borne aircraft attack the US Pacific Fleet at its Hawaiian base at Pearl Harbor. Five battleships are sunk (although three will be subsequently repaired), together with three destroyers and a minelayer.

8 December. At Guam, the US minesweeper *Penguin* is sunk by

Above: An aerial view of 'Battleship Row' taken during the Japanese attack on Pearl Harbor, 7 December 1942. (USN)

Above: The end of battleship USS *Arizona* at Pearl Harbor. Nearly half the US casualties were sustained when the ship exploded. Today *Arizona* rests undisturbed at Pearl Harbour as a memorial to those killed in the attack. (USN)

land-based Japanese Naval Air Force (JNAF) air attack. On the same day, at Shanghai, the British gunboat *Peterel* is sunk by gunfire from the Japanese cruiser *Idzumo*.

10 December. The JNAF land-based anti-shipping units prove every inch as competent as their carrier-borne counterparts when, operating at a range of more than 600 miles from their base, they sink the battleship HMS *Prince of Wales* and the battlecruiser HMS *Repulse* off Malaya.

11 December. The defence of Wake Island in the mid-Pacific results in the first significant defeat for the Japanese. The destroyer *Hayate* is sunk by gunfire from a US Marine Corps shore battery and later beached as a total loss, while on the same day the destroyer *Kisaragi* is sunk by USMC aircraft operating from Wake.

13 December. Force K scores another major success against Axis convoys running petrol and munitions to North Africa when it intercepts two Italian cruisers bound for Tripoli with a cargo of spirit on the night of 12/13 December. The destroyers are operating inshore of the cruisers and thus achieve complete surprise. *Alberico de Barbiano* and *Alberto di Giusanno* are both sunk. The torpedo boat *Cigno* rescues 500 of the 650 survivors but over 900 officers and men are drowned.

19 December. In the Mediterranean, Force K's extremely successful anti-shipping campaign comes to an abrupt end when it runs into an Italian minefield. The cruiser *Neptune* is sunk – only one man out of a complement of 764 is saved – as is the destroyer *Kandahar*, and the

cruisers *Aurora* and *Penelope* are badly damaged. On the same morning, three Italian SLCs penetrate the net and boom defences of Alexandria harbour and succeed in damaging the battleships *Queen Elizabeth* and *Valiant*. These losses, taken with the loss of HMS *Ark Royal* and the elimination of Force K, mean that, in the Mediterranean, the Royal Navy has effectively been neutralised.

21 December. In the Atlantic, HMS *Audacity* is torpedoed while providing cover for convoy HG.76.

24 December. The corvette HMS *Salvia* is torpedoed and sunk by *U568* west of Alexandria. *Salvia* is carrying several hundred survivors from a torpedoed PoW transport, but only wreckage is found.

1942

11/12 February. The German battlecruisers *Scharnhorst* and *Gneisenau* and the cruiser *Prinz Eugen* return to Germany via the English Channel. British attempts to intercept the German squadron fail. However, both battlecruisers are damaged by mines in the North Sea. *Gneisenau* is further damaged in an RAF raid while in dock at Kiel on 27 February. The damage is severe: her bows are blown off and her career is ended.

15 February. The British surrender Singapore to the Japanese.

19 February. Japanese carrier-borne aircraft attack the port at Darwin in northern Australia. The harbour installations are seriously damaged and ten merchant ships are sunk along with the destroyer USS *Peary*. Elsewhere, in the Battle of the Badoeng Strait the Dutch destroyer *Piet Hein* is sunk.

27 February–1 March. The Allied fleet in the Netherlands East Indies is destroyed in a series of engagements with Japanese cruiser and destroyer squadrons in the Battle of the Java Sea. On 27 the Dutch cruisers *De Ruyter* and *Java* are sunk, along with the Dutch destroyer *Kortenaer* and the British destroyers *Electra* and *Jupiter*. The survivors – the cruisers HMS *Exeter*, HMAS *Perth* and USS *Houston* and the destroyers HMS *Encounter*, USS *Pope* and

Above: The British battleship HMS *Rodney* seen in 1942. The unusual arrangement of the main armament in three triple turrets mounted forward of the bridge is quite clear. (USN)

HNethMS *Evertsen* – are sunk on 1 March in a series of engagements with Japanese cruisers and destroyers which rank as one of the most crushing naval defeats of all time.

22 March. The Second Battle of Sirte takes place when four British cruisers and eleven destroyers escorting a Malta-bound convoy hold off an Italian force consisting of a 16in-gun battleship and six cruisers for nearly two and a half hours in rough weather.

28 March. British commandos raid the port of St Nazaire to destroy the dry dock there – the only dry dock in France which can accommodate *Tirpitz*. The destroyer *Campbeltown*, packed with explosive, is rammed into the caisson while commandos destroy the pumping houses and other facilities. The following day *Campbeltown* explodes, destroying the caisson.

29 March. In a series of engagements around convoy PQ.13 to Russia, the German destroyer *Z.26* is sunk by gunfire from the cruiser HMS *Trinidad* and destroyers *Eclipse* and *Fury*. However, *Trinidad* is damaged by one of her own torpedoes which circles after being fired.

March–April. Axis bombing of the island of Malta results in severe losses to British naval units stationed there. On 26 March the destroyer *Legion* is sunk in Grand Harbour. On 5 April the destroyer *Lance* and minesweeper *Abingdon* are sunk. On 11 April the destroyer *Kingston* is sunk.

5 April. A Japanese carrier task force enters the Indian Ocean and attacks the British bases at Ceylon – Colombo on the 5th and Trincomalee on the 9th. The armed merchant cruiser *Hector* and destroyer *Tenedos* are sunk at Colombo and the cruisers *Cornwall* and *Dorsetshire* are sighted by chance at sea and sunk by dive-bombers. The strike on Trincomalee on the 9th is less successful. Shipping has been dispersed and only one merchant ship and a floating dock are sunk. However, the old carrier HMS *Hermes*, destroyer *Vampire* and corvette *Hollyhock* are sunk at sea.

30 April. The cruiser HMS *Edinburgh* is torpedoed and damaged in the Arctic by *U456* while returning to the UK with five tons of Soviet gold (payment for Anglo-American aid) in her bomb magazine. She is scuttled on 2 May after damage control efforts fail to save the ship and after an engagement with German destroyers in which *Hermann Schoemann* is sunk.

5 May. British and Commonwealth forces invade the island of Madagascar to prevent the Vichy authorities allowing Axis navies use of the superb natural harbour of Diego Suarez. In the course of the forty-eight hour operation the French armed merchant cruiser *Bougainville*, the frigate *D'Entrecasteaux* and the submarines *Bévéziers*, *Monge* and *Le Héros* are sunk. In return the British lose the corvette HMS *Auricula*.

7 May. The Battle of the Coral Sea takes place in the Pacific.

11 May. The British destroyers *Lively*, *Jackal* and *Kipling* are sunk in the Mediterranean by air attack while trying to intercept an Axis convoy bound for Benghazi. RAF land-based fighters failed to provide adequate cover.

13 May. The German torpedo boats *Iltis* and *Seeadler* are sunk by British MTBs in the English Channel while escorting a convoy bound for Cherbourg.

14 May. The *Decima Mas* attempt to infiltrate another three SLCs into Alexandria harbour to attack the damaged battleship *Valiant* which is under repair in a floating dock. The attack fails because the harbour defences are on the alert.

14 May. The cruiser HMS *Trinidad* is sunk by German aircraft in the Arctic while returning to the UK.

30 May. A Japanese *Ko-Hyoteki* midget submarine enters the anchorage at Diego Suarez and sinks the tanker *British Loyalty* and damages the battleship *Ramillies*. The crew then abandon the submarine and make their way ashore, where they are hunted down and shot by British patrols.

4 June. The Battle of Midway takes place in the Pacific. Although the American victory at the Battle of the Coral Sea in May checked the Japanese advance, the overall strength and capability of the Japanese Navy was not seriously affected. At the beginning of June the Japanese deploy eight carriers (350 aircraft), eight battleships, nineteen cruisers and seventy-four destroyers to cover the simultaneous occupation of the Aleutians and Midway Island. Against one wing of this armada the USN can deploy three carriers (230 aircraft), eight cruisers and fourteen destroyers. The Americans' great advantage is their ability to read the Japanese naval cypher. The Japanese lose

Above: A Japanese aircraft scores a direct hit on the carrier USS *Yorktown* despite a tornado of anti-aircraft fire. (IWM OEM 3772)

Above: The merchant ship *Orari* discharging her cargo in Malta in June 1942. *Orari* was one of two survivors out of six merchant ships that had sailed to Malta in operation *Harpoon*. (Author)

four carriers (and the cream of the carrier aircrew), together with a cruiser, against American losses of one carrier and a destroyer. The Battle of Midway is the first strategic victory for the Allies in the Pacific War.

June 1942. In order to relieve Malta, two convoys sail to the island simultaneously from Gibraltar ('Harpoon') and Alexandria ('Vigorous'). The 'Harpoon' convoy survives continuous air attacks and an attack by three Italian cruisers and five destroyers on 15 June, but only two of the six merchant ships reach Malta. The destroyers HMS *Bedouin* and ORP *Kujawiak* are sunk in the defence of the 'Harpoon' convoy. The 'Vigorous' convoy is subjected to massive air attack and considerable interference from naval HQ in Alexandria which results in the escorts firing off most of their AA ammunition. The destroyers

Hasty, *Nestor*, and *Airedale* are sunk, along with the cruiser *Hermione*. On 15 June the convoy is ordered to turn back.

4 July. Convoy PQ.17, heading for Murmansk, is ordered to scatter in the face of a presumed threat from the German battleship *Tirpitz*. Of the thirty-seven merchant ships in the convoy, two turn back, eight are sunk by air attack and nine by U-boats and seven are finished off by U-boats having been first damaged by air attack. Losses in cargo amount to 430 tanks, 210 crated aircraft, 3,350 vehicles and 94,000 tons of general cargo.

3 August. Convoy WS.21S, codenamed 'Pedestal', for Malta, consisting of thirteen merchant ships and a tanker escorted by two battleships, four carriers, seven cruisers and twenty-six destroyers, sails from the Clyde. A shortage of escorts has prevented a convoy being sent to the island in July and

the position of the islanders and garrison is desperate.

7 August. In the South Pacific, US Marines land on Guadalcanal, beginning one of the longest and bloodiest campaigns of the Second World War.

9 August. The Battle of Savo Island takes place in the Pacific. One Australian and three American cruisers are sunk in the space of an hour by five Japanese cruisers.

9/10 August. The 'Pedestal' convoy passes the Strait of Gibraltar and its odyssey begins. The aircraft carrier *Eagle* is sunk on the 11th, the destroyer *Foresight* and cruiser *Cairo* on the 12th and the cruiser *Manchester* on the 13th. Nine of the merchant ships are sunk but the first of the five survivors reaches the island on 13th. The climax of the operation is the arrival of the damaged tanker *Ohio* on the 15th, the Feast of the Assumption. The

Above: The German surface group assembled in Altenfiord waiting for the order to sortie against convoy PQ.17. The photograph was taken from *Tirpitz* and shows (from right to left) the cruiser *Admiral Hipper* and pocket battleship *Lutzow*. (*Tirptiz* Association)

Above: The bridge watch of a U-boat keep alert for possible targets, 1942. Note the lookout on the right wearing tinted goggles allowing him to look into the sun. (USNA)

supplies brought by the four freighters and the *Ohio* will enable the island to last out until the autumn.

19 August. Anglo-Canadian forces launch an amphibious assault on the port of Dieppe. The raid proves costly in terms of lives and loss of equipment, particularly landing craft, but only one destroyer, HMS *Berkeley*, is sunk.

24 August. The Battle of the Eastern Solomons in the South Pacific results in the loss of Japanese carrier *Ryujo*.

2 September. Convoy PQ.18 sails from Loch Ewe and is successfully fought through to Murmansk against fierce German air attacks. Thirteen ships of the forty in the convoy are sunk, ten by aircraft and three by U-boat. Nevertheless, the *Luftwaffe*'s anti-shipping units in northern Norway suffer severe losses – forty-one aircraft.

14 September. An ill-planned amphibious raid on the port and town of Tobruk results in the loss of the cruiser HMS *Coventry* and

Above: Convoy PQ.18 on its way to Russia in September 1942. In the foreground is the destroyer HMS *Ashanti*. Behind her a bomb explodes close alongside the destroyer HMS *Wheatland*. (Author)

the destroyers HMSs *Sikh* and *Zulu* along with two motor launches and three MTBs.

15 September. In the South Pacific, the Japanese submarine *I-19* torpedoes the carrier USS *Wasp*, the battleship *North Carolina* and the destroyer *O'Brien* in the same salvo. *Wasp* is scuttled after fires get out of control but *North Carolina* and *O'Brien* reach Noumea. *O'Brien* will be sunk on 19 October while returning to Pearl Harbor.

27 September. The German HSK ship *Stier* is sunk north-west of Tristan da Cunha in the Atlantic in a mutually fatal engagement with the US merchant ship *Stephen Hopkins*, whose gunners score thirty-five hits on the raider before she has to be abandoned.

11 October. The Battle of Cape Esperance takes place in the South Pacific.

26 October. The Battle of Santa Cruz, the critical naval action in the US campaign to hold the beach-head on Guadalcanal, takes place. The Japanese mount a major operation in which their carrier fleet co-ordinates operations with land-based aircraft in support of the Army. However, the US Marines hold the island, and although the Americans lose the carrier *Hornet* the Japanese are forced to withdraw with two of their carriers damaged and heavy losses in aircrew.

8 November. Anglo-American forces land in Algeria and French Morocco. The French naval forces offer stout resistance and both

sides suffer severe losses, but the French are eventually overwhelmed. On 8 November the ex-USCG cutters HMS *Hartland* and *Walney* are damaged by shore batteries off Oran and sunk. The destroyer HMS *Broke* is damaged off Algiers and is subsequently scuttled. In return the French lose the destroyers *Epervier*, *Tramontane*, *Tornade*, *Typhon* and *La Surprise*. Off Morocco the US Navy sink the destroyers *Milan*, *Fougeux*, *Boulonnais*, *Albatros*, *Bestois* and *Frondeur*, along with the cruiser *Primaguet*. At Casablanca the French battleship *Jean Bart* is damaged by 16in gunfire from the battleship USS *Massachusetts*. The Axis response is to concentrate U-boats and aircraft in the area, and from 10

Above: American soldiers come ashore in North Africa in November 1942. Operation *Torch* was the first of a series of successful Anglo-American amphibious operations. (USNA)

November Anglo-American losses mount until the appropriate defensive measures can be implemented.

12–15 November. The Battles of Guadalcanal, over the nights of 12/13 and 14/15 November, cost the US Navy dear. Two cruisers and seven destroyers are lost but the Japanese lose two battleships and fail in their efforts to reinforce the island.

27 November. The French fleet at Toulon is scuttled to prevent it falling into Axis hands following the German invasion of Vichy-controlled France.

30 November. In the South Pacific, the IJN demonstrates that it has not completely lost its capability to strengthen Japanese forces on Guadalcanal. A force of Japanese destroyers delivers drums of fuel to the island and, despite being engaged by a superior US force (which has radar warning of the Japanese approach), fight back with such vigour that only the destroyer *Takanami* is sunk in return for the loss of the US cruiser *Northampton* and damage to the cruisers *Pensacola*, *Minneapolis* and *New Orleans*.

2 December. An Italian convoy of four transports escorted by three destroyers and two torpedo boats is intercepted off the Tunisian coast by the British cruisers *Aurora*, *Sirius* and *Argonaut* escorted by two destroyers. All four transports and the destroyer *Folgore* are sunk. In return, German aircraft sink the destroyer HMS *Quentin*. On the same night RAF aircraft from Malta attack a Naples–Tripoli convoy and sink

both merchant ships. British destroyers from Malta sink one of the escorts, the torpedo boat *Lupo*.

31 December. In the Battle of the Barents Sea, a German striking force consisting of the pocket battleship *Lützow*, cruiser *Admiral Hipper* and six destroyers attacks convoy JW.51B but is held off by the escort until the cruisers *Sheffield* and *Jamaica* arrive. The British lose the destroyer *Achates* and minesweeper *Bramble* and the Germans lose the destroyer *Friedrich Eckholdt*. The convoy is unharmed and the scale of the German rout results in massive changes to the *Kriegsmarine*.

1943

January. Minelaying by the British minelayers *Abdiel* and *Manxman* on the routes used by Axis convoys running between Italy and North Africa results in the loss of seven destroyers and escorts between January and March.

3 January. British Chariots enter the harbour at Palermo in Italy and sink the incomplete cruiser *Ulpio Traiano* and liner *Viminale*.

1/2 February. The Japanese begin the evacuation of Guadalcanal using twenty destroyers to take off their remaining troops.

2–4 March. In an attempt to reinforce their garrison in New Guinea the Japanese dispatch an infantry division from Rabaul in eight transports with a strong destroyer escort. In a series of air attacks which begin on the 2nd and continue until the 4th, all eight transports are sunk together with the destroyers *Shirayuki*, *Tokitsukaze*, *Arashio* and *Asashio*.

11 March. In a unique series of engagements around convoy HX.228 in the Atlantic, the destroyer HMS *Harvester* is badly damaged after ramming *U444* and is then sunk by *U432*. The last is then dispatched by the French corvette *Aconit*.

26 March. Battle of the Komandorski Islands in the North Pacific.

7 April. A Japanese carrier-borne air strike comprising 67 dive-bombers escorted by 110 fighters on the Guadalcanal base sinks the destroyer USS *Aaron Ward* and two auxiliaries

16 April. The British destroyers *Pakenham* and *Paladin* encounter the Italian torpedo boats *Cigno* and *Cassiopea* off the west coast of Sicily and in a brisk engagement *Cigno* and *Pakenham* are sunk.

17 April. Admiral Isoruku Yamamoto is killed when his aircraft is intercepted by USAAC P-38 Lightning fighters and shot down over Bougainville in the Solomons. The Americans had knowledge of Yamamoto's movements through intercepted Japanese signal traffic and set an ambush. It is the only occasion during the Second World War when the Americans deliberately seek to kill a specific enemy commander.

30 April. In a last-ditch effort to resupply the Axis forces in Tunisia, the Italian Navy sends the destroyers *Leone Pancaldo*, *Lupo* and the German-manned *Hermes* in a daylight supply run across the Mediterranean. Fighter cover provided by both the *Luftwaffe* and the *Regia Aeronautica* is brushed aside by the Allied air forces, which sink all three ships.

Above: HMS *Starling* (inboard) and *Wildgoose* (outboard) at Liverpool in June 1943. *Starling* (q.v.) was the leader of the successful 2nd Support Group under the command of Captain F. J. Walker, RN (q.v.) (USNA)

8 May. A minefield laid by three American destroyers on 7 May in the Blackett Strait off Rendova island (a route used by Japanese destroyers engaged in harassing operations in the Solomons) claims the Japanese destroyers *Kuroshio*, *Kagero* and *Oyashio*.

6 July. The Battle of Kula Gulf takes place in the South Pacific.

10 July. Anglo-American naval forces support landings on Sicily –

the first invasion of Axis territory proper. The US destroyers *Sentinel* and *Maddox* are sunk by German aircraft. Allied air supremacy is such that the landings are almost unopposed.

12/13 July. Battle of Kolombangara.

6 August. Battle of Vella Gulf.

27 August. The sloop HMS *Egret* is sunk 30 miles west of Vigo by an Hs 293A glider bomb; she is the

first ship to be sunk by an air-launched guided weapon. The destroyer HMCS *Athabaskan* is damaged by another Hs 293A but rescues *Egret*'s survivors and returns to Devonport under her own power.

28 August. Following the refusal of the Danish Government to accept martial law and the death penalty for acts of sabotage, the German Army takes over the country. As a result, the ships of the Royal Danish Navy are either scuttled or seek internment in neutral Sweden. The loss of the Danish minesweeping force in particular represents a serious blow for the *Kriegsmarine*, which now has to stretch its very limited resources to cover this gap.

3 September. The new Italian Government concludes an armistice with the Allies. A condition of this armistice is that the ships of the *Regia Marina* be transferred to the Allies for internment and subsequent use in the war against Germany. This condition is faithfully observed by the Italian Government and on 8 September every seaworthy ship and submarine sails from La Spezia, Taranto or Genoa for Malta; a few determined units even break out of the Adriatic. Ships which cannot be got away are wrecked; even as far away as Shanghai, the lone Italian warship there, the minesweeper *Lepanto*, is scuttled. The Germans are not prepared to let such a valuable asset escape their grasp and launch a series of attacks on the Italian ships. Italian losses might have been greater were it not for the Anglo-American landings at Salerno and Reggio on the Italian mainland.

Above: A mixture of Douglas Dauntless (q.v.) dive bombers and Grumman Avengers on the flight deck of an American escort carrier in wintry conditions in 1943-44. (USN)

9 September. The corvette *Berencie* is sunk at Trieste by German shore artillery while attempting to escape and the minelayer *Pelagosa* is sunk at Genoa by the same means. The main body of the Italian fleet (three battleships, six cruisers and thirteen destroyers) is attacked by Do 217 bombers of *KG 100* fitted with FX 1200 guided armour-piercing bombs. The battleship *Roma* is sunk. Two Italian destroyers, *Antonio da Noli* and *Ugolino Vivaldi*, which have been deployed to the Bonifacio Strait to prevent German reinforcements moving from Corsica to Sardinia, are sunk by German coastal artillery.

20 September. German U-boats equipped with the new T5 acoustic homing torpedo return to main Atlantic convoy routes after their withdrawal following the May battles. The U-boats score an immediate success against the escorts of convoy ON.202, damaging the frigate *Lagan* and sinking HMCS *St Croix* and HMS *Polyanthus* on the 20th and sinking the frigate *Itchen* on the 22nd. However, only six merchant ships are lost against three U-boats, thus making an Exhange Rate of 3 – hardly a success. Countermeasures produced by WATU soon produce an effective decoy and tactics to deal with the new weapon.

22 September. Six British X-craft are dispatched to Kaafjord to attack *Tirpitz*, *Lützow* and *Scharnhorst*. Two, *X.8* and *X.9*, are lost on the outward journey, *X.5* disappears after being released from the towing submarine and *X.10* abandons the operation after mul-

tiple mechanical failures. The two survivors, *X.6* and *X.7*, successfully place their explosive charges under *Tirpitz*. Both craft are subsequently sunk and their crews taken prisoner. *Tirpitz* is considerably damaged when the charges explode and will not be fit for operations again until the spring of 1944.

26 September. In the Aegean, the Allied occupation of the islands of Kos and Leros results in the loss to air attack of the Greek destroyer *Vasilissa Olga* on the 26th and HMS *Intrepid* on the 27th. This is proof – if any be needed after three years of war – that warships without organic air cover cannot survive in the face of air attack by well-trained aircrew.

September/October. The German Army manages the astonishing feat of evacuating over 280,000 men, 80,000 animals, 49,000 vehicles of all types, 1,800 guns and 115,000 tons of stores across the Kerch Strait from the Kuban peninsula to the east of the Crimea. Only two of the 240 craft involved are sunk. In return, an attempt by Soviet destroyers to interdict the traffic on 6 October results in *Kharkhov*, *Bezposhchadny* and *Sposobny* being sunk by German dive-bombers.

6 October. Battle of Vella Lavella.

23 October. The cruiser HMS *Charybdis* and destroyer HMS *Limbourne* are sunk by German torpedo boats *T.23* and *T.37* in the English Channel.

2 November. Battle of Empress Augusta Bay.

5 November. Aircraft from the US carriers *Saratoga* and *Princeton* attack the Japanese naval base at

Rabaul. No ships are sunk but the cruisers *Maya*, *Takao*, *Mogami*, *Atago*, *Agano* and *Noshiro* are all damaged. The carriers return again on 11 November with a larger striking force but only succeed in sinking the destroyer *Suzunami*.

11 November. British naval forces in the Aegean, without their own air cover, continue to suffer losses at the hands of the *Luftwaffe*. The destroyer HMS *Rockwood* is damaged by an Hs 293A glider bomb; temporary repairs (effected in Turkish waters) allow her to make Alexandria, but she is not returned to service. On the 13th the destroyer HMS *Dulverton* is sunk by an Hs 293A .

24 November. The US Navy's Fifth Fleet launches its main offensive with the invasion of the Gilbert Islands. While the land battle is an extremely bloody affair, with 1,056 US Marines killed in 76 hours, the naval aspect of the operation proceeds with the loss of just one ship, the escort carrier *Lipscombe Bay*: the carrier is torpedoed by the Japanese submarine *I-125*, her bomb magazine explodes and the ship sinks in less than 25 minutes with the loss of 644 officers and men.

25 November. Japanese attempts to evacuate soldiers from Buka, the northernmost island in the Solomons chain, end in near disaster when the destroyers *Onami*, *Makinami* and *Yugiri* are sunk by the American destroyers *Ausburne*, *Claxton*, *Dyson*, *Converse* and *Spence*.

26 December. The Battle of the North Cape results in the loss of the German battlecruiser

Scharnhorst. This is the last action between capital ships in which aircraft play no part.

28 December. A force of German destroyers and torpedo boats sorties into the Bay of Biscay to escort a homeward-bound blockade-runner (which was, unknown to the Germans, sunk by the RAF on the 27th). The German ships are intercepted by the cruisers HMS *Glasgow* and *Enterprise*. The two British ships are resolutely handled and press home their attack, despite repeated attacks by German aircraft armed with glider bombs. The German destroyer *Z.27* and torpedo boats *T.25* and *T.26* are sunk and only the shortage of ammunition pre-

vents the two cruisers from finishing off the rest of the German force.

1944

January. The Anglo-American landings at Anzio result in a number of losses to British and American warships defending the beach-head. On the 22nd the minesweeper USS *Portent* is mined off Anzio. On the 23rd the destroyer HMS *Janus* is torpedoed by German aircraft and sinks with great loss of life, while on the 29th the cruiser HMS *Spartan* is sunk in Anzio Bay by an Hs 293A glider bomb. On 25 February the destroyer HMS *Inglefield* is another victim of a glider bomb.

17 January. The British midget submarine *X.20* conducts a covert reconnaissance off the Normandy coast where COPP parties landed from the submarine over a four day period take soil samples from beaches and measure beach gradients.

17/18 February. US carrier-borne aircraft strike at the main Japanese base of Truk in the Caroline Islands. Although the capital ships and carriers have been withdrawn to Singapore, the Americans sink the cruisers *Katori* and *Naka*, the armed merchant cruiser *Akagi Maru* and the destroyers *Maikaze*, *Fumizuki*, *Oite* and *Tachikaze*, together with a large number of auxiliary vessels.

Above: A periscope photograph shows a torpedo fired by the US submarine *Puffer* hitting the *Ryuko Mizrit* (the ex-French liner *D'Artagnan*) on 1 January 1944. (USN)

Above: Personnel from the US carrier *Guadalcanal* on the barely afloat *U505* which they captured on 4 June 1944. The U-boat was towed some 2,500 miles to Bermuda. *U505* is now on display in Chicago. (USN)

30 March. The destroyer HMS *Laforey* is torpedoed and sunk in the Mediterranean by *U223* during a 5½-hour hunt for the submarine. The U-boat is later sunk by HMS *Tumult*, *Hambledon* and *Blencathra*. HMS *Laforey* is the last British warship to be sunk in the Mediterranean by submarine.

30 March. US carrier-borne aircraft attack Japanese bases in the Western Carolines, particularly the anchorage at Palau. The destroyer *Wakatake* and patrol boat *No 31* are both sunk, along with three oilers (which are almost irreplaceable as far as Japan is concerned) and a fast repair ship.

26 April. The German torpedo boat *T.29* is sunk off the Île de Batz in the English Channel by HMCS

Above: British commandos come ashore at St Aubin sur Mer on 6 June 1944.

Haida. On the 29th *Haida* and her sister ship *Athabaskan* are in the same area supporting a minelaying operation. *Haida* damages *T.27* and drives her aground, where she is subsequently destroyed by the RAF. However, *Athabaskan* has just been torpedoed by the German torpedo boats and has sunk with heavy loss of life.

27/28 April. German *S-boote* encounter a convoy of LSTs engaged in Operation 'Tiger', a rehearsal for the Normandy landings. An LST is sunk off Slapton Sands and 638 US soldiers are killed.

29 May. *U549* torpedoes and sinks the escort carrier USS *Block Island* south of the Azores. *U549* is subsequently sunk by the USS *Elmore*, but not before she has torpedoed and damaged the destroyer escort USS *Barr*. *Block Island* is the only US carrier to be sunk in the Atlantic.

6 June. A fleet of over 5,000 vessels lands British, Canadian and American soldiers on five beaches in the Seine Bay. The *Kriegsmarine* reacts swiftly, but although three torpedo boats find the battleships of the British bombardment group they only manage to sink the Norwegian destroyer *Svenner.* Mines account for the other two casualties on D-Day: HMS *Wrestler* (damaged beyond repair) north of Le Havre and the USS *Corry* off Utah beach; the latter's 260 survivors are rescued by the USS *Fitch* and *Hobson,* which are fired upon by shore batteries. Further mining casualties include the US minesweeper *Tide* (7 June) and the destroyers USS *Meredith* and *Glennon* and destroyer escort *Rich* (lost on 8 June). The only naval loss to air attack is the frigate HMS *Lawford,* sunk on 8 June off 'Juno' beach.

9 June. Fifty-three merchant ships and five old warships are scuttled off the Normandy beaches to form a four-mile breakwater within

Above: A beachmaster's position at Courseeles in the *Juno* sector of the Normandy beachhead, June 1944. The beachmasters played a vital role in maintaining the smooth flow of supplies from ship to shore in an amphibious operation. (ECPA)

which the Mulberry harbours will be constructed.

14 June. US Navy forces land troops and Marines on the island of Saipan in the Pacific.

15 June. The German light forces based in the Channel ports constitute a threat to the invasion fleet both through direct attack and by covert minelaying, and so 325 Lancasters of RAF Bomber Command attack Le Havre and sink the torpedo boats *Falke*, *Jaguar* and *Möwe*, eleven *S-Boote*, twenty miscellaneous patrol craft and nineteen auxiliaries. The tor-pedo boat *Kondor* is damaged beyond repair. German naval forces in France are crippled. The only survivor is *T.28*, which manages to escape from Le Havre in late July.

19 June. Battle of the Philippine Sea.

Above: A damaged Japanese 'Betty' bomber roars over the flight deck of an American carrier in 1944.

21 June. The German minelaying campaign off the Normandy beaches continues to claim a significant number of casualties; the Oyster, or pressure, mine is particularly effective. On 5/6 July the German *K-Verband* launches human torpedoes against the invasion fleet and manages to sink the minesweeepers *Magic* and *Cato* on the 6th, the Polish cruiser *Dragon* and British minesweeper *Pylades* on the 8th and possibly the destroyer *Isis* on the 20th.

22 June. A combined British and Italian operation is mounted against the cruisers *Bolzano* and *Gorizia* at La Spezia to prevent their being sunk as blockships. Two British Chariots are dropped off at the harbour by Italian torpedo boats. *Bolzano* is successfully sunk but the Chariot assigned to *Gorizia* fails to find the target.

2/3 August. The German K-Verband makes its biggest effort yet against the invasion fleet. Fifty-eight *Neger* human torpedoes and thirty *Linsen* are dispatched and sink the destroyer *Quorn*, the trawler *Gairsay* and an LCG. The cost is high: the 'Trout Line' claims forty-one *Neger* and twenty-two *Linsen*.

15 August. Anglo-American forces carry out a largely unopposed landing in the south of France.

18 August. In the Baltic, the German torpedo boats *T.22*, *T.30* and *T.32* are lost when they stray into a German-laid minefield in the Gulf of Narva while supporting Army operations. A total of 393 officers and men are killed. Coming so soon after the loss of every unit west of the Strait of Dover, this represents a major disaster.

25 August. The *Kriegsmarine* scuttles its surviving units in the Channel and Biscay ports in the face of the Allied advance, thus marking the end of German surface operations in this theatre. The destroyer *Z.37* and five minesweepers are scuttled at Bordeaux.

Above: Two men on a raft rescued by the destroyer HMS *Rapid* in 1944 after spending nearly 53 days adrift after their ship was torpedoed. (Author)

August. In the worst 'friendly fire' incident of the Second World War, the British minesweepers *Britomart* and *Hussar* are sunk in error off Cap d'Antifer by RAF Typhoon aircraft. The minesweeper *Salamander* is damaged beyond repair, while the minesweeper *Jason* and the trawler *Colsay* are lightly damaged.

15 September. *Tirpitz* is attacked by RAF bombers and is hit and damaged by a 12,000lb bomb.

23 October. The Japanese battleship *Musashi* is sunk by numerous bomb and torpedo hits from US carrier aircraft.

12 November. *Tirpitz* is sunk by RAF Bombers with 12,000lb bombs.

20 October. US landings on Leyte.

23–26 October. The Battle of Leyte Gulf off the Philipines, the largest naval battle in history. The US ships are engaged by four separate Japanese strike forces. The Japanese plan to destroy the US invasion fleet fails and it is their fleet that is left totally crippled. One disturbing aspect of the battle is the appearance of the Kamikaze suicide aircraft.

Above: Stowing 4in ammunition in racks formerly occupied by torpedoes in the British T class submarine in 1944. In areas where targets were small, the gun became a more important weapon than the torpedo. (Gus Britton)

Above: The gun crew gather round the 3in gun on the casing of the British submarine *Shakespeare* during an action in the Far East on 3 January 1945. Note how little space there is on the casing for the gun's crew to work the weapon. (Author)

25 December. Leyte finally cleared.

1945
30 January. The greatest maritime disaster in history when the liner *Wilhelm Gustlaff*, having just left Danzig with German refugees fleeing the advancing Soviet Army, is sunk by a Russian submarine. 8,000 people lose their lives.
19 February. US amphibious landings on Iwo Jima.
24 March. Iwo Jima declared secure.
24 March. The Kerama Islands captured, marking the beginning of Operation *Iceberg*, the capture of Okinawa.
1 April. The Americans manage to land 50,000 men on Okinawa in one day. The British Pacific Fleet aids the US Fleet during this great battle.
7 April. The Japanese battleship *Yamato* is sunk by 5 bombs and 10 torpedoes from US carrier aircraft.
22 June. Marks the end of the bloody battle for Okinawa.
30 July. The cruiser USS *Indianapolis* is torpedoed by the Japanese submarine *I-58*, off Tinian. The cruiser is on her way to Leyte after delivering to Tinian components for one of the atomic bombs that are later to dropped on Japan. 883 men are lost.

1946
25 August. The Allied Control Commission for Germany formally announces that the *Kriegsmarine* has been dissolved.
22 October. The destroyers HMS *Saumarez* and HMS *Volage* are mined in international waters while passing between the island of Corfu and the Albanian coast. Thirty-six British sailors are killed

and *Saumarez* is declared a constructive total loss. Britain is subsequently awarded damages in the International Court (which have never been paid).

1947

The Royal Navy operates to prevent illegal Jewish immigration into Palestine. These are messy, distasteful and often violent operations in which British boarding parties are issued with cricketers' 'boxes' as an essential item of equipment, the hat-pin being a preferred weapon of the immigrants.

1948

22 November. In the Arab-Israeli War, Israeli commandos using ex-Italian explosive motor boats sink the Egyptian flagship *El Amir Farouk.*

1949

April. The North Atlantic Treaty Organisation (NATO) is founded; members are the USA, Britain, Canada, France, Belgium, Netherlands, Luxembourg, Portugal, Denmark, Iceland and Norway. The organisation will subsequently be enlarged with the admission of West Germany, Italy, Spain, Greece and Turkey.

July. The 'Yangste Incident': the British frigate HMS *Amethyst*, which has been damaged by Chinese communist gunfire while some way up the Yangtse, makes a

Above: Surrender, May 1945. Two German Type VIIC U-boats arrive at Loch Eriboll in Scotland following the German surrender. (Author)

daring dash down the river to safety on the night of 30 July. She re-joins the Fleet the next day, to general acclamation.

1950

25 June. The Korean War breaks out. For the next three years UN naval forces will operate off the east and west coasts of Korea, supporting the land forces with shore bombardment and carrier air strikes and imposing a blockade.

19 September. The US Navy lands US Marines at Inchon on the west coast of Korea in a daring and successful operation to cut the North Korean forces in two.

1951

British naval forces from the Mediterranean Fleet are dispatched to the Persian Gulf on the nationalisation of the Anglo-Iranian Oil Company. The dispute is settled politically and there is no need for the proposed maritime evacuation of British dependents.

1952

February. A strike by employees of the Suez Canal Company leads to the canal being operated by the Royal Navy. In the Atlantic, Exercise 'Mainbrace' demonstrates the capability of the NATO fleet to strike at the USSR from the far north and challenge the Soviet Navy there.

1954

21 January. The launch takes place of the USS *Nautilus*, the world's first nuclear-powered submarine. In the Far East, the Formosa Straits Patrol is established to protect shipping trading between Hong Kong and ports on the Chinese mainland from harassment by Nationalist Chinese forces operating from islands off Formosa.

1955

October. Goodwill visits by British and Soviet warships to Leningrad and Portsmouth respectively are marred by the adventures of and death of Commander 'Buster' Crabbe.

1956

25 July. The Egyptian Government provokes an international crisis by seizing the Suez Canal and outlawing the Suez Canal Company. Colonel Nasser, the Egyptian premier, had declared on 4 June that the Suez Canal Company's concession would not be extended past 1968. On 16 August Nasser walks out of talks held in London to reconcile differences. Britain and France resolve to settle the issue by force in concert with Israel.

31 October. British and French forces bomb Egyptian airfields and, in the first helicopter assault, land troops to take the Suez Canal. The Egyptian flagship *Ibrahim el Awal* surrenders to the French destroyer *Kersaint* off Haifa and is subsequently transferred to Israel. The Egyptians close the canal by sinking blockships.

7 November. US economic pressure forces Britain, France and Egypt to agree a ceasefire. The withdrawal of Anglo-French forces is complete by 22 December and on 27 December UN forces arrive to begin clearance of the Suez Canal.

1957

29 March. The Suez Canal is opened again to small ships and to all shipping from 9 April.

April. A British Defence White Paper adopts a massive-deterrent, short-war strategy. The opportunity is taken to make significant savings in the Defence Estimates by scrapping the Reserve Fleet and Coastal Forces.

1958

1 January. The Indonesian Government announces its decision to extend its territorial waters despite protests and warnings from Britain and the United States.

September. The first 'Cod War' breaks out between Britain and Iceland over fishing rights following the boarding of a British trawler by an Icelandic gunboat on 1 September.

1961

9 September. The USS *Long Beach*, the world's first nuclear-powered warship, is commissioned. Two months later she will be followed into service by the USS *Enterprise*, the world's first nuclear-powered aircraft carrier.

10 February. The US Government relinquishes the base rights in the Caribbean which it acquired under the 1941 'Destroyers for Bases' agreement with Britain.

June. There is a crisis over Kuwait following the Iraqis' declaration that they will annexe the country. On 30 June 42 RM Commando are landed in Kuwait, supported by a carrier task force, but by 13 August the Iraqi threat lessens and the troops are withdrawn.

December. India annexes the Portuguese colonies of Goa, Daman and Diu on the Indian subcontinent. The Portuguese Navy attempts to resist and the frigate *Alfonso de Albuequerque* is sunk on 18 December by INS *Mysore* and INS *Betwa*.

1962

6 April. The Nassau Agreement is concluded between Britain and the USA whereby the latter undertakes to supply the former with the Polaris strategic missile.

22 October. The US Government reveals evidence that the Soviet Union has established missiles on the island of Cuba. On 24 October a naval blockade of the island is instituted. The US Navy identifies further USSR-flag ships heading toward Cuba with missiles lashed to their decks. After a period of considerable tension, these ships turned back rather than test the US blockade and on 2 November the US Government announces that the missile bases have been dismantled.

1964

25 January. Royal Marine Commandos are landed from HMS *Centaur* to suppress an army mutiny in Tanganyika.

2 August. The Tonkin Gulf Incident: North Vietnamese torpedo boats attack the US destroyer *Maddox* on this day and again on 4 August. These attacks precipitate massive US retaliation which results in the destruction of twenty-five North Vietnamese warships.

29 October. The Indonesian Government of General Soekarno begins a series of landing operations to destabilise the new regime in Malaysia. Between 1964 and 1966 the Royal Navy, with growing support from the new Malaysian forces, operates to safeguard the new regime. The Royal Navy's objectives are two-fold: first, by use of the striking power of the fleet carriers (never used but frequently threatened) to deter the Indonesian regime from further aggression; and second, to provide active support at all levels ranging from disembarked helicopter squadrons, which operate in the jungle to great effect, to patrols in coastal waters and the Strait of Malacca to prevent Indonesian landings.

1965

11 November. The Rhodesian declaration of independence leads to the imposition of the Beira Patrol to prevent oil imports.

1966

February. The British Labour Government decides to cancel the CVA-01 aircraft carrier programme and announces that the existing carrier force will be run on until the 1970s and then scrapped without replacement. The Navy Minister and the First Sea Lord resign.

1967

May. The Nigerian Civil War breaks out following the decision of the eastern part of the Federal Republic of Nigeria to secede from the Union and form a separate state, Biafra. The Federal Navy, consisting of a frigate and five small combatants, remains loyal to the government and establishes an effective blockade of the 200-mile Biafran coast, preventing the secessionist government from receiving supplies by sea. The Navy then uses its one landing craft to land troops to capture the oil terminal at Bonny and subsequently at Port Harcourt and Calabar.

8 June. Israeli aircraft and torpedo boats attack the US intelligence gathering ship *Liberty* which is conducting surveillance operations off Sinai. Thirty-seven US sailors are killed in the attack.

2 October. HMS *Resolution*, the first British Polaris submarine, is completed.

21 October. The Israeli destroyer *Eilat* is sunk outside Port Said by Egyptian *Komar* class FACs firing 'Styx' SSMs.

1968

January. A British Defence Review abandons all commitments east of Suez. Henceforth British naval efforts will be directed towards NATO and the Eastern Atlantic.

23 January. North Korean naval forces seize the US Navy intelligence ship *Pueblo*, which is operating in international waters off Wonsan.

1969

8 June. Spain begins a blockade of Gibraltar in support of her claim to the territory.

September. An Israeli armoured battalion is landed in the Gulf of Suez in Egypt for a raid in depth. The operation is very successful.

1971

4 January. US President Nixon warns the Soviet Government about incursions by Soviet submarines into Cuban waters. The British Exercise 'Highwood' exposes the fallacy of the RAF's claim to be able to supply shore-based air cover to ships at sea.

December. The 'Lightning War' erupts between India and Pakistan over the status of East Pakistan. An Indian task force centred on the carrier *Vikrant* blockades East Pakistan and prevents reinforcements and supplies reaching the country by sea. The four Pakistani missile boats and a large number of smaller craft are all sunk by the Indian Navy on the first day of the fighting. Indian Navy 'advisers' have trained *Mukhti Bahini* guerrillas to plant limpet mines on bridges and Pakistani river craft. The Indian Western Fleet also demonstrates its superiority over the Pakistani main force. The Pakistani submarine *Ghazi* is sunk on 4 December as she lurks outside the Indian naval base of Visakhaptnam, while the next day Indian naval forces sink the destroyer *Karachi* and a minesweeper before bombarding the naval base. The elimination of Pakistani naval forces from the Bay of Bengal allows India to concentrate on becoming a regional power in her own right in the Indian Ocean.

1973

September. The second 'Cod War' breaks out between Britain and Iceland. In one confrontation between a British frigate and an Icelandic gunboat British sailors are alleged to have pelted the gunboat's crew with carrots.

October. In the 1973 Yom Kippur War thirteen Israeli fast attack craft with sixty-three Gabriel missile launchers defeat twenty seven Arab *Osa* and *Komar* boats mounting eighty-four 'Styx' missiles. On the first night of the war, off Latakia in Syria, and in what was the first missile-versus-missile surface action in history, five Israeli units evaded two salvos of six 'Styx' missiles and then fire a Gabriel salvo that sinks all three Syrian ships. Two nights later six Israeli craft dodge twelve 'Styx' missiles and sink three out of four Egyptian *Osa* boats off Damietta.

1974

January. A Chinese landing in battalion stength on the Paracel Islands, 225 miles east of Vietnam, is swiftly repulsed by South Vietnamese naval forces. Two Chinese warships are sunk and two damaged in return for one Vietnamese vessel sunk. Chinese warships fire on South Vietnamese warships laying claim to the Spratly Islands in the South China Sea. In the Middle East, RN mine countermeasures teams complete clearance operations in the Suez Canal.

July. Turkish naval forces launch and support an amphibious invasion of Cyprus in order to protect the ethnic Turkish community. On 22 July the Turkish destroyer *Kocatepe* is sunk in error by the Turkish Air Force. UN forces prevent the Greek Navy from intervening and as a result Greece leaves NATO's military structure.

1975

5 June. The Suez Canal is reopened.

September. Civil war breaks out in the former Portuguese colony of East Timor. A force of thirty Indonesian warships gathers offshore to monitor developments.

December. Indonesian warships

HMS *Resolution*, one of Britain's four Polaris SSBS recommissions after a refit at Rosyth in 1984. (MoD)

bombard targets in East Timor in support of airborne and marine landings to capture the island's capital, Dili. Subsequent naval operations, supported by local anti-communist guerrillas, result in the capture of the towns of Maubara and Baucau, the Ocussi Ambeno enclave and the offshore island off Atauro. At the end of 1975 East Timor becomes the twenty-seventh province of Indonesia.

1976

Outbreak of the Third 'Cod War' between Britain and Iceland over fishing rights in the North Atlantic.

4 February. In the South Atlantic, an Argentine destroyer fires at the British research vessel *Shackleton* during a periodic bout of belligerence by the Argentine Government in support of its claim to the Falkland Islands.

1977

A British SSN is deployed to the South Atlantic to deter Argentine aggression against the Falkland Islands.

1980

24 September. War breaks out between Iran and Iraq. The Armilla Patrol is instituted in the Persian Gulf by RN ships in support of British interests.

1981

June. The Israeli fast attack craft hit the PFLP (Popular Front for the Liberation of Palestine) HQ at Tripoli in Lebanon. In Great Britain, the publication of *The Way Forward*, a Defence Review sponsored by Defence Secretary John Nott, is not well received.

1982

2 April onwards. Argentina resorts to force as a means of settling the long-standing dispute with Britain over the Falkland Islands and seizes both the Falklands and South Georgia on 2 April. In response, a task force centred around the carriers *Invincible* and *Hermes* is despatched from the UK to repossess the islands. Britain declares a blockade of the islands and on 2 May the Argentine cruiser *General Belgrano* (part of three-pronged Argentine striking force about to deliver an attack against the British carrier group) is sunk by the submarine *Conqueror*. Two days later the British destroyer *Sheffield* is badly damaged by an Argentine Exocet missile; on 10 May she has to be scuttled. On 21 May the British land at San Carlos on East Falkland and, despite fierce Argentine air attacks on the beach-head which result in the loss of the frigates *Ardent* and *Antelope*, begin an advance on Port Stanley which results in the Argentine surrender on 14 June. However, on 25 May air attacks on British ships result in the loss of the stores ship *Atlantic Conveyor* and destroyer *Coventry* while on 8 June the LSLs *Sir*

Galahad and *Sir Tristram* were both very badly hit with heavy loss of life. *Sir Galahad* is subsequently scuttled. On 12 June HMS *Glamorgan* is badly damaged by an Exocet.

6 June–August. The Israeli Navy makes a massive effort in providing naval gunfire and amphibious lift to support the Israeli Army's invasion of southern Lebanon. The Israeli naval presence off the coast of Lebanon effectively stops the evacuation of Palestinian forces to Cyprus.

28 September. US Marines land at Beirut to resume peace keeping operations. Naval gunfire support is provided by US warships offshore, although there is some criticism over the accuracy (or otherwise) of the *New Jersey*'s 16in gunfire against Druse positions in the hills outside Beirut. The Marines are withdrawn after a suicide bomber kills 90.

1983

October. The US Navy launches the invasion of the island of Grenada to suppress a Marxist-orientated government. The operation is notable for appalling Army–Navy communications.

1985

4 February. Spain formally ends her blockade of Gibraltar.

1986

24 March. The US Navy launches Operation 'El Dorado Canyon' against Libyan naval forces in the Gulf of Sirte in which the FAC *Beir Glulud* and ex-Soviet *Nanuchka* missile corvette *No 419* are sunk by A-6 Intruder aircraft. Another

Nanuchka, No 416, is damaged the next day.

1987

September. The Iranian LST *Iran Ajr* is captured by the US Navy loaded with contact mines ready for laying. The vessel is scuttled on 26 September.

18 October. US warships attack oil platforms in the Straits of Hormuz used by Iranian Revolutionary Guards as bases from which to harass shipping. Two platforms are

shelled after the occupants are given time to evacuate and the third is boarded by US special forces.

1988

Exercise 'Teamwork', a massive demonstration of NATO maritime capability, is held in the Atlantic. **April.** US air and naval forces attack Iranian forces in the Persian Gulf. The Iranian frigate *Sahand* and fast attack craft *Joshan* are sunk on 19 April and the frigate *Sabalan* is damaged.

3 July. In the Persian Gulf, the American destroyer *Vincennes* shoots down an Iran Air passenger plane in error, believing it to be an Iranian F14 aircraft. All 286 passengers and crew are killed.

1990

August. Iraq invades Kuwait. The invasion results in a massive UN response, Operation 'Desert Shield', to defend Gulf States and Saudi Arabia. Sanctions imposed on Iraq lead to a maritime blockade

being established. In Britain, members of the WRNS go to sea in combatant ships for the first time.

1991

January. Operation 'Desert Storm' is launched to liberate Kuwait. Iraq is attacked by aircraft from US carriers operating in the Persian Gulf and by cruise missiles fired by US warships in Gulf and by US submarines in the Red Sea. US warships bombard Iraqi positions in Kuwait – the last occa-

Above: The Dutch *Walrus* class SSK *Tidjerhaai* entering Portsmouth in 1989. These Dutch boats are the most advanced and capable SSKs extant in the world. (Author)

sion on which a battleship fires her guns in action – the way through the Iraqi minefields having been cleared for them by RN mine countermeasures vessels.

1993

The British Government announces massive cutbacks in the operational strength of the Royal Navy, the reduction of the Royal Navy Reserve by one-third and the abolition of the Royal Naval Auxiliary Service. In the Adriatic, as part of UN sanctions against Serbia over her conduct in the Yugoslav Civil War, a naval blockade is established.

1994

19 September. The 330-ton Sri Lankan patrol craft *Sagarwardene* is sunk by Tamil 'Tiger' guerrillas in a suicide attack in the Indian Ocean.

1995

Filipino warships destroy markers left on the Spratly Islands by Chinese forces indicating that the islands are Chinese territory.

1996

March. A US Navy carrier battle group deployed to Taiwan discourages Chinese attempts to influence the outcome of the Taiwanese elections by displays of military force.

17 September. A North Korean *Sang-O* SSK runs aground at Kangnung in South Korea. After protracted negotiations the North Korean Government issues a grudging 'apology' in December.

1997

April. The Italian Navy carries out Operation 'Alba' to land a multinational peacekeeping force in Albania.

May. Protesters on the island of Vietquez in the Caribbean demand the withdrawal of the US Navy which holds massive training areas on the island.

June. Nigerian naval forces support the landing of Nigerian troops to suppress a coup d'etat in the neighbouring state of Sierra Leone.

1998

20 August. US warships in the Red Sea and the Arabian Sea launch cruise missiles attacks against terrorist targets in Afganistan and the Sudan.

Above: The amphibious assault ship USS *Iwo Jima*. Her sister ship, USS *Tripoli*, while acting as a mine countermeasures helicopter carrier, hit a mine on 18 February 1991 during the Gulf War. (IWM GLF 1028)

A depth charge explodes astern of the sloop HMS *Starling*. The floats on top of the depth charge racks are 'Foxer' decoys for use against acoustic homing torpedoes. (USN)

A — Z

A-Arcs. In a warship, the limits to which the gun turrets (q.v.) can be trained. To open A-Arcs is to alter course in relation to the bearing of the enemy so that all the turrets can bear.

AAW. Anti-Air Warfare.

ABDA. American, British, Dutch and Australian command structure established following the Japanese declaration of war in December 1941. Doomed to failure through lack of resources and pitted against a seemingly invincible enemy, it collapsed following the twin defeats at the Battle of the Java Sea and the Battle of the Sunda Strait.

'Abercrombie', Operation. Two small raids in April 1942 at Hardelot between Boulogne and Etaples on the French coast to test coastal defences. Sometimes spelt as Abercromby.

Aboukir, **HMS.** An elderly *Cressy* class armoured cruiser launched on 16 May 1900. By 1914 she was virutally obsolete but with her sister ships *Cressy* and *Hogue* was employed on patrol duties in the southern North Sea. On 22 September 1914 all three ships were sunk by the German submarine *U9* commanded by Leutnant Otto Weddigen, 30 miles west of Ymuiden. The loss of life in the three ships was very heavy, over 1,400 officers and men being killed and only just over 800 saved.

A-Bracket. The triangular bracket, often also known as a sole piece or sole bracket, which extends from the hull of a steam or motor vessel to give support to the propeller shaft where it extends beyond the hull.

'Abstension', Operation. Bombardment of the Italian island of Casteloritzo in February 1941.

'Accolade', Operation. Plan to take the island of Rhodes in advance of the Italian surrender. Cancelled in September 1943.

'Achse', Operation. German countermeasures to seize the Italian Fleet and disarm Italian forces in the event of Italy concluding a separate peace with the Allies. Implemented on 8 September 1943.

'Acid-Drop', Operation. Capture of prisoners and beach reconnaissance at Hardelot and Merlimont in April 1941.

Acoustic housekeeping. The prevention of machinery and equipment noise within a submarine from being transmitted to the hull and therefore to the water outside.

Acoustic mine. A mine activated by sound. The mine listens for the characteristic signature of the desired target. When introduced during the Second World War, the mine merely listened for a general increase in noise but modern acoustic mines can be tuned to a specific range of frequencies. Acoustic activation is often combined with magnetic or pressure sensors.

Action Data Automation Weapon System (ADAWS). A British computerised tactical data system developed for air defence ships. ADAWS 1 was first fitted in the Batch 2 'County' class destroyers and ADAWS 2 to HMS *Bristol*, ADAWS 3 was intended for the abortive CVA-01 aircraft carrier and ADAWS 4 was installed in Batch 1 Type 42 destroyers, ADAWS 5 in Ikara-fitted *Leander* class frigates, ADAWS 6 in *Invincible* and *Illustrious*, ADAWS 7 in the Batch 2 Type 42 destroyers and ADAWS 8 in Type 42 destroyers with Type 2016 sonar. ADAWS 9 was developed for the projected Type 43 destroyer and ADAWS 10 was fitted in HMS *Ark Royal*.

Active sonar. A sonar that detects its target by receiving sound that it has transmitted. It is thus not dependent on any noise emitted by the target, though its use does reveal the user's position.

'Acute', Operation. Cutting of submarine telephone cables in the English Channel between the UK and France in 1941.

AD. Destroyer tender in US Navy classification. The prefix 'A' used in this and other similar classifications designates 'auxiliary'.

ADA. Action Data Automation. An early British computerised tactical data system. The project began in 1954 and first went to sea in the carrier HMS *Eagle*. The system combined information from the ship's own sensors together with those of other ships and aircraft.

It then evaluated threats and calculated interceptions and passed this information to other ships and aircraft. It replaced the sixty or so officers and men which had done this task manually in the AIO.

ADLIPS. Automatic Data Link Plotting System. A Canadian tactical data system begun in 1969, designed as an inexpensive way of replacing manual plotting. First fitted to HMCS *Athabaskan* in 1976, the production equipment was installed in all RCN destroyers between 1981 and 1986.

Admiral. In all maritime nations, the title of the commander of a fleet or a subdivision of it. The word comes from the Arab *Amir*. As early as the twelfth century the commander of Muslim fleets in the Mediterranean had the title of *Amir al Bahr*. This title evolved into the French *Amiral* and the Spanish *Almirante* and, eventually, the English Admiral. The four active ranks, or Flag Ranks as they are known, are, in descending order, Admiral of the Fleet, Admiral, Vice-Admiral and Rear-Admiral. These ranks are found in all navies throughout the world, though in different forms and spellings. The exclusively male tenure of the rank of Admiral was first breached in 1972 when Miss Alene Duerk was promoted to Rear-Admiral as head of the US Navy's Nurse Corps.

Admiral Graf Spee. (see overleaf) A German pocket battleship of 11,900 tons and armed with six 11in guns. Launched on 30 June

1934, she enjoyed a short though highly effective career as a commerce raider in the South Atlantic where, in a two-month period, she sank nine British merchant ships. On 13 December 1939 she was brought to action off the River Plate by the British cruisers *Exeter*, *Ajax* and *Achilles*, commanded by Commodore Henry Harwood, and after an inconclusive action she took refuge in the neutral port of Montevideo. Four days later she put to sea but was scuttled to avoid internment or defeat at the hands of superior British forces waiting outside the harbour. She was the first major German warship to be sunk during the Second World War. Her wreck was subsequently bought by the British and examined. A number of artefacts, including a 15cm mounting and searchlights, were brought back to Britain, but their current whereabouts are unknown.

Admiral Scheer. (see overleaf) Sister ship to the *Admiral Graf Spee*. She was the most successful German warship of the Second World War in terms of tonnage of Allied shipping sunk, with 137,223 tons to her credit. She was eventually bombed by the RAF at Kiel on 9 April 1945. The ship capsized and her hull was subsequently partly broken up *in situ*. The remains were later 'buried' during the building of a new quay.

Admiralty Islands. An archipelago in the Bismarck Sea and the site of the Operation 'Brewer' landings in February and March 1944. US Army units landed on

several islands, beginning with Los Negros on 29 February. The other landing was at Manus: fierce fighting ensued, and the Americans were forced to use flame-throwers and armour to winkle out the most determined of the defenders. The Japanese held out until 18 May, when the islands were declared secure and the Americans could begin to use Seeadler harbour.

'Adoption', Operation. Destruction of enemy shipping in the North Andaman Sea, May 1945.

'Adroit', Operation. Planned occupation of the Canary Islands during the Second World War, subject to Spanish Government invitation.

'Advent', Operation. Offensive sweep of enemy coastal shipping routes in the English Channel by coastal forces in October 1942.

AE. Ammunition Ship. US Navy/NATO classification.

Aegis. The mythical shield of the gods, now chosen as the name for the American Mk 7 AAW weapons system. This is the most advanced AAW system in the world, integrating SPY-1 phased array radars with SM-2 SAMs, and is fitted in US *Ticonderoga* class cruisers and *Arleigh Burke* class destroyers and in the Japanese *Kongo* class destroyers. It consists of a Command and Decision system, Display System and Weapons Control System which together employ seventeen computers and eleven minicomputers. Aegis can handle 128 tracks simultaneously.

Above: German pocket battleship *Admiral Graf Spee* near Merck, Norway, 5 July 1938.
(IWM HU 1029)

Below: The German pocket battleship *Admiral Scheer* in raiding guise with a false bow wave. *Scheer* was the most successful of the three pocket battleships. (Author)

It was first fitted to USS *Ticonderoga* in 1983.

'Aerial', Operation. Evacuation of British troops from France in 1940 from ports other than Dunkirk. Sometimes spelt Ariel.

AEW. Airborne Early Warning. Surveillance radars fitted to fixed-wing aircraft to provide a more comprehensive picture of the air threat, particularly at low level. The American EC-2 Hawkeye is perhaps the most advanced such AEW aircraft in service.

AF. Store ship. US Navy classification.

AFS. Combat store ship. US Navy classification.

'Aflame', Operation. Deception operation off the French coast in October 1942 involving a large naval force and dummy airborne landing near Berck, the object being to draw enemy aircraft into battle.

Africa, **HMS.** British *King Edward VII* class pre-dreadnought battleship. In 1912 she was fitted with a flying-off platform over her forecastle and on 10 January 1912 a Short S.27 aircraft made the first take-off from a British ship while *Africa* was anchored at Sheerness.

Agadir Crisis. July 1911. Caused by the French decision to send troops to intervene in the Moroccan civil war. The German Government responded by claiming that the French action was a violation of Moroccan sovereignty and despatched a gunboat to Agadir in response. Given the overheated state of European diplomacy as a result of the naval race, there was a risk of war but the crisis resolved itself. However, from a British perspective the crisis revealed alarming gaps in the perceptions of the Army and Royal Navy about how and where a European war would be fought.

'Agency', Operation. Plan for the immobilisation of certain British ports in the event of an invasion, 1941.

AGER. Auxiliary Environmental Research Ship. US designation to mask the intelligence-gathering activities of the USS *Pueblo* and *Banner.*

AGI. Intelligence collector. US Navy classification. A term which came to be universally applied to the Soviet 'trawlers' which sprouted a forest of antennae and which lurked outside every major NATO port and base.

Agincourt, **HMS.** A British battleship, known as the "Gin Palace", which served in the Grand Fleet during the First World War. She had been ordered by Brazil as *Rio de Janeiro* but in 1912 the order was cancelled when the bottom fell out of the South American rubber market. She was then bought by the Turks in 1914 and renamed *Sultan Osman I.* However, when it became clear that Turkey was going to side with Germany, she was taken over by the Royal Navy. She was unique in that she mounted fourteen 12in guns in seven turrets – more than any other capital ship. At Jutland it was recorded that when she fired a full broadside it looked as if she was blowing up. She was scrapped in 1922.

A-Go. Japanese name for the Battle of the Marianas in June 1944.

Agouti. British scheme to inject air through a ship's propeller to reduce cavitation that interfered with the ship's asdic operation.

'Agreement', Operation. Sea raid on Axis shipping and port facilities at Tobruk, September 1942.

Ahead Throwing Weapon (ATW). Anti-submarine weapon which throws a projectile ahead of the ship. In a straight forward depth charge attack, the attacking ship must run over the target, thereby losing asdic contact before dropping the charges. The use of ATWs enabled asdic contact to be maintained throughout the attack. *See* Hedgehog, Limbo, Squid.

Aichi D1A. Japanese single-seat biplane dive-bomber based on the German He 66. The D1A1 was one of the first Japanese aircraft to be involved in the Sino-Japanese War and its successor, the D1A2, achieved notoriety by sinking the American gunboat *Panay* on the Yangtse river in 1937. However, by the time of the Japanese attack on Pearl Harbor the aircraft had been withdrawn from front line service. The aircraft received the Allied code-name 'Susie'.

Aichi D3A. Japanese single-engine monoplane carrier- or land-based dive bomber (D3A1 and D3A2) designed to replace the D1A2; a trainer version, the D3A2-K, was also produced. The aircraft first flew in December 1937 and carrier trials were completed in 1940. The fixed undercarriage gave the aircraft a rather outdated look but the D3A, or 'Val' as it was known to the Allies, took part in the attack on Pearl Harbor, the sortie into the Indian Ocean and the campaign in the Solomons. The D3A sank more Allied ships than any other type of Axis aircraft. As the war progressed it was outclassed by newer American aircaft. Eventually many were pressed into service as *Kamikazes*, a role in which they suffered heavy losses for little in the way of result. A total of 1,495 D3As were built.

Aichi E13A. Single-engine, twin-float reconnaissance seaplane (E13A1). Designed for long-range reconnaissance and maritime escort duties, the aircraft could be carried by cruisers and seaplane tenders. In December 1941 E13A1s from the cruisers *Chikuma*, *Kinugasa* and *Tone* flew reconnaissance missions during the attack on Pearl Harbor. E13A1s served wherever the Japanese Navy was active and, despite the aircraft's lack of defensive armament and crew protection, it was very successful in the maritime reconnaissance role. Its maximum endurance of fifteen hours in the air made it very suitable for long patrol missions. The aircraft served for near-

ly four years without alteration but in November 1944 the E13A1a and E13A1b variants were introduced. The E13A1a carried improved radio equipment while the E13A1b carried air-to-surface radar. Some E13As were fitted with a magnetic anomaly detector known as *Jikitanchiki*. The type was known to the Allies as 'Jake', and a total of 1,418 were built.

Aichi H9A. Twin-engine training and anti-submarine patrol flying boat. The aircraft was largely employed around the Japanese coast and remained unknown to the Allies until the end of the war.

Aichi E16A Zuiun (Auspicious Cloud). Single-engine, twin-float reconnaissance seaplane. Designed as a successor to the E13A, it first flew in May 1942 but did not go into production until August 1943, by which time Japan had lost air superiority in the Pacific. The E16A (Allied code-name 'Paul') suffered heavy losses in the Philippines and most of the survivors were expended as *Kamikazes* off Okinawa.

Aichi B7A Ryusei (Shooting Star). Single-engine, carrier-borne torpedo and dive-bomber. The prototype first flew in May 1942 but engine difficulties delayed the production run until April 1944. Production was finally halted by the May 1945 earthquake which devastated the manufacturing plant at Tokai. In any case it was all too late, for the Imperial Navy no longer possessed the carriers from which the aircraft could be flown. The few B7As which were

produced were flown from land bases.

AIO. Action Information Organisation. The systematic organisation of information from radar and other sensors (including the old-fashioned but invaluable 'Mark One Eyeball') to compile a three-dimensional tactical picture. First developed manually during the Second World War, it has now been mechanised with the advent of computerised radar systems.

AIP. Air Independent Propulsion. A propulsion system for non-nulcear submarines that reduces reliance on diesels for charging the batteries or substitutes for diesel propulsion. An early form of AIP was the steam turbine fuelled by hydrogen peroxide, but far more reliable (and safe) forms of AIP include closed-cycle diesels, Stirling engines using liquid oxygen and fuel cells of various types. Stirling engines are fitted in Sweden's *Gotland* class SSKs, and Australia has the option to retrofit Stirling engines into its Swedish-built *Collins* class submarines.

Air Cushion Vehicles. The naval term for the hovercraft. They are capable of high speeds and able to 'fly' over minefields and submerged obstructions. The Soviet navy were the first to employ them in their main order of battle. In 1977 the US Navy tested two, which resulted in orders of such aircraft to be carried in *Wasp* class LHD ships.

Air–Sea Rescue. A service introduced in 1940 by the Royal Air

Force to rescue pilots and aircrew forced to ditch at sea as a result of enemy action or accident. The service was operated by high-speed launches stationed at ports around the British coast, but particularly in the Channel and North Sea where the majority of air combats took place. Aircrew were issued with lifejackets containing a wireless transmitter (inflatable dinghies were similarly equipped) on which the launches could home. In the Pacific the Americans evolved a particularly comprehensive and effective air–sea rescue system involving the use of high-speed launches, submarines and aircraft. From one US submarine, *Tang*, no fewer than 22 aviators were recovered during the operations off Truk. In the post-1945 period the development of the helicopter has revolutionised air–sea rescue and many countries, including Britain, operate them as an emergency service at sea.

Airships. During the inter-war years the US Navy constructed sev-

Above: The US Navy Airship hovers over *U852*, first Nazi submarine to give up to American forces after Germany's surrender.
(IWM NYP 69371)

eral large rigid airships which could carry fighter aircraft for self-defence. After two of these monsters, *Akron* and *Macon*, crashed at sea, the Americans abandoned the rigid airship type. The US Navy was the only service of any nation to operate airships (blimps) during the Second World War (the US Army having surrendered all its airships in 1937). Blimps were employed for coastal anti-submarine patrol and were highly effective in this role. On the outbreak of war in 1941 the US Navy had ten blimps, but by the end of the war there were 167 in service. Although the majority of blimps entered service after May 1943, by which time the U-boats had largely been defeated, no convoy escorted by a blimp suffered any loss. The majority of blimps in service were of K-type the first of which, K-2, first flew in December. The K-type contained 400,000 cubic feet of non-flammable helium and was fitted with two reciprocating engines which gave a radius of 1,500 nautical miles and a speed of 75mph. Blimps carried a modest armament of depth charges and machine guns. Crews flew missions of up to twenty hours from bases in the US, the Caribbean and North Africa. The longest recorded flight was an eleven-day marathon by Commander J. R. Hunt USN, who flew non-stop (and unrefuelled) from the US to North Africa and back via the Caribbean. By the end of the war blimps had logged over 55,000 missions and 550,000 hours in the air. Only one was lost to enemy action: K-74 was shot down by *U134* on 18 July 1943 after her depth charges failed to release. The U-boat rescued all but one of her

crew, although the submarine with her prisoners aboard was sunk on 24 August 1943 by an RAF Wellington in the Bay of Biscay while returning to port.

AIV. Automatic Inboard Vent. A British system whereby the air used to fire a torpedo from a submarine's torpedo tube is drawn back into a tank. If the air were allowed to follow the torpedo out of the tube then it would create a disturbance on the surface which would give the submarine's position away. Similar systems exist for the torpedo-firing systems of other navies.

AK. Cargo ship. NATO classification.

AKA. Attack Cargo Ship. US Navy designation.

Akagi. Japanese aircraft carrier originally laid down as a 41,200-ton battlecruiser of the 8:8 Programme. Her construction was suspended in February 1922 on Japan's ratification of the Washington Treaty. The decision was taken to convert her to an aircraft carrier and she was completed as such in May 1927. Her displacement was 33,821 tons on trials; after major reconstruction between 1935 and 1938 this rose to 40,650 tons. Her maximum aircraft capacity was 91 although 72 was the operational maximum. *Akagi* was Admiral Nagumo's flagship at Pearl Harbor and in subsequent carrier operations in the Indian Ocean. She was sunk on 5 June 1942 during the Battle of Midway. In an attack by SBD-2

Dauntless dive-bombers from *Enterprise* and *Yorktown*, *Akagi* was caught with her air group ranged on deck having their armament changed. Her flight deck and hanagars were wrecked, uncontrollable fires were started and the ship was abandoned and subsequently scuttled.

'Alacrity', Operation. Landing of Allied forces in the Azores at Portugal's request, October 1943.

'Aladdin', Operation. Proposed naval landing in Norway in the Second World War had the Germans evacuated the country while still occupying the rest of Europe.

'Alba', Operation. Italian Navy operation launched in April 1997 to land and cover the EC peacekeeping force in Albania following the breakdown of civil order.

Albacore. British torpedo-bomber of the Second World War intended as a replacement for the Swordfish, but although it was in many ways superior to the Swordfish it never supplanted that aircraft. Albacores entered service in March 1940, but the only occasions on which they made torpedo attacks from carriers were during the Battle of Matapan in March 1941 and in the attack on the *Tirpitz* in March 1942. The Albacore resembled the Swordfish in that it was a biplane with a fixed undercarriage. However the Albacore was faster, had a longer range and an enclosed (heated) cockpit. The aircraft had a top speed of 161mph and a range of

Above: Fleet Air Arm Albacore torpedo-bombers in formation, 22 June 1942.
(IWM A 10686)

930 miles. The crew consisted of pilot, observer and TAG. Six 250lb or four 500lb bombs could be carried or, alternatively, an aerial torpedo. The plane was also armed with two forward-firing .303in machine guns and a .303in machine gun operated by the TAG. A total of 803 Albacores were built before production ceased in 1943.

Alberich. German name for a synthetic rubber (Oppanol) coating applied to a U-boat's hull which would absorb sonar impulses. In 1940 *U11* was coated with 4mm thick Alberich panels. Tests showed that the panels absorbed some 15% of sonar pulse reflectance although performance was affected by water conditions. *U67* was likewise treated but it was found that the coating was compromised as the Oppanol tiles came loose: in one voyage to Norway *U67* lost some 60% of the tiles. As a result the programme was discontinued. The introduction of the snorkel in 1944 revived interest in Alberich since snorkelling boats were forced to remain at periscope depth, which was where Alberich performed best. *U480* was the first operational boat to be given an Alberich coating and in August 1944 she reported that the coating was effective. Another boat so modified was *U110*5, which fell into British hands at the end of the Second World War: the British referred to her as the 'Black Panther' on account of the Oppanol coating. The British failed to solve the problems of adhesion which had bedevilled *U67* and moreover found that the Alberich coating reduced the boat's speed by 1.5kts. Despite the relative failure of Alberich, all modern SSNs are fitted with a hull coating of anechoic tiles to reduce the effectiveness of the opposition's sonar. Judging from the number of photographs of SSNs with one or more anechoic tiles missing, the problem of adhesion remains to be solved!

'Albion', Operation. German operation to capture Osel and Moon Island in the Baltic in September 1917.

Aldis lamp. A hand-held, electric lamp, fitted with a finger-operated shutter used for sending signals at sea.

Aleutian Islands. Chain of islands running east some 1,700 miles from the Alaskan mainland. In June 1942 the islands of Unalaska, Attu, Agattu and Kiska were occupied by the Japanese in order to prevent the Americans using them as a base from which to launch air attacks on Japan. The operation was also intended to draw off the US Fleet from the defence of Midway, but this was unsuccessful because the Americans were able to read the Japanese signal traffic. In order to halt further Japanese penetration of the Aleutian chain, the Americans established a base on Adak island on 30 August from which bombing raids could be launched on the Japanese-occupied islands. On 11 January 1943 US forces landed on Amchitka, 70 miles west of Kiska, and were able to use the island as a base from which they could besiege the Japanese garrison on Kiska. The Japanese' plight was further worsened by their defeat at the Battle of the Komandorskiye Islands (26 March 1943) when US naval forces drove off a Japanese force attempting to resupply the Kiska garrison; henceforth the Japanese were only able to replenish the garrison by submarine. On 11 May the Americans landed on Attu and there was eighteen days of fierce fighting before the island was secure. The Japanese then decided to evacuate Kiska by sea using submarines and transports. The evacuation was carried out successfully without being observed by US troops, so that when the Americans landed on Kiska on 15 August 1943 they found the island deserted. The capture of the Aleutians placed the Japanese Kurile Islands within bombing range and for the rest of the war Japanese bases on these islands were relentlessly attacked.

'Allah', Operation. Establishment of a small headquarters on a northern Dalmatian island–Vis was the site eventually chosen–to report shipping movements and from where sabotage could be organised.

Allied Naval Council. Organisation established in November 1917 under British presidency (France holding supreme command on land) to co-ordinate naval policy among the British, French, Italians, Japanese and Americans. Its deliberations were particularly relevant to the Mediterranean theatre, where the navies of all five powers were employed and where there was no overall commander-in-chief.

'Alloy', Operation. Operation to take the Azores by force should Vichy France declare war. The plan was abandoned in September 1940.

'Alphabet', Operation. Evacuation of Narvik, June 1940.

Altmark. German naval tanker of 8,053 tons and a supply ship to the German pocket battleship *Admiral Graf Spee*. After the latter was scuttled in the River Plate, the *Altmark*, with 299 British prisoners on board and under the command of Captain Dau, made the long and difficult voyage back to Germany across the Atlantic shipping lanes without being detected. It was only as she headed south using Norwegian territorial waters that she was spotted by the British. On 16 February 1940, while at anchor in Jössingfjord, she was boarded by men from the British destroyer HMS *Cossack* and the prisoners were released. Later the *Altmark* became a supply ship for German surface raiders and was renamed *Uckermarck*. She was accidentally destroyed at Yokohama on 30 November 1942.

Amethyst, HMS. Sloop commanded by Lt-Cdr J. S. Kerans RN which after being in action with the Communists in the Yangtse river in April 1949 was held there by the enemy but made her escape in a gallant 130-mile dash to the sea in July of that year.

Amphion, HMS. British *Active* class scout cruiser launched in 1911. She was mined in the North Sea on 6 August 1914, thus becoming the first British naval casualty of the First World War.

'Amrita', Operation. Minelaying operation in connection with Operation 'Neptune'.

'Anakim', Operation. Plan for the recapture of Burma, 1944.

Ancona. Italian liner torpedoed on 7 November 1915 by the German *U38* commanded by *Kapitänleutnant* Max Valentiner. Valentiner avoided the inconvenient fact that Germany was not at war with Italy by flying Austrian colours. It was therefore the hapless Austrians who had to face the wrath of the United States for twenty of the 200 dead were US citizens. The US Secretary of State, Robert Lansing, described the sinking as 'more atrocious than any of the submarine attacks which had previously taken place'.

Andaman Islands. Group of islands in the Bay of Bengal captured by the Japanese in March 1942. An Allied plan to retake the islands, code-named 'Buccaneer', was called off for lack of landing craft. Eventually the Japanese evacuated the islands in late 1944 and they were reoccupied by the British in January 1945.

'Andrew'. Slang term for the Royal Navy. It is said to have originated with the eighteenth-century press-gang officer, Andrew Miller, whose efficiency at finding men for the King's service during the Revolutionary and Napoleonic

Above: *Altmark* aground in Jössingfjord after the rescue of British prisoners. (IWM HU 27803)

AMPHIBIOUS WARFARE

In the wars between Britain and France in the late eighteenth and early nineteenth centuries, the knowledge of how to land troops on a hostile shore was considered as essential as knowledge of how to fight a fleet action. Particularly in America, the Royal Navy was constantly ferrying and landing troops, and had established a set of procedures for doing so. If a naval officer charged with landing General Wolfe's infantry at the foot of the Heights of Abraham at Quebec in 1759 could have been transported to the Normandy Beaches in June 1944, he might be unfamiliar with (or amazed by) the equipment being used but he would understand the basic principles of what was in progress. Between these two events the techniques of amphibious warfare fell into disuse. The Royal Navy carried British troops around the world in a series of police actions against various colonial rebellions but the knowledge of how to conduct a landing in strength on a hostile shore against an enemy well established in defensive positions was all but forgotten. The truth of this statement was tragically shown in the shambles which accompanied the British and Commonwealth landings on the Gallipoli peninsula in April 1915.

It was the requirement to land troops on defended beaches during the Second World War which led to a resurrection of this unique type of naval warfare. If the Allies were to retake Western Europe or advance against Japan across the Pacific, they could only do so by transporting thousands of men and their equipment across the sea and landing them on a hostile shore. Once there, the navy had to support them through the initial stages of the landing until the troops were established ashore. These operations required a fleet of specialised craft ranging from command ships with sophisticated command and control facilities to the humble LBK (Landing Barge Kitchen), which supplied hot meals to landing craft crews with no galley facilities, and from ocean-going transports (APAs), attack cargo ships (AKAs), dock landing ships (LSDs), tank landing ships (LSTs) to small utility landing craft (LCU). During an invasion the APAs and AKAs would disgorge men and supplies into the smaller landing craft – LCIs, LCUs and LCVPS – which would carry them to the beach, opening their bow doors or lowering their ramps to allow men and vehicles to go ashore. Specialised landing craft armed with guns, mortars and rockets would suppress beach defences during the landing phase. This vast fleet of ships was built up in an extraordinary short space of time. As a result the ships were ill-matched. Some were purpose-built to military requirements, others were taken up from trade and needed extensive modification. Nevertheless, it was on the fleet of amphibious ships – that large number of unnamed and often unsung craft – that the Allied victories in Europe and the Pacific were built.

Since 1945, developments in amphibious warfare have been dominated by the US Navy. This is inevitable given America's geographical separation from the scenes of any future war by two oceans. Yet in the immediate post-war period some doubts were expressed about whether there would be any need for the retention of an amphibious capability. The new disciples of air power argued that the large concentrations of warships, landing ships and craft required for a successful landing would be an ideal target for a nuclear strike. A future war would consist of nuclear exchanges between the two superpowers and there would be no place for amphibious landings. This theory was effectively disproved during the Korean War by MacArthur's brilliant amphibious landing at Inchon, which caused the (temporary) collapse of the North Korean forces in South Korea. The twenty-three LSTs which went ashore on the muddy flats of Inchon provided ample proof that amphibious warfare was a vital element of sea power. By 1955 the US Navy's Long Range Objectives Study Group was calling for an amphibious force of four command ships, six APAs, six AKAs, sixteen helicopter carriers twenty-four LSDs and sixteen LSTs together with a host of smaller craft.

The biggest single development in amphibious warfare techniques since the Second World War has been the introduction of the helicopter as a means of landing men and equipment. Helicopters offer a commander speed and flexibility in making an assault from the sea. The first experimental helicopter assault took place in January 1948 when five HO3S helicopters landed sixty-six US Marines on the North Carolina coast from the escort carrier *Palau*. Eight years later the first combat helicopter assault took place when twenty-two Whirlwind HAR.2 and HAR.3 and Sycamore Mk 14 helicopters landed 415 troops and twenty-two tons ▶

Wars led to it being said that he owned the Royal Navy.

***Andrew*, HMS.** Royal Navy 'A' class submarine built by Vickers and launched in 1946. *Andrew* was the last British submarine to

be armed with a 4in gun, and when she fired her last shot in December 1974 an era of submarine gunnery came to an end.

'Anger', Operation. Landing and recovery of a British officer from

the submarine *H43* to determine the state of German defences on Guernsey.

Angled flight deck. The angling of the landing deck of an aircraft carrier some 10° off the centreline so

---

AMPHIBIOUS WARFARE

▶ of ammunition at Suez in less than ninety minutes. Concurrent with the development of helicopters came the development of a specific type of vessel to carry them. At first such helicopter carriers (or LPHs in the acronym-ridden world of amphibious warfare) were converted aircraft carriers. The Americans' first such vessel was the escort carrier *Thetis Bay*, which was converted to carry twenty HRS helicopters and 1,000 troops. Britain went down a similar road, converting the light fleet carriers *Albion* and *Bulwark* to 'commando carriers'. A shortage of amphibious ships in the late 1950s saw the US Navy convert three *Essex* class carriers, *Boxer*, *Princeton* and *Valley Forge* to the role of LPH. These various conversions gave valuable service in the new skills required for helicopter assault. However, they suffered from numerous disadvantages. Troop spaces on board were cramped and units lost cohesion by being spread throughout the ship in order to fill the available bunk spaces. Since these ships were all fitted with warship propulsion plants they were expensive to man and to run. The three *Essex* class CVs converted by the US Navy required a ship's company of 1,500 (even though half the ship's propulsion plant was shut down) in order to

deliver 1,000 men ashore. What was required was a dedicated helicopter assault ship, and this is what the Americans got with *Iwo Jima*. Ordered in 1958, *Iwo Jima* and her sisters carry twenty helicopters and nearly 2,000 troops. Since the troops would be embarked for periods of up to six months, their accommodation spaces are laid out so as to retain unit cohesion.

At the same time as the US Navy was developing the LPH concept, attention was being given to rationalising the large fleet of ships required for an amphibious assault. Such an operation in the Second World War required troops carriers, stores carriers and a miscellany of landing craft. The LPD – Amphibious Transport Dock – was an attempt to merge most of these requirements into a single hull. These ships, of the *Raleigh* and *Austin* classes, have a well-dock, for the embarkation of landing craft, a flight deck and hangar facilities and accommodation for up to 1,000 troops and a force commander with his staff. The dock can hold LCUs and three LCMs or four LCMs and twenty LVTs. More landing craft can be carried on the flight deck and lowered over the side by means of a crane. Forward of the dock is 12,500 square feet of stowage space for vehicles, including main battle tanks. The LPD design has been copied worldwide, notably by Britain with her two *Fearless* class ships and France with

Foudre. LPDs would be used in concert with the LPH. The LPD could approach the shore to offload vehicles and cargo via her landing craft while at the same time helicopters from the LPH could use the LPD's flight deck to pick up troops for landing ashore or return troops and/or casualties. In exercises the LPH/LPD partnership has proved far more effective at landing more troops in less time than had previously been the case.

The LPH/LPD combination resulted in the development of the ultimate amphibious assault ship, the *Tarawa* class LHA. The LHA combines the flight deck facilities of the LPH with the docking facilities of the LPD. Commissioned in 1976, *Tarawa* represented a revolution in amphibious ship design. With a length of 840ft and a displacement of 40,000 tons fully loaded, she is almost the same size as a Second World War battleship. The well deck has 30,000 square feet of vehicle storage space and the dock can accommodate a variety of LCMs, LCUs, LCVPs, LVTs or the LCAC air-cushion landing craft, depending on requirements. The flight deck can accommodate twelve CH-46 medium or nine CH-53 heavy helicopters. An additional nineteen to thirty CH-46s or CH-53s can be kept in the hangar. Alternatively these ships can carry, as *Nassau* did during the 1991 Gulf War, twenty AV-8B Harrier jets. A total of 1,900 troops are

that any aircraft which are not stopped by the arrester wires can simply accelerate and fly off for another attempt. The first angled flight decks were painted on to HMS *Triumph* in February 1952 and USS *Midway*. The first carrier to be given a purpose-built angled deck was USS *Antietam*, which was modified in 1953 with an 8° angled deck.

Anglo-German Naval Agreement. Agreement concluded in 1935 between Britain and Germany whereby the latter voluntarily restricted the size of her navy to 35% of that of the Royal Navy. Submarines were excluded from the agreement and, under certain circumstances, Germany was to be

---

embarked and climate-controlled training areas on board enable them to exercise in the climate of their destination while on passage. Three trauma suites and a 300-bed sick bay cater for the inevitable casualties. A further development of the *Tarawa* class is the *Wasp* class LHD, in which the landing craft are replaced by three air-cushion LCAC craft. These can transport a main battle tank or sixty tons of men and equipment at speeds of up to 40kts, giving them greater immunity from fire from coastal artillery and missile batteries. The LHD also has a subsidiary role as a Sea Control Ship and can embark twenty AV-8B Harriers and six SH-60B ASW helicopters. Modified scales of equipment for the *Wasp* class LHA now include a number of AV-8B Harrier aircraft in order to provide close air support in the absence of an attack carrier wing.

During this period the US Navy also solved one of the problems which had been bedevilling amphibious commanders since the introduction of the first landing craft. The ramp or bow doors, so essential for the loading and discharge of cargo, limited the speed of the craft, and therefore the fleet, to a maximum of 12–15kts. The Americans wanted an amphibious fleet capable of speeds of 20kts, and the only way this could be achieved was by the elimination of the bow doors or ramp. Numerous solutions were applied, but the one that was adopted was very ingenious. The *Newport* class, built in the 1960s, had a conventional hull form above the waterline. Above the bow two prominent, 112ft forks protruded up and out and were joined at their end by a cross-bar. The forks served to lower a causeway down on to the beach by which troops and vehicles could be discharged. However, in this context it is interesting to note that the Soviet landing ship *Ivan Rogov* has bow doors yet can steam comfortably at 23kts.

Another feature of US developments in the amphibious field has been in the introduction of highly sophisticated command ships. Traditionally such functions were exercised from a battleship or a cruiser. Proof of the unsuitability of this arrangement was graphically shown in the 1942 North African landings when the battleship *Massachusetts*, which was carrying General George C. Patton and his staff, had to leave the landing area (with the by now very irate general) to deal with a French battleship, thus depriving the general of tactical control over his formations. Command ships were converted freighters fitted with sophisticated command and communication facilities from where the assault commander could direct affairs until he could move ashore. In the early 1960s two *Iwo Jima* LPH hulls, *Blue Ridge* and *Mount Whitney*, were modified to become command ships.

In 1992 the US Navy announced plans to build twelve new LX class amphibious assault ships which would replace fifteen LPDs, five LSDs, five LKAs and twenty LSTs. The initial specification is for a 23,000-ton ship with a length of 700ft, carrying two LCACs and 900 Marines and having 25,000 cu ft of cargo space. This investment in amphibious shipping paid off during the 1991 Gulf War: thirty-one amphibious ships served in the Persian Gulf and their presence tied down thousands of Iraqi troops – even though there was no landing.

The other great naval power in the post-1945 period, the USSR, invested little in amphibious warfare. Ships similar to the German wartime MFP were built in the 1950s and 1960s but were largely intended for encircling operations in the Baltic and the Black Sea. Throughout the massive expansion of the Soviet Navy in the 1960s, amphibious warfare vessels remained a low priority. The change came in the early 1970s when the Soviets began seriously to consider a war with China. The result of these plans was a class of major amphibious vessels 518ft long and displacing 13,000 tons. The first ship, *Ivan Rogov*, can carry a battalion of naval infantry (500 officers and men) and all their vehicles — ten tanks and thirty armoured personnel carriers and trucks. The superstructure contains a hangar which can accommodate ▶

allowed parity in submarine numbers with the Royal Navy.

Anglo-Japanese Naval Agreement. Agreement concluded between Britain and Japan in 1902, renewed in 1911, whereby Japan undertook to look after Britain's interests in the Far East, allowing Britain to concentrate her strength in home waters. Britain was, however, required to maintain a naval force in the Far East equal to that of any other European power. The abrogation of the agreement in 1922, under pressure from the USA, was to have immense strategic consequences for Britain.

'Anklet', Operation. Plan to cut German communications in northern Norway, December 1941.

Annapolis. Capital of the State of Maryland in the USA and home of the US Naval Academy; the establishment where officers destined for service in the US Navy receive their first training.

Antenna mine. Developed by the US Navy for use in the Northern Barrage during the First World War, the mine is activated by an antenna rather than horns. The antenna can either hang down, to trap submarines trying to dive through a minefield, or float up to the surface, thus simplifying the task of laying mines in deep water. When the target touches or nears

---

AMPHIBIOUS WARFARE

▶ four 'Hormone-C' or 'Helix' helicopters. Bow and stern doors give a ro-ro capability. Three *Lebed* class air cushion vehicles or six *Ondotra* class landing craft can be carried. *Ivan Rogov* has been compared to an LPD or LHD but in reality there is no comparison with the US ships. An interesting feature of the design is the very large armament with an emphasis on AAW and shore bombardment – a recognition of the fact that the ship will have to operate in a high-threat environment.

Other Western navies continued to maintain an amphibious capability after the Second World War (usually with surplus US ships), although as budgets contracted it was often the amphibious warfare capability that was the first to be discarded. Britain built two LPD ships and a class of five civilian-manned LSTs with conventional bow doors. However, the concentration on ASW in the northern and eastern Atlantic left precious little over for Britain's amphibious capability and naval assets declined.

In peacetime exercises it was not unusual to see the Royal Navy chartering ships from the four corners of the world in order to increase its amphibious lift. The 1982 Falklands War showed how inadequate Britain's resources were, as is borne out by the large number of STUFT which were required. France and Italy are the only other European countries to have invested substantially in amphibious ships. France has built the 8,500-ton *Ouragon* class which can carry 250 troops (although nearly 500 can be packed in for a short voyage). *Ouragon* and her sisters, together with the larger follow-on ships of the *Foudre* class, also serve as flagships and mobile repair ships. The Italians have built one LPD, *San Giorgio*, which can carry 500 troops, five CH-47 helicopters and thirty medium tanks. However, the Italian Navy is in the fortunate position of being able to lay its hands on another such ship, the *San Marco*, which is identical in all respects but was built (and paid for) by the Ministry of Civil Protection for use as a disaster relief ship with a secondary wartime amphibious capability.

Amphibious warfare remains a major priority for naval planners. The capability to land a large number of troops with their equipment quickly can be an effective yet non-threatening tool in dealing with recalcitrant countries. An amphibious force can lurk over the horizon, out of sight yet ready to intervene if required. The end of the Cold War has meant an increase in small out-of-area conflicts where amphibious forces are required to land peacekeeping or monitoring troops. The American *From the Sea* policy document asserts that amphibious warfare will grow in importance throughout the 1990s. Britain and France continue to believe in amphibious warfare. A new British LPH, HMS *Ocean*, is about to enter service and France has plans to build larger, more capable LPDs. The nascent Russian capability in this field has declined to the point where future operations will be restricted to the traditional coastal encircling movements. Most smaller navies will continue to build and operate small LSD-type ships. These give the added advantage, for Third World countries, of being able to double as low cost commercial transport.

the antenna it completes the firing circuit.

Anti-Aircraft Cruiser. Cruiser whose main armament was configured for both high- and low-angle purposes. They were intended to provide an increased measure of AA defence for fleets, carrier task groups and convoys, particularly operational convoys. Such ships were either converted from older cruisers, such as the British 'C' and 'D' class conversions, or purpose-built, such as the British *Dido* class and American *Atlanta* class.

Antwerp. Largest seaport in Belgium, situated on the east bank of the River Scheldt. In the First World War Antwerp was intended to be the 'National Redoubt' of the Belgian Government but was poorly garrisoned. British reinforcements could do little to stop the rot and on 10 October the garrison surrendered. The British forces, consisting of 1st Naval Brigade and a Brigade of Royal Marines, played an important role in covering the Belgians' withdrawal. However, the sailors proved to be ill-trained for land warfare and most were taken prisoner or opted for internment in Holland; only the disciplined and aggressive Royal Marines succeeded in fighting their way out to safety. During the Second World War Antwerp fell into German hands in 1940 and the port lay idle for the next four years. As the Anglo-American forces raced north and east following the landings in Normandy, the capture of Antwerp was seen as essential as

it was the only port capable of handling the vast amounts of *matériel* required for the Allied armies in north-west Europe. Although the town was captured on 7 September 1944, the British neglected to secure a bridgehead over the Scheldt; as a result the Germans remained in North Beveland and were able to deny the Allies the use of the port until 4 November. This delay cost the Allies dear.

AO. Oiler. US Navy/NATO classification.

AOG. Gasoline tanker. US Navy classification.

APA. Attack transport. US Navy classification.

Aphrodite (1) Radar countermeasures employed by U-boats and consisting of strips of aluminium suspended from a hydrogen-filled balloon. Preliminary results from using it were very favourable but as the number and experience of RAF patrol aircraft grew throughout 1944 the disadvantages became apparent. The major drawback was that the boat had to be surfaced to use it: instead of just one echo there would be a cluster of them which simply acted as a big 'here I am' signal to any patrolling aircraft. Eventually Aphrodite was due to be replaced by another decoy which could be launched from a submerged submarine – *Thetis*. (2) Allied code-name for the use of radio-controlled bombers packed with 20,000lb-plus of explosive or napalm against U-

boat pens in occupied France and in Germany.

AR. Repair ship. US Navy/NATO classification

Arab-Israeli Wars (1948–1982). Naval warfare in this long running dispute has taken second place to the fighting on land but these conflicts are not without interest. In 1948 Israeli commandos using ex-Italian explosive motor boats sank the Egyptian flagship *El Amir Farouk* and in 1956 the Egyptian flagship *Ibrahim el Awal* was captured by two Israeli destroyers. In the 1967 Six-Day War the lightning achievement of the Army left the Navy virtually unemployed. However, a force of three torpedo fast attack craft reached Sharm-el-Sheikh from Eilat to find that the naval blockade which had precipitated the war no longer existed. At the same time raids by Israeli frogmen in Egyptian harbours did little physical damage but were a considerable morale booster. The 1967–70 'War of Attrition' gave more scope to Israeli's warships. Their vulnerability to modern missiles was dramatically illustrated by the sinking of the destroyer *Eilat*, a lesson that was to be learned and with a vengeance. Meanwhile in September 1969 an armoured battalion was landed in Egypt for a raid in depth – an operation which was very successful and which cost the Egyptian CinC his job. Israeli naval intelligence was less surprised than most by the 1973 Yom Kippur War and events were to vindicate the Israelis' new emphasis on missiles and electronic warfare. Thirteen

Israeli fast attack craft with sixty-three Gabriel missile launchers defeated twenty-seven Arab *Osa* and *Komar* boats mounting eighty-four 'Styx' missiles. On the first night of the war off Latakia in Syria, and in what was the first missile-versus-missile surface action in history, five Israeli units evaded two salvos of six 'Styx' missiles and then fired a Gabriel salvo that sank all three Syrian ships. Two nights later six Israeli craft dodged twelve 'Styx' missiles and sank three out of four Egyptian *Osa* boats off Damietta. Israeli naval operations in the 1980s showed a daring attitude that was only possible with total air superiority. In June 1981 Israeli fast attack craft hit the PFLP HQ at Tripoli in Syria. The following year the Israeli Navy made a maximum effort in sup-

port of the Army's drive on Beirut and in thwarting the subsequent Palestinian attempts at an evacuation.

Arado Ar 196. Two-seat, low-wing floatplane designed in 1937 for operation from German warships and HSKs. The aircraft entered service in the latter part of 1939 and was issued to *Gneisenau, Admiral Graf Spee, Lützow, Prinz Eugen, Scharnhorst and Admiral Scheer*. The battleships *Tirpitz* and *Bismarck* were also issued with the aircraft. While warships were equipped with the Ar 196A-1 a more aggressively armed version was ordered for coastal patrol and reconnaissance. This was the Ar 196A-3 which carried two 20mm cannon in the wings and two paired 7.9mm machine guns in

the rear cockpit. A small bomb/depth charge load could also be carried. On 5 May 1940 an Ar 196A-3 from *Ku.Fl.Gr.706* flown by *Leutnant* Günther Mehrens sighted and attacked the British submarine *Seal* which was on the surface having been damaged by a mine. The crew were badly affected by carbon dioxide poisoning and after a brief attempt at defence the submarine surrendered. Mehrens alighted alongside and picked up the submarine's commanding officer, Lt-Cdr Rupert Lonsdale RN, and flew him to Frederickshaven. The Ar 196A-1s embarked on board *Tirpitz* were used to defend the ship when she was attacked by Albacore aircraft of the Fleet Air Arm in March 1942 – the only occasion on which the battleship received any air defence from the

Above: An Arado Ar 196 over the Aegean Sea, April 1942.
(IWM MH 5837)

Luftwaffe. The Ar 196 was one of most versatile aircraft employed by the *Luftwaffe.* It served in all theatres of war and its roles included anti-submarine work, convoy protection and coast defence. A total of 593 were produced.

Arado Ar 231. Small single-engine floatplane designed to be stowed in a 2m diamter container which could be carried on the casing of a U-boat to provide reconnaissance reports. Six prototypes were built but the aircraft proved extremely cumbersome to handle and took a considerable time to erect and recover – time during which the U-boat would be dangerously exposed on the surface. The programme was abandoned early in 1942 in favour of the Focke Achgelis Fa 330.

Arapaho. Concept developed after the 1982 Falklands War for the conversion of a civilian container ship into an aircraft carrier. The project appeared to offer significant savings in cost but although such ships' hulls and structure proved sound enough for their new purpose the cost of all the 'add-ons' such as command facilities, sensors and a rudimentary EW fit worked out at not much less than for a purpose-built ship.

Archangel. Port on the White Sea used as an alternative destination for Arctic convoys if the port of Murmansk were iced up.

'Archery', Operation. Combined raid on Vaagso, December 1941.

Arctic convoys. Instituted by the Allies to bring aid to Russia dur-

ing the Second World War. The most notorious was the Allied disaster of convoy PQ.17. But aswell as setbacks the Royal Navy had some notable successes The most notable of these being the sinking of the German battlecruiser *Scharnhorst,* aswell as getting a great many merchant ships through with their vital war material.

Argus, **HMS.** The first aircraft carrier with a full length flight deck to enter Royal Navy service. Built on the hull of the purchased Italian liner *Conte Rosso, Argus* commissioned too late for service in the First World War, but in the Second World War she performed a variety of duties including pilot training and aircraft ferry operations to Malta. She was broken up in 1946. The name is currently

Above: HMS *Argus*. (IWM FL 941)

borne by an ex-ro-ro ferry, *Contender Bezant*, acquired in 1984 which, though under RFA control, can operate as an auxiliary carrier providing a 'spare deck'.

Arizona, **USS** (BB39). US battleship launched in 1915 and armed with twelve 14in guns. She was destroyed in the Japanese attack on Pearl Harbor on 7 December 1941 when a 1,750lb bomb dropped by Petty Officer Noburo Kanai's B5N Kate bomber struck the barbette of No 2 14in turret, penetrated deep inside the ship and detonated near the magazine below the turret. The forward part of the ship was wrecked and 1,104 Navy and Marine Corps personnel were killed, including Rear-Admiral Isaac C. Kidd, Commander Battleship Division 1, and the ship's commanding officer, Captain F. van Valkenburgh USN. Both were posthumously awarded the Medal of Honor, as was the senior surviving officer, Lt-Cdr S. G. Fuqua USN. After the war her superstructure and turrets above the water were cleared away and a memorial was erected over the hull. Her remains are treated as a ship in commission: colours are raised and lowered every day and passing warships render passing honours.

Ark Royal, **HMS.** Name given to four British aircraft carriers during the twentieth century. The first was a seaplane carrier purchased in May 1914 and renamed *Pegasus* in 1934. She was eventually sold out of the service in 1946 and was broken up in 1950. The

Above: The second HMS *Ark Royal*, May 1941. (IWM A 4074)

Above: The third HMS *Ark Royal,* February 1978. (IWM MH 25090)

Above: The fourth HMS *Ark Royal* moving slowly up Portsmouth harbour in July 1985. The fourth of the *Invincible* class 'through deck cruisers', as they were quaintly styled on completion. The well on the port quarter of the flight deck is for a Vulcan Phalanx CIWS. A Sea Harrier is mounted on the 'ski-jump' while a Fairey Swordfish rests on the after end of the flight deck. (MoD)

second was a 22,000-ton aircraft carrier built in 1937 which became famous for her service with Force H in the Mediterranean and Eastern Atlantic and particularly for the role her aircraft played in the sinking of the German battleship *Bismarck* in May 1941. She was torpedoed by *U81* off Gibraltar on 13 November 1941; all efforts to save the ship failed

and she sank the next day. The third was a 36,000-ton vessel launched in 1950. Following the decision to end the Royal Navy's aircraft carrier programme in 1966, *Ark Royal* continued in service until 1979 as the last exponent of conventional fixed-wing aviation in the Royal Navy. She achieved national fame featuring in the BBC TV series *Sailor*. The

fourth ship of the name is a 16,000-ton support carrier launched in 1981 and still in commission.

ARM. Anti-radar missile. A missile fired, usually by an aircraft, that homes on to radar emissions by means of a seeker in the missile head locking on to the defender's radar. Such a missile forces the enemy to shut down his radar systems, thus degrading his ability to deal with subsequent attacks.

'Armada', Operation. SOE sabotage of French canals in 1943 to prevent the transfer of midget submarines and S-boats to Italy.

Armed guards. US Navy personnel placed on board merchant ships to man defensive armament.

Armed merchant cruiser (AMC). Passenger liner or merchant vessel taken up from trade, fitted with a rudimentary gun armament and used for naval purposes. The British employed such ships during both world wars on blockade duties in the North Atlantic. Although they proved useful at a time when ships were in short supply, they were unsatisfactory in service, their weak armament, lack of armour protection and great size making them impressive and vulnerable targets. By 1942 nearly all the AMCs then in British service had been withdrawn and converted for other uses. Nevertheless, some of these ships have earned their place in history for their role in sinking German raiders and defending convoys (*see Carmania, Jervis Bay, Rawalpindi*). The Germans and Japanese also made use of AMCs though in a predatory role against Allied shipping.

'Armour', Operation. Re-occupation of Hong Kong in August 1945.

Armistice (1918). Under the terms of the Armistice concluded in the forest of Compiègne, Germany was to surrender the bulk of the High Seas Fleet (10 battleships, 6 battlecruisers, 10 light cruisers 50 destroyers and 176 U-boats). The vessels were to be disarmed and sailed to a nominated port, Rosyth for the ships and Harwich for the U-boats, for internment as a guarantee against the Germans' good beahviour while the peace talks were in progress. The ships duly arrived at Rosyth in a mass surrender on 21 November 1918 and, after inspection, were sent north to Scapa Flow for internment. In the Adriatic similar conditions applied to the Austrian Fleet. However, the breakdown in command following the collapse of the Empire meant that there were insufficient crews to sail the ships to Venice, so they were interned at the ports where they lay under Allied supervision. On 24 March 1919 the Italians staged their own victory parade by sailing a number of ex-Austrian vessels to Venice with Italian crews.

Armistice (1943). On 8 September the provisional government in Italy led by Marshal Badoglio concluded an armistice with the Allies following the ousting of the Mussolini government. As a condition of that armistice the majority of the Italian Fleet was required to sail to Malta and internment. It was a protracted exercise carried out against a background of German opposition. Eventually five battleships, nine cruisers, ten destroyers, ten torpedo boats, six corvettes, thirty-three submarines and one seaplane carrier arrived at Malta. One battleship, *Roma*, and two destroyers, *Vivaldi* and *Da Noli*, were sunk en route while two torpedo boats, *Pegaso* and *Impetuoso*, headed for internment in the Spanish Balearic Islands at Port Mahon but collided outside the harbour entrance and sank.

Armoured deck. Horizontal structure fitted to capital ships, aircraft carriers and cruisers to protect their machinery spaces and magazines from plunging shellfire.

Armoured flight deck. During the Second World War British aircraft carriers were fitted with an armoured flight deck to protect their hangars from aerial attack or plunging shellfire: the three *Illustrious* class vessels, together with *Indomitable* and *Implacable*, had 3in thick armour. In theory it was an admirable concept but the weight of the structure meant that fewer aircraft could be carried than in foreign ships of a similar size. In combat, particularly in the Far East, where British carriers survived several hits by *Kamikaze* suicide aircraft, armoured flight decks proved effective.

'Arsenal', Operation. Diversionary bombardment of Catania, Sicily, in July 1943.

Arctic Convoys. Instituted by the Allies to bring aid to Russia during the Second World War. The most notorious was the Allied disaster of convoy PQ.17. But as well as setbacks, the Royal Navy had some notable successes, the most notable of these being the sinking of the German battlecruiser *Scharnhorst,* as well as getting a great many merchant ships through with their vital war material.

'Artichoke', Operation. Method of protecting convoys against U-boat attack, 1942.

AS. Submarine tender. US Navy/ NATO classification.

'Ascot', Operation. Plan to seize and hold Bodø in northern Norway to use as an advanced base for coastal forces attacking German shipping.

ASDIC. General term for devices using sound for the underwater detection of submarines. From Allied Submarine Detection Investigation Committee of 1917, this was original name for Sonar.

ASDS. Advanced Seal Delivery System. US Navy term for a midget submarine currently under construction which bears a remarkable resemblance to a Second World War British X-craft. The craft can be used to plant mines or to deliver SEALs to the target area.

ASROC. Anti-Submarine Rocket. American ASW missile which is designed to deliver a homing torpedo as close as possible to the target submarine in the minimum time, thus limiting the submarine's ability to take avoiding action or launch a counter-attack. It consists of a Mk 44 or Mk 46 homing torpedo which is fired from a launcher on the deck of a ship to a range programmed by the ship's sonars. After a predetermined flight time, the motor shuts off and the torpedo drops into the sea and activates. A nuclear version was also developed using a 1-kiloton warhead.

'Assassin', Operation. Planned deployment of the Home Fleet in the event of a German invasion, 1941. Also used for the invasion of Ramree Island.

ASTER. An advanced series of French AAW missiles with active terminal guidance for use against both aircraft and missile targets. ASTER 15 is for use against targets out to 15km range and ASTER 30 for targets out to 70km. ASTER will be fitted to the French carrier *Charles de Gaulle* and will form the basis of AAW systems fitted in the forthcoming Anglo-French-Italian 'Common New Generation' frigate.

'Astrologer', Operation. Eastbound convoy to Malta, November 1941. Sometimes also known as 'Bandolier'.

ASW. Anti Submarine Warfare.

ASWORG. Anti-Submarine Warfare Operations Research Group. Established on 1 April 1942 to analyse the effectiveness of anti-submarine weapons, sensors and tactics. It was directed throughout the war by P. M. Morse.

Athenia, **SS.** Passenger liner of 13,581 tons owned by the Don-

Above: The destroyer HMS *Fame* closes on the sinking *Athenia*.

aldson Atlantic Line. On 3 September 1939, while outward-bound for the United States with a full passenger list (mainly women and children), she was torpedoed without warning by the German *U30* commanded by *Kapitän-leutnant* Lemp. Nearly 1,300 passengers and crew were rescued but 112 lost their lives. Although Lemp had acted contrary to the Hague Convention and his own orders, he was exonerated on the grounds that he had thought that *Athenia* was an armed merchant cruiser. However, *U30*'s log was amended to remove all details of the sinking. The British viewed the sinking as an indication that the Germans intended to pursue a campaign of unrestricted submarine warfare as they had in the First World War.

'Athletic', Operation. Naval air attack on shipping at Narvik and Trondheim, October 1944.

Atlantic, Battle of. Two campaigns fought basically between Great Britain and Germany during the First and Second World Wars. They were largely struggles between German submarine forces and Allied merchant ships, with the occasional sorties by German surface units during the Second World War.

During the First World War Allied losses reached a peak of 875,000 tons in April 1917 and the contest was going Germany's way, but after the British instituted the convoy system in May 1917 the losses dropped dramatically, the Allies finally having the upper hand.

With the Luftwaffe assisting the German Navy during the Second World War, this second struggle reached its climax during the spring of 1943, but with the development of the escort carrier and growing Allied air strength (plus Allied knowledge with regard to the German signal codes for the 'Enigma' machine) losses were sharply reduced. The Axis lost 781 U-boats all told, more than half of which were accounted for by air attack. The Allies lost over 23 million tons of shipping, 14 million to submarines.

Atlantis. Armed merchant raider of the Second World War which was the most successful such vessel employed by the Germans in either world war. She was launched in 1937 for the Hansa Line with the name *Goldenfels* but was commissioned into the *Kriegsmarine* as *Handels-Stor-Kreuzer* (commerce disruption cruiser) No 2, alternatively known as *Schiff 16*. Her appearance could be altered so that she resembled the Norwegian MS *Knute Nelson*, the Japanese *Kasii Maru*, the Soviet MS *Kim* or the Dutch MS *Abbkerk*. Her main armament of six 15cm guns came from the pre-dreadnought *Schlesien*. She was also fitted with four 21in torpedo tubes and carried two He 114B seaplanes for reconnaissance. Having sunk or captured twenty-two vessels totalling 145,968grt, *Atlantis* was herself sunk by gunfire from the cruiser HMS *Devonshire* in the South Atlantic on 23 November 1941. In what was a remarkable rescue operation involving eleven U-boats, only eleven of her crew were lost.

Audacious, **HMS.** British battleship launched in 1912 and which was mined on 27 October 1914. The damage was slight, but progressive flooding as the weather worsened meant that the ship became unmanageable and she foundered. The Admiralty had hoped to keep her loss a secret but her last moments were witnessed by the liner *Olympic*, among whose passengers were many Americans. The news was out in less than a month, though to the end of the war the Admiralty maintained that *Audacious* had been but damaged.

Audacity, **HMS.** Former German merchant ship *Hannover*, seized by the British and converted into the first escort carrier. With an air group of six Martlet (F4F-3 Wildcat) fighters, she made just three convoy voyages before being sunk on 21 December 1941 by *U751* while escorting convoy HG.76. Nevertheless, her aircraft played a critical role in guiding escorts on to U-boats and keeping the ever-present Fw 200 Condor shadowing aircraft at bay. The effectiveness of aircraft was fully realised by the Germans, who recognised that if every convoy possessed its own organic air cover the whole nature of the Atlantic battle would be changed.

'Avalanche', Operation. Landings at Salerno and Naples in September 1943.

Aviation Support Ships. Most Western navies ignored aviation support ships in the post-war period. The US Navy discarded all three classes of seaplane carrier it operated during the Second World War when seaplanes were removed from the inventory. However, the Royal Navy was keen to divert flying training away from operational carriers – given the shortage of flight decks available. In 1960 an RFA-manned helicopter support ship, *Engadine*, was completed and she has since been replaced by the former ro-ro ship *Contender Bezant*. Renamed *Argus*, she was chartered during the 1982 Falklands War and purchased outright in 1984. She then under went a four-year refit in which her cargo and vehicle decks were made into a hangar deck for eight Sea Harriers and three Sea King (or similar size) helicopters. Although she lacks a ski-jump, *Argus* can be employed in the combat role.

Aviso Escorteur. Designation used by the French Navy in 1959 for the *Commandant Rivière* class ships.

'Avonmouth', Operation. Narvik expedition as first proposed, to be carried out if the German reaction to 'Wilfrid' justified it.

Awa Maru. Japanese merchant vessel torpedoed by the US submarine *Queenfish* on 1 April 1945. Only one survivor of the 2,404 on board was rescued. Unfortunately *Awa Maru* was sailing under a safe conduct pass since she was officially carrying relief supplies for Allied PoWs in China. In fact American intelligence learned that the Japanese were using the ship's status to carry gold, strategic materials and essential personnel. Although *Queenfish*'s commanding officer, Cdr Charles E. Loughlin, did not receive the signals giving details of *Awa Maru*'s safe conduct or route, he was relieved of his command and court martialled on a variety of charges. He was punished with a letter of admonishment. On the Japanese surrender, the Japanese Government requested $52 million in compensation from the US Government. No reparations were paid.

'Axiom', Operation. Mission sent to London and Washington by Mountbatten to urge the adoption of Operation 'Culverin', February 1944.

AUXILIARIES

Naval auxiliaries have been a major growth area in terms of naval history since the Second World War. Auxiliary warships of many types – colliers, tenders, repair ships – have always been included in the order of battle but the dramatic change in naval warfare during the Second World War created requirements for large fleets of specialised support vessels which were capable of operating at the same speeds and to the same tempo of operations as the main body of the Fleet. Auxiliaries are now so important that in the two major naval conflicts since the end of the Second World War they have outnumbered the combatant vessels. During the 1982 Falklands War a fleet of sixteen RFAs and twenty-five STUFT supported the British fleet of two carriers and twenty-five surface ships. The US Navy in the 1991 Gulf War required no fewer than 25 auxiliaries and thirty ships of Military Sealift Command.

In the early part of this century naval auxiliaries were, by and large, the many bases which the world's naval powers, particularly Britain, maintained around the world. Ships needing replenishment would simply put into one of these bases. All navies maintained a number of sea-going auxiliaries, store carriers and the like, but the concept of underway replenishment was impractical. Food, personnel and ammunition could be transferred at sea, and there were well-established methods of doing so, for example the jackstay transfer. However, until the introduction of oil-fired propulsion ships burned coal and there was no practical means by which sufficient coal could be transferred in sufficient quantities at sea. It might be possible for an individual ship to coal at sea (German raiders did so often), but it was out of the question for a fleet as large as the Grand Fleet or the *Hochseeflotte* (High Seas Fleet) to coal at sea. Thus before the First World War major deployments of warships around the world, such as the Russian Baltic Fleet's ill-fated voyage to the Far East or the US Navy's 'Great White Fleet' world cruise, were marked by frequent port calls for coaling and replenishment. Experiments during the inter-war period had shown that underway replenishment was possible, but in general the world's navies entered the Second World War dependent on land bases for refuelling and maintenance facilities.

Ayesha. Schooner captured by the landing party from the German cruiser *Emden* which had been put ashore on Direction Island to destroy the wireless station there. While the landing party were busy destroying the communications facilities, *Emden* was engaged by the cruiser HMAS *Sydney* and was subsequently beached on North Keeling Island after sustaining massive damage. The landing party, commanded by *Emden*'s executive officer, *Kapitänleutnant* von Mucke, escaped in the *Ayesha* and made their way across the Indian Ocean and thence overland to Constantinople and a warm welcome.

'Backchat', Operation. raid on the Cherbourg Peninsula, March 1942. Also used for interception of E-boats in the western Channel in January 1943.

'Backside', Operation. Operations for the occupation of Madagascar, September 1942.

Badoeng Strait, Battle of. During the night of 19/20 February 1942 the Dutch cruisers *Java* and *de Ruyter* arrived off the island of Bali to destroy Japanese transports which were anchored in the Badoeng Strait which separates Bali from Nusa Besar Island. However, on arrival they found that the main body of the Japanese force had sailed, leaving but one transport and three destroyers. In the resulting engagement the Dutch destroyer *Piet Hien* was sunk by *Asashio*. A second attack made some hours later by the Dutch cruiser *Tromp* and four destroyers was equally unsuccessful: both *Tromp* and the American destroyer *Stewart* were badly damaged. As this force was leaving the Badoeng Strait, it was intercepted by two Japanese destroyers and in the ensuing action *Michisio* was sunk. A third Dutch attempt to find the Japanese force failed to make contact and was withdrawn.

Baja, Battle of. Brief engagement on the River Danube on 25 June 1919 between HMS *Ladybird* and *ML.236* of the Royal Navy's Danube Flotilla and six Hungarian river monitors loyal to the Bela Kun government. After three salvos of 6in shell from *Ladybird* all six Hungarian craft surrendered.

The requirement for auxiliaries was demonstrated very early in the Second World War. Even non-carrier operations demonstrated the need for replenishment ships. German surface raiders, both warships and HSKs, relied on a series of supply ships pre-positioned in various quiet corners of the ocean. The Type XIV U-boat was specifically designed as a refuelling boat for other German submarines engaged in operations in distant waters. In May 1941, following the sinking of the German battleship *Bismarck*, the British battleship HMS *King George V* was so low on fuel that the possibility arose that she might have to be towed home. But it was the demands of long-range carrier operations during the Pacific campaign that led to a requirement for a fleet of auxiliary ships that could sustain the carrier task forces at sea.

The ability of the American carrier task forces to strike rapidly at a particular target and then retire, or remain in an area to carry out a series of attacks, depended on a regular supply of fuel, aviation spirit, ammunition, replacement aircraft, food, Coca-Cola (rum in the case of a British carrier group) and the 1,001 other items which a carrier group requires. By the end of the Second World War the US Navy had commissioned large numbers of oilers (AO; aviation spirit carriers were classed as AOG), ammunition ships (AE), stores ships (AF), stores issue ships (AKS), aviation supply ships (AVS), repair ships, and depot ships (for both destroyers and submarines). Standard operating procedures called for the supply ships (the 'fleet train' in British naval parlance) to operate some distance astern of the strike force. At regular intervals, usually three to five days, components of the strike fleet would be detached to meet the supply ships at a predetermined mid-ocean rendezvous point. It could take anything up to a day to replenish a carrier and several hours for a destroyer. First alongside would be the Aos, transferring fuel via pipes slung from a jackstay. The AOs would be followed by a succession of stores ships transferring everything from 16in shells to the latest Hollywood movie. During this period the fleet had to steam at reduced speed on a steady course and was thus vulnerable to air or submarine attack. When the resupply was complete, the combatant ships would return to the operational area while the supply ships would steam back to a major base to replenish their stocks.

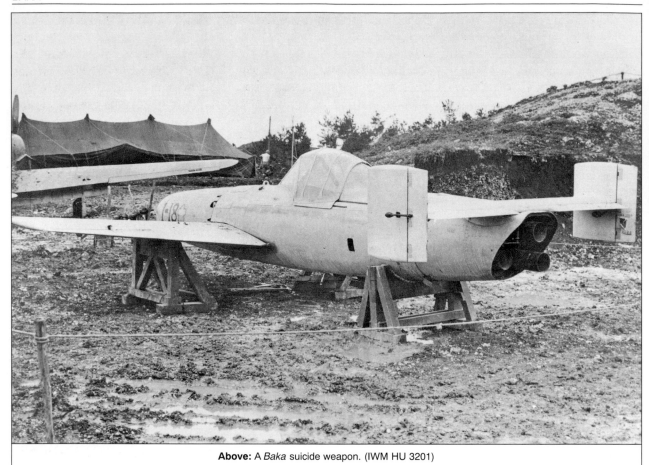

Above: A *Baka* suicide weapon. (IWM HU 3201)

Baka. MXY-7 *Ohka* (Cherry Blossom) was a Japanese suicide weapon used in the final stages of the war, mainly against US ships off Okinawa. The weapon consisted of an aircraft-like body with stubby wings and a small tail. Most of the plane consisted of the 2,646lb warhead. The Baka was fitted underneath a mother aircraft, usually a G4M2 Betty (although a smaller version was developed for the PlY Frances). It was released over the target area. After release the pilot would fire the craft's three rockets, which provided a combined thrust of 1,764lb for eight to ten seconds, giving the craft a maximum range of 22 miles from the point of release. The pilot then selected a target and dived to destruction. Maximum powered speed was 403mph, although higher velocities were undoubtedly reached, though not recorded, during the terminal dive. The first success scored by a Baka was on 12 April when one smashed into the destroyer *Mannert L. Abele* (DD773) which had already been badly damaged by a suicide aircraft. The destroyer sank in less than five minutes. The same day another Baka smashed through the bow of the destroyer *Stanly* (DD478), doing some damage but not affecting the ship's seaworthiness or fighting ability. The Bakas were a considerable nuisance off Okinawa but their effectiveness was blunted because of the vulnerability of the mother planes to attack: too often the Bakas were jettisoned or the mother plane shot down miles from the target.

Balikpapan, Battle of. Also known as the Battle of the Macassar Strait. On 24 January 1942 four American destroyers, *John D. Ford*, *Pope*, *Parrott* and *Paul Jones* made a high-speed run to the important oil port of Balikpapan on the coast of Borneo, where a Japanese force was landing troops. The transports were illuminated by the burning oil installations on shore and four of them, and a Japanese escort, were sunk by torpedoes fired by the US destroyers. The only American casualty was the destroyer *Ford*, which was damaged. Balikpapan was a bright spot in an otherwise dismal campaign for the ABDA forces, but although it was a tactical victory it did not prevent the Japanese conquest of Borneo.

Balkan War. Conflict between Greece and Turkey over territorial possessions in Asia Minor in 1912-13. From a naval perspective the war is of interest in that it saw the first submarine attack and the first use of a seaplane to attack an enemy fleet. The Greek Navy, under Rear-Admiral Paul Kondouriotis, successfully supported the Army in driving the Turks out of Epirus while at the same time imposing a blockade on the Dardanelles through the capture of the islands of Lemnos, Tenedos, Imbros, Strati, Samothrace, Mytilene and Chios. Turkish attempts to break out from the Dardanelles on 14, 16 and 22 December 1912 and on 18 January 1913 were all repulsed. On 9 December 1912 the Greek submarine *Delfin* carried out the first submarine torpedo attack in history when she aimed a torpedo at the cruiser *Medjidieh*. However, the torpedo did not run properly and sank. In February 1913 the Greeks made the first use of aircraft in naval warfare when a seaplane took off from Mudros and dropped four bombs (which missed) on the Turkish Fleet.

Ballistic missile. Missile that throws an unpowered warhead into a ballistic trajectory that will carry it to the target.

'Bamboo', Operation. Operation to establish an advanced naval and air base at Hastings Harbour and Victoria Point, Malaya, to assist operations in Burma and prepare for operations in Malaya, 1944.

'Bandolier', Operation. *See* 'Astrologer'.

'Bangor', Operation. MGB patrol off the Dutch coast in the later part of 1944 to destroy enemy coastal shipping.

'Banjo', Operation. Occupation of the island of Gozo following the success of 'Husky'.

'Banknote', Operation. Plan for attacking certain German and Italian vessels in Spanish (and therefore neutral) waters in the Second World War.

'Baptism', Operation. Air reconnaissance sorties launched from North Russia to photograph the German battleship *Tirpitz*, May/June 1944.

***Baralong*, HMS.** British Q-ship which achieved notoriety for the sinking of *U27* on 19 August 1915. *Baralong* sank the U-boat while the latter was preparing to sink the transport *Nicosian*. Some of the U-boat's survivors swam toward the *Nicosian* and were fired on in the water and while climbing the transport's falls. Four of *U27*'s crew survived this fusillade and took refuge in the

Nicosian's engine room, where they were found and shot by Marines sent over from the *Baralong*. Whether the Germans were shot because they were trying to scuttle the ship or whether they were murdered in cold blood has never been determined.

'Barbara', Operation. Attack on the Laksevaag floating dock at Bergen using the one-man Welman submarine in November 1943. The operation was a failure, three of the craft being scuttled and the fourth captured.

Barents Sea, Battle of the. One of the most outstanding naval actions of the Second World War, centred around the defence of convoy JW.51B bound for Murmansk. On 31 December 1942 the convoy's destroyer escort held off a stong German task force consisting of the pocket battleship *Lützow*, the cruiser *Admiral Hipper* and six destroyers until the British cruisers *Sheffield* and *Jamaica* arrived and drove them off. During the action the destroyer *Achates* was sunk and *Onslow* badly damaged; the latter's commanding officer, Captain R. St V. Sherbrooke, was badly wounded and was later awarded the Victoria Cross. The Germans lost the destroyer *Friedrich Eckholdt*, which made the mistake of closing *Sheffield* thinking she was friendly. The battle had important political consequences. When Hitler learned of this new failure of the *Kriegsmarine* he ordered all the surface ships to be paid off. Faced with this ultimatum Admiral

Above: Damage to the British destroyer *Onslow* sustained in the Battle of the Barents Sea on 31 December 1942. (Author)

Raeder resigned and was replaced by Dönitz.

Barracuda. British Fairey designed naval aircraft used by the Royal Navy during the Second World War. It was the first British monoplane torpedo-bomber to enter British service and some

Above: Fleet Air Arm Barracuda Torpedo Bomber. (IWM A 20180)

2,582 were produced. It had an awkward appearance and never enjoyed the popularity of the Swordfish. It first saw front-line service in September 1943 and its most significant operation was a series of attacks on the German battleship *Tirpitz* beginning on 3 April 1944 in which specially modified aircraft carried 1,600lb armour-piercing bombs. The Barracuda had a crew of three, a maximum speed of 228mph and a range of 685 miles.

'Barrage', Operation. Unsuccessful operation to intercept a Japanese submarine carrying important officials from Germany to Singapore in November 1943.

'Barricade', Operation. Landing on French coast in August 1942 between Barfleur and St Vaast to destroy DF station and AA gun sites.

'Basalt', Operation. Commando raid on the German-held island of Sark, October 1942.

Bat bomb. Proposed weapon system using Mexican free-tailed bats to carry 1oz incendiary weapons to drop on Japanese wood and paper houses. The project was begun in 1943 by the USAAF but was passed to the US Navy, who passed it to the USMC. In August 1944 the project was abandoned, having cost $2,000,000 (at 1944 levels) and an unknown number of bats.

Bat missile. The most sophisticated guided missile employed during the Second World War. Bat, better known as Bomb Mk 57, SWOD Mk 9, was a low angle of glide weapon with a Mk 15 Mod 2 Radar Bombsight working in X-band for active homing. It had a 1,000lb warhead, a glide range of 30–40,000yds and a speed of 300mph. Tests in late 1944 proved satisfactory and in January 1945 three squadrons of PB4Y-2 Privateer aircraft were equipped with the weapon, each aircraft carrying two Bats. The missile was used operationally first on 23 April 1945 at Balikpapan and later at Okinawa. Results, however, did not equal expectations and at the end of the Second World War 7,000 of the 10,000 missiles ordered were cancelled.

***Batfish,* USS.** US submarine which sank three Japanese submarines, *RO.55*, *RO.112* and *RO.113*, during the Second World War – the only one to sink that number. An interesting feature of these attacks was that the initial detection was by

Above: The first battlecruiser, HMS *Invincible*. (IWM Q 21391A)

passive reception of Japanese radar transmissions.

'Bathtub'. Code-name for first US Navy training base established in the UK in 1942.

Battle Honours. Names of battles or individual ship actions in which a warship has taken part, usually displayed on a board in a prominent place in the ship as a source of pride in her name. Battle honours are hereditary and a subsequent ship of the same name usually displays the honours won by her predecessors. This is a normal practice in all navies although in the United States Navy they are known as Battle Stars.

Battle Stars. *See* Battle Honours.

Battlecruiser. Contemporary development of the *Dreadnought* battleship pioneered in Britain. The function of battlecruisers was to act as advanced scouts of the main battle fleet. They were armed with guns of the same calibre as carried by a dreadnought battleship and were some four knots faster. However they lacked the same degree of armour protection. They were the brainchild of Admiral Sir John Fisher, who called them fast armoured cruisers, and it was not until 1912 that they became known as battlecruisers. The change in name was unfortunate since it may have led future fleet commanders to believe that the battlecruiser could take its place in the line of battle whereas in fact their lack of armour protection made them extremely unsuitable for a prolonged engagement. The first battlecruiser to be designed was the British HMS *Invincible* although her sister ship HMS *Indomitable* was the first to be commissioned. The normal development of the type culminated in the super-battlecruiser HMS *Hood*, which was the last ship of the type built for the Royal Navy. During the First World War British and German battlecruisers saw considerable service. At the Battle of the Falkland Islands, on 8 December 1914, the British battlecruisers *Invincible* and *Inflexible* destroyed Von Spee's squadron consisting of the armoured cruisers *Scharnhorst* and *Gneisenau* and the light cruisers *Nürnberg* and *Leipzig*. This action seemed to be a vindication of the battlecruiser concept. In the North Sea battlecruisers saw most of the action, where they were engaged at the Battles of Heligoland Bight on 28 August 1914, Dogger Bank on 24 January 1915 and Jutland on 31 May 1916. At the last battle three British battlecruisers, HMS *Indefatigable*, *Queen Mary* and *Invincible*, were sunk by German

gunfire, thus demonstrating the weakness of this type of ship. The battlecruiser was a valid concept but one that was subsequently misused by those charged with their employment. With the development of reconnaissance by naval aircraft they ceased to have any relevance since aircraft could perform the scouting role more efficiently and cheaply.

Battleship. The largest and most influential surface combatant this century until the aircraft carrier

came of age during the Second World War.

'Bayleaf', Operation. Attack on Axis shipping off Norway.

B-Dienst. Cryptoanalytical service of the German Navy during the Second World War. It was particularly effective in decoding Allied radio traffic to permit the centralised control of U-boat operations against convoys in the Battle of the Atlantic, especially in view of the lack of other intelligence sources on Allied convoy

movements. The service was founded in 1919 – not long after the conclusion of hostilities in the Great War – and enjoyed some success at breaking foreign governments' codes during the inter-war period. The service was successful in reading Allied, especially British, codes up to April 1943, but thereafter the introduction of machine ciphering and better codes on the Allied side combined to reduce its efficiency. The destruction of *B-Dienst's* headquarters, and its records, in Berlin during an air raid in November 1943 reduced its effectiveness still further. Another field in which the *B-Dienst* was less than successful was counter-intelligence. The Germans had no idea that their own codes were being read with regularity by the Allies. Nevertheless, it was undoubtedly the most efficient of all the Third Reich's intelligence services.

Bear Trap. system developed by the RCN for the recovery of helicopters to a small flight deck in bad weather. A harpoon attached to a cable is fired from the helicopter into a meshed area on the flight deck. When the harpoon engages, the helicopter is simply hauled down and secured.

'Begun', Operation. Naval bombardment of Kismayu in Italian Somaliland, January 1941. Sometimes spelt Begum.

Beira. Port in Mozambique, East Africa, which was the subject of a blockade by the Royal Navy from 1966 to 1975. The object of the

Above: End of an era. Two views of HMS *Vanguard*, the last British battleship, as she is broken up at Faslane in 1960. In the upper picture looking forward along the bows, in the foreground, are the trunnions for the two 15in guns of 'A' turret. The lower picture shows the breeches of two 15in guns. (Author)

blockade was to prevent the illegal Government then extant in Rhodesia (now Zimbabwe) from importing oil through the port. The blockade was wholly unsuccessful as the Rhodesian government was getting all the oil it needed via South Africa. For those involved the patrols, usually conducted by one British frigate or destroyer, were a tedious business known as the 'Beira Bore'.

Beira Bucket. Trophy competed for by ships engaged in the blockade of Beira. The competition consisted of a terrifying timed race around the upper deck.

'Bellows', Operation. Aircraft ferry operation to Malta in August 1942 involving the carrier HMS *Furious*. A part of the much larger Operation 'Pedestal'.

'Bellpush', Operation. Series of reconnaissance raids on the north French coast in December 1943 and January 1944.

Benedetto Brin. Italian battleship. On 27 September 1915 she blew up while at anchor at Brindisi with the loss of 596 killed and wounded. Her demise was subsequently attributed to Austrian sabotage.

Bergen. Norwegian seaport lying at the head of Byfjord. During the Second World War it was used by the Germans as a base for warships and submarines. It was the focus for three operations by British midget submarines, all with the object of destroying the Laksevaag floating dock. *See* Operations 'Barbara', 'Guidance', 'Heckle'.

'Berlin', Operation. Commerce raiding operation in the Atlantic in February 1941 by the German battlecruisers *Scharnhorst* and *Gneisenau*. Between them the two ships sank 116,000 tons of Allied shipping.

'Beserk', Operation. High-speed aircraft carrier manouevres in July 1942 prior to Operation 'Pedestal'.

'Betty'. *See* Mitsubishi G4M.

Biber. Beaver. German one-man midget submarine whose design was based on a British Welman

Above: A German *Biber* one man submarine lying on the beach at Fécamp in the summer of 1944. The recess in the craft's hull was for the stowage of a torpedo. (Author)

captured at Bergen in 1943. *Biber*s displaced 6.3 tons, were 9m long and were powered by a 32hp petrol engine and a 13hp electric motor. They were armed with two G7e torpedoes. They were first employed in Normandy and subsequently from bases in the Netherlands, and were spectacularly unsuccessful. They are believed to have accounted for a net-layer, an LST and a merchant ship. As in all such one-man craft the operator had too much to do in order for them to be very effective.

'Bigamy', Operation. Naval aspect of joint SOE/OSS operation against enemy-held islands in the Adriatic in 1943.

Bikini Atoll. Isolated atoll in the Marshall Islands chain selected for the 1946 atomic bomb tests, including tests to ascertain the effects of nuclear weapons on warships. The 167 inhabitants were removed to Rongerik Atoll. See also Operation 'Crossroads'.

Bismarck. German capital ship launched in 1939. She displaced 41,700 tons, was 792ft long and was armed with eight 15in guns. Together with her sister ship *Tirpitz*, she was the first genuine battleship laid down by the Germans since the end of the First World War. A feature of the design was the broad beam of 118ft which made a very steady gun platform even in the heaviest seas. In many ways, however, she was little more than an improved *Baden* class battleship although her fine lines and impressive superstructure gave an appearance of modernity. She was commissioned in August 1940 and nine months later had been sunk. Hers is one of the epic naval stories of the Second World War.

Bismarck action. On 18 May 1941 the German battleship *Bismarck* (*Kapitän zur See* Ernst Lindemann) and the heavy cruiser *Prinz Eugen* sailed from Gdynia, under the command of *Vizeadmiral* Günther Lütjens, to attack Allied shipping the Atlantic. The operation, codenamed 'Regenbogen', followed hard on the heels of the successful Operation 'Berlin' and great things were expected of it. *Bismarck* had the gun armament and protection to enable her to take on any British capital ship escorting a convoy while her

cruiser consort attacked the merchant ships. The Germans' hopes of achieving surprise were soon dashed. Intelligence reports from Sweden and Norway, backed up by aerial reconnaissance photographs of Grimstadtfjord, told the British Admiralty that the German ships had sailed. Admiral Sir John Tovey, Commander-in-Chief of the Home Fleet, took immediate steps to reinforce the units patrolling the exits into the Atlantic, steps which included sending the battlecruiser HMS *Hood* and battleship HMS *Prince of Wales*, under the command of Vice-Admiral Lancelot Holland, to the Denmark Strait between Iceland and Greenland. In misty weather on the evening of 23 May the British cruisers *Suffolk* and *Norfolk*, on patrol in the Denmark Strait, encountered the German ships and began to shadow them. *Hood* and *Prince of Wales* were some 220 miles away to the south-east and course was altered so as to engage the German ships on the morning of the 24th. Shortly before 0600 on 24 May all four ships came into action south of the Denmark Strait. After a brief engagement *Hood* blew up and *Prince of Wales*

Above: *Bismarck* at Bergen, Norway. A photograph taken from the cruiser *Prinz Eugen*. (IWM HU 375)

was hit and forced to retire. However, the German ships had not escaped unscathed. *Bismarck* had taken three 14in hits from *Prince of Wales*, one of which had isolated some 1,000 tons of oil fuel in tanks in the forward part of the ship. The loss of this fuel would have an important bearing on Lütjens' conduct of the operation: *Bismarck* now lacked sufficient fuel for a commerce-raiding operation and was forced to head for a French port. Later on 24 May Swordfish aircraft from HMS *Victorious* made a brave but unsuccessful torpedo attack on the German ships. Meanwhile the Admiralty had ordered Force H to sail north from Gibraltar to intercept the German ships. Early on the morning of 25 May the two German ships parted company: *Bismarck* was heading for Brest while *Prinz Eugen* was dispatched to act independently. At about the same time HMS *Suffolk*, which had been gamely shadowing *Bismarck*, lost radar contact. At first it was thought that the German was heading north-west and ships and aircraft were deployed in that direction to search for her, and it was not until the evening of the 25th that signals intelligence indicated that she was heading for a French port. By that time the British ships were 150 miles astern. All through the 25th and the night of the 25th/26th *Bismarck* was lost. Anxiety mounted and the news that she had been sighted by an RAF Catalina at 1030 on 26th was received with a great deal of relief. Within a few minutes of

the Catalina sighting *Bismarck* was spotted by Swordfish aircraft from HMS *Ark Royal* and the ship was shadowed throughout the day. Aircraft from *Ark Royal* mounted two attacks on *Bismarck* on the evening of the 26th: the first was abandoned after some aircraft attacked the cruiser *Sheffield* by mistake, but in the second attack *Bismarck* was struck by three torpedoes, one of which hit right aft, damaging her propellers and jamming her rudders. *Bismarck* came up into the wind, her speed fell off to six or seven knots and she was unable to steer. It was at this point in the action that her fate was effectively sealed. During the night of 26/27 May *Bismarck* was attacked by British and Polish destroyers of the 6th Destroyer Flotilla. At least five torpedo hits were scored during this phase of the action. The final phase of the action took place on the morning of the 27 May. Throughout the night the British battleships *King George V* and *Rodney* had been closing for the kill. They sighted *Bismarck* shortly after 0800 on the 27th and in less than an hour they had reduced the German ship to a shambles. *Bismarck* was finally sunk by three torpedoes fired by the cruiser HMS *Dorsetshire* and she sank with her colours flying. Only 110 of her ship's company of 2,400 were rescued by *Dorsetshire* and the destroyer *Maori*.

Bismarck Sea, Battle of the. As the Allied forces advanced up the north coast of New Guinea in early 1943 the Japanese made strenu-

ous efforts to reinforce their garrison at the important base at Lae in the Huon Gulf. On 1 March a convoy of eight transports, escorted by an equal number of destroyers under the command of Rear-Admiral Kimura, left Rabaul in New Britain for Lae. Next morning shore-based American and Australian aircraft began three days of concerted air attacks on the convoy. On the night of 3/4 March the aircraft were joined by PT-boats operating from Milne Bay. By the end of the battle the Japanese had lost all eight transports and the destroyers *Shirayuki*, *Arashio*, *Asashio* and *Tokisukaze*, together with 3,000 troops. The Japanese made no further attempts to reinforce their garrison in New Guinea by sea.

'Blanket', Operation. Exercise to test the efficiency of Thames estuary defences against enemy explosive motor boats and midget submarines.

Bletchley Park. Country house in Hertfordshire and site of the British Government Code and Cipher School (GCCS) where German radio traffic was decoded during the Second World War. *See* special section on Codes and Code-breaking.

'Block', Operation. Attack on the Japanese garrison on Ramree Island, January–February 1945.

Blockade. A declaration by a belligerent power forbidding seaborne trade with an enemy. In the nineteenth century blockade was successfully used by the

British against the French in circumstances remarkably akin to a siege: British ships would patrol off French ports and prevent ships leaving or entering. This was known as a close blockade. The development of the mine, torpedo and submarine in the early twentieth century meant that close blockade was no longer a practical proposition. Instead a distant blockade was instituted in which merchant shipping would be intercepted far out at sea. Blockade is universally admitted to be a belligerent right to which neutral countries are bound to submit. It is regulated by the twenty-one articles of the 1909 Declaration of London. During the First World War Britain used the blockade to wage economic warfare on Germany. It was extremely comprehensive and, in addition to the usual searching of merchant ships at sea, included a number of diplomatic measures. These consisted of agreements with the Netherlands and Scandinavian countries to ensure that cargoes consigned to a neutral port (and therefore above seizure) would not be re-exported to Germany. Britain also agreed to buy up surpluses of any commodities in the Scandinavian countries in order to prevent their export to Germany. The end result of these measures was that by November 1918 the German Government was facing mass starvation on the home front even though the German armies were undefeated. Blockade was also employed against Germany in the Second World War though it was less effective, largely because the occupation of most of western Europe meant that Germany was less dependent on food imports. By contrast, both German attempts to blockade Britain were comprehensively defeated. In the Second World War the Americans blockaded Japan by means of sinking her merchant shipping and mining her ports. Japan, an island economy dependent on imports of food and raw materials, could not survive this treatment. Historians continue to dispute whether the dropping of the two atomic bombs in August 1945 was strictly necessary in view of the fact that the blockade had effectively brought Japan to her knees. In the post-war period blockade has been used to enforce sanctions imposed by the United Nations against a particular nation. It was used, most unsuccessfully, against Rhodesia in the 1960s, against Iraq before and after the 1991 Gulf War and against Serbia in the recent Bosnian crisis.

Blockship. Obsolete ship stripped of most of her fittings, filled with cement or other such material and then scuttled either to block access to and from a port or to fill a gap in a breakwater. Perhaps the best known use of such a vessel was in the gallant but unsuccessful raid on Zeebrugge on 23 April 1918. A total of 79 blockships were used in the June 1944 Normandy landings as part of the Mulberry harbours. Blockships were also successfully used by Colonel Nasser's government to close the Suez Canal in 1956.

'Bloodstock', Operation. Capture of Kerkenah Island off the Tunisian coast in April 1943. The island was believed to be a base for German and Italian special forces.

Blücher. Name used for two German warships this century. The first was an armoured cruiser launched in 1908. She was often classed as a battlecruiser although her armament (twelve 8.2in guns) gave her no right to this title. However, she operated with the First Scouting Group of the High Seas Fleet and was sunk during the Battle of the Dogger Bank. The name was used again for a *Hipper* class cruiser launched in 1937. She was sunk on 9 April 1940 by Norwegian coastal artillery in the approaches to Oslo.

'Blues', Operation. Deception operation in the southern North Sea in June 1944 to indicate a likely landing in southern Norway. It was part of the overall deception plan for D-Day, Operation 'Fortitude'.

Bofors. (See overleaf) Swedish armaments company which manufactured a 40mm AA gun that was the most widely used AA weapon of the Second World War and is still in service today.

Bogue, USS. American escort carrier employed in the Battle of the Atlantic whose aircraft accounted for eight U-boats.

'Bolero', Operation. Movement of US troops to the UK by sea in

Above (see previous page): Crewmen of a US Navy PT boat operate the single 40mm Bofors mounting. (NYP20614)
Below: US Navy gunners man a 40mm quadruple Bofors mounting aboard the battleship USS *South Dakota*. (IWM NYF 4723)

advance of the invasion of Normandy.

'Bombardon'. Code-word for a prefabricated concrete breakwater section forming part of the Mulberry harbour.

Bombe. A high-speed electromechanical calculating machine used by British cryptanalysts at Bletchley Park to determine the daily settings of the German Enigma enciphering machine. The order of placing the rotors in the Enigma machine could be varied in sixty different ways. For each order there were 17,576 possible settings. No human brain could reach an answer to mathematical problems of such magnitude.

'Bottom', Operation. Aptly named projected attack on Italian battleships at Taranto using Chariots, scheduled to take place in September 1943. The operation was cancelled when Italy concluded an armistice.

Bottom capture. Term used to describe the seduction of an active sonar homing torpedo by the seabed.

Bouvet. French battleship sunk on 18 March 1915 while returning from the second bombardment of Turkish forts on the Gallipoli peninsula.

Bow transducer. Sonar transmitter/receiver fitted in the bow.

BPK. Soviet designation for a large anti-submarine ship, e.g. the helicopter carrier *Moskva*.

'Brawn', Operation. Abortive carrier-borne attack on *Tirpitz* in May 1944.

'Breath', Operation. Plan for an opposed landing on Sicily.

Bremen. German transatlantic liner and flagship of the Norddeutscher Lloyd Line. On the outbreak of the Second World War she was in New York and risked being interned. However, she slipped out of harbour a few days later and, evading the British patrols, took a northerly route across the Atlantic before arriving at the Soviet port of Murmansk. Some weeks later she sailed for Germany and was sighted by a British submarine on patrol in the Heligoland Bight. The submarine was unable to attack – and was prohibited from doing so by the Hague Convention – and *Bremen* was able to break clear. Although she reached Germany safely she never put to sea again. She was ultimately damaged in an air raid on Bremerhaven on 18 March 1942 and burnt out.

'Bridford', Operation. Series of extremely successful blockade-running operations from Sweden to the UK using converted (and enlarged) MTBs to import ball-bearings and strategic materials from Sweden. The craft could make the journey from the Swedish port of Lysekil to the Humber in a single night under cover of darkness.

Britannia. Name associated with the Royal Navy since 1682 when the first ship of the name was commissioned at Chatham. In the twentieth century the name has been used for a pre-dreadnought battleship launched in 1904 and which was torpedoed by *UB50* off Gibraltar on 9 November 1918 – the last capital ship to be sunk during the First World War. The name subsequently reverted to the naval college at Dartmouth, which had previously been housed in a wooden ship of the line named *Britannia*, but in 1953 a new royal yacht was given the name, the college becoming known as Britannia Royal Naval College (BRNC).

Britannic. 45,000-ton luxury liner owned by the British White Star Company and sister ship to the ill-fated *Titanic*. *Britannic* had been requisitioned by the British during the First World War as a hospital ship plying between the UK and the Eastern Mediterranean. On 2 November 1916 she was mined in the Aegean. Fortunately she was not carrying wounded at the time. Among her survivors was a stewardess, Violet Jessop, who had also survived the sinking of the *Titanic*.

Britomart, HMS. British *Halcyon* class minesweeper sunk in particularly tragic circumstances by the Royal Air Force on 27 August 1944 during the Normandy landings. HMS *Hussar* was sunk in the same incident and HM ships *Salamander* and *Jason* damaged. It was the worst British 'friendly fire' incident of the Second World War.

Broad pendant. Swallow-tailed pendant flown from the masthead and in most navies the distinguishing flag of a Commodore.

Broadside. Full weight of metal which can be fired simultaneously from the guns on one side of a ship.

Broke, **HMS.** British destroyer which on the night of 20/21 April 1918, under the command of Captain Edward Evans RN and in company with HMS *Swift*, fought an action with six German destroyers in the English Channel in which two of the latter were sunk. The action was the last occasion on which men from one of HM ships have boarded an enemy ship while the two were still engaged.

'Broomstick', Operation. Counter-measures designed to prevent a break-out by surviving German naval units in north-west Europe, March 1945.

Brussels. A ferry owned by the British Great Eastern Railway Company whose Master, Captain Charles Fryatt, avoided an attack by *U33* on 28 March 1916 by turning towards the U-boat as if to ram. To the Germans *Brussels* was a marked ship and Fryatt a marked man. On 22/23 June 1916 the *Brussels* was seized by German destroyers and taken into Zeebrugge. Fryatt was tried as a *franc-tireur* before a military court, found guilty and sentenced to death. The British regarded his execution as judicial murder aimed at terrorising merchant sea-

men and the case aroused much international disapproval, particularly in America.

'Bubble', Operation. British plan to mine beaches on the south coast of England in case of German invasion, 1941.

Bubyian Channel, Battle of the. The destruction of the Iraqi Navy during the 1991 Gulf War by Royal Navy Lynx helicopters armed with the Sea Skua missile. On 29 January a convoy consisting of a number of small craft escorted by three ex-Kuwaiti TNC-45 FAC-Ms was attacked by the Lynx helicopters. Two of the FAC-Ms were sunk and a third was damaged. The shipping they were meant to protect was destroyed in a free-for-all in which every Coalition helicopter in the area participated. The following day four RN Lynx, given fire control guidance by a US Navy SH-60B helicopter with a superior radar, attacked a second Iraqi convoy consisting of a T-43 type minesweeper, three ex-Soviet *Polnocy* class LSTs escorted by an ex-Kuwaiti TNC-57 FAC, an ex-Kuwaiti TNC-45 FAC-M and six other Project 205 FAC-Ms. The Lynx fired a total of sixteen Sea Skua missiles, scoring fourteen hits which sank the T-43, two of the Project 205s and the TNC-45 and left the TNC-57 and two of the LSTs dead in the water. Fixed-wing USN aircraft finished off the cripples.

Bulges. Structures fitted to the sides of battleships, aircraft carriers, cruisers and monitors to

increase their protection against torpedo or mine damage. The bulge would absorb the force of the explosion leaving the hull proper undamaged.

Bulwark, **HMS.** British pre-dreadnought battleship which blew up at Sheerness on 26 November 1914 while she was taking on board ammunition. Only twelve of her 750-man crew survived. Sabotage was initially suspected but a subsequent inquiry found that the explosion was due to the instability of the cordite being embarked. The name *Bulwark* was subsequently used for a light fleet aircraft carrier launched in 1948. In 1960 she was converted to a commando carrier, and the ship survived until 1984 when she was sold for breaking-up.

Bunker Hill, **USS** (CV17). An *Essex* class aircraft carrier which was badly damaged on 11 May 1945 by *Kamikaze* aircraft. Two aircraft struck the carrier and it was thought that they had replicated the carrier's IFF for there was no warning of the attack. The General Quarters alarm sounded just as the first *Kamikaze* ploughed into the flight deck. The carrier survived, but 389 of her crew were killed and 264 wounded.

Bureau of Ordnance. Sometimes known as the 'Gun Club', 'BuOrd' is the US Navy organisation charged with the development, testing and issuing of all ordnance – shells, bombs and torpedoes – to ships of the US Navy. During the Second World War it demonstrated an alarming lack of competence in refusing to accept reports from sea that US submarine-launched Mk XIV torpedoes were running 11ft deeper than they were set to run and that the Mk VI Exploder was failing to explode. Crucial evidence from sea was rejected until the submarine force commanders in the Pacific conducted their own trials and presented the Bureau with incontrovertible proof. Another of BuOrd's failings was its refusal to countenance the fact that the IJN possessed a 24in, oxygen-fuelled torpedo (*see* Long Lance).

'Buttercup', Operation. Anti U-boat offensive in the western Channel, January 1942.

C³I. Command / Control / Communications / Intelligence. The synergy of the techniques of managing operations by which commanders can effectively communicate their orders and intentions to their subordinates.

C⁴I. Command / Control / Communications / Computers / Intelligence. As above but with the addition of computers. All modern data systems rely on mechanised data-handling.

CA/CB. Two-man Italian midget submarines developed for harbour penetration and coastal defence during the Second World War. The 12-ton CA type just carried mines but the larger 35-ton CB type could carry two torpedoes or mines. They were an interesting and sophisticated design and, properly handled, could have had a significant effect on the Allied

invasions of Italy. The most interesting aspect of their employment was the proposed use of *CA.1* in an attack on New York – an attack which was cancelled because of the Italian armistice.

CACS. Computer Aided Command System. British tactical data system designed for the Type 23 frigate but which failed all trials and was never put into service.

'Caesar', Operation. Proposed German attack on British and Russian naval forces in the Kola Inlet using *Biber* midget submarines. Six *Biber*s were to be carried to within forty miles of the target by three Type VIIC U-boats, *U295*, *U318* and *U716*. The U-boats left Harstad on 5 January 1945 but the operation was abandoned. The vibration of the U-boats' diesel engines started leaks in the *Biber*s' fuel lines which, despite the efforts of the U-boats' engine room departments, could not be fixed.

CAH. Helicopter carrying heavy cruiser. A version of the US/NATO designation system which has been used to describe the British *Invincible* class 'through deck cruisers' as part of the continuing campaign to convince Whitehall (and the RAF) that the ships are not aircraft carriers.

'Calendar', Operation. Aircraft ferry operation to Malta in April 1942 involving the American carrier USS *Wasp*.

Calibre. Term used for the measurement of guns. It is employed

in two senses but its strict meaning is the length of the gun expressed as a multiple of the bore diameter. In its second sense the word defines the bore of the gun measured at the muzzle.

'Caliph', Operation. Proposed invasion of France on the Biscay coast or the Mediterranean ten days after the Normandy landings to draw off German forces.

'Camera', Operation. Deception operation mounted off Norway to fool the Germans into moving forces there and thus diluting their forces in the Mediterranean just before the landings in Sicily. Sometimes known as Operation 'Governor'.

Camouflage. Method of disguising the size, outline, course and speed of a ship by painting her hull and superstructure in contrasting shapes and colours arranged in irregular patterns. *See also* Dazzle-painting.

***Campbeltown*, HMS.** Former American destroyer USS *Buchanan* built in 1919 and transferred to Britain under the September 1940 'Destroyers for Bases' deal with the USA. On the night of 27/28 March 1942 she was expended in the attack on dock facilities in the French port of St Nazaire. The object of the operation was to destroy the caissons on the Normandie Dock, which was the only such facility on the French Atlantic seaboard capable of servicing large capital ships. While commandos destroyed other dock facilities, *Campbeltown*, her bows packed with high explosives set to detonate after a predetermined time, was driven against the caisson and abandoned. The Germans had no suspicion as to her real purpose and were taken by surprise when the ship blew up on the morning of 28th, completely wrecking the caisson. The dock was not fully repaired until 1948. *Campletown*'s commanding officer was awarded the Victoria Cross and had the unusual distinction of having his citation read to him in his PoW camp.

Calabria, Battle of. Inconclusive action on 8 July 1940 between major Italian naval units and the British Mediterranean Fleet. After unsuccessful attacks are Swordfish torpedo bombers from HMS *Eagle* the opposing forces clashed in the late afternoon. The Italian battleship *Giulo Cesare* was hit by a 15inch shell from HMS *Warspite* and an Italian cruiser was also slightly damaged. The Italian fleet escaped after they laid a smoke-screen. The Italian Air Force then made a number of attacks on the British fleet, the ships only being near missed by the bombers.

Camship. Merchant ship fitted with a catapult mounted on the bows on which was carried a single Hurricane fighter. Their purpose was to provide convoys with a rudimentary air defence against attack or persistent shadowers. It was, however, a 'one-shot' weapon since, once launched, the aircraft could not be recovered. The pilot would have to ditch his aircraft when the fuel ran out and hope that he

Above: A Hurricane fighter on the catapult of a Camship. (IWM A 9422)

would be rescued. Camships were eventually replaced by the more effective and practical escort carriers.

Canberra, SS. Passenger liner built for the P&O company. Following the Argentine invasion of the Falkland Islands in April 1982 she was requisitioned at short notice for service as a troopship. Despite lying at anchor in San Carlos Water throughout numerous Argentine air raids, the 'Great White Whale', as she was known, emerged unscathed and returned to Britain to a rapturous welcome in July 1982.

CAP. Combat air patrol.

Cape Esperance, Battle of. A tactical victory for an American force of cruisers and destroyers against a similar force of Japanese vessels which were intercepted on the night of 11/12 October 1942 while attempting to bombard American positions on Guadalcanal.

Cape Palos, Battle of. The principal naval engagement between Government and Nationalist naval forces during the Spanish Civil War took place on 5/6 March 1938. The cruiser *Balaeres*, in Nationalist hands, encountered three Government destroyers, *Lepanto*, *Artequera* and *Barcaiztegui*, off Cape Palos. Neither side was aware that hostile forces were in the area but victory went to the three Government destroyers who fired torpedoes, one of which struck *Balaeres* in her forward 8in magazine, sinking the ship.

Cape St George, Battle of. Last of seven engagements between American and Japanese forces in the Solomon Islands during 1943. Both this action and that of Empress Augusta Bay arose out of Japanese attempts to counter the American landings on Bougainville, which had begun on 1 November. Operating from their main base at Rabaul in New Britain, Japanese naval forces tried unsuccessfully to reinforce their garrisons. In the early hours of 25 November, a flotilla of five US destroyers, *Charles F. Ausburne*, *Claxton*, *Dyson*, *Converse* and *Spence*, under the command of Captain Arleigh Burke USN, was patrolling between Buka in north Bougainville and Cape St George, New Ireland. They intercepted and attacked five Japanese destroyers which were returning to Rabaul on completion of a stores run to Baku. The Japanese force was taken by surprise and in the ensuing *mêlée* *Onami*, *Makinami* and *Yugiri* were sunk without loss or damage to the American force.

Cape Spartivento, Battle of. Engagement south of Sardinia between British forces consisting of *Renown*, *Ark Royal*, two cruisers and five destroyers under the command of Vice-Admiral Sir James Somerville and units of the Italian Fleet. The British were covering a small convoy of fast transports carrying reinforcements to the Middle East when on 27 November 1940 an Italian force consisting of two battleships, seven cruisers and sixteen destroyers was sighted. Despite

the odds Somerville showed no hesitation in closing the enemy and from 1220 there was a brief engagement in which the British cruiser *Berwick* and the Italian destroyer *Lanciere* were damaged. The Italians then retired with Somerville in pursuit. Two air strikes by aircraft from *Ark Royal* were unsuccessful and Somerville was forced to retire before he came within range of Italian shore-based aircraft. Somerville had succeeded in his primary object, which was the protection of the convoy. However, his conduct was judged unsatisfactory by Churchill who felt that Somerville had not showed sufficient enterprise – a charge which was subsequently disproved.

Captain. In all navies, the commissioned rank below that of Rear-Admiral and by custom the title of the commanding officer of any naval ship regardless of rank.

Captor mine. Mine held by its sinker on the bottom until its sensors (magnetic, acoustic or pressure) detect a target. The mine is then released and heads for the surface and the target. Such mines are impossible to detect by conventional minesweeping methods. Detection by bottom-scanning sonar and subsequent disposal by diver and/or ROV is the only way of dealing with these weapons – a lengthy and time-consuming process.

Cap Trafalgar. German 18,710-ton liner owned by the Hamburg Sud-Amerika line. On the outbreak of the First World War she was in South American waters and was hurriedly requisitioned by the German Naval Attaché in Buenos Aires. She was armed with guns from the gunboat *Eber* which had made a passage across the Atlantic from West Africa to the uninhabited island of Trinidada. However, before she could begin her raiding career she was sunk by the British armed merchant cruiser *Carmania*, which caught her coaling at Trinidada on 14 September 1914.

***Carmania*, RMS.** First Cunard liner to be fitted with turbines instead of triple-expansion reciprocating engines. In September 1914 she was commissioned as an armed merchant cruiser. On 14 September 1914 she fought and sank the German armed merchant cruiser *Cap Trafalgar* after a spirited action. In recognition of the event, the British Navy League presented the ship with a plate from Lord Nelson's dinner service.

***Card*, USS.** American escort carrier employed in the Battle of the Atlantic whose aircraft accounted for eight U-boats.

'Catapult', Operation. Operation in July 1940 following the Franco-German armistice to seize control of French naval forces in the UK, Alexandria and Oran and thus prevent the ships from coming under German control. (*See* Oran for details of events at that port.) At Alexandria, the matter was sensitively handled by the British and the French squadron there was duly interned. In Britain the

large number of French ships were seized without incident except in the case of the French submarine *Surcouf*, when one British officer and a rating were killed.

'Catherine', Operation. Proposed British invasion of the Baltic to cut Germany off from her iron ore supplies from Sweden during the Second World War. The plan involved the use of three old *Royal Sovereign* class battleships, selected for their expendability and specially converted, to smash their way through the minefields of the Skaggerak and Kattegat. The plan was backed by Churchill and confounded by some remarkably devious manoeuvring by Admiral Dudley Pound. It was audacious, perhaps even brilliantly conceived, but hopelessly impractical.

Cattaro, Gulf of (Bocche di Cattaro, now known as Kotor). Port on the southern Dalmatian coast used a base for submarines and light forces by the Austrian Navy during the First World War. The port consists of a number of deep-water fjords surrounded by high mountains and with only one narrow entrance to the sea. The area was a perfect anchorage. In 1914 Cattaro was the scene of some fierce fighting when the Austrians cleared Montenegrin forces from the slopes of Mount Lovcen which overlooked the area. Thereafter the Austrians remained in undisputed possession of the area. Cattaro was home to the three *Helgoland* class light cruisers, destroyers and submarines; the

port was also used by German U-boats. Cattaro was the base from which Austrian forces sortied to attack the Otranto Barrage forces and the Serbian-held port of Durazzo. In February 1918 Austrian sailors on the depot ship *Gaa* mutinied. They were followed by some sailors in the larger ships, but men in the cruisers, destroyers and submarines remained loyal. The mutiny was short-lived and was brutally crushed. Cattaro's use as a base for submarines and light forces made it the focus for continued Allied attacks. A number of French submarines penetrated the Austrian defences and entered the harbour, while British and Italian seaplanes based at Otranto and Brindisi made regular flights over the area. On 2 September 1917 six Short 320 seaplanes based at Brindisi were towed by MLs to a position south of Traste Bay, From there they were to take off and launch a torpedo attack on the submarine base at Teodo. Unfortunately the plan was cancelled because of heavy seas and high winds. The activities of U-boats based at Cattaro was of such concern to the *Entente* powers that in 1918 a landing there by US Marines was proposed but never proceeded with on account of the Armistice.

Cavitation. Loss of effective propeller thrust caused by the blades of a propeller cutting across the column of water sucked along by the propeller instead of working in it. It can be caused by a propeller being too small, or too near the surface, for the head of water pressure to supply a solid stream for the propeller to work in, by poor streamlining of the blades or of the after run of the hull form, or by too thick a leading blade on the propeller itself. The effect of cavitation, besides loss of thrust, is heavy vibration of the ship and noise. It follows that in modern warships and submarines, where a good deal of attention is paid to acoustic housekeeping, the elimination of cavitation is a high priority.

CC. Command ship. US Navy classification.

CDS. Comprehensive Display System. A British pioneering analogue computerised AAW plot-compiling system used in conjunction with the Type 994 three-dimensional radar. It was first fitted to the aircraft carrier *Victorious* in 1957.

'Cerberus', Operation. *Luftwaffe* element of Operation 'Thunderbolt', the escape of the German battlecruisers *Scharnhorst* and *Gneisenau* through the English Channel in February 1942. Under the general direction of *Oberst* Adolf Galland, a massive air umbrella was provided for the ships covering each stage of their voyage. The operation was controlled from Galland's shore headquarters but, to facilitate co-operation on the spot, *Luftwaffe* liaison teams were embarked in each of the German capital ships. The arrangements worked perfectly - none of the air attacks launched by the Fleet Air Arm or

the RAF posed any threat to the German ships. As a side-note, this operation was one of the very few when the *Luftwaffe* and *Kriegsmarine* enjoyed any sort of co-operation. *See also* 'Channel Dash'.

CG. Guided missile cruiser. US/NATO designation. Most DLGs were redesignated CGs on 30 June 1975.

CGN. Nuclear-powered guided missile cruiser, i.e. a nuclear-powered variant of the CG. The USS *Long Beach* has been a CGN all her life and the *California* class were commissioned as such. The other CGNs in service are former DLGNs which have been reclassified.

Chaff. Strips of reflective foil deployed in clouds to confuse radar. They are deployed from rockets and form a plume which confuses the radar homing heads on anti-ship missiles. Chaff confuses an incoming missile by providing multiple targets, seductive echoes and misleading information as to the centre of the radar reflections of the target at which the missile is aimed. Once chaff has been fired the ship has to manoeuvre very carefully in order to stay within the protective cloud of foil.

'Channel Dash'. British name for the escape of the German battlecruisers *Scharnhorst* and *Gneisenau* up the English Channel in February 1942. The two ships, together with the cruiser *Prinz Eugen* and six destroyers, left Brest on 11

February and by the afternoon of the 12th were well up the Channel. Successive attacks by British aircraft, MTBs and destroyers were brushed aside, although both *Scharnhorst* and *Gneisenau* were mined off Terschelling. The German force arrived to a heroes' welcome at Brunsbüttel on 13 February. It was a Pyrrhic victory for the Germans: although they had inflicted a considerable humiliation on the British, the removal of the raiding squadron from the Atlantic ports was one less threat the British had to guard against. *See also* 'Cerberus'.

Chariot. Name given to the two-man British human torpedo. It was roughly the same size as a 21in torpedo but fitted with an electric motor and ballast tank to adjust the trim. The warhead, consisting of a 600lb charge, was detachable and could be secured against the hull of an enemy vessel by magnetic clamps. The two-man crew, wearing special suits and breathing apparatus, sat astride the craft. Chariots were taken to their operational area by submarine (although the use of a Sunderland flying boat for this purpose was investigated) before being released. Although their crews were given training in escape and evasion, it was accepted that the operators would be taken prisoner following their sortie. For this reason, apart from one small raid on Phuket in October 1944, British Chariots were not employed in the Far East for fear of what would happen to a 'Charioteer' should he be taken

Above: A British two-man Chariot running awash on the surface. (Author)

prisoner by the Japanese. After the failure of an operation against *Tirpitz* in November 1942, their principal success was damaging the Italian cruiser *Ulpio Traiano* and liner *Viminale* in Janaury 1943 at Palermo. Chariots represented a hurried attempt by the British to develop a weapon which would emulate the successes of the Italian *Decima Mas*. However, whereas Italian *Maiale* were employed in the relatively warm waters of the Mediterranean, British 'Charioteers' fared less well in the Arctic. British Chariots were interesting and innovative weapons of war, but they did not repay the investment and effort put into their development.

'Chariot' Operation. Commando operation to destroy the dock facilities at the French port of St Nazaire. *See Campbeltown.*

Chatham. Port in Kent, England, on the banks of the River Medway which has been a naval base since 1509. In this century Chatham was one of the three Royal Dockyards and was one of the three manning ports for the Royal Navy. There was substantial investment in the dockyard facilities in the 1960s and 1970s, including the construction of a nuclear submarine refitting complex. The 1980s saw the dockyard falling victim to cuts in defence expenditure and the yard was finally closed in the 1980s, the last ship to be refitted there being the frigate HMS *Hermione*.

Checkmate System. System for verifying the identity of suspicious merchant ships by radioing London.

Chemulpo, Battle of. First naval engagement of the Russo-Japanese War which occurred on 9 February 1904, immediately before the formal declaration of hostilities. On 8 February Japanese transports arrived off the port of Chemulpo on the west coast of Korea near Seoul, escorted by a squadron of cruisers and torpedo boats under the command of Rear-Admiral Uriu. In the harbour were the Russian cruiser *Varyag* and the sloop *Korietz*. By the morning of 9 February the Japanese troops had landed and Uriu informed the Russian commander that war had been declared and that his ships would be attacked at their moorings unless they sailed. When the two Russian ships tried to leave harbour they were attacked and forced back after *Varyag* had been badly damaged. Both ships were subsequently scuttled to avoid capture.

'Chess', Operation. Landing near Ambleteuse on the French coast for the assessment of coastal defences, July 1941.

Chester, HMS. British cruiser badly damaged at Jutland when she was engaged by the Second Scouting Group of the High Seas Fleet and hit seventeen times. *Chester* had been launched as the Greek *Lambros Katsonis* and one of the aspects of her design was that the gunshields for her ten 5.5in guns did not offer the same protection as British patterns. As a result her casualties, 35 killed and 42 wounded, were nearly all among those who worked on the upper deck. *See also* Cornwell in the personalities section.

'Chevaline'. British programme to update the A3 Polaris missile in Royal Navy service with an advanced MRV system capable of defeating Soviet exo-atmosphere anti-ballistic missiles. The programme started in 1972 and the upgraded missile went into service in 1982. 'Chevaline' was carried out in conditions of extreme secrecy and cost some £600m.

'Childhood', Operation. Attack by coastal forces and Chariots on moles and blockships at Tripoli in January 1943 to prevent demolition and the blocking of the harbour.

'Chopstick', Operation. Proposed operation for the capture of the Cape Verde Islands during the Second World War if certain circumstances arose.

CIC. Combat Information Centre. USN term (Operations Room in British parlance) for the compartment below decks where information from the ship's various sensors is handled and the battle fought. It is the nerve centre of the modern warship.

City of Benares. A British flag merchant ship which was torpedoed and sunk by *U48* on 18 September 1940. Among her passengers were child evacuees on their way to Canada. Seventy-seven children and 248 adult passengers and crew were killed.

CIWS. Close-In Weapons System. A last-ditch weapons system designed to deal with missiles or suicide craft which have leaked through the outer layers of defence. Typical examples of CIWS are the Dutch Goalkeeper system and the Vulcan-Phalanx.

CL. US/NATO designation for a light cruiser.

'Cleaver', Operation. Dispatch of naval forces into the Skaggerak and Kattegat and from there to Copenhagen on the conclusion of hostilities in 1945.

CMB. Coastal Motor Boat. Type of small warship used in the Royal Navy during the First World War (1914–18). CMBs were of wooden construction with a single stepped hydroplane hull and were powered by petrol motors. There were two variants of the original design, 40ft and 55ft, with speeds of 30 and 42kts respectively. They carried an armament of depth charges, mines or torpedoes; when armed with torpedoes the 40ft boats carried one and the 55ft boats carried two. A few 70ft craft were built for minelaying duties only. They were employed in operations in the English Channel but undoubtedly their most famous operation was the attack on Bolshevik ships at Kronstadt in June 1919 in which the Soviet cruiser *Oleg* was sunk.

CNO. Chief of Naval Operations. The professional head of the US Navy.

Coastwatchers. Volunteers, mostly from Australia and New Zealand, who hid in the Solomon Islands to report on Japanese shipping movements. The idea was developed by the Australians before the Second World War. The men selected were planters, missionaries or colonial administrators who were familiar with local customs and language and who could harness the goodwill of native populations. The Coastwatchers were of particular importance during the Guadalcanal campaign, when they reported Japanese shipping and aircraft movements down The Slot from Rabaul to Guadalcanal. Admiral Halsey said that 'The Coastwatchers saved Guadalcanal and Guadalcanal saved the Pacific.'

COAST GUARDS AND PARAMILITARY NAVAL FORCES

The post-1945 era has also seen the growth of coast guards and paramilitary naval forces in many countries. Such forces maintain territorial integrity by mounting border patrols, prevent smuggling, control pollution, prevent unauthorised exploitation of offshore economic assets and carry out maritime safety

Coat, Operation. Passage of troops and supplies to Malta in November 1940.

Cod Wars. Name given to the three disputes (1958–1961, 1973 and 1975–1976) between Britain and Iceland over fishing rights in the North Atlantic and resulting from a unilateral Icelandic decision to impose an exclusive economic zone extending for 200 miles around their coastline. British trawlers fishing in these waters were subjected to repeated harassment by Icelandic warships. The Royal Navy was called upon to provide protection and, particularly in the 1973 and 1975–76 'wars', there were numerous confrontations between Icelandic gunboats and British frigates. The Icelandic ships were designed for this sort of work, the British frigates most certainly were not. Every device and manoeuvre short of the use of firearms was employed. Casualties were minimal but the damage to the frigates was not. British ships heading for Icelandic waters had their bows

duties. The United States, Canada, India, Italy and Japan operate substantial coast guard forces. The US Coast Guard is the largest of these and its 'cutters' have always been configured with the auxiliary warship role in mind. The most capable vessels in the USCG's fleet are the *Hamilton* class cutters, which are 3,000-ton vessels with a top speed of 29kts. Possession of a coast guard fleet gives any navy a 'second tier' of warships which can be used in time of war but whose cost is not borne by the defence budget.

reinforced by massive fenders to give added protection. Though a decision reached in 1974 by the International Court of Justice seemed to favour Britain, her fishing rights in Icelandic waters have continued to be eroded.

Colossus. A more advanced electro-mechanical computer than the Bombe. First used in February 1944, it could read some 25,000 bytes per second.

Colours. Name by which the national flag flown by a ship at sea is known. Most nations use their national flag but a number of navies have a special flag for naval vessels, e.g. the Royal Navy's White Ensign.

Combined Operations. A British organisation established during the Second World War to train personnel for and organise operations where one or more service was involved. It was established in 1940 under Admiral of the Fleet Sir Roger Keyes, who was succeeded by Rear-Admiral Lord Louis Mountbatten in October 1941. Its headquarters was known as 'Wimbledon' (after the well-known London tennis club) because, in the words of one officer, 'Combined Ops' was 'All balls and rackets'.

Commando carrier. Aircraft carrier carrying helicopters and a substantial number of embarked troops instead of a fixed-wing air group. The concept was developed by the British in the late 1950s when it became clear that the light fleet carriers, *Hermes*,

Bulwark, Albion and *Centaur* were too small to operate the new generation of carrier aircraft coming into service. The conversion involved the removal of catapults and arrester gear, the fitting of davits for the stowage of landing craft and the modification of messdecks so as to accommodate 733 Royal Marines. The air group now consisted of eight helicopters. The first ship to be thus converted was *Bulwark*: she proved to be such a success that she was followed by *Albion* and *Hermes*. However, plans to convert *Centaur* foundered for financial reasons. Commando carriers saw extensive service 'East of Suez' and on NATO's northern flank, where they would have been used for the rapid reinforcement of Norway in the event of a war with the Soviet Union. They were extremely versatile ships able to deploy (and recover if necessary) large numbers of men and equipment to and from the shore very quickly. They also were very useful in the disaster relief role – *Hermes'* efforts during the evacuation of British nationals from Cyprus in 1974 being just one example. *Albion* was broken up in 1972 and *Hermes* relinquished her amphibious role when she embarked Sea Harrier aircraft in 1980, but *Bulwark* remained in service until 1981. The demise of the commando carrier left a big gap in the Royal Navy's order of battle – consider how valuable *Bulwark* would have been in the 1982 Falklands War – which will not be filled until HMS *Ocean*, currently under construction on the Clyde, is commissioned in 1997.

The commando carrier concept was a typically British way of making the best use of assets which had outlived their original function. The US Navy has since developed the type much further with its *Iwo Jima* and *Tarawa* class landing ships. These vessels combine flight decks for helicopter operations, accommodation for up to 2,000 troops, vehicle stowage below decks and, in the case of the *Tarawa* class, a small well-dock capable of accepting small craft up to LCU size.

Commodore. A rank intermediate between Captain and Rear-Admiral held by a Captain to indicate that he has additional responsibilities. It is not a step on the promotion ladder but relates to the appointment in which the holder is serving. A Commodore holding an appointment afloat flies a broad pendant.

***Compass Rose*, HMS.** Fictional 'Flower' class corvette which is the heroine of the novel *The Cruel Sea*, a book which more than any other encapsulates the nature of the Battle of the Atlantic.

Conning tower. Armoured control centre in a warship from where the ship was navigated in battle. In submarines the conning tower is the structure between the pressure hull and the bridge. In British submarines this consisted of no more than a trunk with an internal ladder and sealed by hatches at the upper and lower ends. However in American, French (in French boats the area was known as the *kiosque*) and German sub-

marines the space was used to house the attack periscope and attack instruments and would be the position from which the commanding officer directed an attack while the boat was dived.

***Conqueror*, HMS.** British *Churchill* class SSN armed with six 21in torpedo tubes. On 2 May 1982 *Conqueror* sank the Argentine cruiser *General Belgrano* during the 1982 Falklands War – the only occasion on which a nuclear submarine has torpedoed another vessel. When *Conqueror* returned to her base at Faslane she flew the Jolly Roger flag traditionally worn by British submarines returning from patrol. The flag was proudly marked with one white bar symbolising the sinking of *Belgrano*.

Contact mine. A mine exploded by contact with the target. Detonation occurs when the target strikes the mine, breaking open the horns and completing the firing circuit. An alternative is the antenna mine.

Contraband. Goods which have been prohibited from entering a belligerent state due to the declaration of a blockade. There are three types of contraband as defined by the 1909 Declaration of London. Absolute Contraband consists of a very short list of items directly associated with the enemy's war effort. Any goods in this category could be seized outright. Conditional Contraband comprises goods which might or might not be relevant to the war effort; fuel and fodder are two examples. If the goods were consigned to an enemy port then they could be seized; if they were consigned to a neutral port, then the cargo was inviolate. Free Goods are goods which are above seizure even though this category includes items such as metal ores, rubber, textiles and machinery, all of which are relevant to the war effort. The categories Conditional Contraband and Free Goods have been the most contentious since all articles in these categories are clearly relevant to the war effort. During the First World War the British Government sought to tighten the blockade on Germany by declaring as many items as possible Absolute or Conditional Contraband.

Convoy. One or more merchant ships sailing in company to the same general destination under naval escort. Convoy has an ancient history: there are references to convoys of merchant ships as early as 1213. Convoy's apogee was undoubtedly the Napoleonic period when all of Britain's considerable maritime trade was conducted under the convoy system. The unwise shipowner who chose to sail his ships independently not only risked their being sunk or captured by a French privateer but was liable to a fine of £100. In the latter half of the nineteenth century the convoy system fell out of favour largely because (in defiance of all the principles of war) it was seen as defensive: active patrolling of the sea lanes was seen as offensive and therefore much more acceptable. There was also the belief, largely fostered by radical liberals, that the convoy

Above: A British convoy to Russia, 4 February to 2 March 1945. A photograph taken from the escort carrier HMS *Campania* showing the sort of weather conditions that could be expected. (IWM A 27518)

system interfered with individual freedoms. Consequently, for the first three years of the First World War the British Admiralty steadfastly refused to adopt the convoy system in the face of mounting losses which very nearly forced Britain out of the war. In the Second World War the British adopted convoy almost immediately but insufficient escort vessels meant that merchant ship losses were very high in the early years. On the other side of the world the Japanese failed to adopt the convoy system until very late in the war. By then it was *too* late: American submarines had decimated Japan's merchant marine. In the post-war period the convoy system has come under scrutiny once again, largely by those advocates of land-based air power who believe that shore-based aircraft are sufficient to protect merchant ships at sea – an argument not proven in various NATO exercises. Various other ancient heresies have also raised their ugly heads on the subject, for example that patrolling and hunting down enemy warships/submarines is preferable to escorting merchant ships. Yet in the 1982 Falklands War and in the Straits of Hormuz in 1988 convoy was used effectively to manage merchant ship movements. The convoy system encompasses all the principles of maritime war. It concentrates one's own forces and compels the enemy to make the first move. To those who decry the value of convoy in the post-1945 period there can be one rejoinder: 'He who forgets history is condemned to repeat it'.

Convoy codes. A system of identifying convoy routes by a series of alphabetical code letters. It was practised largely by Britain and America in both world wars. The principal codes for the First World War are as follows:

HB	New York to Bay of Biscay
HC	Quebec to UK
HD	Dakar to UK
HG	Gibraltar to UK
HH	Hampton Roads to UK
HL	Sierra Leone to UK
HN	New York to UK (East Coast ports)
HS	Sydney (Cape Breton) to UK
HX	New York to UK (West Coast ports)
OB	Lamlash outward-bound
OC	Southend outward-bound
OD	Devonport outward-bound
OF	Falmouth outward-bound
OL	Liverpool outward-bound
OLB	Liverpool outward-bound
OLX	Liverpool outward-bound (fast troop convoys known as the 'Liverpool Express')
OM	Milford Haven outward-bound

Codes for the principal convoy routes in the Second World War were as follows:

AP	UK to Middle East via Cape
BTC	UK coastal after June 1944
GM	Gibraltar to Malta
GUF	Gibraltar to USA (fast)
GUS	Gibraltar to USA (slow)
HG	Gibraltar to UK
HX	Halifax/New York to UK
JW	UK to Kola Inlet (replaced PQ)
KMF	UK to Mediterranean (fast)
KMS	UK to Mediterranean (slow)
MG	Malta to Gibraltar
MKF	Mediterranean to UK (fast)
MKS	Mediterranean to UK (slow)
MW	Alexandria to Malta
OA	UK (Thames) to North America
OB	UK (Liverpool) to North America
OG	UK to Gibraltar
ON	UK to North America (fast) (replaced OB)
ONS	UK to North America (slow)
OS	UK to Freetown
PQ	UK/Iceland to Kola Inlet
QP	Kola Inlet to UK
RA	Kola Inlet to UK (replaced QP)
SC	North America to UK
SL	Sierra Leone to UK
TA	UK to North America (military traffic only)
UC	UK to Caribbean (tanker traffic)
UGS	USA to Gibraltar (slow)
UGF	USA to Gibraltar (fast)
WS	UK to Middle East ('Winston Specials')

Convoy Commodore. Senior naval officer assigned to a convoy to give general direction to the merchant ships and to ensure compliance with regard to station-keeping, signalling and other procedures. In the Second World War British Convoy Commodores were a unique band of men. Many were distinguished flag officers who had already enjoyed long and full careers and who now came back from retirement to serve their country. Despite their advanced years they endured the same privations as men half their age and were an immense source of strength and experience.

COPP. Combined Operations Pilotage Parties. A British organisation of mixed RN, RM and Army personnel who undertook beach reconnaissance before a landing. They were taken to the operational area by submarine, MTB or X-craft. They then paddled ashore in Folboats to take hydrographic data on the beach in question. Among the many tools of their trade were delubricated condoms, which were used for taking soil samples. They were first employed in Sicily in July 1943, and also saw service in Normandy and in the Far East.

COQC. Commanding Officers' Qualifying Course. *See* Perisher.

Coral Sea, Battle of the. The first battle conducted by aircraft carriers in which neither fleet sighted the other. An American force consisting of two carriers supported by cruisers and destroyers was dispatched into the Coral Sea to frustrate a Japanese invasion of New Guinea. Early on 7 May 1942 American aircraft sank the Japanese carrier *Shoho* but it was on 8 May that carrier borne aircraft of both sides came into contact. The Americans damaged the carrier *Shokaku* (losing thirty-three aircraft in the process) and in a counter-strike by Japanese aircraft the USS *Lexington* was damaged and subsequently scuttled. Although US losses (which included the destroyer *Sims* and oiler *Neosho*) were greater, it was a strategic defeat for the Japanese: their southward thrust had been turned back and an invasion of Australia, which would have been

the next step had New Guinea fallen, had been averted.

Corfu Incident. The mining in international waters of the destroyers HMS *Saumarez* and HMS *Volage* which were passing between the island of Corfu and the Albanian coast on 22 October 1946. Thirty-six British sailors were killed and *Saumarez* was declared a constructive total loss. The Albanians claimed the waters as theirs (and had mined them with Yugoslav assistance) and the British destroyers had been ordered to pass through the straits in order to test their right of free passage. It was a classic 'freedom of the seas' operation but one which went disastrously wrong. Britain was subsequently awarded damages in the International Court, but these have never been paid.

Corncob. Blockships sunk as part of the breakwaters in the Mulberry harbour complex.

Coronel, Battle of. First major naval engagement of the First World War and one which ended disastrously for the British. On the outbreak of the First World War the German East Asia Squadron, consisting of the heavy cruisers *Scharnhorst* and *Gneisenau* and two light cruisers under the command of Vice-Admiral *Graf* von Spee, began a long return voyage to Germany via the Pacific and Cape Horn. On 1 November 1914, off Coronel on the coast of Chile, Spee's squadron was brought to action by an ill-assorted British force under the command of Rear-

Admiral Craddock and consisting of the cruisers *Good Hope* and *Monmouth*, the light cruiser *Glasgow* and the AMC *Otranto*. The old battleship *Canopus*, which was supposed to provide heavy support for Craddock's ships, was some 300 miles to the south. When contact was made in the late afternoon both sides believed that only a single enemy ship was present, but when Craddock was informed that he was facing superior force he decided to engage rather than break away and shadow. Von Spee held fire until the British ships were silhouetted against the setting sun and the range was less than 12,000yds. The German gunnery was so superior that the British ships were almost overwhelmed, particularly as the heavy seas meant that they could not work some of their main armament which was mounted in casemates. After a short action *Good Hope* was sunk, followed quickly by *Monmouth*. Only *Glasgow* and *Otranto* survived. The German squadron subsequently rounded Cape Horn, only to be defeated at the Battle of the Falkland Islands five weeks later.

'Coronet', Operation. Planned invasion of Honshu and the Tokyo Plain in the Japanese home islands set for early 1946.

'Corporate', Operation. Tri-service operation mounted by the British in April 1982 for the liberation of the Falkland Islands.

Corvette. Term reintroduced by the Royal Navy in 1940 for the

1,000-ton 'Flower' class. Previously it had been used for small ships employed in coastal work of between 500 and 1,000 tons. In the post-1945 period the French Navy has classed its large destroyer type ships as corvettes, which is a more accurate use of the term since in the days of sail corvettes were merely smaller frigates.

'Cosmic', Operation. British Home Fleet contingency plan to deal with the German battleship *Tirpitz* if she moved south into the North Sea, 1944.

***Cossack*, HMS.** British 'Tribal' class destroyer built in 1937 with a displacement of 1,870 tons and an armament of eight 4.7in guns and four 21in torpedo tubes. Under the command of Captain Philip Vian she became an extremely well-known ship for her part in the liberation of British merchant seaman PoWs from the German tanker *Altmark* on 16 February 1940. She was damaged at the Second Battle of Narvik in April 1940 and played a part in the sinking of the German battleship *Bismarck* in May 1941. On 23 October 1941 she was torpedoed off Gibraltar by *U563* and sank the next day.

'Countenance', Operation. Neutralisation of Iranian naval, land and air forces in August 1941.

'County' class. (see overleaf) A group of eight 'destroyers' (*Devonshire, Hampshire, Kent, London, Fife, Glamorgan, Antrim* and *Norfolk*) built for the Royal Navy between 1960 and 1967 and

undoubtedly the most handsome British ships built since the Second World War. The designation 'destroyer' was chosen to gain Treasury approval for their construction even though they were as large (6,200 tons normal and 505ft long) as a Second World War light cruiser. They were the first British ships designed to carry guided missiles, the Sea Slug and Seacat SAM systems, and were the first to carry a helicopter, a Wessex 3. Four 4.5in guns in two twin mountings rounded off the armament. In the 1970s the second group (*Fife, Glamorgan, Antrim* and *Norfolk*) had their 'B' 4.5in mounting removed and replaced with four Exocet missiles. *Devonshire* was sunk as a target in July 1984, *Hampshire* was broken up after being cannibalised, *London* was sold to Pakistan and *Fife, Glamorgan, Antrim* and *Norfolk* were sold to Chile and remain in commission. *Kent* is the only one of these ships to remain in RN service, as a static training ship at Portsmouth. However, she will have to be renamed when the new *Kent*, a Type 23 frigate, is commissioned.

***Courageous*, HMS.** A British aircraft carrier which was a former light battlecruiser. Completed in February 1916 and lost to *U29* on 17 September 1939, with the loss of 518 lives. Sister ship to HMS *Glorious.* Her conversion to an aircraft carrier was from 1924. As a battlecruiser her main armament was four 15in guns and her top speed was 30.5 knots. As a carrier of 22,500 tons she had a compliment of 48 aircraft.

Creeping attack. Anti-U-boat tactic developed by Captain F. 'Johnny' Walker and designed to prevent the loss of asdic contact caused when the attacking ship ran over the U-boat to drop her depth charges. U-boat commanders were learning to listen for the sound of the escort steadying on a course and increasing speed for the attack run and could make last-minute alterations of course and speed to foil the attack. One ship would hold the U-boat in asdic contact while a second would be directed to make an attack run which she did at slow speed and with her asdic switched off. It was thus hoped to confuse the U-boat about which direction the attack was coming from.

Crete. Island in the Eastern Mediterranean from which the Royal Navy evacuated some 18,000 British and Commonwealth troops following the German airborne attack in May 1941. The evacuation was conducted under extremely difficult conditions, ships being exposed to continuous air attack with no air support of their own. Three cruisers and six destroyers were sunk during the evacuation, while two battleships, an aircraft carrier, five cruisers and four destroyers were damaged. There was nearly a crisis of confidence in the Mediterranean Fleet as a result, but Admiral Cunningham kept his nerve and that of his fleet.

Cross-deck. Movement of men and supplies from ship to ship while both vessels are at sea, a

Above: HMS *Glamorgan*, a County Class guided missile destroyer. She was damaged when hit by an Excocet (q.v.) missile during the Falklands conflict in 1982, but she survived and was capable of continuing the fight. (IWM FKD 582)

process made infinitely easier thanks to the helicopter. One of the most spectacular examples of 'cross-decking' took place on 19 May 1982 when 40 Commando and the 3rd Battalion Parachute Regiment were transferred from the liner *Canberra* to the assault ships *Fearless* and *Intrepid* respectively in mid-ocean before the landings at San Carlos on 21 May 1982.

'Crossroads', Operation. The fourth and fifth detonations of atomic bombs at Bikini Atoll in the Marshall Islands to test their effects on ninety-three American, German and Japanese ships, many of which had live animals tethered to their decks to simulate personnel (animal rights activists in the USA suggested the use of Japanese PoWs or convicts for this purpose), together with items of equipment. Bikini was chosen because it was free from currents and outside the range of the prevailing winds. A task force of 150 ships, seventy-five aircraft and 40,000 men was assembled for the trials, and the 167 inhabitants of Bikini were unceremoniously removed to the island of Rongerik. The 'stars' of the proceedings were the former Japanese flagship, the battleship *Nagato*, and the German cruiser *Prinz Eugen*. Other ships included the battleships *Arkansas*, *New York*, *Pennsylvania* and *Nevada* (the last two being survivors of Pearl Harbor [q.v.]), the cruisers *Salt Lake City* and *Pensacola* and a large number of smaller vessels. Test 'Able' on 1 July 1946 was an airburst atomic bomb dropped

from a B-29 directly over *Nagato*. Test 'Baker' on 25 July 1946 consisted of an atomic bomb exploded 90ft below the surface. The explosion produced a column of water some 7,000ft high and 2,200ft in diameter, and photographs and film of this detonation became an enduring symbol of the awesome power of nuclear weapons. Twenty-one ships had been destroyed in the two explosions. Test 'Charlie' was to be another underwater explosion but was cancelled because the 'Baker' test had spread contaminated water far and wide. Long after the tests the US Government has continued to reject claims that many personnel participating subsequently developed various cancers. In later years a further twenty-two atomic and hydrogen weapons were tested at Bikini.

Cruise missile. Long-range missile that flies to its target using aerodynamic surfaces for lift and is powered by a jet engine. The term is particularly associated with weapons such as the US Navy's Tomahawk.

Cruiser. Traditionally a large surface combatant capable of operating independently and used for both fleet reconnaissance and trade protection. In the inter-war period cruiser construction was regulated by the Washington and London Naval Treaties, which laid restrictions on both size and gun calibre. By the end of the Second World War these restrictions had gone by the board and cruisers displaced anything between 8,000 and 16,000 tons. As post-war

economies bit into naval budgets, the term began to die out but it was reintroduced in the 1970s to classify the large DL/DLG type ships which were comparable in size to cruisers of the early part of the century. A modern definition of a cruiser might read as a large surface vessel with a comprehensive range of capabilities including area air defence, of at least 7,000 tons' standard displacement to give sufficient room for all systems.

Cuba. Island in the Caribbean which was the scene for an American blockade from 22 October to 20 November 1962. Aerial reconnaissance photographs revealed the presence on Cuba of Soviet missiles capable of reaching the United States. The Americans reacted by blockading the island and warning the Soviet Union that they would prevent, using force if necessary, Soviet ships reinforcing the missile stocks on the island. The Soviet Union backed down , it was the worst crisis between the two super-powers since the 1949 Berlin Crisis.

Cudgel. Two-kiloton nuclear mine designed for use with the British *X-51* midget submarines and intended for laying in Soviet harbours. The weapon was based on the 2,000lb Red Beard free-fall bomb. Development stopped in 1955 owing to a shortage of fissile material.

'Cultivate', Operation. Relief of the Australian garrison at Tobruk and running of supplies into

Tobruk from Alexandria, October 1941.

Cunard Line. Transatlantic steamship company founded in 1840 by Samuel Cunard. The company grew steadily throughout the nineteenth century, determined to dominate the profitable North Atlantic seaway against whatever opposition presented itself. The company stole a clear march on its competitors with the construction of the liners *Mauretania*, *Lusitania* and *Aquitania*. These liners set new standards in size, comfort and speed. *Mauretania* held the coveted 'Blue Riband' for a large part of her existance. In wartime many of Cunard's ships were taken up by the Admiralty. *Mauretania* and *Lusitania* had been built with government subsidies to serve as armed merchant cruisers, but in the event they proved unsuitable for service in this role though found alternative work as troopships and hospital ships. *Lusitania* was sunk in controversial circumstances in April 1915 but her two running mates went on to dominate the Atlantic passenger trade until the 1930s, when they were replaced by the *Queen Mary* and *Queen Elizabeth*. In the Second World War the two 'Queens' were taken up for service as troopships. Both vessels played an important role in the movement of American soldiers to Britain in preparation for the invasion of Europe. They sailed unescorted as their great speed meant that they could evade submarine attack. The decline in the Atlantic passenger trade in the post-war period saw Cunard sell off most of its large liners, including the two 'Queens' and the old *Aquitania* and by the 1960s the company had but one large ship in service, the *Queen Elizabeth 2*. She alternated summer cruising with Atlantic voyages but in May 1982 she was hurriedly requisitioned to take 5 Infantry Brigade to the Falkland Islands. She was considered too valuable to risk inside the confined waters of San Carlos but instead went straight to South Georgia, where her troops were 'cross-decked' to the *Canberra* and the *Norland*.

'Curfuffle', 'Clunk' and 'Clong'. Three of the many onomatopoeic words used to describe and identify transient noises heard by a passive sonar operator.

Curie. French submarine of the *Brumaire* class launched in 1912 and captured on 20 December 1914 while trying to enter the Austrian base at Pola. Her commanding officer, *Lieutenant de Vaisseau* Gabriel O'Byrne, was allowed visits from his wife while in an Austrian PoW Camp. *Curie* was subsequently commissioned into the *KuK Kriegsmarine* as *U14*. She was returned to France after the war and finally broken up in 1928.

'Cutting', Operation. The cutting and picking up of the undersea telephone cable between Dakar in West Africa and Pernambuco in Brazil in August 1941.

Cuxhaven. The Zeppelin sheds at Cuxhaven in Germany were the target for a British seaplane raid on 25 December 1914. Seven seaplanes from the carriers *Engadine*, *Riviera* and *Empress* took off before dawn. Only one of them found the sheds, but the pilot failed to recognise the target for what it was. Nevertheless, the aircraft flew around the Cuxhaven area dropping their bombs. One plane flew over the High Seas Fleet in Schillig Roads, where its appearance caused a good deal of alarm. The aircrew were all rescued by the carriers or submarines deployed for that purpose. In return the carriers were attacked by Zeppelin *L5* as they searched for their aviators. The raid was a preview of the great air–sea battles of future wars.

CV. USN/NATO designation for large aircraft carriers with general-purpose capabilities, including ASW as well as strike and AAW.

CVA. Attack aircraft carrier. USN term used in the 1950s to reflect the role of its carriers in delivering nuclear weapons. The classification lasted until 30 June 1975 when CVAs were redesignated CV.

CVAN. Nuclear-powered attack aircraft carrier. Now designated CVN.

CVE. Escort carrier.

CVL. Small aircraft carrier. Used for the USN's *Independence* class aircraft carriers during the Second World War and subsequently for the British light fleet carriers of the *Colossus*, *Majestic* and *Hermes* classes.

CVS. ASW support carrier. Originally applied to the USN's *Essex* class carriers converted for this role in 1953, it is now applied to the three British *Invincible* class ships since it is now judged politically safe enough to refer to them as aircraft carriers.

'CW/CX', Operation. Anti-U-boat operation in UK waters, 1944–45.

Cyprus. Island in the eastern Mediterranean and the focus of Greek–Turkish tension. In 1975 the Turkish Government launched an invasion of the northern, and ethnic Turkish, side of the island and established a separate regime. The only naval casualty of the assault was the Turkish destroyer *Kocatepe*, sunk in error by the Turkish Air Force in mistake for a Greek ship of the same class.

DA. Director angle. The amount of 'aim-off' applied during a submarine attack to allow for the target's speed.

Damage control. The means by which damage to a ship can be repaired and contained. It includes fire-fighting, the shoring up of bulkheads, plugging of holes in the side and the restoration of essential services and supplies. Effective damage control can make all the difference between a ship sinking and surviving.

Dakar. Port in French West Africa and scene of an abortive attempt by the British and their Free French hirelings to persuade the Vichy governor to declare for the Free French cause. *See* 'Menace'.

Dardanelles. Narrow strait which separates Turkey in Europe with Turkey in Asia and links the Sea of Marmara to the Mediterranean. In 1915 it was the scene of bitter fighting when British and French forces tried to force a passage to Constantinople and thereby drive Turkey out of the war. A naval bombardment of the forts guarding the entrance to the Dardanelles failed and three battleships, the British *Ocean* and *Irresistible* and the French *Bouvet*, were lost on 18 March 1915 to mines laid by the Turks. Instead British forces landed at Cape Helles and French troops at Kum Kale on the Asiatic shore. The landings were notable for the gallantry displayed in appalling conditions by the British, Australian and New Zealand forces. However the Turks held on and by the middle of summer 1915 the Allies were no nearer achieving their goal. A further landing at Suvla Bay in July 1915 with the intention of outflanking the Turks failed. With no end to the campaign in sight and with the approach of winter, the government took the courageous decision to evacuate the peninsula. It was ironic that out of the whole sorry shambles of the Dardanelles campaign, the evacuation was successfully carried out with the loss of only one life. The last troops left the peninsula on the night of 16 January 1916. From a naval perspective the Dardanelles campaign showed that all the lessons of amphibious warfare learned by the British in the Revolutionary and Napoleonic wars, where amphibious operations had been an integral part of naval warfare, had been completely forgotten. As Lloyd George succinctly commented, 'There was no co-ordination of effort. There was no connected plan of action. There was no sense of the importance of time.'

DASH. Drone Anti-Submarine Helicopter. An imaginative but unsuccessful American attempt to employ an unmanned helicopter to deliver a homing torpedo within 200yds of a submerged submarine 10,000yds away. Many ships in the USN and MSDF were fitted to carry DASH but the system was prematurely withdrawn since it proved extremely difficult to control the drones in flight. Of the 746 DASH drones built, over half were lost at sea in accidents.

Data shock. Paralysis of an electronic processing system – or the operator – due to information overload.

DATS. Deep Armed Team Sweep. Method of minesweeping in waters as deep as 200m. A wire with two explosive cutters is deployed between two vessels with 'kites' to depress the sweep to the required depth.

Dauntless. *See* SBD.

Davis Submarine Escape Apparatus (DSEA). British equipment used for escaping from sunken submarines. Developed in 1929, it consisted of a breathing bag and an oxygen cylinder containing thirty minutes' supply. Oxygen was bled from the cylinder into the breathing bag and was then inhaled by the wearer using a mouthpiece. The exhaled air was passed through a cylinder containing a purifying agent, usually soda lime, before being returned to the breathing bag. Each set came complete with goggles, a nose clip and a drogue or apron for the wearer to check his ascent on leaving the submarine and thus avoid lung damage. DSEA sets were first used in the escape of four men from the British submarine *Poseidon* which sank on 9 June 1931. The sets also proved useful in a number of other applications, notably human torpedo operations and shallow-water diving.

Dazzle-painting. Method of deceiving an enemy as to a ship's course, speed and size by means of painting the hull and superstructure in contrasting colours applied in irregular shapes. A ship scientifically disguised by dazzle painting could be made to look smaller than she actually was, steaming faster than she was actually steaming and steering an entirely different course. It was widely used in both world wars to complicate the task of submarine commanders when trying to calculate the correct amount of DA.

DCB. Distance Controlled Explosive Motor Boat. British term for an unmanned, remotely controlled fast motor boat (*Fernlenkboot*) packed with explosives which the Germans used against British monitors in the English Channel during the First World War. The boats were 43ft long, weighed six tons, had a speed of 30kts and were packed with 750kg of high explosive. They were controlled from the shore by means of a thirty-mile

long trailing cable in accordance with instructions radioed to the shore controller from an aircraft. As they were unmanned the intention was to crash them into the sides of a monitor, when it was hoped that the charge would blow a hole sufficiently large in the monitor's side to sink it. The first DCB used against the Royal Navy blew up when it was inadvertently steered into Nieuport pier in March 1917. However, later attacks on the ships of the Dover Patrol were more troublesome. Cutting the control cable or shooting down the directing aircraft only led to the DCB careering about out of control. The only sound method of ensuring their destruction was shooting them up with close-range armament. DCBs were an interesting concept, but given the extensive anti-torpedo protection with which all monitors were equipped they were less than successful. On 28 October 1917 the monitor HMS *Erebus* was struck by a DCB but was not seriously damaged as the anti-torpedo bulge took the full force of the blast. The Germans abandoned use of DCBs at the end of 1917.

DD. Destroyer. USN/NATO classification.

D-Day. For planning purposes, the day selected for the start of an operation. Planning can then be organised in terms of D-1, D+3 etc. without being committed to a specific date.

DDE. Fast destroyer/anti-submarine destroyer. USN/NATO classification.

DDG. Guided missile destroyer. USN/NATO classification.

DDH. Helicopter-carrying destroyer. USN classification.

DDR. Radar picket destroyer. USN/NATO classification.

DE. *See* Destroyer escort.

'Deadlight', Operation. The scuttling of German U-boats in December 1945 and January 1946 in deep water to the north of Malin Head. The U-boats were those not required by the Allies for trials purposes or war booty, and a decision taken at the Potsdam Conference required that all such surplus U-boats be destroyed.

Decima Mas. The Italian 10th Light Flotilla, an élite unit specialing in operations involving the use of hu,man torpedoes and assualt frogman.

Defence, HMS. Name which has been used for six vessels in the Royal Navy of which only one has been in commission this century. This was an armoured cruiser built at Pembroke Dock in 1907 and which was sunk with all hands at the Battle of Jutland. As a matter of record, she was the last large warship built for the Royal Navy with reciprocating engines as opposed to turbines.

DEG. Guided missile destroyer escort. USN classification. Replaced by FFG on 30 June 1975.

Degaussing. Method whereby ships can be rendered relatively

Above: Landing craft packed with vehicles and troops of the US lst Infantry Division await the order to sail for Normandy at Portland on the south coast of England in June 1944 during the D-Day operations (see previous page).

immune to the attentions of a magnetic mine. Once the polarity of the magnetic mine was known it was a relatively easy matter to reverse the polarity of the ship's magnetic field by passing a current through an electric cable encircling her hull. Degaussing did not offer complete protection but it considerably reduced the risk of detonating a mine and increased the confidence of ships' companies when sailing through waters known to be mined.

Delfin (Dolphin). Name used by a number of countries for, appropri-

ately enough, submarines commissioned into their naval service. It was Greek submarine named *Delfin* which carried out the first submarine torpedo attack in history on 9 December 1912. *Delfin*, under the command of Lt-Cdr Paparrigopoulos, was on station at the seaward end of the Dardanelles when she sighted the Turkish cruiser *Medjidieh* escorted by five torpedo boats. Paparrigopoulos closed to 500yds before firing one 17.7in torpedo which, in the best traditions of the torpedo, failed to run properly and sank.

Deptford. One of oldest naval dockyards in Britain. By the twentieth century most of the dockyard facilities had been moved elsewhere, but Deptford remained the Royal Victualling Yard where most of the Royal Navy's food, drink, clothing and furniture was manufactured and stored. The yard was finally closed in 1965.

Depth Charge. Weapon designed during the First World War for use against submerged submarines. It consists of an explosive-filled canister fitted with a hydrostatic fuse which is set to explode at a given depth. The fuse is activated by water pressure against a spring, tension on the spring being varied to correspond to the depth at which the charge is required to explode. Until the development of ahead-throwing weapons, depth charges could only be dropped over the stern of the ship or fired on the beam by means of depth-charge throwers. During the Second World War lightweight depth charges were developed for dropping from aircraft. Another Second War development was a British depth charge which weighed one ton and was fired from a torpedo tube: it was designed for use against a submarine which had dived extremely deep to evade attack. Post-war developments include the introduction of nuclear depth charges which widen the lethal radius of the explosion and are for use against fast, deep-diving nuclear submarines, and the fitting of an active homing device to attract it to the vicinity of the target before it explodes. The first submarine to be sunk by a depth charge was *UB29*, sunk on 13 December 1916 by the destroyer HMS *Landrail*.

Derfflinger, SMS. German battle-cruiser launched in 1913 and armed with eight 30.5cm guns. At the Battle of Jutland *Derfflinger* sank the British battlecruiser *Queen Mary* in eleven salvos with little damage in return. However, in the rest of the battle she sustained massive damage. She was hit by no fewer than ten 15in, one 13.5in and ten 12in shells. Interned at Rosyth and later at Scapa Flow on the signing of the

Armistice, she was subsequently scuttled at Scapa Flow on 21 June 1919. Her hull was raised in 1934 although she was not broken up until after the Second World War. As she lay alongside at Faslane awaiting the welder's torch, the ship secured ahead of her was HMS *Iron Duke*, Jellicoe's flagship at Jutland.

'Dervish', Operation. The first convoy to Russia in August 1941 by northern route, around the north of Norway to the port of Murmansk. The convoy comprised six merchant ships and a tanker.

Destroyer. Formerly a destroyer of torpedo boats, latterly a general-purpose surface combatant of between 2,500 and 7,000 tons, capable of the most demanding combat operations, including the screening of fast carrier groups. A large destroyer differs from a small cruiser in that the former lacks a comprehensive capability; for example, she has no area defence system. A large frigate differs from a small destroyer in that the frigate has a lower speed and a simpler engineering plant.

Destroyer Escort (DE). Escorts built in great quantity by the Americans for convoy escort duties during the Second World War in order to make good the shortfall in destroyers. The US Navy had produced a design for such a ship as early as 1939 but it was felt that it sacrificed capability for little in the way of cost savings. British experience in the Second World War convinced the USN otherwise and in January 1942 it

increased an original order for fifty DEs to 300. The DE construction programme was unique in that it was considered 'common' in that both navies could take ships as required. DE construction was carried out using modern techniques of prefabrication at factories often hundreds of miles from the sea, followed by final assembly at one of seventeen yards around the country. The record time for construction was fifty-four days from keel-laying to commissioning. Seventy-eight of the ships went to Britain, where they were known as 'Captain' class frigates. Six went to France, six went to Brazil and the remaining 460 served in the USN. In action the DEs proved remarkable anti-submarine ships. In the Atlantic they formed 'hunter-killer' groups with escort carriers while in the Pacific the USS *England* (DE635) sank six Japanese submarines in May 1944. Their moment of outstanding glory came during the Battle of Leyte Gulf in October 1944 when a force of nine destroyers and fourteen DEs screening eighteen escort carriers ran into a force of four Japanese battleships and eleven cruisers. In a heroic operation the escorts, armed with no greater calibre weapon than a 5in gun, successfully screened the withdrawal of the carrier group. The original DE design was a 1,150-ton ship, $289\frac{1}{2}$ft long and armed with three 3in guns. The length was later increased to 306ft and the displacement to between 1,100 and 1,450 tons, and some of the ships carried the more powerful 5in gun. All carried a large number of depth charges. In 1943, with the submarine threat declining, fifty of the hulls under construction were completed as high-speed transports (APDs), while forty-five were converted from existing hulls. These ships were used to deliver UDT teams to the beach in advance of an amphibious landing. The APDs were all long-hull ships given a minimal armament for self-defence but fitted with four pairs of davits to carry LCAs and accommodation for 160 troops. Nine US DEs and one US APD were sunk during the Second World War, and two DEs and two APDs were damaged beyond repair. Ten of the British DEs were sunk. After the war some DEs were converted to radar-picket ships while others were distributed to US client states as part of mutual aid programmes. Britain disposed of her surviving sixty-eight ships remarkably quickly, preferring to keep the shoddy UK-built 'Loch', 'Castle' and 'Bay' class frigates.

Destroyer leader. Destroyer fitted with command facilities to co-ordinate the operations of a flotilla.

'Destroyers for Bases'. Anglo-American agreement of 24 July 1940 whereby the United States exchanged fifty superannuated destroyers in exchange for sovereign rights to bases in Antigua, the Bahamas, British Guiana, Jamaica, St Lucia and Trinidad. The gift of bases in Argentia (Newfoundland) and Bermuda were arranged at the same time but were not part of the deal. The first ships were handed over the British on 9 September 1940 and, of the fifty ships, seven were Canadian-manned and a number transferred to the Dutch and the Norwegians. All were given names of towns in both the US and the UK. On 30 May 1944 nine were handed over to the Soviet Union. Eight were lost during the war.

Deutschland. Lead ship of the three pocket-battleships built by Germany during the inter-war period. She had a nominal displacement of 10,000 tons, was armed with six 11in and eight 5.9in guns and was powered by diesel machinery. In December 1939 she was renamed *Lützow* since it was feared that the propaganda effect in Germany of losing a ship with such a prestigious name would be disastrous. *Lützow*'s subsequent career did not involve going in harm's way. She spent most of the war hiding in various Norwegian fjords and in May 1945 she was scuttled at Swinemünde after being damaged by the RAF.

Devastator. *See* TBD.

Dieppe. Port in France which was the scene for an amphibious landing on 19 August 1942. The purpose of the operation remains unclear. It may have been to battle-

DEPOT AND REPAIR SHIPS

Small naval combatants such as destroyers, minesweepers, fast patrol craft and submarines lack organic maintenance and repair facilities. Large repair and maintenance tasks beyond the capacity of the ship's staff had to be undertaken by the nearest shore base. Deployments of these ships away from dockyard facilities led to the development of repair ships equipped with a full range of workshops, foundries, forges, electronic repair facilities, optical laboratories, laundries and

stores facilities. A second function of these vessels was to exercise administrative command over destroyer and submarine squadrons or flotillas. During the First World War many pre-dreadnought battleships which were unsuitable for service with the battle fleet enjoyed a new lease of life acting as depot ships in faraway places. The British battleship *Queen* supported an array of destroyers, drifters, trawlers, motor launches and submarines from her anchorage at the Italian harbour of Taranto. Depot ships have the space to embark a squadron (or fleet) commander and his staff. Between 1980 and 1985 the American depot ship *Puget Sound*

acted as flagship of the Sixth Fleet in the Mediterranean, accommodating the flag staff of ninety officers and men. When she was replaced by the cruiser *Belknap* sixty of the staff had to move ashore since the cruiser could only accommodate a flag staff of thirty. Britain has used the depot ships *Maidstone* and *Tyne* for similar purposes. The Soviet Navy used the *Ugra* and *Don* class depot ships as *stationnaires* in harbours from where Soviet submarines operated. These ships provided a dual function, supporting the ships and submarines allocated to them and acting as a centre for the spreading of Soviet influence ashore.

harden the large number of Canadian troops in England (who so far in the war had found little employment except annoying the miltary police), or to demonstrate Allied amphibious capability and hearten the inhabitants of occupied Europe by showing them that liberation would, eventually, come. The operation was a failure: surprise was lost and the troops landed on the beaches adjacent to the town to face a murderous crossfire from the defenders. Shortly after 0900 the order to withdraw was given, but it was not until after midday that the last troops were off the beach. 3,188 officers and men were killed or taken prisoner, of whom 2,900 were Canadians. The affair has been the source of bitter argument among the protagonists and historians ever since. In the long run, however, the operation convinced the Germans that, when it happened, the Allied invasion of Europe would involve the capture of a major port. This false deduction contributed much to the German assessment of where the landings would ultimately take place.

Director sight. The means whereby the main armament of a ship can be controlled from a single master sight. It was introduced into the Royal Navy in 1912 following much research and experimentation by Admiral Sir Percy Scott, one of the greatest gunnery experts in the Navy. Previously guns had been aimed and fired by the individual gunlayer, but this led to unco-ordinated firing. Scott's system consisted of a single telescopic sight, mounted high up in the ship in the foretop where it would be well clear of funnel and gun smoke. Details of the target's range, course and speed where passed electrically to the transmitting station, a compartment deep inside the ship which contained the fire control computer. This was an electrically driven mechanical device which calculated the correct turret training and gun elevation. These values were transmitted to the turrets where the turret trainer and the individual gunlayers simply lined up their gunsights with a pointer on a dial. The guns were then all fired simultaneously by the gunlayer in the foretop so that all the shells in the salvo fell together and were thus easier to spot. Although there was significant opposition to the introduction of the director system, trials between the director-fitted HMS *Thunderer* and the unmodernised HMS *Orion* in November 1912 showed an immense improvement, the former ship emerging with six times as many hits. By the time of the Battle of Jutland all but two of the British capital ships in the Grand Fleet were fitted with directors. The director system was subsequently adopted by most of the world's navies, with modifications to suit individual nations' requirements.

Discrete frequency peaks. Distinctive high spots on a noise frequency spectrum recorded by passive sonar produced by rotating machinery and hull resonances.

DLG. Generic term for ships which in terms of size fall between a large destroyer and a small cruiser and which are equipped with an area defence SAM system. The British designated their 'County' class ships DLGs and kept the term for the Type 42 air defence ships – although the use of the term may have had more to do with persuading Parliament that they were getting a cheap and cheerful ship! DLGs were reclassified CGs on 30 June 1975.

DLGN. As above but nuclear-powered.

Dogger Bank, Battle of the. During the night of 23 January 1915 the German battlecruisers *Seydlitz* (flying the flag of Vice-Admiral Franz Hipper), *Moltke*, *Derfflinger* and *Blücher* sailed from Wilhelmshaven supported by a number of light cruisers and torpedo boats to attack the British fishing fleet off the Dogger Bank early the next day. Through intercepted German radio traffic the British knew of Hipper's departure and the Battlecruiser Fleet consisting of *Lion* (flying the flag of Rear-Admiral David Beatty), *Tiger*, *Princess Royal*, *New Zealand* and *Indomitable*, sailed from Rosyth to intercept them. Beatty aimed to dispose his ships across Hipper's route back to Wilhelmshaven. Early the next morning Hipper's ships were sighted north-east of the Dogger Bank. Shortly after 0900 HMS *Lion* opened fire and action was joined as both squadrons proceeded at high speed. Nearly an hour later *Seydlitz* was hit by *Lion* and lost the use of her after 11in turrets;

it was only prompt flooding of the magazines which prevented the loss of the ship. The slower *Blücher*, which was unable to keep up with her faster consorts, was also hit and began to fall behind. At this critical juncture – with the advantage resting fairly with the British – *Lion* was hit by three shells fired by *Derfflinger* and was forced to drop out the line. Command of the British ships passed to Rear-Admiral Moore in HMS *New Zealand*. Moore misinterpreted Beatty's intentions and instead of pursuing the Germans concentrated on sinking *Blücher*, which eventually capsized and sank after absorbing tremendous punishment. By the time Beatty re-joined the main force in a destroyer it was too late to catch Hipper. The sinking of *Blücher* and the photographs of her stricken hull which appeared in the press constituted a considerable propaganda *coup* for the British. However, they also served to hide serious deficiencies in Beatty's command, particularly in signalling, and the fact that a great opportunity of destroying the enemy had been lost.

Dogger Bank Incident. On 13 October 1904 the Russian Baltic Fleet sailed from Libau to reinforce the garrison at Port Arthur, 17,000 miles away. As it passed down the North Sea on the night of 22 October jumpy look-outs sighted some Hull trawlers and reported them as Japanese destroyers. In the confusion the whole fleet opened an indiscriminate fire in which four trawlers

were damaged and another was reduced to a sinking condition. The incident aroused great passions in Britain and the Russian Fleet was harassed by the Royal Navy as it passed down the Channel and Bay of Biscay.

Dolphin, HMS. Headquarters of the British submarine service at Fort Blockhouse, Gosport. There have been twenty-two ships in the Royal Navy which have borne the name *Dolphin*, the twentieth being a sloop built in 1882 which in 1912 became the first submarine depot ship at Fort Blockhouse. She was replaced in 1925 by HMS *Pandora*, which was then renamed *Dolphin*. Since then a number of small craft have borne the name *Dolphin* for the submarine base as all facilities are housed ashore. Under the current rationalisation of defence estates in the UK *Dolphin*'s role as a submarine base is to end and the establishment will become a Joint Services Medical Centre.

Doolittle Raid. The first bombing raid on Japan, conducted by sixteen B-25B Mitchell bombers trained and led by Lt-Col James Doolittle USAAF. No US aircraft had the range to reach Japan from any US or Allied base, so the aircraft were launched from the carrier USS *Hornet* on 18 April 1942. The Mitchell was not a carrier aircraft and the bombers had to contend with a take-off run of only 450ft as opposed to the usual 1,200–1,500 feet from a conventional runway. All the aircraft took off and bombed Tokyo, Kobe, Nagoya and Yokohama.

Dornier Do 17. German twin-engine bomber widely employed in a number of roles. The role for which it will be remembered in naval warfare is its carriage of the Hs 293A guided missile which sank the frigate HMS *Egret* on 27 August 1943. Subsequently Do 217s armed with the Fritz X missile sank the battleship *Roma* on 9 September 1943 and damaged *Italia*. Subsequent Do 217/Fritz X attacks sank the cruiser HMS *Spartan* and damaged the battleship HMS *Warspite* and the cruiser USS *Savannah*.

Dover. English seaport at the eastern end of the English Channel and one of the five Cinque Ports. At the end of the nineteenth century Dover was selected by the British Admiralty for use as a naval base, it being well situated between the Channel and the North Sea. During the First World War the base was the home of the famous Dover Patrol commanded by Vice-Admiral Sir Reginald Bacon. During the Second World War Dover was no less busy. It was the main port involved in the evacuation of the British Expeditionary Force from the French coast in 1940 and thereafter was an important convoy port and base for coastal forces.

Dover Barrage. System of minefields and nets laid in the Dover Strait to prevent U-boats using the English Channel and a route to their patrol areas when proceeding to and from their Belgian bases. The nets and minefields were backed up by the forces of the Dover Patrol. It became formidably effective when Keyes, who replaced Bacon, ordered the nets to be intensively patrolled during the day and illuminated at night. Strong tides made the task of maintaining the minefields extremely difficult, and had the war lasted into 1919 a series of fixed structures would have been established in the Channel to act as local anti-submarine stations. The only one to be built was the Nab Tower, which is still standing.

Dover Patrol. Heterogeneous collection of monitors, destroyers, motor launches, barrage vessels and other small craft based at Dover during the First World War and responsible for naval operations in the English Channel. Under the command of Vice-Admiral Sir Reginald Bacon the Dover Patrol was involved in the transportation and supply of the British Army in France, the protection of Allied shipping in the Channel, the enforcement of the blockade of Germany, the harassment of the right flank of the German Army in Flanders and the barring of the Dover Strait to U-boats operating from Bruges and Zeebrugge. The best known of the Dover Patrol operations are those of the 6th Destroyer Flotilla. Their numerous and stirring engagements with German destroyers based at Ostend and Zeebrugge were the subject of numerous books during the interwar period. However, the Dover Patrol has never really been recognised for its development and use of new technology in pursuit of its operations. Considerable pioneering work

was done in the fields of long-range shore bombardment, submarine beach reconnaissance, air reconnaissance and combined operations. Perhaps the least known of the Dover Patrol's operations was the projected 'Great Landing' on the Flanders coast in the autumn of 1917. The plan was for two infantry divisions to be landed on the Belgian coast behind the German lines, the landing being timed to co-ordinate with the offensive at Ypres launched by the Army. The object was to capture the submarine base at Ostend/ Bruges and mount guns ashore which could bombard the base at Zeebrugge. It was also hoped that the landing would turn the right flank of the German Army in Flanders. Alas, the Army offensive at Ypres did not make the requisite progress and the 'Great Landing' was called off. It remains one of the great 'what ifs?' of the First World War. Bacon was relieved of command of the Dover Patrol in November 1917 on account of failure to stop U-boats using the Dover Strait as a route to and from the Western Approaches. His replacement, Rear-Admiral Roger Keyes, was an extremely popular and aggressive commander but lacked Bacon's intellectual qualities. Keyes inherited Bacon's plan for a blocking operation against Zeebrugge which was launched on 23 April 1918. Though the operation failed in its primary objective, it was a source of considerable inspiration throughout the country. On the conclusion of hostilities in 1918, the Dover Patrol was disbanded.

Dover Strait, Battle of. A clash between British and German destroyers in the Channel on 20/21 April 1917. The Germans planned a major raid on the Dover Barrage forces using two destroyer flotillas. The British, for once, had no inkling of what was afoot and only six British destroyers were at sea. On the morning of the 21st there was a violent action at close range between the destroyers of both sides in which guns, torpedoes and ramming were used. The German destroyers *G42* and *G85* were sunk and the British destroyer *Broke* badly damaged. However, there were no further German destroyer raids on the Barrage for nearly a year.

Downs, The. Anchorage on the east coast of England which lies inside the Goodwin Sands and between the North and South Foreland. The Goodwins provide shelter from all easterly winds, while the area is sheltered from westerly winds by the land. During the First and Second World Wars the area was a convenient convoy assembly point and also an area where the Examination Service would clear neutral ships heading for ports on the Continent.

'Dragoon', Operation. Anglo-American landing on the south coast of France, August 1944.

***Dreadnought*, HMS.** Name used nine times in the Royal Navy. The best known ship was the eighth to bear the name, the battleship launched in 1906. She was a

Above: An E-Class submarine passes a fishing boat. (IWM SP 778)

design which revolutionised capital ship construction: her main armament was all of the same calibre and she was the first capital ship to be powered by steam turbines. Her progenitor, Admiral Sir John ('Jacky') Fisher, described her as the 'hard boiled egg – because she can't be beat!' She gave her name to the type of capital ship which succeeded her. HMS *Dreadnought* served with the Grand Fleet and on 18 February 1915 rammed and sank *U29* in the Pentland Firth, the only time a battleship has sunk a

submarine. In May 1916 she moved south to Sheerness as flagship of the 3rd Battle Squadron but re-joined the Grand Fleet in March 1918 as flagship of the 4th Battle Squadron. She was sold for breaking up in 1920. The ninth HMS *Dreadnought* was a nuclear fleet submarine launched on 21 October 1960. Although her armament and control systems were British in design, her nuclear reactor and propulsion system were those of an American *Skipjack* class subma-

rine. She was decommissioned in 1982 and her present status is uncertain.

Dresden, **SMS.** German cruiser launched in 1907. At the beginning of the First World War she was operating in support of German interests in Mexico. Avoiding British forces searching for her, she met with the German East Asia Squadron and survived the Battle of the Falkland Islands. She was scuttled on 14 March 1915 at the island of Mas e Fuera when found by overwhelming

British Expeditionary Force (BEF) following the collapse of Anglo-French forces in France and Belgium. In a nine-day operation an armada of warships, merchant ships and small pleasure steamers of all sizes evacuated 338,226 men from the beaches around Dunkirk.

Durazzo. Port on the Albanian coast used for the evacuation of the Serbian Army in the winter of 1915-16.

'Dynamo', Operation. Evacuation of the British Expeditionary Force (BEF) and such French and Belgian troops as wished to be evacuated from ports along the French Channel coast, particularly around Dunkirk and La Panne, May–June 1940.

'E' class submarines. Class of 57 submarines which bore the brunt of British submarine operations in the First World War; 26 of them were lost. They served in all theatres of war, and of the five Victoria Crosses awarded to British submariners three went to 'E' class commanding officers. The boats displaced 655/796 tons (*E.9* onwards 667/807 tons) and were armed with four (*E.9* onwards five) torpedo tubes. *E.24*, *E.34*, *E.41*, *E.45* and *E.51* had their beam torpedo tubes removed and replaced by vertical mine wells, ten each side, carrying twenty mines. *E.22* even carried two Sopwith Schneider seaplanes.

British forces. Her mascot, a pig named *Tirpitz*, survived and lived to a ripe old age at HMS *Excellent*, the Royal Navy's gunnery school.

Drifter. Fishing vessel which operated around the coast of the UK. Drifters were taken up from trade in large numbers during the First and Second World Wars to serve in a variety of roles.

'Dryad', Operation. British raid on the Casquets lighthouse in September 1942 to recover prisoners and confidential books. HMS *Dryad* is the Royal Navy's School of Maritime Operations.

DUKW. Code letters used for an amphibious military vehicle capable of being driven normally across land while being able to swim in rivers and estuaries.

Dunkirk. Port on the north-east coast of France which was an important centre of naval operations during the First World War. It sprang to fame in the first year of the Second World War as the scene of the evacuation of the

***Eagle*, HMS.** Ship's name which has been used more than twenty times in the Royal Navy. It has been used twice in the twentieth century, both ships being aircraft carriers. The first of these was laid down as the battleship *Almirante Cochrane* for the Chilean Navy but was taken over while under construction and launched on 8 June 1918 as *Eagle*. She was sunk by *U73* on 11 August 1942 while escorting the 'Pedestal' convoy to Malta. The second *Eagle* was launched in 1946, was completed in 1951 and underwent major reconstruction between 1959 and 1964. After reconstruction she operated thirty-five fixed-wing aircraft and ten helicopters. In 1966 *Eagle* was a victim of the decision to scrap aircraft carriers then in service. In *Eagle*'s case the rather spurious excuse was that the ship could not operate the F-4 Phantom aircraft, but in fact the carrier had already operated this aircraft and needed but minor modifications to her flight deck equipment to do so. Although *Eagle* was the only modern carrier in the Royal Navy she was paid off in 1972 and progressively cannibalised to provide spares to keep the older *Ark Royal* running. After presenting a sorry sight swinging round a buoy in the Hamoaze River for a number of years, *Eagle* was eventually broken up in 1978.

Eastern Solomons, Battle of the. One of the six major engagements fought between the Americans and the Japanese in 1942 for control of the Solomon Islands. The dispatch of a Japanese task force from its main base at Truk to an area north-east

of the Solomons to cover a troop convoy headed for Guadalcanal provoked a response from Vice-Admiral Fletcher's carrier group, *Enterprise*, *Saratoga* and *Wasp*. The result was a two-day duel between the aircraft of both sides. On the morning of 24 August Fletcher's aircraft found and sank the light carrier *Ryujo* but that afternoon *Enterprise* was badly damaged in attacks by Japanese aircraft. Meanwhile the troop convoy had been attacked by American aircraft based on Guadalcanal: two of the ships were sunk and the remainder turned back. The result was inconclusive but in the long term the losses in aircrew suffered by the Japanese would significantly affect their ability to counter the American carrier task groups which were growing in size and capability.

East Timor. Scene of naval operations by Indonesia following the outbreak of civil war in this former Portuguese colony in 1975. In September 1975 Indonesian naval forces gathered off the island to monitor developments. In December 1975 Indonesian warships bombarded targets in East Timor in support of airborne and marine landings to capture the island's capital, Dili. Subsequent naval operations, supported by local anti-communist guerrillas, resulted in the capture of the towns of Maubara and Baucau, the Ocussi Ambeno enclave and the offshore island off Atauro. At the end of 1975 East Timor became the twenty-seventh province of Indonesia.

'Eclipse', Operation. Plans and preparations for operations in north-west Europe in the event of a German surrender following shortly after 'Overlord'.

Egret, HMS. First warship to be sunk by a guided missile. The sloop *Egret* was sunk by an Hs 293A guided missile in the Bay of Biscay on 27 August 1943.

Eilat (*Elath*). The ex-British destroyer HMS *Zealous* which was transferred to Israel in 1955. On 21 October 1967 she was off Port Said when she was engaged and sunk by Egyptian *Osa* class fast attack craft firing 'Styx' missiles from inside the harbour. Casualties were forty-seven killed and ninety wounded out of a complement of 199. This was the first occasion in which a warship had been sunk by a ship-launched missile. Her loss persuaded the Israeli Navy that significant attention had to be paid to missile design and development and electronic warfare (EW).

'El Dorado Canyon', Operation. Operation by the US Sixth Fleet in March 1986 to enforce the freedom of the seas in the Gulf of Sirte following a Libyan claim that the entire Gulf was Libyan territorial waters.

Electro submarine. Term for Type XXI and Type XXIII German U-boats which had considerably enhanced underwater speed and endurance compared with other submarines.

ELINT. Electronic Intelligence. The gathering of intelligence from the receipt of emissions in the electro-magnetic spectrum. This can range from direction-finding or threat-warning using the existence of a radio or radar signal to detailed code-breaking analysis of hostile communications.

EMCON. Emission Control. The prevention or reduction of radio, radar or sonar emissions to pre-clude their detection by the enemy.

Emden, **SMS.** German light cruiser of 3,600 tons which became the best known German surface raider of the First World War. While the rest of the German East Asia Squadron headed for Germany (and destruction at the Battle of the Falkland Islands), Emden was released for com-merce-raiding operations in the Indian Ocean. In a cruise lasting from the outbreak of war until 9 November 1914 she sank a light cruiser, a destroyer and twenty-three merchant ships totalling 101,182 tons. She was finally sunk on 9 November 1914 by the Australian cruiser *Sydney* at Keeling Island, where Emden had gone to destroy the cable station. *Emden*'s commanding officer, *Korvettenkapitän* Karl von Müller, had conducted his operations with full respect for international law and a desire to avoid unnec-essary loss of life. As a result he is still recognised as one of the greatest seamen of his age.

EMP. Electro-magnetic pulse. The pulse of high electro-magnetic energy caused by the interaction of the radiation of a nuclear weapon with the earth's atmos-phere. EMP can cause serious damage to electrical circuits unless the appropriate 'hardening' measures have been carried out.

Empress Augusta Bay, Battle of. Night action fought in the Solomons on 2 November 1943 between an American force con-sisting of the cruisers *Montpelier* (flag of Rear-Admiral Merrill), *Cleveland, Columbia* and *Denver* with eight destroyers which was escorting an amphibious force landing on Bougainville and a Japanese force consisting of the cruisers *Myoko* (flag of Vice-Admiral Omori), *Haguro, Agano* and *Sendai* with six destroyers. In a short action the Japanese retired, having lost *Sendai*, which had been overpowered by American gunfire, and the de-stroyer *Hatsukaze*. The Americans lost the destroyer *Foote*. The bat-tle was notable for the success of new night-fighting techniques introduced by the Americans and it showed that the Japanese were not invincible in a night engage-ment.

Endurance, **HMS.** Ice patrol ship operated by the Royal Navy in the South Atlantic. The first ship of the name was the former Danish *Anita Dan* and was pur-chased in 1967. In 1982 the deci-sion to scrap the ship as part of a defence review was a prime fac-tor in influencing the Argentine Government's decision to invade the Falkland Islands. During the campaign which followed the landings on the Falkland Islands *Endurance* hid in the wastes of the South Atlantic while her Royal Marine detachment put up a stout defence of Grytviken on South Georgia. *Endurance* was sold for breaking up in 1991. Her replacement, which still bears the distinctive paint scheme of red hull, white upperworks and yellow funnel, is the ex-*Polar Circle*.

Engadine, **HMS.** South East & Chatham Railway cross-Channel steamer taken over by the Royal Navy in 1914 for conversion to an aircraft carrier. She carried four seaplanes in a hangar construct-ed on the stern and she was fitted with cranes for their launch and recovery. *Engadine* participated in the Cuxhaven Raid of 25 December 1914, the attack on Tondern on 4 May 1916 and the Battle of Jutland, where one of her seaplanes sighted the High Seas Fleet, but poor communica-tions failed to get the message through. She then towed the damaged cruiser *Warrior* and saved over 600 lives when the cruiser foundered. She was returned to her civilian owners in 1919. The name was subsequent-ly used for an RFA helicopter training ship.

England, **USS** (DE635). A US Navy destroyer escort commissioned on 10 December 1943 which in the course of a twelve-day period in May 1944 sank six Japanese sub-marines – *I-16* on 19 May, *RO-106* on 22 May, *RO-104* on 23 May, *RO-116* on 24 May, *RO-108* on 26 May and RO-105 on 31 May. This is a record tally unequalled by any ship of any Navy.

Enigma. A coding machine used by the Germans for all military communications which provided electro-mechanical enciphering through non-repeating ciphers. Three (later four and five) interchangeable rotors and numerous plug connectors provided up to 20 quintillion permutations.

Eniwetok. Amphibious operation undertaken in February 1944 to complete the conquest of the Marshall Islands. The Eniwetok group of islands consists of three islands, Engebi, Eniwetok and Parry, rising from a circular coral reef enclosing a lagoon some seventeen miles wide. After an entrance to the lagoon had been cleared of mines and artillery had been established on the coral reef, US troops landed on Engebi on 18 February 1944 and on Eniwetok on the 19th. Engebi was secured the same day but on Eniwetok the Japanese resisted until the 21st. Troops landed on Parry on the 22nd and the island was secured that day. After the war Eniwetok was selected as the site for the explosion of the first American hydrogen bomb in 1952.

Enterprise, USS. Name which has been used eight times by the US Navy. The seventh *Enterprise* was a 20,000-ton aircraft carrier launched on 12 May 1938 and known as 'Big E'. She served throughout the Second World War and was decommissioned in 1947, having earned twenty Battle Stars. She served at the Battle of Midway and the Philippine Sea as well as in eighteen other actions against the enemy. She was followed by the

Above: An Enigma machine used by the Germans to cipher and dicipher radio signals. The Germans thought their codes invulnerable; Allied codebreakers proved otherwise. (USN)

eighth ship of the name, an 89,084-ton aircraft carrier and the first such ship to be nuclear-powered. At the time of writing she is still in commission.

'Enthrone', Operation. The laying of navigational beacons in the English Channel prior to 'Overlord'.

Environment. An area of growing importance for navies as concern is expressed about the disposal of

nuclear waste and redundant reactors. Over the next ten years up to 200 nuclear submarines, some with two reactors, are due for decommissioning. In September 1995 the fifteen countries bordering the Atlantic signed the Paris Convention, accepting a fifteen-year total ban on the dumping of nuclear waste at sea, although Britain and France held out for the dumping of large items such as reactors. The initial Soviet denial that they had dumped nuclear waste at sea was found to be less than correct. According to a Russian Government report, twenty-one reactors from submarines and the icebreaker *Lenin* have been dumped in the Kara and Barents Sea, some in only 20m of water. On a more mundane note, all navies have to pay attention to environmental concerns and nearly all now have varieties of 'good neighbour' policies to ensure that the environment and wildlife around naval bases are not adversely affected.

Escort. Generic name for ships of all types whose main employment is the protection of single ships or convoys. The name embraces various types of vessel and includes trawlers, corvettes, frigates, cutters, minesweepers and sloops.

Escort carrier. Auxiliary aircraft carrier developed using a merchant ship hull and propulsion. The first escort carrier, HMS *Audacity*, was converted from the hull of the German merchant ship *Hannover* and had a brief but successful career before she was sunk on 21 December 1941. With the United States in the war construction accelerated rapidly, despite an early lack of interest in the type shown by the USN. A total of 115 such ships were built, of which twelve went to the Royal Navy. Their most important contribution was in the Battle of the Atlantic, where, in addition to pro-viding convoys with air cover, they formed 'hunter-killer' groups whose aircraft were able to 'close the gap' in mid-ocean beyond the reach of land-based aircraft. In the Pacific escort carriers provided close air support in numerous amphibious campaigns.

ESM. Electronic support measures. The provision of receivers to identify and classify electronic emissions to give warning of an attack and to provide passive detection of ships and aircraft beyond the horizon.

Essex, **USS.** Lead ship of a class of twenty-four large carriers, of 34,000 tons, which formed the backbone of the US Navy's fast

Above: The *Essex* Class carrier, USS *Franklin*, badly listing after receiving bomb damage which started massive fires and explosions, March 1945. The fires were eventually put out and she made it back to Pearl Harbor. (IWM NYF 70547)

carrier task groups in the Pacific and the basis of the post-war US carrier fleet. The ships were essentially larger versions of the *Yorktown* but freed of treaty restrictions. The ships displaced 27,208 tons (standard) and were 820ft long at the waterline. High-pressure steam machinery gave a top speed of 32kts (*Intrepid* made 32.7kts on trials) and they each carried about ninety-five aircraft.

EW. Electronic warfare. The exploitation of the electro-magnetic spectrum for miltary purposes. It includes the gathering of ELINT of all kinds and the application of countermeasures such as jamming and the generation of false targets.

Excellent, **HMS.** Royal Navy's gunnery school at Whale Island in Portsmouth. The establishment had an awesome reputation for standards of drill and discipline. Its gunnery functions have ceased, but it is now the General Naval Training Centre and home to a number of specialist training establishments.

'Excess', Operation. Complicated series of fleet movements carried out by the British Mediterranean fleet in January 1941 – troops to Greece, supplies to Malta and aircraft for Alexandria.

Exchange rate. A useful formula for determining the success or otherwise of a commerce raiding campaign. It is obtained by dividing the number of merchant ships sunk by the number of raiders lost. An exchange rate of more than 100 indicates that the campaign is going spectacularly well, a rate of about 25 is average while a rate of less than 10 means that the campaign is in deep trouble.

Exeter, **HMS.** A British cruiser completed July 1929 and lost during the battle of the Java Sea in 1942. Half-sister ship to HMS *York*, her main armament was six 8in guns and her top speed was 32 knots. Her most notable action was her involvement in the battle with the German pocket battleship *Admiral Graf Spee* in 1939, during

Above: An Excocet missile being fired from HMS *Norfolk*. (IWM TR 44834)

which the British cruiser was very badly damaged.

Exocet. French-built sea-skimming missile that has acquired an awesome reputation. It can be fired from ships, launched from helicopters or aircraft or fired from a submarine. The weapon has an active radar-seeking homer, a range of between 42 and 70km depending on the variant and a warhead of 165kg. The potency of the weapon was first illustrated when the British Type 42 destroyer HMS *Sheffield* was sunk after being struck by a single air-launched Exocet on 10 May 1982 during the Falklands War. On this occasion the missile's warhead did not explode but the kinetic energy of the missile striking the ship and the ignition of its remaining fuel started a fire which eventually caused the ship to be abandoned. The US frigate *Stark* was wrecked by two Exocets fired at her by an Iraqi aircraft in the Persian Gulf on 17 May 1987.

Explosion vessel. *Ad hoc* weapon for destroying or damaging ships or harbour installations. It was usually an old ship with her own propulsion but filled with explosive or combustibles. The ship was then run alongside the ship or target to be destroyed and the charge fired. It was a weapon more commonly found being used in the seventeenth and eigh-teenth centuries, but there have been two spectacular examples of the use of this weapon this century, firstly the use of the submarine *C.3* to destroy the viaduct at Zeebrugge on 23 April 1917 and secondly the use of the old destroyer HMS *Campbeltown* to destroy the dock caissons at St Nazaire in 1942. The Royal Navy also had plans to employ 'explosion vessels' in the English Channel at the height of the invasion scare in 1940 to disrupt German invasion shipping.

F2A Buffalo. Lacklustre US Navy single-seat carrier fighter characterised by a short stubby fuselage and a large radial engine. It had a maximum speed of 300mph and a

Above: The Brewster Buffalo. (IWM CH 1101)

range of 1,000 miles. It was completely outclassed at Midway by Japanese aircraft and was withdrawn from service in September 1942.

F4F Wildcat. US Navy single seat carrier fighter of the Second World War which though not particularly distinguished in terms of performance more than held its own against Japanese aircraft. It flew at Wake Island, Midway, Coral Sea, Guadalcanal, the Solomons and in the Atlantic. It was replaced in US Navy fleet carriers in the Pacific in 1942 by the F6F Hellcat but continued to be employed on escort carriers, particularly in the Atlantic, where it was used to suppress

flak from U-boats while the ASW Avengers delivered their ordnance. The F4F had a speed of 318mph and a combat range of 770 miles. It was armed with six .50-cal machine guns but could carry two 250lb bombs or six 5in rockets.

F4U Corsair. A large and powerful US Navy single-seat carrier fighter which was in continuous production longer than any other Second World War-era aircraft. A total 12,570 were built. The Corsair was distinguished by a long nose, making take-off difficult, and an inverted gull-wing with the main legs of the landing gear located at the wing knuckles. The aircraft had a fearsome reputation among

pilots, one British pilot confessing that, after seeing a Corsair for the first time, he wanted to make his will. Poor cockpit visibility caused the US Navy to reject the aircraft for carrier service but it saw extensive use by Marine Corps squadrons in the ground support role. The Royal Navy used Corsairs from carriers and subsequently the US Navy flew the modified F4U-1A from carriers and the F4U-2 fitted with AI radar for night operations. The F4U-4 variant had a maximum speed of 446mph and a combat range of 1,000 miles. It was armed with six .50-cal machine guns but could also carry two 1,000lb bombs. In post-war service the F4U was flown by the French in Indo-China, and during

Above: F4F Wildcat fighters in British service, where they were called 'Martlets'. (IWM A 15114A)

Above: F4U Corsair. (IWM OEM 5539)

the Korean War a US Navy F4U shot down a Soviet-built MiG-15 fighter.

F6F Hellcat. The first US Navy carrier fighter that could equal the Japanese A6M Zero under all conditions. The F6F was credited with 4,947 of the 6,477 enemy aircraft destroyed by US Navy pilots. It

Above: F6F Hellcat. (IWM NYF 28563)

was developed from the F4F Wildcat but had larger and cleaner lines; a total of 12,274 were built for US and British service. The F6F-5 variant had a top speed of 380mph and a combat range of 945 miles. Armament consisted of six .50-cal machine guns or two 20mm cannon and four machine guns.

F7F Tigercat. Twin-engine carrier fighter intended for deployment in the *Midway* (CV41) class carriers. The war ended before they could see service but some flew in the Korean War in the ground support role.

F8F Bearcat. The penultimate piston-engine fighter delivered to the US Navy. It had outstanding performance though at some cost in range. It was too late to see service in the Second World War, but some were flown by the French in Indo-China.

FAC. Fast attack craft (FAC-M indicating a craft armed with missiles), the post-1945 successor to the wartime MTB/MGB/PT boat/ *Schnellboot* types. What differentiates the FAC from its predecessors is that the introduction of surface-to-surface guided missiles, such as the Soviet P-15 'Styx', French Exocet and American Harpoon, means that the FAC does not have to close to suicidally short ranges in order to engage the target but can stand off and fire the missile from long range. The potency of these craft was shown by the sinking of the Israeli destroyer *Eilat* by an Egyptian FAC in 1967. A typical contemporary FAC would be the Swedish *Spica III* class which have a standard displacement of 310 tons, are 152ft long and are powered by a three shaft CODAG system giving a top speed of over 32kts. Armament consists of eight RBS-15 SSMs, one 57mm Bofors, one 40mm Bofors, four ASW-600 A/S rockets and two 21in torpedo tubes. Two of the SSM canisters can be replaced by mine rails. As FACs have developed they have also grown in size. The Israeli *Sa'ar V* is a 1,200-ton, helicopter-carrying ship armed with eight Harpoon and eight Gabriel SSMs. Just as the destroyer replaced the torpedo boat it was developed to counter, so the

FAST MULTI-PRODUCT SUPPORT SHIPS

The most important post-war development was that of the fast multi-product support ship. Wartime auxiliaries were mostly conversions of basic, mass-produced freighter and tanker designs. They were slow (their maximum speed was around 11kts, compared to over 25kts of their combatant 'clients') and were modified to take just one category of item. With slow speeds and type-loaded ships, resupplying a carrier group could take days. The German Navy introduced the concept of the multi-product support ship. Since it lacked a large merchant fleet and it was impractical to disperse a large number of auxiliaries around the ocean, the Germans built their oilers with a capacity to dispense other items, carrying food, ammunition and spare parts in different holds. Two of these ships, *Ditchmarschen* and *Nordmark*, were allocated to the United States and Britain after the Second World War and were renamed *Conecuh* and *Bulawayo* respectively. In a series of exercises both ships proved the viability of the multi-product ship. The impressive performance of these two ships coincided with a requirement for carrier task groups to steam at even greater speeds. A fast multi-product supply ship was seen as the only way of providing the attack carrier groups with the supplies they needed. In 1959 the Americans issued a requirement for such a ship, and this emerged as the USS *Sacramento* (AOE-1). *Sacramento* has a displacement of 53,600 tons and a speed of 26kts. She carries 177,000 barrels of fuel, 2,150 tons of ammunition and 750 tons of stores, including 250 tons of refrigerated food. She can replenish another vessel at speeds of up to 20kts. The inclusion of a flight deck and hangar capable of accommodating two UH-46 Sea Knight helicopters gives another dimension to the resupply process: while supplies and fuel are being transferred via the jackstay, smaller, lighter and high-value items can be flown over to the receiving ship by helicopter. The *Sacramento*s were followed by the *Mars* class combat stores ship (AFS), which combines the facilities of an AKS, AF and AVS within one hull. *Mars* can carry 25,000 types of spare parts. Slightly smaller versions of the *Sacramento*, the *Wichita* class AOR, were built to maintain the US Navy's ASW carrier groups. Since the ASW groups did not have the same intensive operational cycle as the attack carrier groups, a smaller supply ship was required. Even so, the

FAC has grown into the large surface combatant that was its original target.

Fairmile. British boat-building company which specialised in the construction of coastal forces craft for the Royal Navy as well as small pleasure craft. Fairmile 'A' and 'B' types were 110ft/112ft motor launches used for a variety of roles including general harbour duties, boom defence, surveying, air–sea rescue and special operations. All the Fairmile 'A's were converted to coastal minelayers. The Fairmile 'C' type was a 110ft MGB. The Fairmile 'D' was built as a 115ft MGB but nearly all were converted to MTBs or air–sea rescue craft for the RAF. It was a very successful and rugged design if somewhat slow. As an MTB the boat's armament consisted of two 18in or 21in torpedo tubes or four 18in, two 6pdr Mk II, two or three 20mm, four 0.5in machine guns, four 0.303in machine guns and two depth charges. The Fairmile 'F' was a 115ft MGB and the Fairmile 'H' a 105ft LCI.

Falkland Islands. Group of islands belonging to Great Britain in the South Atlantic about 200 miles east of the nearest part of South America. The first European to find the islands was John Davis in 1592; two years later they were sighted by Sir Richard Hawkins. In 1598 they were named the Sebald Islands after the Dutch seaman Sebald de Wert but they were renamed the Falkland Islands in 1693 after Lord Falkland, the then First Lord of the Admiralty, by Captain John Strong, who made the first recorded landing on the islands. Between then and 1766 the islands were alternately 'discovered' and 'claimed' by France and Britain. At that period the islands were of little or no strategic value and these 'claims' were not taken too seriously. Following the break-up of Spain's Latin-American empire, the islands were claimed and occupied by Argentina. British rule was restored in 1833 and the islands were finally ceded to Britain in 1771 by Spain. It was the advent of steam navigation that gave the islands an important position. They became a convenient coaling station near Cape Horn, although

Wichitas carry 175,000 barrels of fuel oil, 600 tons of ammunition and 500 tons of dry and refrigerated stores.

The Vietnam War demonstrated the utility of these ships. One AOE and one AFS operated with the carrier task groups between 1964 and 1973. In a three-week cycle the ships would divide their time between the carriers engaged in operations off North Vietnam and the other surface ships off South Vietnam. At the end of the three-week cycle the ships would return to Subic Bay in the Philippines for a four-day replenishment period in port. During these operations the AOE/As would either act as 'delivery boys' by visiting individual ships or as 'grocery stores', remaining in a particular location or position within a fleet while the receiving ships detached from their stations to rendezvous with her. During the 1980s the US Navy gave all its replenishment ships the capability to supply multiple products.

Developments in Western navies mirrored those in the US Navy. However, the smaller size of most other NATO navies, and budget restraints, meant that most could not afford the luxury of purpose-built supply ships. Britain had a host of converted tankers and cargo ships but from the late 1960s the Royal Navy has concentrated on two types of auxiliary: the fleet oiler (AO); and the replenishment ship (AFS) carrying food, spares and ammunition, the first of which, RFA *Regent* and *Resource*, entered service in 1967. A feature of Western replenishment ships is their multiplicity of functions. The French *Durance* class AORs can carry up to 100 men in excess of complement and have the facilities to act as flagships. The Canadian *Protecteur* class AORs can carry four LCVPs and 60 troops. These vessels can also act as combatants in their own right: British, Canadian, Dutch and French AORs all carry helicopters for ASW duties. The former Soviet Navy was a late convert to the idea of replenishing its ships at sea. Generally the Soviets preferred to conduct such operations at an anchorage in a friendly port. When they did replenish at sea, matters were carried out via the slow and cumbersome astern method, which requires both ships to steam very slowly – 5kts or less – in very calm weather. It was a feature of Western observation of Soviet naval exercises to note the number of ruptured fuel lines and similar disasters. However, the Soviets began to develop the capability of underway replenishment in the late 1960s with the construction of the six *Boris Chilikin* class AORs, followed in 1978 by the 40,000-ton *Berezina*, the largest such ship built outside the United States.

parsimony on behalf of successive British governments meant that the dockyard facilities on the islands were never fully developed. During the First World War the islands were the scene of a naval action on 8 December 1914 when the German East Asia Squadron was destroyed by a British force under the command of Vice-Admiral Doveton Sturdee. The Second World War almost passed the islands by except for a brief scare in 1942 that the Japanese were proposing to invade them. The Argentine Government had never abandoned its claim to the islands and the dispute was a running sore between the two governments. As much as anything else, the Argentine Government's claim served as a useful distraction from its appalling human rights record at home, and in the spring of 1982 it took military action and invaded the islands. In the subsequent Falklands War the British dispatched a task force and successfully recovered the territory. The diplomatic position of the Falkland Islands remains unsettled. The possibility that vast deposits of oil and/or natural gas may lie beneath the surrounding sea has given the islands a new importance. Moreover, in the event of the Panama Canal being incapacitated or destroyed by terrorist action, the Falklands may yet resume their role as a 'convenient coaling station near Cape Horn'.

Falkland Islands, Battle of the. Engagement on 8 December 1914 off the Falkland Islands in which the German East Asia Squadron

under Admiral *Graf* Maximilian von Spee was scattered and destroyed. Spee had decided to bombard Port Stanley but was surprised to find two battlecruisers, *Invincible* and *Inflexible*, and the cruisers *Carnarvon, Cornwall, Kent, Bristol* and *Glasgow*, which had been assembled in the South Atlantic to search for the German squadron. The German ships reversed course but their end was inevitable. The action was a vindication of the battlecruiser concept

for the two British ships, despite being caught coaling when the German ships were sighted, were able to close their opponents at great speed and destroy them with long-range gunfire. *Scharnhorst* and *Gneisenau* were sunk by the battlecruisers, *Leipzig* was sunk by *Glasgow* and *Cornwall* and *Nürnberg* was sunk by *Kent. Dresden* escaped.

Falklands War. The British campaign from 2 April to 14 June

Above: HMS *Ardent,* her stern badly damaged by Argentine air attacks, in San Carlos Water, 21 May 1982, during the the short war for the Falkland Islands. She subsequently sank. (IWM FKD 146)

1982 to recover the Falkland Islands following the Argentine invasion. It took place in three parts. The first was the assembly of forces and their dispatch to the South Atlantic. Given that, at the time, the Royal Navy was being run-down as a result of yet another Defence Review, this was no mean achievement. The second phase began when the Task Force entered the Total Exclusion Zone established around the islands and commenced a series of opera-

tions designed to whittle down the strength of the Argentine forces while at the same time conducting reconnaissance prior to the landing. The highlight of this phase was the sinking of the cruiser *General Belgrano* on 2 May 1982 by HMS *Conqueror.* This had the effect of keeping the Argentine Navy in port or within their coastal waters for the rest of the war. The third phase began on 21 May 1982 with the landings at San Carlos and lasted until the

Argentine surrender on 14 June. During this phase the Navy was wholly dedicated to supporting the troops ashore through providing air defence, conducting bombardments, screening supply convoys and inserting and recovering special forces.

Farnborough, HMS. British Q-Ship which sank *U83* in an epic engagement on 17 February 1917. Despite being torpedoed in the engine room, *Farnborough's* crew remained at their gun positions until *U83* surfaced less than 100 yards away and then sank her in a hail of gunfire. *Farnborough*'s commanding officer, Captain Gordon Campbell, was awarded the VC while awards to the rest of the crew totalled two DSOs, three DSCs, ten DSMs and twenty-four 'Mentions in Despatches'. However, such was the secrecy surrounding the sinking that the circumstances of the award were not disclosed and thus Campbell became known as 'the Mystery VC'.

Fast Battery Drive. Term used by the Royal Navy for the post war 'T'-Conversion and 'Super-T' class submarines which had increased battery capacity and were capable of greater underwater speeds.

Fernlenkboot. See DCB.

FF. Frigate. US Navy classification, adopted to replace DE on 30 June 1975.

FFG. Guided missile frigate. US Navy classification adopted on 30 June 1975 to replace DEG.

Fido. Code-name for an air dropped acoustic torpedo developed during the Second World War by the US Navy; the weapon was also known, for security purposes, as the Mk XXIV mine. Fido's guidance was based on four passive hydrophones. When dropped into the water, the torpedo dived to a preset depth and began to search for its target. In theory the weapon had a detection range of 1,500yds, though poor conditions could shorten this considerably. If the torpedo failed to detect a target it would go into a circling pattern which it could maintain for ten to fifteen minutes: *U296* was sunk by a Fido after a run of thirteen minutes. The torpedo was 84in long, weighed 680lb and carried a 92lb torpex warhead. It was first used in 1943, some 340 were dropped and it enjoyed a 22% 'kill rate' as opposed to 9.5% for depth charges.

Fifi, **HMS.** The German gunboat *Kingani*, captured on Lake Tanganyika on 26 December 1915 and recommissioned into the Royal Navy.

'Fireball', Operation. Mine-clearance operations in the approaches to Rotterdam, May–June 1945.

Firefly. British two-seat carrier fighter designed and manufactured by Fairey which was particularly successful in the night fighter, photo-reconnaissance and strike roles.

Fishery protection. Use of naval forces to enforce fishery protection regulations.

Flag of Convenience. Term used to describe ships registered in certain small countries, notably Panama and Liberia, by owners who are not nationals of that country. It is usually done as a means of avoiding high wages and regulations imposed by traditional maritime countries. The practice began in the shipping slump in the 1920s and 1930s but became much more commonplace after the Second World War when a considerable amount of surplus merchant tonnage was available. 'Flagging out' is a practice which has serious implications for countries like Britain which depend on maritime trade: in January 1996 over half of UK-owned merchant shipping was registered outside the country.

Flasher, **USS** (SS249). US submarine which sank the greatest tonnage – *Tautog* (SS199) sank the most ships – during the Second World War. She carried out six patrols, sinking two light cruisers, two destroyers, two gunboats, five tankers and ten other merchant ships – a total of twenty-one vessels totalling 100,231 tons. A *Gato* class diesel-electric submarine, *Flasher* displaced 1,525/2,425 tons, was 311¾ft long and was armed with ten (six bow and four stern) torpedo tubes. She was launched in 1943, placed in reserve in 1946 and broken up in 1959.

'Flaxman', Operation. *See* 'Gauntlet'.

Fleet Air Arm. Since 1924 the name by which the air wing of the Royal Navy has been known. Naval aviation in Britain dates from 1912, when the naval component of the Royal Flying Corps (RFC) broke away to form a separate organisation called the Royal Naval Air Service (RNAS), which was controlled by the Royal Navy. However, on 1 April 1918 the RFC and RNAS were amalgamated to form one independent service called the Royal Air Force. All aircraft, establishments, air crew and ground crew of the RNAS were transferred *en bloc* to the new organisation. All naval flying and procurement of aircraft was controlled by the RAF. This was an unfortunate state of affairs, to say the least, since all questions concerning naval aviation took second place to the RAF's obsession with strategic bombing. This resulted in the design and procurement of aircraft which were unsuitable for sea service. In an attempt to satisfy naval concerns on the subject the RAF established the Fleet Air Arm of the RAF to train naval officers for flying duties. However, discontent with the split arrangement continued and in 1937 the Fleet Air Arm was placed under the direct control of the Admiralty, where it has remained ever since. Today the Fleet Air Arm consists of two naval air stations, Culdrose and Yeovilton, which support the sea-going squadrons of Sea Harrier fighter aircraft and Sea King, Merlin and Lynx helicopters.

Fleet-in-being. A battle fleet which seldom strays from its harbour but which performs a useful function in tying down large numbers of the opposition's forces. During the First World War the Austrian battle fleet of four dreadnoughts and three pre-dreadnoughts tied down a large number of British, French and Italian warships in the Adriatic. However, by far and away the most successful example of the concept is the German battleship *Tirpitz*, which dominated British naval planning and operations in northern waters during the Second World War from her

arrival in Norwegian waters in 1942 until she was sunk two and half years later.

Fleet train. Generic term for a group of auxiliary vessels such as oilers, stores ships, repair ships, ammunition ships, water carriers and tugs which allow a fleet to remain at sea and on operations for long periods without having to return to port and replenish.

Fleet Rehabilitation and Modernisation Program. A massive American programme to modernise surface ships undertaken as a result of a 1958 study which found that the US Navy was not 'in an acceptable state of readiness'. In November 1958 three levels of modernisation were announced: FRAM-1, nothing less than a complete modernisation to give eight more years of life; FRAM-2, sufficient modernisation for five more years; and FRAM-3, the minimum work required to give three more years' service. Budget constraints quickly forced the FRAM-3 conversion to be dropped, but the FRAM-1 and FRAM-2 conversions were accorded the highest priority – equal to that of the Polaris programme. Seventy-nine *Gearing* and *Carpenter* class destroyers were given a FRAM-1 upgrade; and eight carriers and sixteen *Gearing* class, thirty-one *Allen M. Sumner* class and three *Fletcher* class destroyers received the FRAM-2 conversion, along with eight 'Guppy' submarines, four APDs and seven LSDs.

Flexible Response. A strategy involving a number of responses

to a particular kind of attack ranging from the minor conventional to all-out nuclear war which was developed by the USA in the 1960s and formally adopted by NATO in 1967.

FLIR. Forward Looking Infra-Red. Equipment which allows night vision by the use of infra-red sensors projecting an image on to a cathode ray tube.

Flotilla Defence. Strategic concept advocated before the First World War whereby massed flotillas of destroyers and submarines would be built instead of capital ships to counter the threat posed by an enemy battle fleet. In Britain the concept had many strong supporters, including Winston Churchill, who was prepared to switch funds from capital ship construction to destroyers and submarines.

'Flower' class corvette. British escort constructed in large numbers during the Second World War and employed principally on convoy escort duty in the Battle of the Atlantic. The design was based on that of the whalecatcher *Southern Pride* and had the advantage that it could be built simply and cheaply by yards which had no previous experience of warship construction. The design also proved capable of absorbing substantial modification as a result of war experience. The 'Flowers' were not ideal escorts but they held the ring in the Atlantic until more sophisticated ships were completed. A standard 'Flower' class corvette had a standard displacement of 925 tons, was 205ft long and was

Above: The Flower Class corvette HMS *Dianella* (ex-*Daffodil*). (IWM A 12313)

armed with one 4in gun, forty depth charges and a variety of close-range weapons.

Focke Achgelis Fa 330. Captive autogyro carried by large Type IX U-boats for reconnaissance.

Folboat. Canoe used by British SBS and COPP parties for special operations during the Second World War. It could be folded – hence the name – for compact stowage in a submarine.

'Forager', Operation. Naval air strike on the Marianas Islands in June 1944.

Force H. British naval force based at Gibraltar for operations in the eastern Atlantic and Mediterranean which was established in June 1940. Although a number of ships served in Force H for specific operations, the core of the force was the aircraft carrier *Ark Royal*, the battlecruiser *Renown* and the cruiser *Sheffield* under the command of Vice-Admiral Sir James Somerville. Its most notable operations were the bombardment of the French Fleet at Oran in July 1940, various convoy operations in the Mediterranean and the strike against the German battleship *Bismarck* in May 1941. In 1943 Force H was quietly absorbed by the comprehensive Allied naval structure in the Mediterranean.

Force K. British naval force based at Malta between 1940 and 1942 and consisting of a number of light cruisers and destroyers. Of all the forces based on the island of Malta, Force K was the most effective in terms of sinking Axis supply ships bound for North Africa.

Force multiplier. Sensor or weapons system which not only provides capability itself but enhances the value of other systems. For example, a 'home on jamming' capability in one missile of a salvo is a force multiplier for a standard radar homer head in another missile of the same salvo. Whether the enemy decides to use jamming or not is immaterial: one missile will hit.

Force Z. The battleship HMS *Prince of Wales* and battlecruiser HMS *Renown*, which were dispatched to the Far East in 1941 as a 'deterrent' to the Japanese, and which were sunk by Japanese aircraft off the east coast of Malaya on 10 December 1941.

Former Naval Person. Code-name used in correspondence by Winston Churchill.

Formidable, HMS. British aircraft carrier launched in 1939. After service in the Mediterranean, where she was badly damaged, she joined the British Pacific Fleet. On 4 May 1945, while operating off the Sakashima Gunto, she was struck by a *Kamikaze* on the flight deck near the island structure. The ship's armoured flight deck saved her from more serious damage but the flight deck was holed and dented over a large area and eleven aircraft were wrecked beyond repair. Eight men were killed and forty-seven wounded. Nevertheless, six hours later, the ship was flying-on aircraft. On 9 May *Formidable* was struck by a second *Kamikaze* which ploughed into the after deck park. There was little structural damage though seven aircraft were destroyed and two damaged. However, the blast blew out some rivets in the flight deck and burning petrol poured down into the hangar. The sprinkler system was turned on and a further twelve aircraft were destroyed either by burning petrol or by the firefighting efforts. After the *Kamikaze* attack on 4 May *Formidable*'s commanding officer reportedly roared at his USN liaison officer, 'What do you think of our flight decks now!' and received the reply, 'Sir, they're a honey!' The US navy previous to this had not thought very highly of them. *Formidable* displaced 23,000 tons, was 753ft long and could carry thirty-three aircraft (compare these figures with those of the US *Essex* class). She always enjoyed a reputation as a happy ship to serve in and was broken up in 1953.

Formosa. Island off the east coast of China and the scene for potential conflict since 1949 when the Chinese Nationalist forces established a government-in-exile there following the communist victory on the mainland. Nationalist naval forces have harried communist merchant shipping, while in recent years the People's Navy has carried out exercises in waters between Formosa and the Chinese mainland as a means of intimidating the Nationalist government.

'Fortitude', Operation. Large-scale deception operation to indicate to the Germans that the invasion of Europe would be in the Pas de Calais area. On the naval side it involved the assembly of dummy landing craft in the Thames and Medway estuaries, the creation of bogus radio traffic to indicate the presence of non-existent units and the use of MTBs fitted with radar augmenters to enable them to masquerade as larger vessels.

Foucault. French submarine sunk in the Adriatic on 15 September 1916 by Austrian seaplanes. The seaplanes sighted the submarine at periscope depth, the waters in the eastern Adriatic being especially clear, and bombed her. The submarine was damaged, surfaced and surrendered. The seaplanes took the commanding officer, *Lieutenant de Vaisseau* Devin, and his executive officer back to Durazzo as 'samples' while destroyers picked up the rest of the crew. *Foucault* was the first submarine to be sunk in a deliberate air attack.

Foxer. Noisemaker streamed astern of a warship to decoy acoustic torpedoes.

FR-1 Fireball. First USN jet-powered aircraft to make a landing on an aircraft carrier.

Franklin, USS (CV13) US *Essex* class aircraft carrier which sustained massive damage on 19 March 1945 when she was struck by two bombs. The bombs exploded in the hangar, starting massive

Above: The commanding officer and first lieutenant of the French submarine *Foucault* pose with aircrew of the Austrian seaplane L.135 which had sunk the submarine.

fires which burned for five hours. Firefighting was made the more hazardous by the explosion of ordance (including the 11in 'Tiny Tim' air-to-ground rockets with their 150lb warheads) fitted to aircraft awaiting take-off. She was eventually saved, though only 55 miles from Japan at the time of the attack, but 832 of her crew were killed and 270 injured. She returned to the US under her own power but was never recommissioned.

'Frankton', Operation. Commando raid on German shipping in the Gironde estuary and Bordeaux in December 1942.

Free French. An anti-German, anti-Vichy French government-in-exile established in London by General Charles de Gaulle in 1940. As such it disposed substantial naval forces either given to them by Britain or mobilised from surrendered French warships.

Friedrich der Grosse, **SMS.** German *Kaiser* class battleship launched in 1911. She displaced 24,330 tons, was 565ft long and was armed with ten 12in guns. *Friedrich der Grosse* was the flagship of the High Seas Fleet at the Battle of Jutland. At the end of the war she was interned at Scapa Flow and scuttled there on 21 June 1919. Her wreck was subsequently raised and broken up, although in a gesture of goodwill her ornate bell was returned to Germany.

Frigate. A medium-size surface combatant of between 1,750 and 3,000 tons designed primarily for convoy escort duties. Between 1955 and 1975 the term was used by the US, Britain and France (who still use the term) for destroyer-type ships, largely to convince reluctant legislatures that they were getting something for (nearly) nothing. The modern use of the designation comes from a need formally to designate ships which

Above: The Type 23 class frigate HMS *Westminster* photographed on completion in 199

The VLS Seawolf missile launchers are located behind the 4.5in MK.VIII gun mounting. (MoD)

have their ancestry in the large, ocean-going, twin-screw corvettes of the Second World War. The Royal Navy now classifies as frigates all surface ships whose primary mission in ASW.

Fritz X. Highly effective German air launched, radio controlled, anti-ship guided missile. Its operational début occurred on 9 September 1943 when it was used to sink the Italian battleship *Roma*, and on 11 September a Fritz X damaged the US cruiser *Savannah*. The weapon weighed 3,454lb and had a range of 5½ miles if dropped from 26,000ft. Range decreased if the missile was released from a lower altitude. Flares on the missile's wings enabled the controller flying in a Dornier Do 217 aircraft to track and guide the missile. It had great potential as an anti-shipping device although its effectiveness was blunted by the superiority of Allied fighter forces which prevented the 'mother' aircraft coming close enough to a target to launch the weapon.

Frogmen. *See* UDT.

FSU. Forward Support Unit. British unit supporting MCMV ships deployed out of area or away from their home port. Typically such a unit would carry sufficient spares and stores to keep the ships running, along with workshop facilities. The FSU deployed to the Persian Gulf for the 1991 Gulf War consisted of sixteen containers carrying 200,000 items of stores (worth £1.5m), workshops, a power supply and communica-

tions. It was manned by forty senior ratings. Since this unit was accommodated in an LSL there was no need for the accommodation or sanitary units, but these could be supplied if necessary.

'Fuller', Operation. Plans to deal with the German battlecruisers *Scharnhorst* and *Gneisenau* should they attempt to pass up the English Channel.

Fulmar. Royal Navy's first monoplane carrier fighter. It was a two-seat Fairey aircraft armed with eight .303in machine guns and was particularly effective against Italian aircraft in the Mediterranean; it was less effective against the faster German types which entered that theatre from January 1941. It was manoeuvrable, well armed with a good rate of climb. However, it lacked speed – the most essential quality in a fighter – due to the presence of a navigator. Unless the pilot hit the target with his first burst he rarely had a chance of a second shot. The first production Fulmar survives and is displayed in the FAA Museum at Yeovilton.

Fünf Minuten Schiffe. Five-Minute Ships. The unkind name given to the six pre-dreadnought battleships of the 2nd Squadron of the German High Seas Fleet, that being their life expectancy in action with the Royal Navy.

'Galvanic', Operation. US plans for the capture of the Gilbert Islands in the South Pacific, November 1942. *See* Cromwell,

Richard P., in the Personalities section.

Gambier Bay, **USS.** The only US aircraft carrier to be sunk by Japanese gunfire during the Second World War. She was dis-

Above: Fulmar (foreground) and Wildcat fighters on the flight deck of HMS *Illustrious* in the Indian Ocean, 22 December 1942. Astern of the carrier is HMS *Valiant* on a practice shoot. (IWM A 15153)

patched on 25 October 1944 by 8in gunfire from Japanese cruisers during the Battle of Leyte Gulf. *Gambier Bay* capsized and sank at 0907 with the loss of 100 officers and men after her machinery spaces had flooded and her dam-

age control parties had been unable to contain the fires.

Gamma. Italian term for highly trained assault swimmers. Armed with limpet mines, they were employed at Gibraltar, Algiers and

Alexandretta against Allied shipping.

'Gardening'. Minelaying operations by RAF Bomber Command at the Admiralty's request during the Second World War.

Above. The USS *Tang,* one of the very successful *Gato/Balao* class. It was an outstanding design which proved capable of absorbing many wartime modifications. (USN).

Below: New uses for old boats. The US *Balao* class submarine *Cusk* in 1950. The 'hangar' aft of the conning tower contains a Loon missile. On 12 February 1947 *Cusk* became the first submarine to fire a guided missile. (USN)

Gato/Balao Class. One of the most successful submarine designs of World War Two. US ship yards built a total of 77 *Gato* class and 120 *Balao* class boats. Their surfaced displacement was just over 2,000 tons, they had a surfaced range of 11,000 miles and an endurance of 75 days. The only significant difference between the two classes was that the *Balao* class had a deeper operational depth because of the use of high tensile steels. The *Gato* class felt the full weight of Japanese ASW effort, nineteen boats being lost; nine boats of the *Balao* class were lost. After the war many of the *Balao* class were modified and served on for a good many more years.

'Gauntlet', Operation. Destruction of mines and machinery at

Above: The launch of the *Gato* class submarine USS *Flying Fish* on 7 December 1941 at Portsmouth Navy Yard. (USN)

Spitzbergen and the evacuation of Russian and Norwegian personnel to the UK in August/September 1941.

General Belgrano, ARA. Argentine cruiser, formerly the USS *Phoenix*, built in 1938, a survivor of Pearl Harbor and transferred to Argentina in 1951. On 2 May 1982 she was torpedoed and sunk by the British submarine HMS *Conqueror* south-east of the Falkland Islands with the loss of 321 of her crew of 1,042 officers and men. The sinking attracted considerable criticism from left-wing and pacifist groups in the UK on the grounds that it took place outside the Exclusion Zone established around the islands by the British Government. However, in August 1995 the Argentine Government declared that the sinking of *Belgrano* was a legitimate act of war.

German East Asia Squadron. Unit of the Imperial German Navy deployed to the Far East to protect the German colony at Tsingtau in China and Germany's possessions in East Africa and Polynesia before the First World War. It consisted of the armoured cruisers *Scharnhorst* and *Gneisenau*, the cruisers *Emden*, *Nürnberg*, *Leipzig* and *Königsberg* and the Austrian gunboat *Kaiserin Elizabeth*. At the beginning of the First World War the bulk of the squadron attempted to return to Germany around Cape Horn but *Scharnhorst*, *Gneisenau*, *Leipzig* and *Nürnberg* were sunk at the Battle of the Falkland Islands.. *Kaiserin Eliz-*

abeth was scuttled at Tsingtau. *Emden* had been detached for commerce raiding in the Indian Ocean and was finally sunk on 9 November 1914 by HMAS *Sydney*. *Königsberg* was at Dar-es-Salaam in East Africa and after a brief raiding career took refuge up the Rufiji River, where she was destroyed by gunfire from British monitors and finally scuttled on 11 July 1915.

'Gibbon', Operation. Control and surrender of the Italian warships and merchant ships at the time of the Italian Armistice in September 1943.

Gibraltar. Strategically important British possession (since 1715) overlooking the strait between the Mediterranean and the Atlantic. In both world wars it provided an invaluable harbour and air base and was the staging port for the invasion of North Africa in November 1942. It was also the scene for a series of determined attacks by Italian assault swimmers and human torpedoes which were either launched from a submarine or from the Italian tanker *Olterra* moored in Algeciras harbour. In the post-war period the base's usefulness to NATO has been compromised by Spanish demands for the return of the 'Rock' to Spanish control.

Gibraltar Underwater Working Party. British unit of divers established at Gibraltar in 1942 to counter the operations of Italian assault swimmers and human torpedoes operating from Spain.

Gilbert Islands. An important group of islands lying directly across the route between Hawaii and Australia. They were seized by Japan on 9 December 1941. In November 1943 the Americans landed on Tarawa, Makin and Apamama in Operation 'Galvanic'.

GIUK Gap. The sea passage between Greenland, Iceland and the UK. A strategically important area through which Soviet ships and submarines would have to pass en route for the Atlantic. This area was therefore the focus of much NATO activity, including the laying of SOSUS chains.

Glitra. British merchant ship sunk on 20 October 1914 by *U17*. She was the first merchant ship to be sunk by a U-boat. *U17*'s commanding officer behaved in accordance with international law in stopping and searching the *Glitra* for contraband – even though the boarding officer is alleged to have torn up the Red Ensign and stamped on it – before sinking her.

Glorious, HMS. A British aircraft carrier which was a former light battlecruiser, sister ship to HMS *Courageous*. Launched 1916 and sunk by the *Scharnhorst* and *Gneisenau* on 8 June 1940.

Glowworm, HMS. A name that has been used twice by the Royal Navy this century. The first *Glowworm* was an 'Insect' class river gunboat launched in 1915 which spent the First World War as an AA battery at Lowestoft. In the inter-war period she served on the Danube and it was into the care of her commanding officer, Captain Arthur Snagge RN, that the ex-Emperor Karl of Austria-Hungary was surrendered on 21 November 1921. Karl gave his parole to Captain Snagge that he would not escape; the only other occasion on which an ex-sovereign has surrendered to a British warship was when Napoleon gave a similar undertaking to Captain Maitland of the *Bellerophon* in 1815. *Glowworm* was broken up in 1925 and the name was given to a 'G' class destroyer launched in 1935. On 8 April 1940 she was sunk in action with the German cruiser *Admiral Hipper*, an action for which her commanding officer, Lt-Cdr G. Roope RN, was posthumously awarded the Victoria Cross.

GNAT. Allied term for the German T5 'Zaunkonig' acoustic torpedo – German Naval Acoustic Torpedo. The T5 was specifically developed to deal with escorts by homing in on their propeller noises. It was first used on 20 September 1943 when the frigate HMS *Lagan*, escorting convoy ON.202, was damaged by *U270*. In the next three days T5s were used to sink a destroyer, a frigate a corvette and two other escorts. The British had learned of the deployment of the T5 through Ultra and interrogation of PoWs. WATU was able to promulgate countermeasures, which included the deployment of noisemakers or Foxers and low speeds at which it was judged that the T5's hydrophones would not be able to detect engine noise.

Gneisenau. A name that has been used three times this century for German warships. The first was a 12,781-ton armoured cruiser launched in 1906 and sunk at the Battle of the Falkland Islands on 8 December 1914. The second was a 34,841-ton battlecruiser launched in 1936. She took part in the 1940 Norwegian campaign, sinking the British aircraft carrier *Glorious* on 8 June 1940. She participated in Operation 'Berlin' before returning to Germany in the Channel Dash. She was badly damaged in an RAF raid on Kiel in November 1942. Although plans existed to repair the ship, she was eventually scuttled as a blockship at Gotenhafen, where her wreck was broken up between 1947 and 1951. One of her triple 11in mountings exists as a coast defence weapon in Norway. The third *Gneisenau* was the ex-British 'Hunt' class destroyer HMS *Oakley*. She was acquired in 1958 and broken up in 1977.

Goa. Portuguese colony on the Indian subcontinent which together with the enclaves of Daman and Diu was annexed by India in December 1961. The local Portuguese naval forces offered resistance, which was swiftly crushed, and the Portuguese frigate *Alfonso de Albuequerque* was sunk on 18 December by INS *Mysore* and *Betwa*

Goeben, SMS. German battlecruiser launched in 1911. She displaced 22,616 tons, was 611ft long and was armed with ten 11in guns. On the outbreak of the First World War she was in the

Mediterranean and she made a celebrated dash for Constantinople. She was nominally transferred to Turkey, and renamed *Yavuz Sultan Selim* (although she retained her German crew), as compensation for the two battleships under construction in Britain which had been seized by the British. Her arrival in Turkish waters was instrumental in persuading the Turkish Government to join Germany and Austria. After the First World War she became Turkish property and was finally decommissioned in 1960. A number of attempts were made to save the ship for preservation, but she was broken up in 1971.

'Goodwood', Operation. British carrier strike on the German battleship *Tirpitz* in the summer of 1944.

Gooseberry. Artificial breakwater to create anchorages off the Normandy beachhead in the summer of 1944.

Graf Zeppelin. One of four aircraft carriers to be built for the German Navy under the Z Plan of 1938. She was launched in 1936 but her construction was suspended, when she was 85% complete, on Hitler's order in April 1940. Work was ordered to commence again in May 1942 but was halted in January 1943 in order that all resources be concentrated on U-boat construction. In April 1943 she was towed to Stettin, where she was scuttled in January 1945. She was raised by the Russians and was to be taken to Leningrad but foundered en route, possibly as a result of striking a mine. *Graf Zeppelin* displaced 28,090 tons, was 820ft long and would have carried 43 aircraft, Bf 109T fighters and Ju 87 dive-bombers. The completion of the carrier would have posed an additional threat to the Royal Navy in home waters but, in view of the fact that the German Navy had no experience of operating carriers or carrier aircraft (by 1939 Britain, the USA and Japan had had over twenty years of practical experience), her potential effectiveness must be considered dubious.

Great Landing. Proposed amphibious operation on the coast of Belgium in September 1917 to coincide with the British Army's offensive at Ypres. Two divisions would be put ashore between Ostend and Nieuport. They would have the opportunity of turning the German flank, destroying the coastal batteries and then linking up with British troops advancing from the south. The troops would be landed from 540ft long pontoons pushed by two monitors and supported by tanks. The plan was bold and ambitious and stood an above average chance of breaking the hideous stalemate on the Western Front. However, the British Army failed the make the necessary gains in their offensive by 20 September 1917, after which time favourable conditions of tide, weather and daylight hours were vanishing. The plan was called off on 2 October.

'Great Marianas Turkey Shoot'. *See* Philippine Sea, Battle of the.

Great White Fleet. The name given to the sixteen American warships which made a round-the-world cruise in 1907–09. Though the voyage was dogged by mishap and scandal it was striking proof that the US Navy was capable of projecting naval power into the Far East.

Greenland. Strategically important island in the North Atlantic as a source of cryolite (used in aluminium production) and as an excellent site for meteorological stations. Although a Danish possession, it was annexed by the United States on 9 April 1941 with the agreement of the Danish government-in-exile. The Allies established a number of weather stations there, as did the Germans, who also planned to build an air base there supplied by U-boats. However, the German stations were quickly neutralised by the US Coast Guard.

Greer, USS (DD145). The first US warship to attack a U-boat during the Second World War. On 4 September 1941 *U652* was attacked by *Greer*, on passage to Iceland. The destroyer dropped a number of depth-charge patterns and *U652* fired a torpedo, but both sides escaped without damage. 'From the date of the *Greer* incident,' wrote Samuel Eliot Morison, 'the United States was engaged in a *de facto* naval war with Germany on the Atlantic Ocean.'

Greif. German commerce raider of the First World War. She was a nondescript-looking steamer of 5,000 tons but was armed with four 5.9in guns and two torpedo tubes. On her first voyage out into the Atlantic she was intercepted by the armed merchant cruiser *Alcantara* on 29 February 1916. In a fierce action, fought virtually at point-blank range, *Greif* was so badly damaged that she nearly sank before she was able to sink her opponent with a torpedo. The armed merchant cruiser *Andes* and cruiser *Comus* then appeared, to give the *coup de grâce* to the raider.

Grillo. One of four 'climbing boats' (the others being *Cavaletta*, *Pulce* and *Locusta*) built by the Italian Navy during the First World War. They were basic 8-ton, 52ft torpedo boats but fitted with caterpillar tracks on their port and starboard sides to enable them to climb over net and boom defences guarding the Austrian base at Pola. *Pulce* and *Cavaletta* were scuttled during an attack on Pola on 13 April 1918. *Grillo* was damaged by Austrian gunfire and scuttled off Pola on 14 May 1918; she was subsequently raised by the Austrians, who tried to develop their own such craft. *Locusta* was broken up in 1921.

GRP. Glass reinforced plastic. Material used extensively in the construction of minehunters. The first GRP warship was the British minesweeper HMS *Wilton*, which was built using a single GRP skin over a wooden framing and proved very successful, surviving a small fire and two collisions with minimum time spent under repair. The British 'Hunt' class minesweepers/

hunters which followed are the largest GRP warships in the world. Although they attracted considerable criticism on the grounds of cost, the cost of the GRP hull was only 7% of the total and certain items (such as non-ferrous anchors and anchor cable) were more expensive than the hull. The Italian Navy has since developed a thick (140mm) monocoque construction technique which requires no framing for its *Lerici* class MCMVs, and this technique has been adopted by the US Navy for its *Osprey* class MCMVs.

Guadalcanal. On 7 August 1942 US Marines landed on Guadalcanal in the southern Solomons and began a desperate struggle for possession of the island which would involve six naval battles, Savo Island, Eastern Solomons, Cape Esperance, Santa Cruz Islands, Guadalcanal and Tassafaronga. From the outset Japanese naval forces based on Rabaul used the channel between the Eastern and Western Solomons, known as The Slot, to send down reinforcements by sea. These convoys were known as the 'Tokyo Express'. Another focus of naval activity was Sealark Channel between Guadalcanal and Florida Island, which was renamed Ironbottom Sound.

Guadalcanal, Battle of. One of the most bitterly fought battles of the Second World War, this American victory marked the end of Japanese attempts to use battleships and cruisers to support their forces at Guadalcanal. On the night of 12 November 1942 a Japanese task force consisting of

two battleships, three cruisers and fourteen destroyers roared down The Slot to bombard the American beach-head. In the darkness the Japanese encountered an American force and sank the cruiser *Atlanta* and four destroyers; the cruiser *Juneau* was torpedoed the next morning. However, the Japanese turned back after this engagement and on the morning of the 13th American aircraft found one of the Japanese battleships, *Hiei*, and sank her. Both sides then brought up reinforcements and the following night a Japanese force set off to cover a landing force consisting of eleven transports escorted by eleven destroyers. The Japanese bombarded the beach-head but lost seven transports to air attack. However, they did manage to beach four of the transports and get the troops ashore. The final Japanese attempt was made on the night of 14/15 November. Admiral Kondo entered Iron-bottom Sound in the battleship *Kirishima* with four cruisers and a number of destroyers to bombard the beach-head but he ran into the American battleships *South Dakota* and *Washington*. An electrical power failure left *South Dakota* with no main armament but *Washington*'s radar-directed gunfire demolished *Kirishima* in seven minutes.

Guam. Largest of the Marianas Islands, Guam surrendered to the Japanese on 10 December 1941. US Marines landed on the island on 21 July 1944 and Guam was declared secure on 10 August. The fighting had been savage, with the

Japanese losing more than 5,000 men. With the island secure, Seabees began turning it into a port and airfield from which the final stages of the war against Japan would be directed.

Gulf of Siam, Battle of the. *See* Koh Chang, Battle of.

'Guppy'. Acronym for Greater Underwater Propulsive Power. Reconstruction programme undertaken by the United States post World War Two for the large number of war-built diesel-electric submarines. All fittings and equipmemt external to the casing were removed and the casing given a more streamlined form. All masts were enclosed in a lightweight structure called a fin. 'Guppy-Is' were conversions of existing submarines but 'Guppy-IIs' were purpose-built.

Habbakuk. Ingenious plan to create floating airfields in the Atlantic during the Second World War made out of sawdust and water frozen together, a mixture known as Pykrete after its creator Geoffrey Pyke. As Pykrete melted the fibrous content formed an outer surface which held the material together. A scale model was built and tested in Canada. A full size Pykrete 'carrier' would have had a displacement of one million tons, be self-propelled and be fitted with accommodation, workshops and all the other facilities for the operation of aircraft. The idea won Churchill's enthusiastic backing and support but the development of VLR aircraft caused the project to be dropped.

Above: USS *Tiru*, an American 'Guppy' type SSK (see previous spread). This photograph was taken in San Francisco Bay in 1969. Note the streamlined hull form. (USN)

Hague Convention. Peace conference held at The Hague, the Netherlands, in 1907 whose object was the limitation of armaments, especially naval armaments. A previous conference held in 1899 had collapsed but, largely as a result of Russian initiatives, a second conference was held in 1907. Any attempt to limit naval armament foundered completely when the Germans refused even to discuss the subject. However, some progress was made in the field of international law as it applied to naval and military operations. In particular, the Convention governed the circumstances under which merchant shipping could be sunk in war, in particular that merchant ships suspected of carrying contraband must be visited and searched and adequate arrangements made for the safety of the crew. The Convention also amended international maritime law to the effect that a declaration of war must be preceded by an ultimatum or adequate notice. An unsuccessful attempt was made by some neutral countries to secure exemption from seizure for their ships during war, even if these ships were carrying contraband. Not surprisingly this proposal met with robust opposition

doned the Hague Convention throughout the war.

'Halberd', Operation. British west-bound convoy to Malta in September 1941.

***Hampshire*, HMS.** British armoured cruiser launched in 1903. On 5 June 1916 she left Scapa Flow carrying Lord Kitchener and a military mission to Russia for talks. Three hours after clearing the Hoxa Gate, the cruiser ran on to a mine laid by *U75* a week earlier. Only fourteen men survived the sinking; neither Kitchener nor any member of his staff survived. Kitchener's death was the cause of many rumours that there was more to the affair than met the eye, but the circumstances of his death and *Hampshire*'s loss were purely accidental: *U75*'s commander had observed British warships passing close inshore off the Orkneys on a previous patrol and these observations determined where he would lay his mines.

'Hangman'. Code-name for a clandestine British organisation in occupied Norway to report the movement of German warships.

from all the major naval powers and was defeated. In one respect the Convention took a retrograde step. The Declaration of Paris of 1856 had abolished the *guerre de corse*, but the Hague Convention authorised the use of armed merchant raiders. Many observers correctly predicted that in practice the provisions of the Hague Convention would be unworkable, particularly those which related to

the sinking of merchant ships. In both World Wars the Hague Convention was virtually ignored by both sides. In the 1945 Nuremberg Trials there was the ridiculous spectacle of one defendant, Admiral Karl Dönitz, being charged with violations of the Hague Convention and entering in his defence an affidavit from Fleet Admiral Chester Nimitz confirming that the Americans had aban-

'Happy Time'. Generic term for two periods during the Battle of the Altantic during the Second World War when the German U-boat fleet was particularly successful against Allied shipping. 'The First Happy Time' was June 1940 to May 1941 when the main part of the campaign was fought out in the Western Approaches, close to the Britsish Isles. 'The Second Happy Time' was from

February to October 1942 when the combat was concentrated in the eastern coastal waters of the United States.

Harpoon. A high-subsonic anti-ship tactical cruise missile. Designed and produced in the United States, it is in service with a number of navies around the world. In its various configurations it is capable of being launched from surface ships, submerged submarines and aircraft. It has a range of over 50 miles.

'Harpoon', Operation. British westbound convoy to Malta in June 1942. This convoy sustained heavy losses and of the five merchant ships and a tanker involved only two merchant ships reached Malta.

Hartlepool. Port on the north-east coast of England which was bombarded (along with Whitby and Scarborough) by units of the High Seas Fleet on 16 December 1914. There was considerable damage to property and many civilian casualties. Despite British howls of outrage about dastardly German behaviour, under International Law the High Seas Fleet was allowed to bombard Hartlepool since the town was defended by a battery of coast defence guns.

Haruna. Japanese fast battleship launched in 1913 and the only Japanese capital ship to be damaged during the First World War: in September 1917 she struck a mine laid by the German raider *Wolf.* On 10 December 1941 she was reported as being sunk in a suicide attack by Captain Colin Kelly USAAF when in fact she was peacefully at anchor off Hiroshima at the time. *Haruna* survived the Guadalcanal campaign and Leyte Gulf and was sunk in shallow water near Kure on 28 July 1945. Her wreck was subsequently broken up *in situ. Haruna* was a *Kongo* class fast battleship and had a displacement of 27,500 tons. Her main armament consisted of eight 14in guns. She was the only one of the four ships to survive the war.

Harwich Force. A force of light cruisers and destroyers commanded by Commodore Reginald Tyrwhitt based on the British East Coast port of Harwich for operations in the southern North Sea. Known as the 'Outer Gabbard Yacht Club', the Harwich Force was unique among British destroyer commands in that its ships were trained in offensive action rather than the shepherding of big ships.

'Headache'. Specialist teams of German-speaking communicators embarked in British warships during the Second World War to provide translations of German voice and plain text communications.

Heavy cruiser. Cruiser whose main armament consists of guns of 8in calibre or above.

'Heckle', Operation. British X-craft operation against the floating dock at Bergen in Norway in September 1944. A previous attack in April resulted in the destruction of the steamer *Barenfels* but the dock escaped unscathed. On this occasion there was no mistake and the dock was destroyed by HM Submarine *X-24.*

Hedgehog. A 24-spigot anti-submarine mortar firing 7in diameter contact-fused projectiles weighing 65lb with a 35lb charge. It was designed to be fired ahead of the attacking ship and thus gave the advantage that the ship did not lose asdic contact with the target during the final attack run. It was fitted to destroyers and frigates and by the end of the Second World War had been installed in 500 ships.

Helgoland, **SMS.** Austro-Hungarian light cruiser which played a significant role in operations against the Otranto Barrage forces. Launched in 1912, she was armed with nine 10cm guns. At the end of the war she was ceded to Italy and recommissioned as *Brindisi.* She was paid off in March 1937.

Heligoland. German island in the North Sea, 20 miles north of the Elbe, Jade and Weser rivers. Heavily fortified, it was used as a U-boat base during the First World War. Under the terms of the Treaty of Versailles its fortifications were to be demolished, but it was refortified in time for the Second World War and for a second time the fortifications were destroyed at the end of the conflict.

Heligoland Bight, Battle of the. Confused action in the Heligoland Bight on 28 August 1914 in which the Harwich Force, comprising two light cruisers and thirty-one destroyers, was dispatched into the Bight to attack German patrols. The Germans had had an inkling of what was afoot and reinforced the patrols. In a series of inconclusive engagements, fought in poor visibility, between 0800 and 1130, Tyrwhitt was hotly engaged with eight German light cruisers. Although the German cruiser *Frauenlob* was badly damaged, Tyrwhitt's forces were in danger of being overwhelmed. At 1125 Tyrwhitt requested assistance from the 1st Battle Cruiser Squadron (Vice-Admiral Beatty) which was forty miles north of Heligoland and unaware of Tyrwhitt's predicament. Nevertheless, Beatty steamed into the Bight, disregarding the threat posed by U-boats and minefields, rescued Tyrwhitt's forces and sank three German light cruisers, *Köln*, *Ariadne* and *Mainz*. The remaining German ships scattered and returned to port. Though not resulting in a spectacular victory, Beatty's decisive intervention caught the public's imagination and reinforced the image of the Royal Navy as the dominant power at sea.

Heligoland, action off. Inconclusive action on 17 November 1917 between British and German forces. A British force consisting of two battlecruisers, eight light cruisers and destroyers, supported by six battleships, six battlecruisers and twenty destroyers, was sent into the Heligoland Bight to attack German heavy units covering the minesweepers engaged

in the perpetual task of maintaining the German minefields and clearing the British ones. The plan succeeded in the primary aim of surprising the minesweepers, but the British commander, Vice-Admiral T. W. D. Napier, failed to pursue his advantage. It was the last engagement between British and German capital ships during the First World War.

Hellcat. *See* F6F.

Helldiver. *See* SB2C.

HF/DF. High-frequency direction-finding, or 'Huff-Duff'. A way of locating a target by means of its radio transmissions. It was of particular use in locating German U-boats during the Battle of the Atlantic. The homing signals broadcast by U-boats and the frequent signals they were required to send to U-boat HQ made them particularly vulnerable to this form of detection. Equipment developed in Britain and Canada recorded and plotted the bearing of even the briefest radio signal. Should one or more ships in the convoy be fitted with HF/DF, it would be possible to triangulate and establish the position of the emitter. Using the equipment in service during the Second World War, if HF transmissions from a U-boat were detected, it meant that the U-boat was no more than 15 to 20 miles away and an escort, or aircraft (if the convoy had air cover), could be dispatched down the bearing. Even if the escort or aircraft failed to sink the submarine, by forcing her to dive and cease broadcast-

ing the enemy's homing transmission would be interrupted, possibly allowing the convoy to alter course and escape. The Germans consistently underestimated the effectiveness and role of HF/DF in U-boat sinkings.

H-Hour. Term used when planning amphibious operations to determine the time at which the landing will begin. All times can therefore calculated as H-3, H+2 etc. See also D-Day.

'Highball'. A 1,280lb bouncing bomb developed for use against the German battleship *Tirpitz*. The bomb would be dropped from a height of 60ft while the aircraft, a modified Mosquito, flew at 360mph. The bomb would bounce across the water before striking the ship's side. It would then sink to a depth of 30ft and explode alongside and beneath the target. No 618 Squadron was formed to deliver the weapon but disbanded in September 1943 when *Tirpitz* moved to northern Norway and thus out of range of the Mosquito. However, the unit was re-formed in 1944 with Fleet Air Arm pilots, embarked in escort carriers, and sent to the Far East to use the weapon against Japanese warships. The squadron thus became the first unit to operate twin-engine aircraft from an aircraft carrier. Although the weapons arrived in-theatre before the end of hostilities, they were never employed operationally, largely due to American resistance, and the squadron was disbanded and the bombs destroyed in June 1945.

High Seas Fleet (*Hochseeflotte*). Principal German fleet in the North Sea throughout the First World War. At the Battle of Jutland the High Seas Fleet consisted of sixteen dreadnought battleships, five battlecruisers, six pre-dreadnoughts, eleven light cruisers and sixty-one destroyers.

HMS. Prefix placed before the name of a British warship to indicate that she is Her (or His) Majesty's Ship. An equivalent used in the Imperial and Austro-Hungarian and Imperial German navies was SMS, *Seiner Majestät Schiff*.

Hong Kong. Former British possession in China and major naval base in the Far East. Under an agreement that was concluded in 1984 Hong Kong reverted to Chinese ownership on 31 July 1997.

***Hood*, HMS.** A British battlecruiser launched in 1918 which epitomised the strength and might of the Royal Navy in the inter-war period. Her reputation – 'The Mighty Hood' – was inflated by the press who equated size with fighting power and efficiency. However, by 1939 her public 'persona' hid a multitude of problems and defects which included nearly twenty-one years of active service without a major refit, mess decks which were insanitary and in places breeding grounds for TB bacilli and a machinery plant which was, literally, falling to pieces. There were so many coats of paint on the ship, required for a smart appearance, that her displacement began to be affected and the above-water torpedo-tube doors could not be opened because they were jammed with paint. Plans existed for the ship to be taken in hand for a major refit, but when war was declared in September 1939 she could not be spared from operational commitments. She served in the North Sea and in the Mediterranean, where she led the assault on the French fleet at Oran in July 1940. She was sunk on 24 May 1941 in action against the German battleship *Bismarck* in the Denmark Strait with the loss of all but three of her crew of 95 officers and 1,324 men. The cause of her sinking has been hotly debated and was the subject of two internal British inquiries, both of which failed to come to any definite conclusions. A considerable amount of contemporary research has been carried out into her loss and the following set of circumstances is advanced as the most likely cause of her sudden end. *Hood* was just turning to port to open her A-arcs when *Bismarck*'s fifth salvo landed alongside her port quarter. It has been suggested that one of the shells from this salvo penetrated *Hood*'s side beneath her armour belt and exploded in the area of the two after 15in magazines and a 4in AA magazine. Such a scenario is not as implausible as it sounds: when HMS *Prince of Wales* was docked after the *Bismarck* action an unexploded 15in shell from *Bismarck* was found lodged in her double bottom. It had struck the water and then gone through *Prince of Wales*' side beneath the armour belt and come to rest. The explosion of *Bismarck*'s shell is unlikely to have caused a sympathetic detonation of those magazines – shells are notoriously difficult to explode other than in the way for which they are designed. What the explosion would have done is to start a huge fire among the 115 tons of cordite stored in those magazines. This fire would have produced masses of gas. For a while this gas would have been contained within the magazine structure – hence the delay between the fall of *Bismarck*'s fifth salvo and the explosion which marked *Hood*'s end – but when the pressure became too great it would have taken the line of least resistance and burst forward into the engine room before rushing up through the exhaust vents located on the upper deck. The effect of this explosion of cordite gas on the ship would have been to cause a massive structural failure causing the ship to split in half. HMS *Hood* had a standard displacement of 42,670 tons, was 860ft long and had a main armament of eight 15in guns.

***Hornet*, USS.** An aircraft carrier of the *Yorktown* class completed in December 1940 with a complement of nearly 100 aircraft and a top speed of 32 knots. It was from her flight deck that the famous Doolittle Raid was launched. She was at the Battle of Midway and was sunk at the Battle of Santa Cruz by a combination of bombs and torpedoes.

Hospital ships. Ships which are either specifically built or taken up from trade for the purpose of receiving the wounded from either a land campaign where medical facilities on land are poor or from ships operating far away from the facilities of a base hospital. During the First and Second World Wars many luxury liners were requisitioned for this purpose. Under the Geneva Convention hospital ships enjoy immunity from attack provided they are correctly marked (painted white overall with a green stripe down the side punctuated by prominent red crosses), sail illuminated at night, contain no belligerent personnel (or stores) and have no communications facilities other than what are necessary for the safety of the ship and her patients. However, hospital ships were sunk during both world wars, with German U-boats being the main culprits. The worst such case was the sinking of the *Llandovery Castle*. After the Second World War the hospital ship enjoyed a surprising renaissance. The USN maintained three on station off the coast of Vietnam during the 1960s; it was reckoned that with helicopter casualty evacuation a wounded man could find himself on board a hospital ship less than an hour after being wounded. The USSR operated several hospital ships off the coast of Angola in the late 1970s for Cuban 'volunteers' wounded during the 'War of Liberation'. During the Falklands War the Royal Navy took up the liner *Uganda* (despite having a dedicated hospital ship in the shape of the Royal Yacht *Britannia*) for use as a hospital ship. Operating from her Red Cross 'box' off the Falkland Islands, she took care of British and Argentine wounded alike. Likewise the Argentine Navy declared two vessels, the icebreaker *Almirante Irizar* and the supply vessel *Bahia Buen Paraiso*, hospital ships. During the remarkable US Navy build-up in the 1980s concern was expressed about the lack of medical facilities to support an amphibious operation. Military Sealift Command bought two tankers in 1983 and converted their tank spaces into medical areas by the insertion of prefabricated compartments. *Mercy* and *Comfort*, as the ships are named, have twelve operating theatres, four X-ray rooms, 1,000 beds, an 80-bed intensive care unit, a specialist burns unit and a 50-bed triage area. Flight decks allow casualties to be flown on board, although both ships carry a large number of boats for more conventional embarkation. The ships are said to be among the most modern medical facilities in the United States.

HSK. *Handels-Stör-Kreuzer* (commerce disruption ship). German term used in the Second World War for commerce raiders. All merchant ships taken up from trade by the *Kriegsmarine* were allocated a simple number – *Schiff 1*, *Schiff 2* and so forth – for administrative purposes. Those selected for commerce-raiding operations retained their *Schiff* pendant numbers for security reasons but were also given an HSK designation and pendant number. The name of the ship was left to the discretion of the commanding officer, as was the nature of the disguises he adopted when on the high seas. HSK ships were given a concealed armament of 15cm guns, mine rails and aircraft for spotting duties. They also carried large supplies of paint, plating and canvas so as to be able to alter their appearance as quickly as possible. The ships may have been selected for their nondescript appearance but they were manned by the best sailors the *Kriegsmarine* could provide. HSK ships proved quite successful in the early years of the war but attempts to send out better-equipped ships after 1943 failed. Those HSK vessels which survived found other duties as depot, training or fighter-direction vessels.

Hunter-killer. Term used for USN escort carrier anti-submarine groups in the Battle of the Atlantic during the Second World War. Also used in Royal Navy parlance to describe a nuclear-powered fleet submarine.

Hurricane bow. An aircraft carrier bow with continuous plating from the flight deck to the waterline. It was first introduced in the British *Ark Royal* launched in 1937.

'Hurry', Operation. Aircraft ferry operation to Malta involving the carrier HMS *Argus* in July/August 1940.

'Husky', Operation. The invasion of Sicily in July 1943.

Hydrophones. Early form of underwater listening apparatus developed by the British during the First World War.

I-400. A class of Japanese submarine (three were built, *I-400, I-401* and *I-402*) which were the largest undersea craft in service during the Second World War. The *I-400*s had a displacement of 3,530/ 6,560 tons and could carry three Aichi M6A1 Seiran floatplanes. They were also armed with eight 21in bow tubes, one 5.5in gun and ten 25mm AA guns. They were designed to launch aircraft against New York and other US cities but this role was scaled down to attacks on the Panama Canal. A strike on the Panama Canal was planned with *I-400* and *I-401* launching six bombers between them but the war ended before it could be implemented. The submarines received the recall order at sea and after destroying their torpedoes and aircraft surrendered to US forces. All three boats were evaluated by the US Navy and then sunk.

'Iceberg', Operation. Capture of Okinawa and the surrounding islands in the Kerama Retto group and the neutralisation of Japanese air assets on Formosa, March/June 1945.

IFF. Radar device to indicate the presence of friendly ships or aircraft. Each plane or ship carries a transponder which when interrogated by a search radar triggers a response, indicating to the operator that the particular ship is friendly.

IJN. Imperial Japanese Navy. The designation was abolished in 1945, but given the almost relentless growth in size and capability of the 'Maritime Self-Defence Force' the possibility that it might be revived is by no means implausible.

Ikara. Anti-submarine missile developed in Australia which could drop a lightweight homing torpedo on a sonar contact at ranges of up to ten miles from the firing ship. It was fitted in Australian 'River' class frigates, in British *Leander* class frigate conversions and in HMS *Bristol*, the sole Type 82 class destroyer. Although it was an effective weapon, it was largely superseded by the helicopter which could perform other missions and could also deliver other ASW ordnance.

***Illustrious,* HMS.** British aircraft carrier launched in 1939. In November 1940 she launched the first carrier strike in history when her Swordfish aircraft attacked the Italian Fleet at Taranto. On 10 January 1941 she survived an intense dive-bombing attack from the *Luftwaffe* which put her out of action for 10½ months. She displaced 23,000 tons standard, was 673ft long (pp) and could carry thirty-three aircraft.

Immune zone. The range at which a ship's armour will protect her against both plunging shellfire and shellfire with a flat trajectory.

'Implement', Operation. British submarine campaign against shipping carrying iron ore from Spanish ports to France in May 1944. The campaign ceased when HMS *Sceptre* torpedoed a ship which was lying at a buoy in a Spanish harbour.

Inchon. Port on the west coast of Korea which was the scene for a brilliantly conceived landing by the US Marines in the Korean War. With the bulk of UN forces demoralised and pinned down by the North Koreans around the port of Pusan, General MacArthur planned a landing in the rear of the North Korean Army which would cut their forces in two and force them to retreat. If ever a port were totally unsuitable for an amphibious landing, that port was Inchon. Every hazard to a landing force, both man made and natural, existed here. Yet on 15 September 1950 the US 1st Marine Division stormed ashore and within days had advanced to liberate Seoul, capital of South Korea.

***Indefatigable,* HMS.** British battlecruiser launched in 1909. She was sunk on 31 May 1916 at the Battle of Jutland by gunfire from the German battlecruiser *Von der Tann*. There were only two survivors from her ship's company of over 1,000. The name was subsequently borne by an aircraft carrier launched in 1942 and broken up in 1956.

***Independence,* USS** (CVL22). Lead ship for a class of nine small or light aircraft carriers, built on the hulls of *Cleveland* class cruisers, which along with the larger *Essex* class formed the core of US carrier task forces in the Pacific. They had distinctive appearance with their flight decks ending some 40ft short of their bows and a small island structure with four stubby funnels angled outboard. They carried forty aircraft, F6F Hellcat fighters and TBF/TBM Avenger bombers. They had a standard displacement of 11,000 tons and were 622½ft long; they had a top speed of 31.6kts. They served in all the major carrier battles of the Pacific War and one of their number, *Princeton* (CVL23), was the only US carrier sunk after the Battle of Midway.

***Indianapolis,* USS** (CA35). The last major US warship sunk in the Second World War. She was torpedoed on 30 July 1945 by the Japanese submarine *I-58* (Lt-Cdr Mochitsura Hashimoto IJN) after delivering components for the atomic bomb to the US base on Tinian. She was struck by two torpedoes and sank within two minutes without being able to send a distress call. Communications errors meant that her absence was not noted, and it was not until 2 August that her survivors were sighted by a Catalina on routine patrol. Only 318 of her crew of 1,199 officers and men were saved; many had survived the sinking of the ship but had been eaten by sharks while awaiting rescue. See also McVay, Charles B., in the Personalities section.

Indonesian Confrontation (1964–66). Following the creation of the state of Malaysia, the Indonesian Government of General Soekarno began a series of landing operations to destabilise the new

regime. The Royal Navy, with growing support from the new Malaysian forces, operated to safeguard the new regime. The Royal Navy's objectives were twofold: first, by use of the striking power of the fleet carriers (never used but frequently threatened), to deter the Indonesian regime from further aggression; and secondly to provide active support at all levels ranging from disembarked helicopter squadrons, which operated in the jungle to great effect, to patrols in coastal waters and the Malacca Strait to prevent Indonesian landings. The campaign was a considerable success and resulted in the internal overthrow of the Soekarno regime.

Indo-Pakistan Wars. Following the partition of British India in August 1947, the two independent states of India and Pakistan have been uneasy neighbours. There have been a series of border disputes, of which three have been large or serious enough to warrant the description of a war. The first, in November 1947 was over Kashmir and was settled in January 1949. In April 1965 fighting in the disputed Rann of Kutch led to a second all-out war which lasted 22 days before the UN arranged a ceasefire. The third war, or 'Lightning War', was in December 1971 over the demands of East Pakistan to declare an independent republic. It lasted thirteen days before Pakistan capitulated. In terms of naval operations, the 1971 conflict was the only one in which naval operations played an important role. An Indian task

force centred on the carrier *Vikrant* blockaded East Pakistan and prevented reinforcements and supplies reaching the country by sea. Four Pakistani missile boats and a large number of smaller craft were all sunk by the Indian Navy on the first day of the fighting. Indian Navy 'advisers' trained Kukhti Bahini guerrillas to plant limpet mines on bridges and Pakistani river craft. The Indian Western Fleet also demonstrated its superiority over the Pakistani main force. The Pakistani submarine *Ghazi* was sunk on 4 December 1971 as she lurked outside the Indian naval base of Visakhaptnam while the next day Indian naval forces sank the destroyer *Karachi* and a mine sweeper before bombarding the naval base. The elimination of Pakistani naval forces from the Bay of Bengal allowed India to concentrate on becoming a regional power in her own right in the Indian Ocean.

Industrial-Military Complex. Phenomenon identified by President Eisenhower whereby close collaboration between defence contractors and the military results in defence procurement programmes regardless of whether an impartial assessor would judge the expenditure to be in the national interest. In the naval world the most interesting manifestation of this phenomenon would be in 1910 when the CinC of the Austro-Hungarian Navy, Admiral Montecuccoli, under pressure from the STT shipyard at Trieste (who wanted the work), ordered the hulls of the first two

Austrian dreadnoughts on his own authority without having sought political approval.

'Infatuate', Operation. Capture of the island of Walcheren prior to clearing the River Scheldt and opening of the port of Antwerp in November 1944. 'Infatuate I' was a secondary landing on Flushing and 'Infatuate II' a landing on Westkapelle.

Infra-red (IR). The portion of the electro-magnetic spectrum between the wavelengths of 1.5 and 14 microns. It can be used for surveillance, target-acquisition, tracking and weapon guidance and communications. Surveillance requires either active or passive IR. Active IR requires a source to illuminate the target and a viewer to look at it. Passive IR simply converts received IR emissions to images. The most common type of weapon guidance is a passive IR homer fitted to a missile head. IR systems are degraded by bad weather, clouds and fog. They are equally vulnerable to IR countermeasures (IRCM).

Inshore Patrol Flotilla. Innocuous sounding cover name for a Royal Navy unit which, during the Second World War, was responsible for running a clandestine transport service between its British base on the Helford River in Cornwall and occupied France. Captured French fishing vessels were the usual means of conveyance, although MGBs were also used. The Flotilla operated under Admiralty control although its clients were SOE (Special Op-

erations Executive) and MI6 (the Secret Intelligence Service of the Foreign Office)

Intelligence ships. The growing use of electronic systems for communications and surveillance and the reliance on naval forces to serve as part of the strategic balance led to the development of an entirely new category of naval auxiliary in the post-1945 period – the intelligence ship. Both the United States and the Soviet Union (particularly the latter) invested heavily in a fleet of dedicated intelligence ships. The first Soviet intelligence ships (AGI) began to appear off the eastern coast of the USA in the late 1950s. Although they were converted deep-sea trawlers they were easily recognisable by the forest of antennae which they sprouted. The first purpose-built AGIs to appear were the seven 500-ton *Lentra* class, followed by the fifteen 700-ton *Okean* class. In the 1970s six 3,500-ton *Primorye* class vessels were built, which had the facility to process the intelligence they collected. They were followed by the three *Balzam* class ships, which represent the last word in shipborne intelligence-gathering. At the height of the Cold War Soviet AGIs were a ubiquitous feature lurking outside every major port, particularly carrier and SSBN facilities, and trailing along behind carrier battle groups. The US Navy used former destroyers and converted cargo craft. However, after the attack on the *Liberty* and the seizure of the *Pueblo*, the US Navy has fitted

warships and submarines with temporary intelligence-gathering cells.

Invincible, HMS. A British battle-cruiser launched in 1907. *Invincible* displaced 17,373 tons, was 567ft long and was armed with eight 12in guns. She participated at the Battle of the Falkland Islands but was sunk two years later at the Battle of Jutland. Under fire from the German battlecruisers *Lützow* and *Derfflinger*, she was struck on 'Q' turret. The explosion ignited charges stored in the turret and the ammunition trunk and the ship was blown in half. For a while her bow and stern remained above the water. All but three of her crew were lost.

Iowa, USS (BB61). Name-ship of the last class of battleships built for the US Navy and the largest battleships built for any navy other than the two Japanese super-battleships *Musashi* and *Yamato*. The four ships of the class were *Iowa* (BB61), *New Jersey* (BB62), *Missouri* (BB63) and *Wisconsin* BB64). Another two ships were cancelled at the end of the Second World War. As completed the ships were armed with nine 16in guns, twenty 5in guns and over 100 40mm and 20mm close-range AA weapons. They had a standard displacement of 45,000 tons, were 887ft long and had a top speed of 33kts. Wartime complement was 2,900 officers and men. All four ships served in the Pacific. However, *Iowa* was selected to take President Roosevelt and the Chiefs of Staff to North Africa in

Above: The *Iowa* class battleship *Wisconsin* (BB64) firing her main armament during fire support operations during the Gulf War in early 1991. (IWM GLF 1016)

November 1943 for the Casablanca Conference. During the voyage her career was nearly ended prematurely when an armed torpedo was 'accidentally' fired at her by an escorting destroyer during an exercise. The torpedo exploded in *Iowa*'s wake with no damage other than to the destroyer CO's career. In the Pacific the battleships were used to provide AA firepower for the fast carrier groups. On the one occasion they were tasked to engage Japanese capital ships, during the Battle of Leyte Gulf on 25 October 1944, the Japanese ships turned back before contact was made. At the end of the war *Missouri* was chosen as the setting for the signing of the Japanese surrender. Post-war *Missouri* was retained in the training role while the other three were mothballed. The Korean War (1950–53) saw all four reactivated, while *New Jersey* was reactivated for shore bombardment duty during the Vietnam War in 1968. In the build-up of US forces sanctioned by the Reagan presidency all four were reactivated. Their secondary battery was reduced to twelve 5in and supplemented with thirty-two Tomahawk and sixteen Harpoon missiles, while their radar and EW suites were upgraded. *Missouri* and *Wisconsin* served in the 1991 Gulf War. On 31 January 1995 all four ships were stricken and their futures are uncertain. Plans exist to offer them as museum ships (in 1997 it was announced that *Missouri* would be preserved at Pearl Harbor), while a small but determined lobby in the US Congress is advocating their reactivation.

Iran Ajr. Iranian ro-ro LST built in Japan in 1978. In September 1987 she was captured by the US Navy in the Persian Gulf and found to be loaded with contact mines ready for laying. She was scuttled on 26 September, together with her cargo.

Iran–Iraq War. One of longest and costliest wars this century. It began with an Iraqi invasion in 1980 and lasted until 1988 when an armistice was signed. At the time of writing a formal peace treaty has yet to be signed. From a maritime view there is little reliable information on naval operations except Iraqi claims to have sunk two Iranian landing craft and a fast attack craft in 1980 and two frigates in 1982. At the same time Iran claimed to have destroyed at least fifteen minor Iraqi war vessels. However, the importance of the Persian Gulf and Straits of Hormuz as an export route for oil going to the West brought other nations, principally the United States, into the conflict. The maverick Iranian Government began indiscriminate minelaying in the Gulf. In September 1987 Iranian denials that they had been minelaying were blown away when the LST *Iran Ajr* was captured by the US Navy loaded with contact mines ready for laying. The Iranian use of oil platforms in the southern Persian Gulf as bases from which to harass tanker traffic finally provoked the US Navy into action. In April 1988 US air and naval forces struck, sinking the frigate *Sahand* and fast attack craft *Joshan* on 19 April 1988 and damaging *Sabalan*.

Ironbottom Sound. American term for the passage between Guadalcanal and Florida Island in the Solomons group. As many as forty-eight American, Australian and Japanese warships lie there, sunk between August 1942 and early 1943. The scene was recently investigated by the American underwater archaeologist Dr J. Ballard, who brought American, Australian and Japanese veterans together and filmed the wrecks of their ships.

'Ironclad', Operation. Capture of the island of Diego Suarez, Madagascar, March–May 1942.

Iron Duke, HMS. British battleship launched in 1912, one of a class of four. She displaced 25,000 tons, was 622ft long and was armed with ten 13.5in guns. She was the flagship of the Grand Fleet at the Battle of Jutland. She survived the purge of Britain's capital ships in the inter-war period, having been converted to a boys' training ship, and served throughout the Second World War as a depot ship at Scapa Flow. She was broken up in 1946 at Faslane. The name is currently borne by a Type 23 frigate launched in 1991.

Italo-Turkish War. War fought between Italy and Turkey in 1911–12 for Turkey's possessions in North Africa. The Italian Navy achieved complete domination over the Turks in actions fought at Prevesa (29–30 September 1911), Santa Maura and along the Syrian coast. In North Africa Tobruk was taken on 4 October 1911 and Tripoli the day after. On 16 April

1912 the Italian Fleet massed at the entrance to the Dardanelles. On 5 November the Italian Government announced the annexation of Tripolitania, Libya and Cyrenaica.

Iwo Jima. Pacific island lying 600 miles from Japan and the scene of one of the costliest amphibious operations of the war. The capture of the island was required as it was an ideal location for an airfield for B-29 bombers requiring emergency landing; the island would also serve as an advanced base for P-47 and P-51 fighters which could cover the bombers all the way to Tokyo if based on Iwo Jima. Air bombardment prior to the landings lasted for seventy-four consecutive days – the longest pre-invasion bombardment of the war. UDT teams surveying the beaches suffered 170 casualties. The Marines of the 4th and 5th Divisions went ashore on 19 February 1945 but it was not until 16 March that the island was declared secure. The Japanese resistance was intense and formidable: 6,821 US Marines gave their lives on Iwo Jima and twenty-seven Medals of Honor were awarded – more than for any other single operation of the war. 'Uncommon valour was a common virtue,' was Admiral Nimitz's verdict on the campaign. The sacrifice was not in vain. B-29 bombers made 2,400 emergency landings on Iwo Jima with their crews, totalling more than 24,000 men. The taking of Iwo Jima, which had been so costly, undoubtedly saved many more

lives. The battle is chiefly remembered for the photograph by Joseph Rosenthal showing the raising of the Stars and Stripes on Mount Suribachi on 23 February 1945 by US Marines and Navy Corpsmen. The photograph is one of the great images of the Second World War and formed the basis for the US Marine Corps memorial in Washington.

Jane's Fighting Ships. An international yearbook listing and commenting on the strengths and weaknesses of the world's navies. It should be used with caution since, being a contemporary publication, it is subject to the dictates of security and to the inflated claims made by governments and defence contractors alike about the performance of their products.

Japan Sea, Battle of the. Engagement on 14 August 1904 between the Russian Vladivostok Squadron, consisting of the armoured cruisers *Rossiya*, *Gromoboi* and *Rurik*, and Japanese warships during the Russo-Japanese War. The Russians were seeking to join with the Port Arthur Squadron and were unaware that the latter had been destroyed in the Battle of the Yellow Sea two days earlier. On 14 August, north-east of Tsushima, they encountered a force of four Japanese cruisers under Admiral Kamimura. Early the action *Rurik*'s steering gear broke down and she was repeatedly hit. Kamimura's ships concentrated on finishing her off, thus allowing *Rossiya* and *Gromoboi* to escape.

Java Sea, Battle of the. The last obstacle facing a Japanese invasion of Java was the ramshackle American, Australian. British and Dutch naval squadron based at Surabaya under the command of Rear-Admiral Karel Doorman. This consisted of two Dutch cruisers *Java* and *De Ruyter*, the Australian cruiser *Perth*, the British cruiser *Exeter* and the USS *Houston*. The force also possessed nine destroyers (two Dutch, three British and four American) but no air cover. On 27 February 1942 Doorman sailed to intercept a Japanese force reported northwest of Surabaya and throughout the next seven hours there was a series of savage engagements. The destroyers *Kortenaer* and HMS *Electra* were torpedoed and sunk and the cruiser *Exeter*, damaged, had to withdraw. Doorman broke off, hoping to run around the rear of the Japanese formation, but in doing so ran into one of his own minefields and lost the destroyer HMS *Jupiter*. Undaunted, Doorman attacked the Japanese fleet for a second time and in a fierce night action both Dutch cruisers were sunk with the loss of Doorman and many of their ships' companies. Only the USS *Houston* and HMAS *Perth* escaped. They arrived at Batavia in the early hours of 28 February but sailed again that afternoon for the Sunda Strait, acting on reports that a large Japanese landing force was in the area. They sank four Japanese transports but were overwhelmed that night by a superior Japanese force and were sunk. Meanwhile the damaged *Exeter* and two destroy-

Above: The last moments of HMS *Exeter* (left) during the Battle of the Java Sea, 27 February 1942. (Author).

ers were trying to escape through the Sunda Strait. On the morning of 1 March the ships were discovered by Japanese aircraft, bombed and sunk.

Jervis Bay, HMS. Armed merchant cruiser sunk by the German pocket battleship *Admiral Scheer* on 5 November 1940 while protecting convoy HX.84. Her commanding officer, Captain Fogarty Fegen (posthumously awarded the VC) deliberately sacrificed his ship in order that the convoy might have time to scatter.

Jikitanchiki. Japanese term for airborne MAD equipment.

Jeune École. French school of naval thought which advocated commerce warfare against the British rather than France building

a comparative fleet of capital ships. So great was the debate aroused by the *Jeune École* that French naval policy was in turmoil for the last twenty years of the nineteenth century, which resulted in the French Navy entering the twentieth century with a motley collection of ships contemptuously dubbed 'a fleet of samples'.

'Jubilee', Operation. Raid on the French port of Dieppe in August 1942.

Jutland, Battle of. The Battle of Jutland was the long-awaited clash between the British Grand Fleet and the German High Seas Fleet. For various reasons neither side won the outright victory they had been hoping for. In May 1916 Admiral Reinhard Scheer, Commander-in-Chief of the Ger-

man High Seas Fleet, sought to whittle down the superiority of the British Grand Fleet by using a portion of his fleet, in this case the five battlecruisers comprising the 1st Scouting Group under the command of Vice-Admiral Franz Hipper, as a bait to lure the Grand Fleet out of harbour. Scheer then hoped that U-boats would be able to sink a number of the British battleships and that the High Seas Fleet would be able to detach and destroy a portion of the Grand Fleet, particularly Vice-Admiral Sir David Beatty's battlecruisers. The High Seas Fleet sailed from the Jade and Elbe estuaries in the small hours of 31 May. Hipper's battlecruisers were to proceed north up the Skagerrak, while the main body of the High Seas Fleet gave cover off the Jutland coast. The British

Admiralty were aware that an operation by the High Seas Fleet was in the offing through interception of their radio traffic and as a precaution the Grand Fleet (Admiral Sir John Jellicoe, q.v.) and the Battle Cruiser Fleet (Vice Admiral Sir David Beatty, q.v.) were ordered to sea on the evening of 30 May. Neither side realised the full extent of the opposing commitment, with the result that by midday on 31 May 1916 the fleets were approaching each other at right angles entirely ignorant of each other's presence. The sea was calm. The visibility, quite good in the beginning, deteriorated as the afternoon wore on. A combination of mist, funnel and cordite smoke reduced visibility to a maximum of seven miles and at times to less than half that distance. A small Danish steamer, the *N. J. Fjord*, provided the point of contact between the two fleets. British destroyers sighted her blowing off steam as she stopped to be inspected by German destroyers. As the British ships closed, they sighted Hipper's battlecruisers and the action began. The first phase of the action was characterised by the Germans heading south-east to lure the British towards the main body of the High Seas Fleet. German gunnery and fire control was excellent and the Germans had the added advantage of the light. British fire control and gunnery was less impressive. Two British battlecruisers, HMS *Indefatigable* and HMS *Queen Mary* were sunk. This phase came to an end when Beatty's ships sighted the main

body of the High Seas Fleet at 1633. The roles were now reversed, with the British battlecruisers leading the German fleet north to the main body of the British Grand Fleet. Contact was made at 1756. The engagement between the two fleets was inconclusive. Twice Jellicoe managed to 'cross the T' of the German fleet yet on each occasion Scheer extricated his fleet by skilled manoeuvering. Neither commander seemed prepared to close the range and risk a torpedo attack from the opposing side's destroyers. The fleet action ended at 1922 when Jellicoe turned away from the German fleet to avoid a torpedo attack. In the night action the German fleet, heading back to the Jade and the Ems estuaries, slipped round the rear of the Grand Fleet which was heading south to cut the Germans off. There was a series of short and intense engagements in which superior German training in recognition, signalling and night fighting paid off. Moreover, failures in British signalling procedures ensured that Jellicoe was never informed of the situation, with the result that the High Seas Fleet slipped away. The Grand Fleet and Battle Cruiser Fleet returned to their bases at Scapa Flow and Rosyth respectively. They arrived on 2 June and at 21.45 Jellicoe reported that the Grand Fleet and Battle Cruiser Fleet were ready at four hours' notice for sea. The High Seas Fleet, however, would not be ready for sea until mid-August. Churchill's verdict that 'the High Seas Fleet has assaulted its jailer

but remains in jail' is still the most accurate summary of the battle. Despite inflicting greater losses on the British than it suffered, the High Seas Fleet did not venture forth again to seek a decisive engagement with the Royal Navy.

Jutland Controversy. Controversy which divided the Royal Navy in the inter-war period concerning the relative merits of Jellicoe and Beatty as commanders at Jutland. Though the commanders did not get involved themselves, both had their partisans and versions of the battle appeared in print which favoured each side. The controversy was adjudged so great that it was decided not to name two battleships of the *King George V* class *Jellicoe* and *Beatty* for fear of rekindling the passions.

'JV', Operation. Attack on shipping in Boulogne harbour in April 1942 using divers equipped with limpet mines.

'K' class submarines. British steam-driven submarines designed for service with the fleet as an advance scouting screen. One observer commented that they resembled the result of 'an unholy union between a destroyer and submarine' and they acquired an unenviable reputation for accidents. Of the eighteen boats in the class, eight suffered disasters and there were sixteen major accidents and an untold number of minor incidents. They were the largest submarines built for the Royal Navy to date and displaced 1,980/ 2,566 tons, were 338ft long

Above: The British steam driven-submarine *K.15*. The design was ahead of its time and the *Ks* had a terrible record for accidents.
(Author)

and were armed with ten tubes. It was their propulsion plant which made them unique – Brown Curtis or Parsons steam turbines for surface power and electric motors for submerged drive. A top speed of 24kts could be achieved on the surface. Their construction represented an immense technological achievement for British industry.

Kairyu (Sea Dragon). Japanese two-man midget submarine order-ed in quantity (750+ units) at the end of the Second World War. They were a suicide weapon – the only Japanese midget submarines so designed – and were armed with two 457mm torpedoes or one 600kg explosive charge. *Kairyu*s displaced 18.94/18.97 tons, were 17.2m long and had a top speed of 7.5kts on the surface and 10kts submerged. Only 212 had been delivered at the end of the war and none was used operationally.

A three-man version, fitted with a periscope, was also developed for training purposes.

Kaiser Wilhelm der Grosse, SMS. German 14,349-ton liner owned by Norddeutscher Lloyd and which won the Blue Riband on her maiden voyage in 1897. At the beginning of the First World War she was employed as a commerce-raider but she was never very successful. Her career was

his craft via a watertight tunnel. When released by the parent submarine, he would start the engine and simply head for the target at top speed, running awash on the surface. In theory *Kaiten* operators were provided with the means to leave the craft before the final impact (although the explosion of the 1,500kg warhead would have probably killed them), but in practice all rode the craft to oblivion. They were unsuccessful operationally since their high speed of 30kts+ made them very difficult to control and their large wake made them easy to spot. Their total successes amounted to a fleet oiler and a destroyer sunk; in return, approximately fifty *Kaiten* had been expended and eight of the parent submarines sunk with the loss of 900 lives. A later version was developed powered by a hydrogen peroxide engine giving a top speed in excess of 40kts, but only a couple of these craft were built.

Kamikaze. Organised Japanese naval suicide attacks using aircraft, human torpedoes and explosive motor boats and named after the typhoon which scattered the Mongol invasion fleets in 1274 and 1281. Although suicide had long held an honoured place in the Japanese (and Western) military tradition, organised suicide attacks using aircraft packed with explosive or petrol against US warships began on 25 October 1944 during the Battle of Leyte Gulf. The Japanese believed that such desperate tactics could reverse the tide of the

dominated by an insatiable appetite for coal and she only sank two ships and a trawler. On 26 August 1914 she was caught coaling in Spanish territorial waters at Rio de Oro by the cruiser HMS *Highflyer*. The British ship disregarded Spanish neutrality and inflicted such damage that *Kaiser Wilhelm der Grosse* was scuttled. The British Government apologised but the damage was done.

Kaiten (Heaven Shaker). Japanese one-man human torpedo based on the successful Type 93 Long Lance torpedo. *Kaiten* had a displacement of 8.2 tons, were 14.75m long and were armed with a charge of 1,550kg. They were carried by larger submarines and launched in the target area. On sighting a target the submarine's commander would give the target data to the *Kaiten* operator, who would then board

Above: A remarkable photograph showing the final moments of a Japanese *Kamikaze* attack on an American battleship in 1944. (USN)

war. The first *Kamikaze* attacks were flown when twenty-four volunteer pilots of the Japanese Navy's 201st Air Group flying A6M Zero fighters attacked a group of US escort carriers. Lt Yukio Seki smashed into the USS *St Lo*, which erupted in explosions and sank in an hour. During the battles for the Philippines, Iwo Jima and Okinawa the Japanese dispatched 2,257 aircraft in organised suicide attacks. Of these, 936 returned to base, leaving a net expenditure of 1,321 aircraft. In return these aircraft sank twenty-six warships and damaged 300 others. British and American casualties amounted to 3,000 dead and twice that number wounded. The Japanese also developed other suicide weapons including the *Baka* bomb, the *Kaiten* human torpedo and the *Shinyo* explosive motor boat.

'Kennecott', Operation. Escorts for Operation 'Torch' convoys sailing from the UK to North Africa.

'Keyhole', Operation. Operation launched by the Royal Navy in June 1982 to recover the island of Southern Thule after the Falklands War.

'Kingdom', Operation. Seizure by the Royal Navy of French ships interned at Alexandria following the fall of France in June 1940. Unlike events in Britain and at Oran, the French squadron at Alexandria was dealt with carefully and tactfully and there were no casualties. The name was also

Above: The scene of the flight deck of the British aircraft carrier HMS *Formidable* on 9 May 1945 after a *Kamikaze* attack off the Sakashima Gunto during the Okinawa campaign. The British carrier's armoured flight deck saved her from more serious damage.

used for the safe return of HRH Prince Haakon, Crown Prince of Norway, and his staff to Oslo in May 1945.

King George V classes. Two classes of British battleship. The first class of four ships was completed during 1912-13, their main armament being ten 13.5in guns and their top speed – 21-22 knots. HMS *Audacious* was sunk by mine off Lough Swilly in 1914. The other three ships of the class saw action at the Battle of Jutland.

HMSs *King George V* and *Ajax* were sold for scrap in 1926. and *Centurion* was expended as a block ship during the Normandy landings.

The second class of five ships, HMSs *King George V, Prince of Wales, Duke of York, Anson* and *Howe,* was completed during 1940-42. Their main armament was ten 14in guns and their top speed was 29 knots. HMSs *Prince of Wales* and *King George V* both saw action with the *Bismarck* during her sortie, *King George V* being

involved in the German ship's sinking; *Duke of York* was crucial to the sinking of the *Scharnhorst.* HMS *Prince of Wales* was sunk by bombs and torpedoes from Japanese aircraft off the coast of Malaya in December 1941. The four remaining ships were sold for scrap 1957–58.

Kocatepe. A US *Gearing* class destroyer launched in 1945 as the USS *Harwood* and transferred to Turkey in December 1971. On 22 July 1971 she was sunk in error by the Turkish Air force during the invasion of Cyprus when pilots mistook the ship for a similar *Gearing* class destroyer in the Greek Navy (Greece had seven of the same type of ship in commission at the time).

Koh-Chang, Battle of. Engagement between French and Siamese forces. In November 1940 the Siamese Government sought to take advantage of French weakness by invading French Indo-China. However, French naval forces in the area were more than a match for the Siamese Navy and in a brief night engagement on 16/17 January 1941 the Siamese coast defence ships *Sri Ayuthia* and *Dhonburi* and three torpedo boats were sunk by the French cruiser *Lamotte Piquet*.

Ko-Hyoteki. Japanese two-man midget submarine. Developed before the Second World War and designed to be used before the decisive engagement between the Japanese and American battle fleets, these craft were to be launched from special transports and were intended to whittle down the strength of the enemy fleet before the action and deal with the cripples afterwards. The Japanese decision to launch a surprise air attack on Pearl Harbor removed their *raison d'être* but Admiral Yamamoto was persuaded to allow them to be used in the harbour penetration role – a role for which they were not suited and for which their crews were not trained. Of the twenty built, five were lost at Pearl Harbor, three at Diego Suarez on 30 May 1942,

four at Sydney on 31 May 1942, eight off Guadalcanal in 1942 and three in the Aleutians. The *Ko-Hyoteki* was a technically very sophisticated craft. The Type A variant displaced 46 tons submerged, was 23.9m long, had a 600hp electric motor giving a top speed of 23kts on the surface and 19kts dived and was armed with two 457mm torpedoes. Larger and more sophisticated variants were built, one Type B and fifteen Type C. Eight were lost off the Philippines, the remainder being broken up after the war. Their biggest success was the torpedoing of the British battleship *Ramillies* at Diego Suarez on 30 May 1942.

Kolombangara, Battle of. An American task force consisting of the cruisers *Honolulu* and *St Louis* and the New Zealand cruiser *Leander* attempted to stop a Japanese force of four destroyer-transports covered by the cruiser *Jintsu* and four destroyers from landing reinforcements on Kolombangara island in the Solomons. The forces met in the early hours of 13 July 1943 off the northern tip of the island, and although *Jintsu* sank with great loss of life (483 dead) the three Allied cruisers were all torpedoed and the destroyer *Gwin* sunk. It was a tactical victory for the Japanese, won through their use of the impressive Long Lance torpedo, but they failed in their primary objective of landing troops on the island.

Komandorski Islands, Battle of. This was an unusual battle in the Pacific campaign in that neither

aircraft nor submarines were employed. A force of four Japanese cruisers and four destroyers under Admiral Hosogaya was escorting two large troopships to the Aleutians on 26 March 1943 and was attacked by a US squadron consisting of the cruisers *Salt Lake City* and *Richmond* and four destroyers. Despite its numerical inferiority, the American force pressed home its attack with such determination (even though at one stage the *Salt Lake City* was lying dead in the water through damage) that Hosogaya turned away and the Japanese made no more attempts to reinforce the Aleutians by sea.

Komet. German HSK ship of the Second World War. Commissioned in June 1940, *Komet* was the smallest but best equipped of all the HSK ships. She broke through into the Bering Strait via the Arctic (with a good deal of Sovet assistance) and then sank ten ships totalling 21,378grt before she returned to Norway in July 1940. In October 1942 she attempted a break-out into the Atlantic via the English Channel but was sunk on 14 October 1942 by *MTB236* with the loss of all her crew of 269 officers and men. *Komet* had a standard displacement of 7,500 tons and was armed with six 15cm, one 60mm, two 37mm and four 20mm guns. She carried two pairs of 21in torpedo tubes, two Ar 196A-1 aircraft and a small *Schnellboot* named, appropriately, *Meteorit* by her crew.

Komsomolets. Soviet submarine of the Project 685 *Plavnik* class

(NATO designation 'Mike'), built with a titanium hull to test new technologies. She was sunk on 7 April 1989 off the Norwegian coast after a fire erupted in a machinery space and went out of control. *Komsomolets* was able to surface and the fire was fought for several hours before the submarine began flooding and sank. Of sixty-nine men on board, four apparently died in the fire and four in the ejected rescue chamber because of toxic gases and other problems, and another thirty-four died in the water from hypothermia, heart failure or drowning; one man survived the ascent in the escape chamber (of five who were inside when the submarine exceeded her operating depth). *Komsomolets* carried ten torpedoes at the time of her loss, two of which had nuclear warheads. The Russian Government has sought foreign funding to salvage the submarine. However, it is questionable whether the Norwegian Government would allow salvage to proceed, fearing a radiation threat if a lift were attempted.

Koryu (Scaly Dragon). Japanese five-man midget submarine designed at the end of the Second World War. It was not a suicide weapon like the *Kaiten*. *Koryu* craft displaced 58.4 tons submerged and were 26.2m long. They had a speed of 8/16kts and were armed with two 457mm torpedoes. They were intended for use against the US invasion fleets, but of the 540 units ordered only 115 were built and none saw action.

KuK Kriegsmarine. The formal title of the Austro-Hungarian Navy, translated as Imperial and Royal Navy. It refers to the divided nature of the Austrian monarchy whereby the monarch was Emperor of Austria but King of Hungary. Unlike the Austrian Army, where national groups were organised into individual battalions, the Navy was a microcosm of the Empire. In a single ship the crew could be made up of over a dozen ethnic groups each speaking their own language. To resolve the formidable problem in Austrian ships, all ratings had to be able to understand orders given in German, which was the command language, but officers had to be able to speak German, Croat (the language of the largest ethnic group) and one other language. So long as Emperor Franz Josef reigned the system worked, held together by the Emperor's personality. However, on his death in November 1916 the Navy could not manage to contain the nationalist pressures building up in the Empire.

Kula Gulf, Battle of. A Japanese attempt to reinforce their garrison on the island of Kolombangara on 6 July 1943 using seven destroyer transports screened by three destroyers. The Japanese force was intercepted by the cruisers *Helena, Honolulu* and *St Louis* and four destroyers. The Japanese destroyer *Niizuke* was overwhelmed by gunfire but the other Japanese ships delivered a volley of Long Lance torpedoes which struck and sank *Helena*. A second Japanese destroyer, *Nagatsuki*,

went aground on Kolombangara island, could not be refloated and was destroyed by US aircraft the next day.

Kuril Islands. Island chain north of the Japanese home islands. The islands, together with the southern half of Sakhalin, had been ceded to Japan after the 1904-05 Russo-Japanese War. In late November 1941 the Japanese task force for the attack on Pearl Harbor assembled in Hittokapu Bay off the Kuril island of Etorofu. After the Second World War the islands, together with Sakhalin, were taken by the Soviet Union. Japan still lays claim to the islands and they are, therefore, a source of potential conflict as the military capacity of Russia declines while that of Japan continues to grow.

Kwajalein. A large atoll in the Marshall Islands group, selected for invasion in the next step of the US Central Pacific Campaign after the capture of the Gilbert Islands. Weeks of bombing by US carrier-borne aircraft culminated in landings by US Marines and the US Army's 7th Division on 31 January/1 February 1944. The Japanese fought savagely and over 8,400 of the 10,000 defenders were killed before the Americans declared the islands secure.

Laconia. One of the most controversial events in the Battle of the Atlantic. The 19,659-ton *Laconia* was sunk by *U156* (*Korvettenkapitän* Werner Hartenstein) on 12 September 1942 in the South Atlantic. At the time of her loss she was carrying 2,228 passengers and crew, including eighty women and children and 1,800 Italian PoWs. When Hartenstein found the sea full of Italians he sent out distress calls *en clair* asking for assistance (these signals were received at Freetown but considered to be a trap) and began rescuing people from the water and taking the lifeboats and rafts in tow. He was joined by *U506* and *U507* and the Italian submarine *Cappellini* but on 16 September *U156* (which was wearing a large red cross on her forward casing) was attacked by a B-24 Liberator of the 343rd Bombardment Squadron flying from Ascension. Hartenstein had no choice but to put the survivors back in the water, cast off the lifeboats and dive. Eventually Vichy French warships from Dakar rescued over 1,000 of the crew and passengers.

Laconia Order. Signal sent by Dönitz on 17 September 1942 following the attack on *U157*. In it he stated that 'Rescue contradicts the most fundamental demands of war for the annihilation of enemy ships and crews.' This seemed to advocate the deliberate killing of survivors in the water, and many U-boat commanders were unclear as to the meaning of this passage. At the Nuremberg trials the Laconia Order was used to indict Dönitz with war crimes and might well have sent him to the gallows were it not for an affidavit from Fleet Admiral Chester Nimitz that US submarines had followed the same policy throughout the war.

Lagosta. Island in the Adriatic which the Italians planned to occupy in July 1915 following the capture of Pelgosa. However, because of operations by Austrian and German submarines, in particular their sinking of the cruisers *Amalfi* on 7 July and *Garibaldi* on 18 July, the Italian command decided that the undertaking was too risky and had to be postponed. Their indecision, particularly so soon after the capture of Pelagosa, caused Captain Herbert Richmond, the British liaison officer to the Italian Fleet, to comment that 'These people had better sell their fleet and take up their organs and monkeys again for, by heaven, that seems more their profession than sea fighting!'

LAMPS. Light Airborne Multi-Purpose System. US designation for a shipborne helicopter used for ASW and ASuW over-the-horizon targeting. LAMPS-1 was the Kaman SH-2F Seasprite while LAMPS-2 is the Sikorsky SH-60B Seahawk.

Landing barge. Barge either taken up from trade or purpose-built to support amphibious operations during the Second World War. The principal variations of landing barges and their code designations were:

Code	Description
LB	Landing Barge
LBE	LandingBarge Emergency Repair. Containing a small workshop.
LBF	Landing Barge Flak
LBG	Landing Barge Gun
LBK To	Landing Barge Kitchen. provide hot meals for boats' crews whose craft did not possess a galley.
LBO ing	Landing Barge Oiler. To provide fuel for landing craft.
LBR	Landing Barge Ramped
LBV(1)	Landing Barge Vehicle Mk 1
LBV(2)	Landing Barge Vehicle Mk 2
LBW To	Landing Barge Water. provide fresh water.

Above: A British Landing Craft Flak, a converted LCT, one of the myriad of specialised support landing craft constructed during the Second World War to support amphibious operations. (Author)

Landing craft. Short-ranged craft for amphibious operations produced in large numbers by all belligerents, but especially the United States and Britain, during the Second World War. As the designations listed below show, landing craft not only put troops and vehicles on the beach, they gave gunfire support before and in the early stages of a landing and provided essential command and communications facilities until the situation ashore had stabilised. They were, and are, an essential ingredient in amphibious operations. The principal variants used in Allied service during the Second World War and their code designations were:

Code	Description
LCA	Landing Craft Assault
LCA(FT)	Landing Craft Assault (Flame Thrower)
LCA(HR)	Landing Craft Assault (Hedgerow)
LCA(OC)	Landing Craft Assault (Obstruction Clearance)
LCC	Landing Craft, Control
LCCS	Landing Craft, Casualty Clearing Station
LCE	Landing Craft, Emergency Repair
LCF(2)	Landing Craft, Flak Mk 2. Later LCF(L).
LCF(3)	Landing Craft, Flak Mk 3. Later LCF(L).
LCF(4)	Landing Craft, Flak Mk 4. Later LCF(L).
LCF(L)	Landing Craft, Flak (Large)
LCG(L)(3)	Landing Craft, Gun

	(Large) Mk 3
LCG(L)(4)	Landing Craft, Gun (Large) Mk 4
LCG(M)(1)	Landing Craft, Gun (Medium) Mk 1
LCH	Either Landing Craft, Headquarters, or Landing Craft, Hospital
LCI(L)	Landing Craft Infantry (Large)
LCI(S)	Landing Craft Infantry (Small)
LCI(Press)	Landing Craft Infantry (Press)
LCI(Smoke)	Landing Craft Infantry (Smoke)
LCI(Stores)	Landing Craft Infantry (Stores)
LCM(1)	Landing Craft, Mechanised, Mk 1
LCM(2)	Landing Craft, Mechanised, Mk 2
LCM(3)	Landing Craft, Mechanised, Mk 3
LCM(4)	Landing Craft, Mechanised, Mk 4
LCM(5)	Landing Craft, Mechanised, Mk 5
LCM(6)	Landing Craft, Mechanised, Mk 6
LCM(7)	Landing Craft, Mechanised, Mk 7
LCM(8)	Landing Craft, Mechanised, Mk 8
LCM(Smoke)	Landing Craft, Mechanised (Smoke)
LCN	Landing Craft, Navigation Leader
LCP(1)	Landing Craft, Personnel, Mk 1
LCP(2)	Landing Craft, Personnel, Mk 2
LCP(L)	Landing Craft, Personnel (Large)
LCP(M)	Landing Craft, Personnel (Medium)

LCP(R)	Landing Craft, Personnel (Ramped)
LCP(S)	Landing Craft, Personnel (Stores)
LCP(Sy)	Landing Craft, Personnel (Supply)
LCQ	Landing Craft Administration
LCS(L)(1)	Landing Craft, Support (Large) Mk 1
LCS(L)(2)	Landing Craft, Support (Large) Mk 2
LCS(M)(1)	Landing Craft, Support (Medium) Mk 1
LCS(M)(2)	Landing Craft, Support (Medium) Mk 2
LCS(M)(3)	Landing Craft, Support (Medium) Mk 3
LCS(R)	Landing Craft, Support (Rocket)
LCT(1)	Landing Craft, Tank, Mk .1
LCT(2)	Landing Craft, Tank, Mk 2
LCT(3)	Landing Craft, Tank, Mk 3
LCT(4)	Landing Craft, Tank, Mk 4
LCT(5)	Landing Craft, Tank, Mk 5
LCT(6)	Landing Craft, Tank, Mk 6
LCT(7)	Landing Craft, Tank, Mk 7. US Navy only,
LCT(8)	Landing Craft, Tank, Mk 8. Royal Navy only.
LCT(CB)	Landing Craft, Tank (Concrete Breaker)
LCT(E)	Landing Craft, Tank (Emergency Repair)
LCT(H)	Landing Craft, Tank (Hospital)
LCT(HE)	Landing Craft, Tank

	(High explosive)
LCT(Loco)	Landing Craft, Tank (Locomotive)
LCT(R)(2)	Landing Craft, Tank (Rocket) Mk 2
LCT(R)(3)	Landing Craft, Tank (Rocket) Mk 3
LCT(SV)	Landing Craft, Tank (Tank Salvage)
LCU	Landing Craft, Utility
LCV	Landing Craft, Vehicle
LCV(M/S)	Landing Craft, Vehicle (Minesweeper)
LCW	Landing Craft, Air-Propelled

Landing ship. Larger vessel used to support amphibious operations. Generally speaking, landing ships were capable of undertaking an ocean voyage on their own while landing craft needed to be carried on a larger vessel. The LST(III) deserves special mention as it was the workhorse of Allied amphibious operations in the Mediterranean, north-west Europe and the Pacific. The principal variants used in Allied service during the Second World War and their code designations were:

Code	Designation
LSC	Landing Ship, Carrier
LSD	Landing Ship, Dock
LSE	Landing Ship, Emergency Repair
LSF	Landing Ship, Fighter Direction
LSG	Landing Ship, Gantry
LSH(L)	Landing Ship, Headquarters (Large)
LSH(S)	Landing Ship, Headquarters (Small)
LSI(H)	Landing Ship, Infantry (Hand-Hoisting)
LSI(L)	Landing Ship, Infantry

(Large)
LSI(M) Landing Ship, Infantry
        (Medium)
LSI(S) Landing Ship, Infantry
        (Small)
LSS   Landing Ship, Stern
        Chute
LST(1) Landing Ship, Tank, Mk 1
LST(2) Landing Ship, Tank, Mk 2
LST(3) Landing Ship, Tank, Mk 3.
        Royal Navy only.

Langley, **USS** (AV3, ex-CV1). The
US Navy's first aircraft carrier,
affectionately known as the

'Covered Wagon'. Originally built
as a naval collier, she served as a
trials carrier from 1922 to 1927
before her conversion to a seaplane tender. She was bombed by
Japanese aircraft on 27 February
1942 and had to be scuttled 74
miles from Java.

Lanikai, **USS.** Sailing vessel chartered and commissioned in the US
Navy in December 1942 to report
on Japanese fleet movements in
the west China Sea and Gulf of
Siam. Following the attack on

Pearl Harbor she was recalled to
Manila and then escaped from
Java, under constant air attack,
and reached Australia. On 22
August 1942 she was transferred
to the Royal Australian Navy,
under the same name, and
employed on boom defence
duties. Her commanding officer,
Lt Kemp Tolley USN, described her
exploits in *Cruise of the Lanikai.*

'Large Lumps', Operation. In-
triguing British Second World War
plan, never implemented, to deliv-

Above: HMS *Duckworth*, an American built Destroyer Escort supplied under Lend-Lease (see overleaf) to the Royal Navy. The Destroyer
Escorts were extremely effective escorts and far surpassed anything produced by British shipyards. (USN)

er Chariots to their operational area by transporting them suspended from a Short Sunderland flying boat.

Large Slow Target. The derogatory nickname for the Landing Ship Tank Mk 2, which has a good claim to be recognised as the single most important ship type in the Allied war effort. Over 1,000 of these vessels were built and they proved most versatile. They were 328ft long and had standard displacement of 4,080 tons when fully loaded. A large tank deck fitted with bow doors and a ramp for beaching allowed a cargo of 2,100 tons to be carried. However, for quick unloading on the beach 500 tons of cargo (typically eighteen 30-ton tanks or their equivalent in soft-skin transport) was a more realistic load. Vehicles could also be parked on the upper deck and driven down on to the tank deck via a ramp in the early ships and a lift in later ships. Between two and six landing craft could be carried, and an LCT could also be carried on the upper deck. In addition to accommodation for their crew of 210, LSTs had bunk space for an extra 160. Variants of the LST(3) were fitted out to carry railway locomotives and rolling stock, horses, prisoners of war and any other cargo required. Some were also fitted out as hospital ships although they rolled wickedly, making conditions for wounded and medical staff on board very difficult.

'Largesse', Operation. Commando landing to destroy the Italian communications centre at Sfax in North Africa coinciding with the

Above: HMS *Broadway*, one of the fifty ex-US destroyers leased to Britain.

advance of the 1st Army from Tunisia in January 1943.

Laser dazzle sight. Weapon designed to use a laser beam to dazzle enemy pilots. It was first deployed on board the frigate HMS *Plymouth* during the 1982 Falklands Conflict. Sometimes also known as DEC.

'Leader', Operation. Rescue of British and Commonwealth per-

sonnel from Crete using coastal forces craft in April 1942.

Lend-Lease. US programme to provide Britain with military aid while the US was officially neutral. Three hours after signing the Act into law Roosevelt ordered thirty-eight USN PT and PTC boats transferred to the Royal Navy. The total amount of Lend-Lease aid received by Britain and the Commonwealth was $31,392,361,000. In naval

This was in September 1940 as part of the 'Destroyers for Bases' deal. (USA)

terms, Lend-Lease aid consisted of US-manufactured ships, munitions and naval aircraft.

***Lexington*, USS** (CV2). One of the two largest US aircraft carriers of the Second World War. She had been ordered as a battlecruiser but her construction was halted by the Washington Naval Treaty of 1922. Her conversion, and that of her sister ship *Saratoga*, to aircraft carriers was permitted.

Launched on 3 October 1925, she had a standard displacement of 37,681 tons and was 888ft (oa) in length. Armed with eight 8in guns, she could carry eighty aircraft. *Lexington* was sunk on 8 May 1942 during the Battle of the Coral Sea when she was attacked by Japanese aircraft and hit by two torpedoes and three bombs. Fires got out of control and she had to be abandoned. She was scuttled by the destroyer USS *Phelps*

(DD360) and thus became the first US carrier to be sunk during the Second World War.

Leyte Gulf, Battle of. Following the US landings on the Philippines on 20 October 1944 the Japanese launched a complex naval offensive, named *Sho-Go*, using their carrier force (four aircraft carriers under the command of Admiral Ozawa) to decoy the US Fast Carrier Force while two powerful surface task forces, supported by shore-based air power, would destroy the transports and supporting warships. The Centre Force, commanded by Admiral Kurita and consisting of five battleships, twelve cruisers and fifteen destroyers, would enter Leyte Gulf via the Sibuyan Sea and San Bernardino Strait. The Southern Force, comprising two battleships, four cruisers and eight destroyers split into two divisions under Admirals Nishimura and Shima, would approach from the south via the Sulu and Mindanao Seas. The plan went awry almost immediately when the US submarines *Bream*, *Dace* and *Darter* attacked Kurita's force on 23 October, damaging the cruisers *Aoba* and *Takao* and sinking *Atago* and *Maya*. Submarine reports allowed the Fast Carrier force to attack Kurita's ships throughout the 24th. Losses were less severe than might have been expected but included the battleship *Musashi*, hit by torpedoes and bombs and the destroyer *Wakaba*. However, the significant factor of these attacks was that they delayed Kurita by some seven hours – he had reversed course while waiting for news that Ozawa's carriers had succeeded in decoying the Americans – thus upsetting the timetable for the operation. Halsey believed that the main Japanese threat lay to the north and dispatched all his forces in that direction, leaving the exit from the San Bernardino Strait completely unguarded. In the early hours of the 25th Kurita's ships passed unchallenged down the San Bernardino Strait and

headed for Leyte. En route, off Samar Island, he encountered Rear-Admiral Clifton Sprague's escort carrier group consisting of six escort carriers and their destroyer screen. Sprague radioed for support from Halsey but he was 400 miles away to the north chasing Ozawa. The Americans defended themselves doggedly despite the overwhelming odds, but three destroyers, *Johnston*, *Hoel* and *Samuel Roberts* (which received twenty hits from major-calibre shells) were sunk, along with the escort carrier *Gambier Bay*. However, shortly after 0900 Kurita broke off the action, re-entered San Bernardino Strait and retired from the action, although two of his cruisers, *Chikuma* and *Chokai*, were damaged by US aircraft that afternoon. Later the same day Sprague's forces received the first *Kamikaze* attack, in which the carrier *St Lo* was sunk. Meanwhile, to the south, an American force consisting of six battleships (some of them veterans of Pearl Harbor) under the command of Rear-Admiral Jesse Oldendorf ambushed Nishimura's ships as they passed through northern exit of the the Surigao Strait. The battleships *Fuso* and *Yamashiro* were sunk, along with the destroyers *Michisio*, *Yamagumo* and *Asagumo*, and the cruiser *Mogami* was crippled. Only the destroyer *Shigure* escaped to warn Shima. The third section of the action was fought far to the north, where Halsey had been chasing Ozawa. At dawn on the 25th Halsey's aircraft located Ozawa's carriers off Cape Engaño on the island of Luzon and sank

the carriers *Zuikaku*, *Chiyoda* and *Zuiho*. The surviving escorts were harried by Halsey's cruisers and destroyers and chased over a submarine patrol line. The cruiser *Tama* and the destroyer *Akzuki* were sunk on the 25th and the cruisers *Noshiro*, *Kinu* and *Abukuma* sunk on the 26th, together with the destroyers *Nowaki*, *Uranami* and *Hayashimo*. The Battle of Leyte Gulf marked the end of the Imperial Japanese Navy as a sea-going fighting force. The Japanese had lost three battleships, four carriers, nine cruisers and nine destroyers sunk and two cruisers damaged beyond repair. The Americans had lost three carriers and three destroyers.

Liberty, USS. A converted cargo ship commissioned in the US Navy as an intelligence-gathering vessel. In June 1967 she was attacked by Israeli aircraft and torpedo boats while conducting surveillance operations off Sinai during the Six-Day War. The Israelis later apologised, claiming a case of mistaken identity, but the ship had been intercepting Israeli communications at a time when the Israeli Army was about to deliver the knock-out blow to the Syrian Army on the Golan Heights. Thirty-seven American sailors died in the attack. *Liberty* was not repaired and was decommissioned after the attack.

Liberty ships. Mass-produced merchant ships based on a British design for a standard tramp steamer dating back to 1879. The plans were modified to

Above: A Liberty ship being launched. (IWM MH 30726)

make construction of the various parts of the hull such that they could be manufactured by any engineering plant. Nineteen American shipyards built a reported 2,700 such ships, each one taking an average of twenty-seven days on the slip followed by fourteen days' fitting out. The record time taken to build one was seven days, fourteen hours and twenty-three minutes on the slip! Liberty ships were 441½ft long and had a deadweight ton-

nage of 10,920. A total of 195 Liberties were lost as a result of enemy action and accidents/collisions while another 133 were converted by the US Navy for a variety of roles including repair ships, water carriers, PoW transports, mule carriers and hospital ships. After the Second World War Liberty ships made an important contribution to rebuilding the merchant fleets of those countries whose merchant marines had suffered most. The US

Navy converted sixteen to radar picket ships – an early form of BMEWS to warn of a Soviet missile attack.

Light cruiser. Cruiser of any size with a main armament of 6in calibre guns or less.

Light fleet carrier. British term for aircraft carriers of the *Colossus*, *Majestic* and *Hermes* classes laid down between 1942 and 1945 which were smaller than large air-

Above: The Light Fleet Carrier HMS *Glory*, May 1945. (IWM A 28926)

craft carriers yet still capable of participating in fleet operations.

Lion, HMS. British battlecruiser launched in 1910 with a displacement of 26,270 tons and armed with eight 13.5in guns. She was known as one of the 'Splendid Cats' and flew the flag of Vice-Admiral Sir David Beatty at the Battles of Heligoland Bight, Dogger Bankand Jutland. At Jutland she was hit by thirteen 12in shells and badly damaged. The most serious was a hit on 'Q' turret which could have resulted in the loss of the ship had not the magazine been flooded by Major Francis Harvey of the Royal Marine Light Infantry, who lost his life in doing so and was posthumously awarded the Victoria Cross. *Lion* was sold for breaking-up in January 1924. The name *Lion* was subsequently used for a *Tiger* class cruiser launched in September 1944 as *Defence* and completed in July 1960. She was broken up in 1975.

Llandovery Castle. British liner owned by the Union Castle Line which was taken up for war service as a hospital ship during the First World War. On 27 June 1917 she was returning to the UK with just her ship's company and medical staff on board when she was torpedoed by *U86* off the Fastnet Light and sank within ten minutes. At the time of the attack the *Llandovery Castle* was wearing the livery of a hospital ship and was fully illuminated in accordance with regulations. The U-boat then surfaced and her CO, *Kapitänleutnant* Helmut Patzig, interrogated the Master and accused him of having combatant personnel on board. Captain Sylvester denied the charge and pointed out the nurses in the boats. Patzig then manoeuvred *U86* at speed among the rafts and boats, smashing them to pieces. He then fired on the survivors in the water, killing all 234, including 14 nurses. Only one boat, containing the Master and 23 others, was rescued. After the war Patzig and two of his officers were indicted for trial but Patzig escaped to the 'free city' of Danzig (beyond German jurisdiction). His two officers were found guilty by a German court of homicide (their defence of only obeying superior orders was not allowed – an interesting judgement for a German court to reach in view of what was to follow) and each was sentenced to four years' imprisonment. Feelings in Germany against the verdict ran high and it was therefore unsurprising when one of the defendants 'escaped' after serving four months and the other after serving six months. Patzig was never brought to trial and later re-emerged as a counter-intelligence officer in the *Abwehr*.

LOFAR. Low Frequency Analysis and Recording. The processing and integration of narrow-band passive sonar data to provide detection of quiet underwater targets. LOFAR techniques have allowed the development of long-range passive sonars of all types, including towed arrays.

Long Beach, USS. The world's first nuclear powered warship, the cruiser *Long Beach* was launched in 1959 and commissioned in September 1961. Her powerplant consists of two C1W reactors and two GE steam turbines, producing 80,000shp for a top speed of 30kts. She has a standard displacement of 15,111 tons and is 690ft long. Her armament consists of two Terrier SAM launchers with 120 missiles, one Talos SAM with 52 missiles (later replaced by Harpoon missiles), one eight-barrel ASROC launcher, two 5in guns and six 12.75in torpedo tubes. While operating in the Gulf of Tonkin during the Vietnam War in May and June 1968 *Long Beach* shot down two MiGs over North Vietnam at ranges of about 65 miles. *Long Beach* underwent a three-year refit from 1980 to 1983 but plans for a further modernisation in 1993, in which she was to be fitted with the Tomahawk cruise missile, were cancelled and the ship paid off.

Long Lance. The Japanese Type 93 Long Lance was the most famous of all torpedoes used by any navy during the Second World War. It was driven by oxygen, ironically because a Japanese naval attaché had seen an oxygen generator on the deck of the British battleship *Rodney* and assumed that the Royal Navy had oxygen driven torpedoes. Development took some time and there were endless teething troubles, but so sure was the IJN that Britain possessed such a weapon that they kept with the project. Long Lance, which was released to the Fleet in 1935, satisfied the Japanese requirement for a very fast, wakeless, long-range torpedo which, when used by cruisers and destroyers, could counter an adversary's superiority in capital ships. It was fitted in all sixteen of the IJN's heavy cruisers, selected light cruisers and all destroyers from the *Hatsuhara* class onwards. Cruisers carried between 16 and 24 torpedoes; destroyers carried 16 or less. Long Lance was used with devastating effect at the Battles of the Java Sea, Savo Island, Tassafaronga, Kula Gulf and Kolombangara. Before the war both the British and the Americans had discounted rumours about Japanese oxygen-driven torpedoes. One American admiral commented that the Bureau of Ordnance only accepted the details about Long Lance's impressive performance 'when the Japanese started blowing the tails off our cruisers down in the Solomon Islands'. It was only superior radar which eventually gave the Americans the edge enjoyed by the Japanese using the Long Lance. The weapon was subsequently used as the basis for the *Kaiten* suicide weapon. Long Lance was 29ft 6in long, 24in in diameter and weighed, with its warhead, 5,952lb. Its range varied with the speed setting: 21,900yds at 48-50 knots; 35,000yds at 40-42 knots and 43,700yds at 36-38 knots. It carried a warhead of 1,080lb.

LORAN. Long-Range Navigation. A US Navy system of radio navigation beacons used by Allied navies during the Second World War.

Lowestoft. Port on the East Coast of England which, together with Yarmouth, was bombarded by four German battlecruisers on 25 April 1916. The German force was engaged by the weaker Harwich Force but lacked the killer instinct to close and destroy them. However, Tyrwhitt's flagship, the light cruiser HMS *Conquest*, was hit by five 12in shells and badly damaged.

LQ. US Navy code-name for a Q-ship project in 1942.

'Lucid' Operation. Deployment of fireships in the Channel in 1941. Also used for a diversion created at Ostend to cover an attack on Calais and Boulogne in November 1940.

Lusitania. Cunard liner sunk by *U20* on 7 May 1915 with the loss of 1,201 lives. In peacetime the 30,396-ton *Lusitania*, with her sister *Mauretania*, dominated the transatlantic passenger trade. Although both ships had been built with an Admiralty subsidy in case they should be required for war service, *Lusitania* was homeward-bound for Liverpool on a scheduled passenger service when she was sunk. The explosion of the torpedo was followed by a secondary explosion. At the time the Germans alleged that the second explosion was ammunition carried on board as cargo and used this interpretation to justify the sinking. However, the latest research would suggest that it was coal dust in the liner's almost empty bunkers which ignited. The sinking brought howls of protest from the Americans since 128 of the dead were US citizens.

LUT (*Langen Unabhängiger Torpedo*). German pattern-running torpedo developed to permit long-range attacks on convoys. Once fired the torpedo proceeded on a straight course and then began to run in a series of loops across the convoy's mean course, the size of the loops being preset so that they covered all the convoy's track. Trials in the Baltic showed that such torpedoes had a 95% hit rate. The LUT was introduced in 1944 but the limited number of U-boats available and the high state of Allied ASW prevented it from having a significant effect on events.

Lützow, SMS. German *Derfflinger* class battlecruiser built in 1913. She displaced 26,318 tons, was 690ft long and was armed with eight 12in guns. At the Battle of Jutland *Lützow* was responsible for the loss of HMS *Defence* and HMS *Invincible* but in return she took massive punishment. She was hit by at least 24 heavy shells, believed to number four 15in, twelve 13.5in and eight 12in. The worst damage was from flooding started by the explosion of two 12in shells from *Invincible*. The flooding became uncontrollable and eventually reached the upper edge of the barbette for 'B' turret. By this stage she was lying dead in the water, virtually awash and with little reserve of buoyancy. She was scuttled on the morning of 1 June 1916 by a torpedo fired by the destroyer *G38* and she was the only German dreadnought to be sunk in the battle. *See Deutschland* for the ship of the same name which served in the Second World War.

MAC Ships. Merchant aircraft carriers were bulk grain carriers or oil tankers with their superstructures removed and replaced with a flight deck (some also had hangar facilities) for operating four Swordfish aircraft. They successfully combined the functions of merchant ship and aircraft carrier without detriment to either. Six grain carriers and thirteen tankers were thus converted. Though their aircrew and supporting personnel were from the Royal Navy, they were civilian owned and manned by the Merchant Navy. Some MAC ship aircraft were spotted with 'Merchant Navy' painted on the fuselage instead of the more usual 'Royal Navy'. No convoy escorted by a MAC ship was ever attacked by a U-boat. It was a useful concept but the conversion work took a considerable time and when escort carriers became available from the USA on Lend-Lease the programme was abandoned.

MAD. Magnetic anomaly detector. Equipment fitted to an aircraft or helicopter to detect fluctuations in the earth's magnetic field caused by a submerged submarine. It was first employed by the USN in 1943 and also by the Japanese who developed their own version. It was a Japanese MAD-fitted aircraft which is believed to have accounted for HMS *Porpoise*, the seventy-fifth and last British submarine to be sunk during the Second World War. In Allied service MAD was used in conjunction with retro-bombs and was, and is, never more than a short-range guide to classification of a contact and not a detector in its own right.

Madagascar. French colonial possession in the Indian Ocean which was the objective of the first major British amphibious opera-

Above: A Merchant Aircraft Carrier (MAC Ship); these were introduced by the British to give Atlantic convoys some degree of air cover. (Author)

tion of the Second World War. On 5 May 1942 British troops were landed on the island to prevent the Vichy administration from offering base facilities to the Japanese. The defenders offered some resistance but capitulated on 7 May. The operation was notable for two reasons. It was the first occasion on which one of the new British designed LSTs was employed; and after the landings a Japanese *Ko-Hyoteki* two-man midget submarine commanded by Lt Saburo Akeida succeeded in damaging the battleship HMS *Ramillies* and sinking the tanker *British Loyalty*.

Magnetic mine. A mine activated by the magnetic field of a passing target. Every ship has a distinctive magnetic signature and magnetic mines can be 'tuned' accordingly. Magnetic activation can sometimes be combined with other forms of activation such as acoustic or pressure. Magnetic mines were first employed by the British in the Dover Barrage during the First World War.

Maiale (Swine.) Italian name for the SLC human torpedo. It derived from an occasion when one slipped away from an operator during training. The operator exclaimed, 'That swine got away!' *See* SLC for details.

Makin Island. Japanese-held atoll in the Gilbert Islands which was the scene for a raid by 221 US Marines in August 1942 to distract Japanese attention from the landings on Guadalcanal. The Marines were landed from the submarines *Nautilus* and *Argonaut* and succeeded in doing considerable damage to shore installations. Twenty-one Marines were killed or drowned in the heavy surf and nine who were captured were executed by the Japanese.

Above: An Italian Maiale human torpedo on display at the Naval Museum in Venice. The craft is shown with the 300kg warhead attached. (Museo Storico Navale, Venice)

Malta. Island in the Mediterranean and British possession from 1814 to 1964. During the First World War the island was Britain's most important naval base and dockyard in the Mediterranean and served as a home for ships operating in the Aegean and the Adriatic. It also served as the headquarters of the Director General for ASW in the Mediterranean. In the Second World War Malta's position became precarious. The island was only fifty miles from Sicily and suffered massive air raids, often as many as thirteen in a night, which reduced the island's capital, Valetta, to rubble. To keep the island supplied the Royal Navy fought through a series of convoys against intense opposition: *see* the entries for Operations 'Harpoon', 'Pedestal' and 'Vigorous'. Submarines and fast minelayers were also used to bring cargo to the islands. In return British aircraft, ships and submarines based on Malta (supplemented by British reading of Axis signal traffic allowing them to dispose their forces most advantageously) gave the British unrivalled control over the central Mediterranean. Axis convoys taking men and supplies to their armies in North Africa had to run the gauntlet of British attacks from Malta-based forces. The 'siege' of Malta is adjudged to have ended in November 1942. From then the island played a role as a forward base for the landings in Sicily and Italy. It was very appropriate that Malta was the port chosen for the internment of the Italian Fleet in September 1943: 'Be pleased to inform Their Lordships that the Italian Fleet

Above. A view of the submarine base at Malta in October 1941 showing British *U* class submarines secured.

now lies at anchor under the guns of the fortress of Malta' was the signal sent to London by Admiral Cunningham. In the post-war period the island gained its independence in 1964 although Britain retained bases there. In 1971 a neutralist government led by Dom Mintoff called for a British withdrawal and nationalised the dockyard. In 1976 it was decided that Britain would vacate her bases on the island by 1979, although this decision was made on the grounds that she could no longer afford to maintain a permanent Mediter-

ranean presence east of Gibraltar rather than as a result of any pressure from Mr Mintoff. On 1 April 1979 the White Ensign came down for the last time and the destroyer HMS *London* carried away the last British personnel. In the 1980s visits to the island by British warships have resumed, much to the delight of the islanders.

Manta. One of a series of interesting but ultimately impractical German midget submarine designs produced at the end of the

Second World War. *Manta* was capable of speeds of over 50kts on the surface and over 30kts submerged using a Walther turbine but was also fitted with an electric motor for creep speeds. The armament consisted of four G7e torpedoes or a 500kg mine which the craft would tow behind her and release in the path of an oncoming ship.

'Maple', Operation. Minelaying effort in support of Operation 'Neptune'. To prevent U-boats, *S-boote* and destroyers interfering

Above. The minelayer HMS *Welshman* arrives at Malta with urgently needed supplies on 15 June 1942. *Welshman* was able to use her phenomenally high speed of 36 knots to make the passage independently. On this occasion she was given false funnel caps and a painted break in the forecastle in order to disguise her as a Vichy French destroyer. (Author)

with the landings, large minefields were laid to the west of the invasion area.

Marder. German one-man human torpedo. *See Neger.*

Mariana Islands. Strategically important island group 1,500 miles east of the Philippines and the same distance from Tokyo. As part of the US Central Pacific Campaign they were seized in July and August 1944 to act as a forward base from which B-29 bombers could attack the Japanese home islands. The pre-invasion moves by the Americans stimulated a response by the Japanese which resulted in the Battle of the Philippine Sea, the last major carrier-versus-carrier battle of the Second World War. *See also* Guam, Saipan, Tinian.

Maritime Self-Defence Force. The formal name for the post-1945 Japanese Navy and somewhat of a misnomer in view of the fact that the MSDF is the third largest in the world and lacks only aircraft carriers and SSNs.

Marmara, Sea of. Lying between the Dardanelles and the Bosphorus, the Sea of Marmara was the scene for the first campaign by British submarines against Turkish shipping taking supplies to the Gallipoli Peninsula in 1915–16. To reach the Marmara the submarines had to make the hazardous passage of the Dardanelles which were defended by nets and minefields. Four British and three French submarines were lost during the campaign but the

Turks lost a battleship, a destroyer, five gunboats, nine transports and thirty steamers. Three Victoria Crosses were awarded to British submariners. Recent research suggests that the campaign was less effective in starving the Turkish Army of supplies than has been previously thought since the Turks proved very ingenious at salvaging both ships and cargoes and, in any case, moved most of their supplies by road. However, the campaign was the first major success for the British Submarine Service and did much to enhance its reputation both within the Service and among the public.

Marshall Islands. A cluster of thity-one atolls in the western Pacific held by Japan after the First World War and secretly, and illegally, fortified by them. During the Second World War they were the Japanese 'unsinkable aircraft carriers' from which aircraft and submarines could launch attacks on Allied shipping. After the conquest of the Gilbert Islands the Marshalls were selected as the next objective and were taken in February 1944. After the Second World War the Marshalls became an independent republic, athough the USA remains responsible for defence and supplies economic aid. The US has also agreed to meet all claims filed in association with the postwar nuclear test programme at Bikini and Eniwetok.

Mary Rose, HMS. A British destroyer completed in 1916 and sunk on 17 October 1917 by the German minelaying cruisers

Brummer and *Bremse* while protecting a Scandinavian convoy. As she sank her commanding officer, Lt Charles Fox RN, shouted, 'Get her going lads – we're not done yet!'

MAS (*Motoscafo Anti-Sommergibile*). Fast Italian motor boats used to great effect during the First World War when they sank two Austrian battleships, SMS *Wien*, sunk by *MAS.9*, and SMS *Szent Istvàn*, sunk by *MAS.15*. There were many variations on the basic design but the 252 Italian-built MAS varied between 11 and 20 tons displacement, were around 53ft long and were armed with a mixture of torpedoes, depth charges and close-range weapons. They were powered by petrol engines, giving a top speed of 28kts, but were also fitted with an electric motor for silent approach. During the Second World War the basic design remained the same though slightly enlarged.

'Mascot', Operation. Attack by carrier-borne aircraft on the German battleship *Tirpitz* in July 1944.

Matapan, Battle of. Towards the end of March 1941 the Royal Navy learned of a planned Italian sweep to the south of Crete. When three Italian cruisers were sighted west of Crete steering SE on 27 March Admiral Cunningham disposed four cruisers and four destroyers under Vice-Admiral Pridham-Wippell off Gavdos (a small island off Crete) as a reconnaissance screen and that evening he put to sea with his fleet consisting of the battleships *Warspite* (flag), *Valiant* and *Barham*, the aircraft carrier *Formidable* and nine destroyers. Early the next morning *Formidable*'s aircraft and Pridham-Wippell's cruisers found the Italian ships, which, after a brief engagement, promptly retired. Coming up behind them was the battleship *Vittorio Veneto* (the only undamaged Italian battleship after Taranto, q.v.), five cruisers and a screen of destroyers. At 1100 *Vittorio Veneto* opened fire on Pridham-Wippell's ships, which fell back on Cunningham. A series of air attacks was launched and a torpedo struck *Vittorio Veneto*, reducing her speed to 19kts. This hit forced the Italians to retire. In a later strike the cruiser *Pola* was hit and disabled. The Italian commander, Iachino, ordered the cruisers *Zara* and *Fiume* and four destroyers to remain with their damaged consort. Cunningham pressed on after *Vittorio Veneto*, ignoring the conventional wisdom which held against a night action. Just after 2230 the battleship's radar detected first the crippled *Pola* and then the returning *Zara* and *Fiume*. The ships were illuminated with searchlights and were taken completely by surprise, their guns trained fore and aft. *Zara* and *Fiume* were sunk immediately, together with the destroyers *Vittorio Alfieri* and *Giosue Carducci*. In the early hours of 29 March the wreck of *Pola* was found and dispatched by the destroyers *Jervis* and *Nubian*. Matapan was a most decisive victory which confirmed Britain as the pre-eminent power in the Mediterranean.

MATCH. Manned Anti-submarine Torpedo Carrying Helicopter. A British concept developed during the 1960s to use a shipborne helicopter to deliver ASW weapons out to the detection ranges obtained with the new sonar sets which were then coming into service. The first MATCH helicopter was the Westland Wasp, which entered service in 1961.

MDAP. Mutual Defense Aid Program. An American programme begun in the early 1950s to supply defence equipment to Cold War allies.

'Measure', Operation. Naval contingency plans had the Germans invaded Eire.

'Medium', Operation. Attack by fireships on shipping at Cherbourg in October 1940.

'Menace', Operation. Abortive operation to capture the port of Dakar using Free French troops backed up by British units in September 1940. After conducting an unsuccessful bombardment of Dakar's forts from the sea, during which the battleship HMS *Resolution* was torpedoed by the French submarine *Bévéziers*, the British withdrew on 25 September. Had they but known it, at the moment of their withdrawal the French governor was considering how best to effect a surrender.

Mers-el-Kebir. *See* Oran.

MFP (*Motorfahrprahme*). German flat-bottomed transport craft used extensively in the Mediterranean during the Second World War.

MGB. Motor gun boat.

Midway, Battle of. A defining point in the Pacific War. As part of the larger plan for an invasion of Hawaii the Japanese sought to take Midway Island. The Americans were aware of the Japanese plan through intercepted signals and disposed the carriers *Enterprise*, *Hornet* and *Yorktown* to the east of the island. On 3 June 1942 US B-17 aircraft based on Midway attacked Admiral Nagumo's four aircraft carriers (*Kaga*, *Akagi*, *Soryu* and *Hiryu*) without success. On the next day US carrier planes struck but their first attack, by forty-one TBD Devastator torpedo-bombers, was unsuccessful and thirty-seven of the aircraft were shot down. The second strike, by fifty-seven Dauntless dive-bombers from *Enterprise* and *Yorktown*, was a devastating success: the four Japanese carriers were caught with their aircraft ranged on deck being refuelled and rearmed for a second strike on Midway. More importantly, the Japanese CAP had been drawn down to low level to meet the threat from the torpedo-bombers and had not returned to their station in order to meet the new threat from the dive-bombers. Between 10.25 and 10.30 *Kaga*, *Akagi* and *Soryu* were crippled and sunk; only *Hiryu* managed to fly off her aircraft, and they so damaged *Yorktown* that she was found and sunk by the Japanese submarine *I-168* two days later. However, *Hiryu* did not escape: on the afternoon of 4 June she was found and sunk by dive-bombers from *Enterprise*. The Japanese loss was immense: their four largest aircraft carriers and over 250 aircraft and their irreplaceable crews. It was the first defeat suffered by Japanese maritime forces since 1592 and marked the limit of their expansion in the Pacific.

Mignatta. Italian human torpedo developed during the First World War. Based on a standard B57 torpedo, it was fitted with handholds for the two operators and two detachable 170kg charges which were held to the target by magnets. Two were used in the attack on Pola on the night of 31 October/1 November 1918: one sank the battleship *Virbus Unitis* while the other was abandoned and left to circle in the harbour, eventually hitting and sinking the accommodation ship *Wien*. *Mignatta* was the precursor for the extremely successful *Maiale* used during the Second World War.

Mikasa. Japanese battleship launched in 1900 and was the flagship of Admiral Togo at the Battle of Tsushima. She was disarmed in 1922 and preserved as a museum ship at Yokosuka.

Milch-Cow. Allied term for the Type XIV tanker U-boat employed to refuel and re-supply other U-boats at sea, thus extending their patrols. The were unarmed, other than with flak guns, but carried

500 tons of fuel which was sufficient to give twelve Type VIIC U-boats an extra four weeks on patrol. The first at-sea replenishment was carried out by *U459* on 22 April 1942 500 miles northeast of Bermuda. She subsequently refuelled another fourteen U-boats in a two-week period before returning to France. However, the extensive use of wireless required to co-ordinate and arrange mid-ocean rendezvous was liable to interception by the Allies – with disastrous consequences. Only nine Type XIVs were built and all nine were sunk.

'Mincemeat', Operation. Allied deception plan. A corpse was procured from a London mortuary, the family being assured that the body was required for 'active service' and that it would, in time, receive a Christian burial. The body was then clothed in the uniform of a Major in the Royal Marines with personal identification as Major William Martin, official number 148228, and the sort of trivial items that he might have been expected to carry around in his pocket – including a letter from his bank manager complaining about his overdraft! 'Major Martin' was put in the sea from the submarine *Seraph* off the Spanish port of Huelva on the morning of 30 April 1943. *Seraph*'s commanding officer, Lt N. Jewell RN, deviated but once from his orders and that was to recite such words as he could remember from the burial service as the body was slid into the sea. The position had been chosen in the knowledge that the tide would carry the body ashore. Attached to the body was a brief-

case packed with forged documents, including letters from the Chiefs of Staff indicating that Sardinia and the Peloponnese rather than Sicily were the target for the next Allied invasion. Once the Spanish reported that 'Major Martin' had been washed ashore, the British Naval Attaché in Madrid, who was not privy to the plan, was sent a series of increasingly anxious signals from London concerning the missing briefcase. His concern was instrumental in persuading the Spanish that the documents were real. The Spanish authorities behaved as predicted and granted the German authorities a sight of the documents (the Germans were given a sight on 9 May and an appreciation of their contents was circulated within OKW on the 14th) before they were returned to the British Naval Attaché in Madrid. Signals intelligence told the British that the Germans had been totally deceived by the documents. As a result German forces in Italy and Sicily were dispersed and the landings on Sicily later in the year met with comparatively little opposition.

Mine. A mine is an underwater weapon consisting of an explosive charge fitted with a device that causes it to explode when a ship or submarine makes contact with it or enters into close proximity. The mine is anchored in place by a length of cable. A very destructive yet relatively cheap weapon, mines have more than proved themselves effective naval weapons, from the Russo-Japanese War to the more recent conflicts in the Persian Gulf.

Above. A German submarine-laid mine and its sinker displayed on the casing of the captured *UC5* in 1916. (Author)

MIDGET SUBMARINES

The midget submarine is one of the most potent weapons of war developed in the twentieth century. Yet it is an extremely old form of naval warfare with the first, albeit unsuccessful attack being launched in 1776. In the early days of submarine warfare this century, all submarines were midget craft. But as the submarine grew, there arose a requirement for small craft which could penetrate a defended harbour and attack shipping. This single requirement has since been expanded to include a host of other roles. Experience with the midget submarine showed that these small craft could accomplish operations of considerable strategic importance with effects out of all proportion to their small size.

It was the stalemate in the Adriatic during the First World War which gave the stimulus for the development of these weapons. Neither the Austrian nor the Italian Fleet would venture out from behind their protective nets and minefields, so the Italians strove to find ways of attacking the Austrian ships in their bases. The *Grillo* 'climbing tank' was one such, unsuccessful weapon, but the *Mignatta* achieved its aim, and pointed a finger to the future, by sinking the Austrian battleship *Viribus Unitis* on 1 November 1918.

During the Second World War many of the major belligerent navies employed midget submarines or specially trained assault frogmen. The absence of France from this field is easily explained – the capitulation of the country in June 1940 effectively removed it from the war.

The United States possessed conventional forces in abundance and thus did not need to resort to this form of warfare. However the absence of the Soviet Union from this area of operations is puzzling, given the pioneering work done by Russian engineers in submarine development. Perhaps the highly individualistic nature of midget submarine operations was not one that sat easily alongside the centralised Soviet command structure.

Three kinds of midget submarine made their appearance during the Second World War: human torpedoes (the Italian *Maiale* and British Chariot); small submersibles (the German *Neger* and associated craft and the Japanese *Kaiten*); and true midget submarines (the Japanese *Ko-Hyoteki*, the Italian CA/CB types, the British X-craft and the German *Seehund*). These craft can also be further divided into the practical and therefore successful (British X-craft, Italian *Maiale*); the enthusiastically designed but impractical (British Chariot, Japanese *Ko-Hyoteki*, German *Biber*); and the suicidal, either by accident or design (British Welman, German *Neger*, Japanese *Kaiten* and its various derivatives).

It was the Italians who led the way in this field. The *Regia Marina* was the only major navy to possess a unit, the *Decima Mas*, which was dedicated to special operations. The *Mignatta* had evolved into the *Maiale*, a two-man human torpedo, which was used to such deadly effect at Alexandria and Gibraltar. The activities of the Italian CA/CB midget submarines are less well known but worthy of attention, particularly the operation to attack shipping in New York – an operation which would have had the most seri-

ous effects in America but which was cancelled on the Italian armistice.

Japan was another of the early pioneers in this field. Before the war the Japanese developed the excellent two-man *Ko-Hyoteki*, an extremely advanced midget submarine. Japanese war plans concentrated on the great battleship engagement between the American and Japanese fleets which would decide the course of the war. To whittle down the American superiority in capital ships, *Ko-Hyoteki* were to launch mass torpedo attacks. It was an ingenious idea and may well have worked. However, the Japanese decision to destroy the US fleet by a carrier strike removed their *raison d'être*. Instead they were employed in harbour penetration, a task for which they were not suited and at which they were less than successful. As the tide of the war went against Japan, the Japanese resorted to suicide weapons such as the *Kaiten* and *Kairyu*. These were intended to overwhelm the Americans by sheer weight of numbers, but once deployed these craft proved no match for the range of anti-submarine measures employed by the Americans.

It was Italian activities in the Mediterranean which spurred the British into the field. Britain had traditionally made no attempt to develop this sort of weapon – as the Royal Navy was the pre-eminent naval force in the world there was no requirement for it. It was only the need to attack the German battleship *Tirpitz* which pushed a reluctant Admiralty in this direction. The British initially copied the Italian two-man human torpedo, the Chariot, but these craft proved unsuccessful and never justified the time and resources devoted to them. Far more successful was the X-craft, a potent four-man midget submarine which could be put to a variety of uses. At the other end of the scale was the Welman, a useless craft whose design shows the effects of allowing enthusiasm to triumph over practicalities. British midgets saw action in all three theatres of war, and their most significant success was the crippling of the German battleship *Tirpitz* in September 1943.

The Germans were the last into this field. While the U-boats were scoring significant successes in the Atlantic, the *Kriegsmarine* showed no interest in midget craft, and it was only when the Germans were staring at the prospect of an Allied invasion of Europe that their attitude changed. In many ways the German attitude mirrored that of the Japanese and was a tacit admission that their naval strategy had failed. German midgets were weapons of desperation, founded in the hope that if used in sufficient numbers they would interrupt the Allied cross-Channel supply lines. With the exception of the excellent *Seehund* two-man submarine, German midgets were poorly constructed and most were as lethal to their crews as they were intended to be to the opposition.

The operations of the various midget submarines during the Second World War remain some of the must supreme examples of cold-blooded courage in history. In a war which became dominated by technology and weapons of mass destruction, the achievements of the midget submariners of all countries stand out and hark back to an earlier and more honourable age, where individual courage and skill-at-arms were the attributes which won wars. Following the failure of the Japanese attack on Sydney, Rear-Admiral Stuart Muir-

head-Gould, in charge of the harbour defences at Sydney, paid the following tribute to the Japanese officers and men who had perished in the attack: 'Theirs was a courage which is not the property, or the tradition or the heritage of any one nation. It is the courage shared by the brave men of our own countries as well as of the enemy and, however horrible war and its results may be, it is courage which is recognised and universally admired. These men were patriots of the highest order. How many of us are really prepared to make one-thousandth of the sacrifice these men have made?'

The post-1945 period has seen the midget submarine occupy an ambivalent place in the orders of battle of the world's navies. Britain and America professed interest in such craft in the immediate post-war period but soon abandoned their interest in this type of craft. The midget submarine was then taken up by some of the world's smaller navies – Yugoslavia, Colombia and Pakistan to name but a few. Other regimes, those of North Korea, Libya and Iran for example, have invested in midget submarines, and their possession of these craft, in view of the unsavoury nature of these regimes and their predilection for supporting international terrorism, must be viewed with the greatest suspicion. The USSR/Russia is a major player in the field of midget submarines, and, given the chronic cash shortage affecting all aspects of the Russian Government, the sale of Russian technology in this field to the highest bidder must be accepted. The USA gave up on midget submarine development with the failure of the *X-1* craft in favour of concentrating on the carrier, SSBN and SSN pro-

grammes. The end of the Cold War now means that the US Navy must adopt a more flexible approach and prepare for more limited operations, possibly in shallow coastal waters, where SSN deployment would be inappropriate. The US Navy is currently developing the ASDS, Advanced Seal Delivery System, a midget submarine with a marked resemblance to a British X-craft which can carry mines or swimmers.

One aspect of midget submarine operations which has survived almost unaltered since the Second World War is a successor to the wartime *Maiale* and Chariots, now known as Swimmer Delivery Vehicles (SDV). These are now far more sophisticated than the weapons in which Greenland and Visintini went to war, but the basic principles are the same. They can be carried by submarines: a number of former SSBNs 'disarmed' by the SALT and START agreements are enjoying a new lease of life as assault swimmer carriers. The USS *Sam Houston* (SSBN609) and *John Marshall* (SSBN611) of the *Ethan Allen* class were converted to carry sixty-seven SEAL swimmers in double dry deck shelters fixed to the casing when it proved impossible to replace their Polaris missiles with the larger Poseidon system. Conversion started in 1984 but both boats were decommissioned, in September and November 1991 respectively. They were replaced by *Kamehameha* (SSBN642) and *James Polk* (SSBN645) of the *Lafayette* class. On the Soviet side a number of Project 66A boats (better known in the West as the 'Yankee' SSBN) have been refitted for other duties by having their central section (containing the sixteen SS-N-4 missiles) removed, the ▶

MIDGET SUBMARINES

two halves of the boat being welded together. Nearly all modern submarines have escape chambers which can easily double as exit/re-entry chambers for divers, while some 'conventional' submarines, such as the British *Otus* and *Opossum*, are fitted with five-man exit/re-entry chambers built in to their fins. Whatever the refinements made to the *matériel* in modern submarines, the principles are the same as those under which *Decima Mas* operated so successfully. There is nothing very new in the midget submarine world that has not been done before.

Midget submarines have three advantages on their side. The first is the advantage of surprise: they would choose the place and time for an attack. The second is the absence of any form of harbour defence: boom defence has all but been forgotten as an aspect of naval operations since 1945. The third is that the operators of these craft are fanatics, whether they be communist functionaries or Muslim zealots. The belief that death in action will lead to a Marxist or Islamic nirvana will overcome a good deal of inadequacy in training. It only takes one midget to get through with her cargo for the mission to succeed. One can only speculate as to the result of such an operation – a wrecked off-shore oil installation in the Persian Gulf; an American aircraft carrier mined while at anchor in the Bay of Naples or a chemical/biological (or nuclear) device detonated in an Israeli harbour.

The most exciting and promising developments centre on the field of robotic, unmanned craft which would be rather like homing torpedoes but with a passive/active search capability of their own. The British company Scion has developed Spur (Scion's Patrolling Undersea Robot), while the Americans have investigated Small Mobile Sensor Platforms (SMSPs) deployed from torpedo tubes. In March 1990 the American Defense Advanced Research Projects Agency (DARPA) ordered two prototype Unmanned Undersea Vehicles (UUV) and an SSN, USS *Memphis* (SSN691), has been converted to act as a sea-going test-bed for advanced submarine technology, including the launch and recovery of UUVs. The UUV is designed as a tactical system which can be deployed from submarines, surface ships or direct from the shore and can perform a number of functions including mine detection, underwater surveillance (including ASW) and communications. The key to the performance of these functions is advanced electronic systems which include 'artificial intelligence' algorithms that work in the same way as human thought processes. In order to guard against computer failure, the vehicle will employ three fully redundant computers which will use a 'voting' approach to system management on board the craft. All three computers must 'agree' on how the craft is run; if only two agree then the craft will continue to operate but in a degraded mode.

The UUV is 36ft long and 44in in diameter. Considerable attention has been paid to limiting the overall size of the craft by use of advanced technology and reducing the size of the power-plant. An internal pressure hull will house the mission payload, which will occupy a 5ft long section. This will consist of the appropriate software and components for surveillance, communications or mine detection duties. In the case of the last, the package includes an ultra-thin cable containing a fibre-optic communications link required for the transmission of commands from a surface ship or submarine. The propulsion system, consisting of a 12hp electric motor and a motor controller, will occupy the after 12ft of the vehicle. The motor is built to operate even when completely flooded with sea water. Bearings are fabricated with a special non-corrosive alloy, and the copper windings that carry power to the motors are impervious to wear. During normal operations, the internal volume of the motor is filled with oil in order to equalise pressure between the inside and the outside of the motor, permitting the use of a thinner and lighter housing. Unmanned vehicles such as SMSPs and UUVs would enable a relatively small number of SSNs to 'control' a large area of ocean through which enemy forces would have to pass. They also offer considerable advantages in the field of mine detection and electronic surveillance, and they have the advantage of being capable of unlimited under-ice operations – a field denied to manned midget submarines.

A number of conclusions can be drawn about midget submarine operations which are extremely relevant today. First, operations require thorough and realistic training if they are to be successful. British and Italian operators were well trained, and this was reflected in their achievements. German operators were flung into battle with hardly any training at all and achieved little as a result.

However, the ability of the fanatic to score one decisive hit at the cost of his own life cannot be ignored. Secondly, midget submarines can be built quickly, cheaply and in large numbers – and they are extremely easy to hide. Thirdly, almost any merchant ship or submarine can be adapted to carry a midget submarine. Fourthly, no defences have ever stopped a midget submarine attack. They have been a hindrance and have deterred an attacker, but a small number of the midgets have always got through. As noted, modern bases are virtually defenceless against this form of attack. Faced by the midget threat, simple last-ditch measures such as spilling oil fuel on the surface of the water will render a small periscope useless: the 'green lobby' would hate it, but against a

simple craft dependent on periscope observation of the target it would be highly effective. Fifthly, one-man operated craft are doomed to failure. A man on his own has to much too do and loses heart. There should be at least two in the crew, and for an operation of any duration at least four are required. Lastly, the quality of the operators – the 'human resources' – is vital. Men best suited to midget submarine operations are those least likely to fit in with the routines of a peacetime navy. It is interesting to note from the British perspective that Australians, New Zealanders and South Africans, whose antipathy to the Naval Discipline Act was legendary, were extremely competent X-craft personnel. The risks implicit in training for midget submarine operations mean

that such men have to develop a team spirit unique to their formation; this is what distinguished *Decima Mas* from the rest of the *Regia Marina* and what distinguishes Russian special forces from the run-of-the-mill conscript.

In 1907 the eminent historian Arthur Thayer Mahan wrote, in *From Sail to Steam*, that 'It is now accepted, with naval and military men who study their profession, that history supplies the raw material from which they are to draw their lessons, and reach their working conclusions. Its teachings are not, indeed, pedantic precedents, but they are the illustrations of living principles.' There is no doubt that midget submarines are still a force to be reckoned with. The development of new technologies will make them even more effective.

Above. A North Korean *Sang-O* midget submarine. These small craft are designed specifically for infiltration and surveillance operations against South Korea.

Mine belt. GRP canisters fitted to the sides of some contemporary German-built submarines. Because these submarines have 'swim out' torpedo tubes they are unable to carry some types of mine. Instead the mines are carried in GRP containers which are simply bolted on to the boat's side.

Minehunting. As distinct from minesweeping, minehunting is the practice of actively seeking mines by means of bottom-scanning sonar and then destroying them by using divers or ROVs.

'Minerva', Operation. Embarkation of General Giraud from southern France in November 1942. Giraud was thought to be the only French general who could command the loyalty of French forces in North Africa in the event of an Anglo-American landing, so he had to be smuggled out of France. The only problem was that he flatly refused to deal with the British. Consequently the submarine HMS *Seraph* was hurriedly recommissioned as the USS *Seraph* and Captain J. V. Wright USN placed 'in command' and given a commissioning document which was a picture of a well-known actress in an advanced state of undress. *Seraph*'s crew developed and practised what they thought was American slang. Giraud (who was thought not to speak English) was duly picked up on 6 November 1942, whereupon it was discovered that he did speak excellent English and had no particular objection to a British submarine!

Minesweeping. Searching for mines by towing paravanes or streaming an electrically charged cable through the water.

***Missouri*, USS.** The last battleship completed for the US Navy, *Missouri* was launched at the Brooklyn Navy Yard on 29 January 1944. She is best known as the ship selected for the signing of the surrender with Japan in Tokyo Bay on 2 September 1945 (Missouri was President Truman's home state).

Mitsubishi G4M. Highly successful twin-engine bomber (Allied code-name 'Betty') used by the Japanese Navy during the Second World War. It could carry either a bomb or a torpedo armament and at the end of the war was modified to carry the *Baka* suicide device. A total of 2,416 of the G4M2 version were produced – more than any other Japanese bomber. The G4M2 had a speed of 272mph and a range of 2,260 miles and had a crew of seven.

MMS. Motor minesweeper. Small British minesweeper built in large numbers in the UK and Canada during the Second World War. There were two main variants. MMS1–118/123–312 were 105ft long and displaced 250 tons while MMS 1001–1090 were 126ft long and displaced 360 tons. Ships of both types remained in service until the late 1950s.

Mobility kill. Action damage to a warship which, whilst not sinking her, renders her incapable of further movement.

Molch. German one-man midget submarine developed in 1944. *Molch* was a development of the *Biber* but had solely electric propulsion. It displaced 2.7 tons, was 7.6m long and was armed with two torpedoes. Nearly 400 were built but there are no figures for how many were lost in action. They were certainly widely dispersed: after the war the Allies found numbers in Germany, Holland, Denmark, Heligoland and Norway.

Monitor. Shallow-draught warship with immense beam and armed with one or two capital ship guns for shore bombardment purposes. During the First World War the Royal Navy made extensive use of

Above. HMS *Cottesmore* photographed in 1993. A highly sophisiticated, and expensive, Hunt class minehunter, her hull is built out of glass reinforced plastic. (MoD)

Above. A World War Two British *Halcyon* class class minesweeper.

Above. The British monitor HMS *Lord Clive* showing the massive single 18in gun mounting at the stern. fitting this massive weapon caused the ship to settle a further 4½ feet in the water at the stern. (Author)

monitors armed with 12in, 14in or 15in guns to provide cheap, expendable but effective shore bombardment in areas (Gallipoli, Macedonia, the Adriatic and the English Channel) where it would be unwise to employ a capital ship. Two British monitors, HMS *Lord Clive* and HMS *General Wolfe*, carried a single 18in gun – the largest ever employed in British naval service.

Montreux Convention. International agreement concluded in 1936 by which Turkey is allowed to fortify the Bosphorus and Dardanelles while allowing free passage to merchant ships and also to warships of other countries under strictly controlled condi-

tions. It particularly affects Russia and the CIS since the only access to the Mediterranean for ships based in the Black Sea is through Turkish-controlled waters.

Moving haven. Imaginary box established around a friendly submarine to protect her from the attentions of her own side. Inside the 'haven' attacks on all submarines are prohibited. The position of the haven is adjusted each day to allow for the submarine's movement. Moving havens did not always guarantee immunity: on 8 July 1944 the French submarine *La Perle* was sunk by British aircraft while proceeding across the Atlantic and protected by a moving haven.

Möwe. German commerce-raider of the First World War. She was a 4,500-ton steamer armed with four 5.9in guns, one 4.1in gun, two 21in torpedo tubes and 500 mines; she also carried a large stock of paint, sheet metal and wooden panelling to enable her to change her appearance frequently. On 29 December 1915 she left the Elbe, returning home on 4 March 1916 having accounted for eleven British merchant ships of 57,000 tons and her mines for the battleship HMS *King Edward VII*.

MPA. Maritime Patrol Aircraft. Land-based, long-range aircraft such as the Neptune, Shackleton, Nimrod, P-3 Orion and Atlantique used for for maritime reconnaissance.

MSC. Military Sealift Command. *See* MSTS.

MSTS. Military Sea Transportation Service. The US Navy's post-war sealift organisation created on 1 October 1949 out of the wartime Naval Ocean Transport Service. In 1950 MSTS assumed responsibility for the US Army's ocean-going ships and transports. On 1 August 1970 it became the Military Sealift Command (MSC). MSC is commanded by a serving flag officer but nearly all of its staff are civilian.

MTI. Moving target indicator. A general term for the filtering out of 'clutter' on radar screens so that moving targets can be followed. It implies some kind of

memory within the radar system so that the progress of successive radar scans can be compared.

MTM (*Motoscafo Turismo Modificato o Migliorato*). An Italian assault craft used extensively by *Decima MAS*. It was an 18ft speedboat packed with 660lb of explosive. The operator would aim the MTM at the target ship, run it up to high speed (as fast as 33kts), lock the controls and throw himself over the stern when he was sure the craft would strike. He would paddle away on a small raft which formed the backrest of his seat. There were a number of derivatives of the MTM design but all had the same principle – a large explosive charge, high speed and a means for the operator to abandon the craft before the final impact. MTM boats were used with

some success at Suda Bay in Crete on 25/26 March 1941 when they sank the British cruiser *York* and tanker *Pericles*. However, in an attack on Malta on 27 July 1941 all nine MTM boats were sunk before they could enter the harbour: the British defenders had the advantage of possessing radar and were able to spot the assault forces assembling outside the harbour.

Mulberry. An artificial harbour designed and built by the British to support the Normandy landings.

Murmansk. Russian port in the Kola Inlet on the Barents Sea. It is Russia's only ice-free Arctic port and was the destination for nearly all the PQ and JW series convoys. It was never the most appealing of places, and heavy bombing had

Above. An aerial view of the Allied Mulberry Harbour at Arromanches, June 1944. (USNA)

turned it into a wilderness. In the Royal Navy it was said that 'If the Kola Inlet was the a*** of the world, then Murmansk was five miles up it.' Today it is the base for Russia's Northern Fleet, with a massive submarine base built into the hills at nearby Severomorsk.

Musashi. Sister ship to the *Yamato*

'Musketeer', Operation. 31 October to 6 November 1956. The crisis over the nationalization of the Suez Canal by the Egyptian Government led to military action by Great Britain, France and Israel against Egypt. During the first night the British cruiser HMS *Newfoundland* sank the Egyptian frigate *Domait*. British and French aircraft operating from aircraft carriers and land bases eliminated the Egyptian air force. This was followed by a parachute and then an amphibious assault, and the first helicopter borne assault in history was flown from British aircraft carriers lying offshore. Militarily the operation was successful but politically it was a disaster.

'Musketoon', Operation. Landing of commandos from the French submarine *Junon* in September 1942 to destroy a power station in Norway.

'Musketry', Operation. Anti U-boat air operations carried out by RAF Coastal Command in the Western Approaches and Bay of Biscay.

NACDEV. Naval Allied Commission for the Disposal of Ex-Enemy Vessels. Inter-Allied commission established in 1919 to ensure that the provisions of the Treaty of Versailles regarding the disposal of the surviving ships of the German and Austro-Hungarian fleets were carried out. Its chairman was the British Vice-Admiral Dudley de Chair.

'Nakhimov', Operation. Russian plan to land an Army Corps on the coast of Anatolia to cut the Angora–Constantinople railway line in October 1917. The Corps would be provisioned for a two- to three-month campaign on Turkish territory. However, a shortage of shipping caused the plan to be revised to a raid by eight infantry battalions, eight cavalry squadrons and a battalion of cyclists to release British PoWs held nearby. The October Revolution put paid to this and all other such plans.

Narvik, Battles of. On 9 April 1940 German troops were landed from ten destroyers at Narvik in order to seize the town and the port. The port's importance lay in that during the winter it handled nearly all of the vital Swedish iron ore exports to Germany. At dawn on 10 April the five destroyers of the British 2nd Destroyer Flotilla under Captain Warburton-Lee passed down Ofotfjord to attack the German force at Narvik. Despite the odds the action was initially successful and the German destroyers *Wilhelm Heidkamp* and *Anton Schmidt* were sunk. However, the German superiority finally told and the British were forced to retire, though not before HMS *Hardy* had been beached and disabled (and Warburton-Lee killed) and *Hunter* disabled by a torpedo. Three days later Vice-Admiral Whitworth returned with the battleship *Warspite* and nine destroyers. First the German destroyer *Erich Koellner* was found lurking in an inlet off Ofotfjord and sunk, then the destroyers *Erich Giese, Diether von Röder* and *Hermann Künne* were sunk off Narvik and finally the destroyers *Wolfgang Zenker, Georg Thiele, Bernd von Arnim* and *Hans Lüdemann* were pursued to the head of Rombaksfjord and sunk. As a bonus the Swordfish aircraft from HMS *Warspite* sank *U64*. Virtually the entire *Kriegsmarine* destroyer fleet had been eliminated at a stroke.

NATEKO (*Nautische-Technische-Kommission für Schwarze Meere*). Commission established by the Germans, Austrians and Turks following the Treaty of Brest-Litovsk with Russia in 1917 to secure all warships of the former Russian Black Sea Fleet and ready them for service. Its chairman was the German Rear-Admiral Albert Hopmann. Although it was a tripartite body, the Germans regarded themselves as *primus inter pares* and paid little attention to the sometimes quite legitimate Turkish claims for a share of the spoils.

NATO. North Atlantic Treaty Organisation. Established in 1949 to provide a common defence structure for the West against growing Soviet aggression. Its members are the USA, Britain,

Belgium, the Netherlands, Germany (admitted in 1954), Spain, Luxembourg (not a great player in naval affairs), Denmark, Norway, Iceland, Canada, Italy, Greece and Turkey. France was an original member but opted out of the organisation's military structure in 1969, although the process of French withdrawal had begun as early as 1959. With the break-up of the Warsaw Pact, NATO is under pressure to admit former Warsaw Pact member states such as Poland and Czechoslovakia. In naval terms NATO provides for a unified command structure in the Eastern Atlantic and standing multi-national naval forces in the Atlantic, English Channel and Mediterranean.

Nautilus, USS. Launched in 1954, *Nautilus* was the world's first nuclear-powered submarine. She displaced 3,533/4,092 tons, was 319ft long and was armed with six bow torpedo tubes. Propulsion was a single S2W reactor which gave a top submerged speed of 23kts. She first got under way on 17 January 1955 and signalled 'Under way on nuclear power' and on 3 August 1958 made the first submerged transit of the North Pole.

Navajo Indians. Used by the US Marine Corps as radio operators speaking in their own language. The Navajos, working in pairs as transmitter and receiver, were able to speak *en clair* and their language baffled Japanese eavesdroppers. About 300 Navajos joined the Marine Corps, some as young as sixteen, and their skills

gave Marine commanders a priceless asset – secure battlefield communications with no risk of their being decoded by the opposition.

Naval Air Squadron (NAS). Term used by the Fleet Air Arm to distinguish its squadrons from those of the Royal Air Force. Thus a Fleet Air Arm squadron is referred to as, for example, 849 Naval Air Squadron.

NCTR. Non Co-Operative Target Recognition. Post-1945 means of solving the identification problem and thus avoiding 'blue-on-blue' incidents. Unfortunately NCTR usually entails some means of identifying which type of aircraft, submarine or ship is the contact. This was acceptable in the Cold War when NATO used Western-built equipment and the Warsaw Pact used Soviet-built equipment. That situation is now not likely to be the case. Russia could be on the side of the West, having sold her equipment to any nation with the ability to pay for it. As an additional complication, buyers of Western-built equipment (for example, Argentina, Iraq or Iran) could be on the other side.

Neger. German one-man human torpedo which consisted of two G7e torpedoes mounted one above the other. The upper torpedo contained the operator and his rudimentary navigation instruments (which consisted of an aiming spike and a compass, but little else) and the lower torpedo was the weapon. The operator made his way quietly to the

target area either running just below the surface or with his perspex canopy awash, and when he had selected a target he simply started and released the lower torpedo. On a number of occasions the lower torpedo started but failed to release, thus carrying the luckless operator into oblivion. Some 200 *Neger* were built and 140 were lost on active service. The *Marder* was an improved *Neger* and could dive to 30m; some 300 were built but the numbers lost are not known. *Neger/Marder* were employed off Anzio but were most successful off the Normandy beaches, where they sank three minesweepers, an LCF, a balloon ship and two destroyers and damaged a cruiser and a destroyer.

'Neptune', Operation. The naval component of the Normandy landings and the largest amphibious operation in history. In terms of sheer numbers it involved seven battleships, two monitors, twenty-one cruisers, 133 destroyers, sixteen sloops, thirty-four frigates, seven destroyer escorts, seventy-three corvettes, sixty-six ASW trawlers, 353 coastal forces craft, 307 minesweepers, two midget submarines, 511 miscellaneous naval craft, sixty-three escorts providing an anti-submarine screen in the Western Approaches, seventy-seven infantry assault ships, 326 large stores ships, 415 short sea cargo ships, 237 LSTs, 1,464 landing craft, eight AA ships, seventy-nine blockships, ten survey vessels, seven cable ships, eleven colliers, thirty-eight HQ ships 136 depot and service craft, twelve hospital carriers, twelve mooring layers, fourteen naval stores ships, twenty-six PLUTO ships, twenty-two pumping vessels, thirty salvage vessels, 190 tankers, 102 trawlers for smoke-laying, 166 tugs and fifteen wreck dispersal vessels – a total of 5,015 vessels, excluding the landing craft embarked in infantry transports and landing ships.

NGS. Naval gunfire support. The provision of naval gunfire to assist land operations.

Nigerian Civil War. In May 1967 the eastern part of the Federal Republic of Nigeria sought to secede from the Union and form a separate state, Biafra. The Navy, consisting of a frigate and five small combatants, remained loyal to the Federal government. The Biafran Foreign Minister unwisely joked 'What Navy?' but even these few ships established an effective blockade of the 200-mile Biafran coast and prevented the secessionist government receiving supplies by sea. The Navy then used its one landing craft to land troops to capture the oil terminal at Bonny and subsequently at Port Harcourt and Calabar. These assaults and the effectiveness of the blockade helped to force the capitulation of the rebels.

'Nightshirt'. British project to reduce propeller noise by masking the ship's propellers with a curtain of air bubbles.

Normandie. A fast transatlantic liner owned by the French CGT company, and one of the most beautiful ships ever built, *Normandie* was interned in New York on the fall of France. When the USA entered the conflict she was taken over, transferred to the US Navy on 24 December 1941 and renamed *Lafayette*, and designated a troop transport. While under conversion she caught fire on 9 February 1942 and subsequently capsized alongside the pier. Although she was salvaged she was never returned to service, either military or civilian, since the fire damage was too great. She was broken up in 1946.

North Cape, Battle of the. The last capital ship action in European waters during the Second World War. The German battlecruiser *Scharnhorst* had put to sea to intercept the homeward-bound Arctic convoy RA.55A and outward-bound JW.55B. Once again interception of German signals meant that the British could make their dispositions accordingly and on 26 December 1943 substantial forces were at sea. At 0830 *Scharnhorst* ran into Rear Admiral Burnett's 10th Cruiser Squadron (*Belfast, Norfolk* and *Sheffield*) but retired after a brief engagement. She then renewed her attempt to reach the convoy but found her path blocked by Burnett's cruisers for a second time. After a second engagement *Scharnhorst* retired once more and headed south-east back to Norway. This time Burnett decided to shadow her, for approaching from the west was the battleship HMS *Duke of York* and *Scharnhorst* was heading straight for her. *Duke of York* was in radar contact with *Scharnhorst* at 1615 and when she opened fire shortly afterwards the German ship was taken completely by surprise, her guns trained fore and aft. At first it seemed as if *Scharnhorst* might use her superior speed to escape, but a lucky hit from *Duke of York* slowed her down and torpedo attacks by destroyers reduced her speed still further. In a final gun action she was reduced to a shambles by gunfire before being dispatched by a torpedo. Only thirty-six of her crew of over 1,800 were rescued. The action emphasised the importance of radar to naval warfare: without radar it would have been impossible to find, let alone fight, *Scharnhorst* in the darkness of an Arctic winter.

Northern Barrage. An attempt to bar the exit of U-boats from the North Sea during the First World War by means of minefields laid from the Orkney Islands to the limits of Norwegian territorial waters (Norway being neutral) off Hardanger Fjord to the south of Bergen. It was an American proposal and agreement to it at the inter-Allied conference in London in September 1917 was contingent on the US providing the necessary mines (some 100,000) since factories in Britain were fully stretched. It aroused considerable opposition from the British Grand Fleet which claimed that the mines (and the new American antenna mines were distrusted) would do no more than severely restrict the Grand Fleet's sea room in the event of a German break-out. The Barrage consisted of three areas: Area A, the central area 30 miles long and laid with shallow mines; Area B, the western sector laid with deep minefields and patrolled so that U-boats would be forced to dive into the mines; and Area C, nearest to the Norwegian coast and laid with both deep and shallow mines. In September 1917 the Norwegian Government, under British pressure, declared that they would extend Area C throughout their own waters using British-supplied mines. Minelaying began in Area B on 3 March 1918 and in Areas A and C on 8 June. The Barrage consumed 70,263 mines and cost $40m at 1918 prices. It claimed six U-boats sunk and possibly a seventh with two or three damaged. The Northern Barrage was typically American – a tremendous effort, a grand design and hugely expensive – but it has to be said that the results were certainly not in proportion to the effort.

Nousret. A Turkish minelayer built in 1912 in Germany. On the night of 16/17 March 1915 *Nousret* laid a field of twenty mines parallel to the shore in Eren Keui Bay in the Dardanelles. On 18 March the Anglo-French fleet engaged in attempting a forced passage of the Dardanelles ran into this field with disastrous results. The British battleships *Irresistible* and *Ocean* and the French *Bouvet* were sunk and the battlecruiser *Inflexible* was damaged.

Oerlikon 20mm gun. Swiss-designed rapid fire anti-aircraft gun extensively used by all sides during the Second World War and after. It had the advantage of being very light, with a good rate of fire (450–480rds/min) and could be simply bolted to the deck of almost any kind of ship or submarine. However its relatively short range, 4,000yds, and small size of the projectile gave it only limited effectiveness against aircraft, particularly *Kamikaze*s.

Ohio. Tanker which was part of the 'Pedestal' convoy to Malta in August 1942. She was struck by

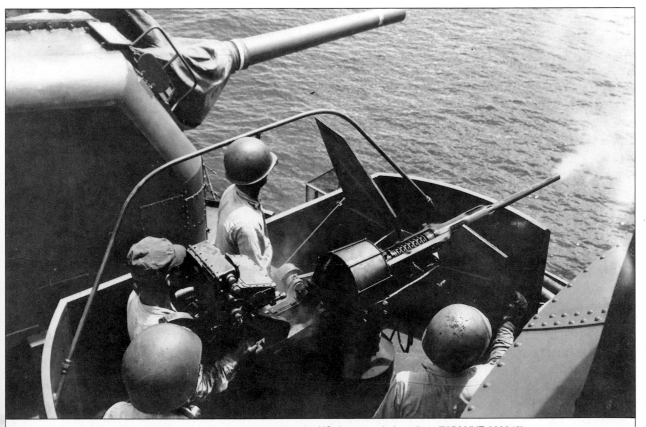

Above. A 20mm Oerlikon in action aboard a US destroyer during 1944. (IWM NYF 283342)

one torpedo, further disabled by near misses from bombs and had a German aircraft crash on her deck. She eventually reached Malta under tow by the destroyers *Penn* and *Ledbury*, where her arrival on 15 August 1942, the Feast of the Assumption and the Maltese National Holiday, was taken by many of the Maltese as a sign of divine intervention on the Allied side. Her Master, Captain D. W. Mason, was awarded the George Cross.

Oiler. General term for a tanker for refuelling ships either in harbour or while under way at sea.

Okinawa. Strategically important island (together with the Kerama Retto archipelago to the west and the island of Ie Shima) lying to the south of Japan and scene of the last amphibious operation undertaken before the projected invasion of Japan. After a massive pre-invasion bombardment US Marines and US Army troops landed on 1 April and met little opposition. Once inland, they found well-prepared Japanese defensive positions and it took three months of bloody fighting before the island was declared secure. From a naval point of view the campaign is of interest because of the losses inflicted by the Japanese. Of the 525 fighting ships in the Fifth Fleet at the onset of the campaign, twenty-two were sunk and 254 damaged; amongst landing craft and auxiliaries, fourteen were sunk and 117 damaged; while US Navy losses were 4,907 killed or missing and 4,824 wounded – the only occasion on

which the dead have outnumbered the wounded. In no previous operation had US naval losses in ships and men been so high, despite the relative inactivity of the Japanese surface fleet, the total lack of success of the submarines and relative decline in Japanese air power. Against these factors have to be set the proximity of Okinawa to the Japanese home islands, the high proportion of Japanese effort expended in suicide attacks, and the length of time that Allied shipping had to lie off the beaches supporting the troops. The capture of Okinawa provided the US forces with air and naval bases within 350 miles of Japan. A major fleet anchorage and 26 potential airfields were available for the final assault.

Oleg. Russian *Bogatyr* class cruiser launched in 1903 which was sunk in a daring night torpedo attack by British CMBs at Kronstadt on 17 June 1919 during the Russian Civil War.

Oliver Hazard Perry class. A class of fifty-one frigates built for the US Navy between 1976 and 1988. They were an attempt to provide the USN with a capable but relative inexpensive warship which could be built in large numbers.

Olterra. A 4,500-ton Italian tanker interned in Algeciras on the outbreak of the Second World War. From September 1942 she was converted, with the tacit knowledge of the Spanish authorities, to act as a forward base for *Decima MAS* forces attacking shipping at

Gibraltar. The ship was fitted with an exit/re-entry port so that SLCs and *Gamma* frogmen could leave and re-enter the ship unobserved. Three operations were launched from *Olterra* before the Italian Armistice in September 1943 brought her activities to an end. The British had their suspicions about *Olterra* but could find no definite proof. A request that British frogmen 'examine' *Olterra* was turned down by the Cabinet on the grounds that such an operation would infringe Spanish neutrality! *Olterra* was handed over to the British in September 1943, when her secrets were finally exposed.

Olympic. British liner launched for the White Star company in 1909. She served as a troopship during the First World War and enjoyed the singular distinction of ramming and sinking *U103* on 12 May 1918.

Operational Research (OR). The application of organised and systematised analysis to specific situations. It was first used by the British in 1937, and by the time the Second World War had ended there was no area of operations on the Allied side (OR was almost unknown on the Axis side) immune from the scrutiny of the analysts. One aspect of OR will suffice: OR scientists analysed air attacks on U-boats and found that between the aircraft sighting and the attack there was an average period of two minutes. The depth charges carried by the aircraft were set to explode at a depth of 100ft. OR calculated that U-boats

Above. The USS *Taylor*, an *Oliver Hazard Perry* class frigate

Above. The Italian tanker *Olterra*, interned in the Spanish port of Algeciras, which acted as a base for *Maiale* operations against British shipping at Gibraltar. (Gus Britton)

were escaping because they were nowhere near 100ft when the charges exploded. Accordingly depth charges were reset to explode at 25ft, with immediate results.

OPV. Offshore patrol vessel. A lightly armed and equipped vessel – such as the British 'Island' class (displacement 1,000 tons, armament one 40mm gun, endurance 11,000 miles at 12kts) – but with sufficient endurance and sea-keeping qualities for ocean constabulary duties such as protecting oil and gas fields and enforcing fishing regulations.

Oran. French naval base in North Africa. After the fall of France in 1940 the bulk of the French Fleet, consisting of two fast battleships, two old battleships, eleven destroyers and five submarines, was gathered there to await events. The British were concerned that the Germans might take control of these ships and so on 2 July 1940 Admiral Sir James Somerville was dispatched from Gibraltar with Force H to offer the French commander, Admiral Gensoul, three alternatives: to join the British; to disarm his ships and sail them into internment in a neutral port; or to scuttle his ships where they lay. If Gensoul declined to accept these terms his ships would be sunk. Negotiations continued throughout 3 July without result and at 1800 Somerville's ships opened fire. After a brief bombardment the battleship *Bretagne* blew up and sank with the loss of over 900 lives and the battleship *Provence*

and fast battleship *Dunkerque* were damaged and beached. Only the fast battleship *Strasbourg* and six destroyers escaped to Toulon. The action was a desperately sad episode which aroused, and arouses, the deepest antagonism in French naval circles. It was probably unnecessary, for the French had no intention of letting their fleet fall into German hands, and some say, cynically, that the action was undertaken to show America that Britain was serious about staying in the war.

Orion. German Second World War commerce raider known to the Germans as HSK.1 or *Schiff 36.* She was commissioned in December 1939 and during her career sank five ships totalling 33,340grt, while her mines were responsible for the loss of five others. She made but one cruise before serving as a repair ship and a gunnery training ship. She foundered on 4 May 1945 north of Swinemünde in the Baltic after being bombed by the RAF. *Orion* had a standard displacement of 15,700 tons and was armed with six 15cm, one 75mm, four 37mm and four 20mm guns. She also carried six 21in torpedo tubes and 228 mines. An Arado Ar 196A-1 seaplane was carried but this was replaced by a Japanese Nakajima floatplane in February 1942.

Oropesa float. Torpedo-shaped float used to support standard contact-wire minesweeping gear. Originally such equipment was towed by two ships, but the Oropesa float substituted for the second ship. *Oropesa* was the

name of the British minesweeper in which the equipment was first fitted.

OS2U Kingfisher. US Navy float-plane used during the Second World War for reconniassance and gunnery spotting. It was carried on board battleships and cruisers, three or four aircraft being carried on each ship. It was a low-wing monoplane with a radial engine. A large single float beneath the fuselage was balanced by small stabilising floats under each wing. The aircraft had a top speed of 164mph and a range of 800 miles. On 30 April 1944 an OS2U flown by Lt (jg) John Burns rescued nine naval airmen from Truk. Unable to take off, he simply taxied out to sea and rendezvoused with a submarine.

'Oscar'. US Navy/NATO designation for the very capable Soviet Project 949 *Antey* cruise missile submarine. An 'Oscar' displaces 12,500/14,000 tons (the 'Oscar II' is heavier at 13,900/16,000 tons), is 143m long and is armed with twenty-four SS-N-19 cruise missiles, two 533mm and four 650mm tubes with twenty-four torpedoes.

Osel. Island in the Gulf of Riga captured by the Germans in October 1917 in Operation 'Albion'. This was the major German operation of the war in the Baltic and was intended to protect the left flank of the German Army from naval gunfire from Russian ships and also from batteries mounted on the Sworbe peninsula.

Ostend. Port in Belgium used extensively by the Germans as a destroyer and U-boat base during the First World War. The port was continually bombarded by long-range gunfire from British monitors of the Dover Patrol but in 1918 was attacked twice with blockships to block the entrance to the harbour and thereby prevent the Germans from using the port. The first attempt on 23/24 April 1918 was a failure. The wind changed, denying the British the use of a smokescreen, and the Germans had shifted the light buoy marking the harbour entrance a mile to the east. The result was that the blockships *Sirius* and *Brilliant* were sunk a mile to the east of the harbour. A second attempt on 10/11 May was no more successful. *Vindictive* entered the harbour but grounded and was sunk by her crew in a position that blocked a third of the channel. A third attack was cancelled on the conclusion of the Armistice in November 1918.

Ostfriesland. A German *Helgoland* class battleship launched in September 1909. After the First World War she was ceded to the United States. The US Navy used the ship in a series of trials to demonstrate the effect of aerial bombing on ships in order to test horizontal protection schemes. Their plans were grievously upset when aircraft commanded by Colonel 'Billy' Mitchell disregarded the rules for the trials, dropping their ordnance from a much lower height than had been ordered, and sank the ship, thus denying the USN any chance to assess the effectiveness or otherwise of the trial. As completed *Ostfriesland* had a standard displacement of 22,440 tons, was 548ft long and had a main armament of twelve 12in guns and a secondary battery of fourteen 5.9in guns.

OTH radar. Over-the-horizon radars bounce beams off the ionosphere to detect targets beyond the line off sight. These require extremely large arrays and therefore can only be employed ashore. However, the information can be sent to ships at sea via data link.

OTHT. Over-the-horizon targeting. The planning of long-range missile engagements so as to

Above. The shell-swept deck of the old British cruiser *Vindictive* after her second attack on Ostend in June 1918. (Author)

exploit the maximum potential of weapons such as the Tomahawk. During the 1960s the US Navy developed a system for such engagements, intelligence information being stored on a database exploited by a Force Over-the-Horizon Track Co-ordinator (FOTC). The database is maintained by merging intelligence from various sources linked by satellite. The USSR developed much cruder systems in the 1960s using reconnaissance aircraft and direct data linkage to allow OTH engagements by SSGNs.

Otomat. Franco-Italian anti-ship missile. A turbojet engine gives a very long range – 180km in the Mk 2 version. It is used by both the French and Italian Navies and has been widely exported.

Otranto Barrage. Attempt to block the exit of U-boats from the Adriatic to the Mediterranean by blocking the Straits of Otranto (between Italy and the Dalmatian coast) with nets and mines. It was indeed an ambitious undertaking: the Straits are over forty miles wide, the depth of water is over 3,000ft in the middle and the area is subject to sudden storms of great intensity. The Otranto Barrage was not a success. It originally consisted of drifters towing indicator nets. As it became clear that U-boats were still getting through the Barrage, forces were repeatedly strengthened until in February 1918 over 200 ships and seventy aircraft were involved in its maintenance. Moreover, the Barrage constituted a tempting target for Austrian light forces based at Cattaro and there were a number of tip-and-run raids culminating in the action of 15 May 1917. By March 1918 the Barrage consisted of a submarine patrol off Cattaro, a destroyer screen further south, then two lines of trawlers between Cape Linguetta and Corfu equipped with hydrophones and depth charges and finally a line of American submarine-chasers working from Corfu. Despite this impressive array, U-boat commanders still boasted that they could slip through on the surface at night. In over three years of war only two submarines was sunk by the Barrage forces – the Austrian *U6* on 13 May 1916 and the German *UB53* on 3 August 1918. Two other submarines, the German *UB44* and Austrian *U30*, disappeared and may have fallen victim to mines while outward-bound through the Straits. A fifth U-boat, *UB52*, was sunk by the British submarine *H.4* to the north of the Barrage on 23 May 1918.

'Oyster'. British nickname for the German pressure mine.

Panama Canal. Strategically important 51-mile link between the Atlantic and Pacific Oceans across the isthmus of Panama. The canal and the zone around it were administered by the US Army until 1979. Then, as a result of a treaty between Panama and the USA, the Panama Canal Zone ceased to exist as an independent jurisdiction and the Panama Canal Company, a wholly US-owned organisation, was replaced by the joint US-Panamanian Panama Canal Commission. The canal is an important route for commercial traffic not wishing to make the long voyage around Cape Horn. From the US Navy's point of view, the canal is of some importance. Although the US Navy maintains powerful and self-contained fleets in both the Atlantic and the Pacific, the Canal acts as a quick and convenient short cut for ships and supplies moving between the two oceans.

Pacific Campaign. The war against Japan, 1941–45, fought by American, British and Commonwealth forces in the Pacific. It was a campaign based on the use of sea power for amphibious operations, for the provision of carrier aircraft to cover such operations which lay beyond the reach of land-based aircraft and for the defeat of the Japanese Navy, which was the means by which Japan had extended and then maintained her conquests. Following on from victories in New Guinea and Guadalcanal the campaign divided neatly into two offensives. The South-West Pacific Campaign, conducted by General Douglas MacArthur, was a US Army-run campaign pushing up through New Guinea to the Philippines. The Central Pacific Campaign was a USN/USMC campaign (though with US Army participation) which pushed up through the Gilbert Islands, the Marshalls, the Marianas and Iwo Jima. Both campaigns were then brought together for the landings on Okinawa in April 1945

Panay, USS. The first US warship to be sunk this century by enemy action. *Panay* was a shallow-draught river gunboat and was bombed and sunk by Japanese aircraft – despite the fact that two enormous Stars and Stripes were spread on her awnings – above Nanking on 12 December 1937. Three US sailors were killed and forty-three wounded. One civilian was killed and five wounded. After a prompt American protest the Japanese Government accepted responsibility and paid an indemnity of $2,200,000 in April 1938.

Pantellaria. A rocky island in the Mediterranean, 70 miles southwest of Sicily. It had been well fortified by Italy and its capture was regarded as a prerequisite for any invasion of Sicily. On 11 June 1943 a five-day naval and air bombardment began, after which the island surrendered.

Panzerschiff. Armoured ship. German term for *Admiral Graf Spee*, *Admiral Scheer* and *Deutschland/Lützow*. Wth their 11-inch gun armament they were armed as a capital ship but displaced no more than a cruiser; thus they fitted none of the accepted classifications for warships.

PAP (*Poisson Auto Propulseur*). French-designed, remotely controlled mine destruction and inspection system. Fitted in the 'Circe' and 'Eridan' class minehunters of the French Navy.

Paracel Islands. An uninhabited chain of islands 225 miles east of Vietnam. In January 1974 the islands were invaded by the Chinese but the invaders were swiftly evicted by South Vietnamese Government forces. Two Chinese ships were sunk and two damaged in return for one South Vietnamese vessel sunk.

'Paraquat', Operation. Operation launched by the Royal Navy in April 1982 to recover the island of South Georgia prior to the recapture of the Falkland Islands. Despite being, in the words of one participant, 'a military cock-up', it was ultimately successful and was a demonstration of Britain's intention and capability to recover the Falklands.

Passive sonar. Sonar that listens for sounds produced by other ships and submarines. It was originally known by the British term hydrophone. Its capabilities have been significantly enhanced by modern systems of signal processing (e.g. LOFAR, q.v.) that permit the detection of very quiet targets at long range. Passive sonar is preferred by users in that it does not reveal the position of the user.

Pathfinder, HMS. British light cruiser launched in 1904 and displacing 2,940 tons. *Pathfinder* was torpedoed off St Abb's Head on 5 September 1914 by *U21* with the loss of 259 officers and men. She was the first warship to be sunk by a submarine.

Patrol frigate. A term adopted by the US Navy in the 1970s for 'austere' frigate designs such as the *Oliver Hazard Perry* class.

'Paukenschlag', Operation. German U-boat offensive against merchant shipping along the USA's eastern seaboard in early 1942 – the second 'Happy Time'.

PB4Y-2 Privateer. US Navy version of the B-24 Liberator extensively modified for maritime patrol and ASW operations. Few of the production aircraft were completed before VJ-Day and those that were operational were employed exclusively in the western Pacific.

PBM Mariner. Twin-engine flying boat which succeeded the PBY Catalina as the US Navy's principal maritime patrol aircraft. It was the world's largest twin-engine flying boat and was renowned for its range, bomb load, ruggedness and seaworthiness. The PBM-3D variant had a maximum speed of 211mph and a range of 2,240 miles.

PBY Catalina. The most successful flying boat ever developed by any nation. The PBY 'Cat' was employed in the ASW, bombing, search and rescue and transport roles. Radar-equipped PBYs, painted black and known as 'Black Cats', carried out night operations against Japanese shipping. More Catalinas were produced than any other flying boat in history. PBYs were flown by the USA, Britain, the USSR and a number of other Allied nations. It was a Catalina of No 209 Squadron RAF which spotted the German battleship *Bismarck* on 26 May 1941 and it was a PBY which made the first sighting of the Japanese carrier force at Midway. The PBY-5A variant had a

Above. A PBY Catalina, in British service, moored to a buoy. (IWM CH 2448)

maximum speed of 179mph, a cruising speed of 117mph and a range of 2,545 miles.

Pearl Harbor. A major US Navy and air base on the Hawaiian island of Oahu. On 7 December 1941 a force of six Japanese aircraft carriers launched an air attack on the US Pacific Fleet. The attack was supposed to have gone in after (though only just after) the Japanese had formally declared war, but the Japanese diplomats in Washington failed to deliver the ultimatum on time, so there was no warning of the attack. The results were catastrophic. The battleships *Arizona* and *Oklahoma* were sunk and

California, *West Virginia*, *Pennsylvania*, *Tennessee*, *Nevada* and *Maryland* were damaged. However, all these ships, except *Arizona* (now maintained as a memorial in commission at Pearl Harbor) and *Oklahoma*, were repaired and took part in the war against Japan. Other casualties included the target ship *Utah* sunk, three cruisers sunk or damaged and three destroyers sunk or damaged; 188 aircraft of all types were destroyed on the ground; and 2,403 US servicemen and civilians were killed and 1,104 wounded. The Japanese lost 27 out of the 183 aircraft employed. A second air strike, aimed at dock and harbour instal-

lations (including the oil depot) was cancelled by the Japanese commander. Fortunately for the Americans, the three Pacific fleet carriers, *Enterprise*, *Lexington* and *Saratoga*, were not in the harbour at the time.

Pearl Harbor Investigations. A series of eight investigations designed to discover who was responsible for the disaster at Pearl Harbor. They were ultimately fruitless.

'Pedestal', Operation. Convoy to Malta in August 1942. Thirteen merchant ships and a tanker were escorted by one of the most powerful forces the Royal Navy

Above. An Italian aerial photograph showing an attack on the *Pedestal* convoy to Malta in August 1942. (Author)

had assembled in European waters and which included all three operational fleet carriers. The convoy battered its way through, enduring attacks from German and Italian aircraft, submarines and coastal forces. Five of the thirteen merchant ships, including the tanker *Ohio*, arrived but the cost was high: an aircraft carrier, two cruisers and a destroyer sunk. However, the supplies brought by the survivors enabled Malta to carry on until the winter.

Above. Another (though indirect) casualty of *Pedestal* was the Italian cruiser *Muzio Attendolo,* shown here without her bows after being torpedoed by the British submarine *Unbroken* in August 1942. (Author)

Pelagosa. Island captured by the Italians in July 1915 as part of a plan to establish a chain of observation posts across the Adriatic. The island, 300m wide and 1km long, was captured on 11 July and the lighthouse-keepers were summarily evicted. However, the Italian decision not to proceed with the next step in the plan, the capture of Lagosta, left the garrison exposed. On 17 August the island was bombarded by an Austrian force and the fresh water tank destroyed; all fresh water now had to be brought in tank ships as there was no natural supply. The island was evacuated the next day.

Peleus. Greek merchant ship sunk on 13 March 1944 by *U852*. After the ship had gone down *U852*'s CO, *Kapitänleutnant* Heinz Eck, had the survivors machine-gunned and their rafts destroyed with grenades. Only three men survived, by feigning death, to relate what happened. Eck and three of his crew stood trial for murder and he, together with the 2nd Watch Officer and the surgeon, were sentenced to death.

Peleliu. Island in the Palau group which was attacked by the Americans on 15 September 1944 as part of operations designed to protect the flank of American forces preparing for the invasion of the Philippines. The Japanese resisted stoutly, aided by the island's many caves, which made excellent defensive redoubts. The US 1st Marine Division lost 53% of its strength, the 5th Marine division lost 42.7% and the 7th Division lost 46.2%. Nineteen Medals of Honor were awarded to the US 1st Marine Division in the Pacific, eight of them being won on Peleliu. Even after organised Japanese resistance ended on 27 November, isolated pockets continued to conduct guerrilla operations until 1945. The courage displayed in taking the island is undiminished by a bitter truth: the landings were unnecessary. Peleliu posed no threat to MacArthur and could have been by-passed with safety.

'Perisher'. Royal Navy term for the Commanding Officers' Qualifying Course for prospective submarine commanders. Allegedly the term came from the saying that a course member either 'passed or perished'. Only one attempt at a 'Perisher' was allowed and thereafter the unsuccessful candidate was returned to general service and never served in submarines again.

'Perpetual', Operation. British aircraft ferry operation to Malta in November 1941. It is most noteworthy in that while returning to Gibraltar after the operation, the aircraft carrier HMS *Ark Royal* (which had already been claimed as sunk by the Germans on at least five occasions) was torpedoed and foundered.

Peterel, HMS. British river gunboat built in 1927 whose bold but futile resistance at Shanghai in December 1941 aroused the respect of the Japanese. *Peterel* was acting as a wireless link for the British consulate at Shanghai when she was boarded by a Japanese naval delegation who demanded her surrender. Lt-Cdr Polkinghorn, *Peterel*'s CO, politely refused and then saw his visitors over the side with the appropriate honours due to foreign naval officers. He then cleared for action. When the Japanese ultimatum expired the little gunboat was overwhelmed by gunfire from the cruiser *Idzumo* and sank beneath the muddy waters of the Whangpo River. Polkinghorn's conduct and brave stand ensured that he and his men were treated better than might otherwise might have been the case.

Philippines. Archipelago in the Pacific which was ceded to America in 1898 by the Spanish. The islands were captured by the Japanese in 1942 and their reconquest by the Americans, which began in October 1944, was the cause of the Battle of Leyte Gulf,

one of the greatest naval engagements in history. Although the islands became a self-governing republic in 1946 the USA continued to retain base facilities at Subic Bay, which were only given up in 1992.

Philippine Sea, Battle of the. The American invasion of the Mariana Islands in the central Pacific in early June 1944 induced the Japanese Combined Fleet under Vice-Admiral Ozawa to seek a decisive battle with the US Fifth Fleet. Nine Japanese aircraft carriers, supported by land-based aircraft from Guam and Truk, launched a series of mass attacks on the American carrier force on 19 June. In an epic air engagement, known subsequently as the 'Great Marianas Turkey Shoot', over 300 Japanese aircraft were shot down. Moreover, two Japanese carriers, *Taiho* and *Shokaku*, were sunk by American submarines. The battle continued at long range throughout the next day as US planes harried the retreating Japanese. The Japanese carrier *Hiyo* was sunk, though the Americans lost many aircraft trying to return to their carriers in the darkness.

Phoney War. Term used to describe the period of seeming inactivity in the war during the winter and spring of 1939/40. At sea there was nothing 'phoney' about this period, which saw the Battle of the River Plate, the Royal Navys loss of one aircraft carrier, a battle ship, a number of lesser warships and the heavy fighting of the Norwegian campaign. Also a large number of merchant ships were to lost to U-boats.

Picket ships. *See* Radar picket ships.

Pinguin. German Second World War commerce-raider known to the Germans as HSK.5 or *Schiff 33.* During a 357-day cruise in which she covered 59,188nm she sank 26 vessels totalling 136,642grt. She was sunk by the cruiser HMS *Devonshire* on 8 May 1941 with the loss of 241 of her crew of 401. *Pinguin* was commissioned in February 1940. She had a standard displacement of 17,600 tons and was armed with six 15cm, one 75mm, one 37mm and four 30mm guns. She also carried four 21in torpedo tubes, 300 mines and one Ar 196A-1 floatplane.

PLARB. Soviet designation for an SSBN.

PLUTO (Pipe Line Under the Ocean). Imaginative attempt to deliver POL goods from the UK to France by means of a cross-Channel underwater pipeline dur-

ve. The Japanese aicraft carrier *Shokaku*. She was sunk at the Battle of the Philippine Sea by the submarine USS *Cavalla*. (IWM MH 5931)

ing the Second World War. The PLUTO scheme provided for the laying of ten 3in diameter flexible pipelines from Sandown on the Isle of Wight to the port of Querqueville near Cherbourg. The first pipleline was to be in place on D+20 and the last by D+75. The theoretical delivery capacity of each of the ten lines was 300 tons per day. The first pipeline was ready on D+19 (25 June) but the plan did not fulfill its creators' hopes. There were several pipeline failures and it was found that flexible steel pipes run out from the Normandy beaches to offshore mooring buoys where tankers could tie up provided 600 tons per hour per ship. In October 1944 a second series of pipelines was laid from Dungeness to Boulogne. PLUTO only ever produced 700 tons per day – far short of what was required.

'Pocket battleship'. Term given by journalists to the three German *Panzerschiffe*, *Admiral Graf Spee*, *Admiral Scheer* and *Deutschland/Lützow*.

Pola. Port at the northern end of the Adriatic and the main base of the *KuK Kriegsmarine* until the collapse of the Fleet in 1918. A superb natural anchorage, it was the scene of the first human torpedo attack on the night of 1 November 1918 when the battleship *Viribus Unitis* was sunk. Between the wars the town and port declined under Italian governance but after the port reverted to Yugoslavia in 1947 a naval dockyard was re-established. The

port now lies in Croatia and efforts are being made to restore and revive some of the town's naval heritage.

Polaris. The first American type of underwater, submarine-launched ballistic missile. There were three types: A-1, with a range of 1,200nm; A-2, with a range of 1,500nm; and A-3 (also used by the Royal Navy), with a range of 2,500nm. The A-3 variant carried three multiple re-entry vehicles (MRVs) instead of a single warhead.

***Pommern*, SMS.** A *Deutschland* class pre-dreadnought launched in 1905. On the morning of 1 June 1916, after the Battle of Jutland, she was torpedoed and sunk by the British destroyers *Faulknor*, *Obedient*, *Marvel* and *Onslaught*. One or two of the torpedoes fired struck the old batrleship and her magazines exploded, justifying her description as one of the Germans' *Fünf Minuten Schiffe*. The ship disappeared in a massive fireball. There were no survivors.

Pom-pom. British term for the 2pdr AA gun fitted in single, quad and eight barrel mountings, so called because of the 'pom-pom' noise made by the weapon when firing. It was also known as the 'Chicago Piano'. It was the major British close-range AA weapon until 40mm Bofors guns became available in numbers. The single and quad mountings were fitted in smaller ships, the eight-barrel version in aircraft carriers and capital ships. It was designed to put up a

barrage of anti-aircraft fire at incoming aircraft. Each barrel had a rate of fire of 100rds/min which was fed from 114- or 140-round loading trays. It had a range of 6,800yds. Early mountings were manually trained and elevated but later versions were given a powered drive. The eight-barrel powered version weighed eleven tons and it was said that the gunlayers for these weapons, who required exceptional qualities of hand and eye co-ordination, were born and not made.

Port Chicago explosion. Ammunition explosion at Port Chicago, California, on 17 July 1944 which killed 202 sailors (all black) and injured 233 others (mostly black). One merchant ship was vaporised in the blast another was damaged beyond repair and several building were damaged. The black sailors refused to return to the depot after the disaster: 258 were subsequently court-martialled and all were found guilty. Fifty were dishonourably discharged and given prison sentences of up to fifteen years, the remaining 208 were dishonourably discharged. The US Navy subsequently commuted most of the prison sentences. The affair had considerable influence on the acceleration of racial integration in the US Navy.

Preventive attack/strike. Attack based on the assumption that the enemy is about to launch an attack or to disable the enemy's forces concurrent with (or just before) a formal declaration of hostilities.

Pressure hull. The basic hull of a submarine designed to withstand high underwater pressures.

Pressure mine. A mine which is activated by the change in water pressure caused by a ship passing overhead.

Prince of Wales, HMS. British battleship of the *King George V* class. She was launched on 3 May 1939 and even before she was fully operational saw action against the *Bismarck*. She later took Churchill to Placentia Bay in Newfoundland for the 'Atlantic Charter' meeting with Roosevelt before proceeding to the Far East with HMS *Repulse* to form Force Z – a 'deterrent' to the Japanese. On 10 December 1941 she was sunk by Japanese aircraft off the east coast of Malaya, having sustained six torpedo hits and one or two bomb hits. 1,285 of the 1,612 officers and men were rescued.

'Principal', Operation. British Chariot attack on Italian warships at Maddalena and Palermo. Although the liner *Viminale* and the cruiser *Ulpio Traiano* were damaged at Palermo, the submarine carrying the Chariots to Maddalena, HMS *P.311*, was sunk before she could launch her craft. The result of the operation must hang in the doubt: in return for the damage to the *Viminale* and *Ulpio Traiano*, the British lost *P.311* at a time when submarines were worth their weight in gold as well as the submarine *Traveller*, lost in a pre-operation reconnaissance of Taranto.

Principles of war. First enunciated in a training manual in 1921, these encompass the ten most important means of successfully waging war. They are: selection and maintenance of the aim; maintenance of morale; surprise; economy of effort; concentration of force; security; seizing and holding the offensive; flexibility; co-operation; and administration.

Princeton, USS (CVL23). An American *Independence* class carrier sunk at the Battle of Leyte Gulf in October 1944. She was bombed by Japanese aircraft and set on fire. Damage control could not halt the spread of the flames and eventually her torpedo magazine exploded, yet of her ship's company of over 1,500 only 106 men died. Casualties were more severe in the cruiser USS *Birmingham* (CL62) which was alongside fighting the fire: she lost more than 200 men when *Princeton* exploded. Captain John M. Hopkins USN, who was on board *Princeton* as prospective commanding officer, had his foot amputated in hurried circumstances by the medical officer wielding a sheath knife. Hopkins survived to command the next USS *Princeton* (CV37).

Prinz Eugen. A *Tegetthoff* class battleship of the Austro-Hungarian Navy launched in 1912 and scuttled off Toulon in June 1922. The name was revived for a German *Hipper* class cruiser in order to assuage Austrian sensibilities following the *Anschluss* and the ship was launched by Admiral Horthy on 22 August 1938. *Prinz Eugen* was the 'lucky ship' of the German Navy, participating in nearly every major operation, including the *Bismarck* sortie and the 'Channel Dash'. She surrendered at Copenhagen in May 1945 and following the Potsdam Conference was ceded to the United States. After a period of examination she was selected for destruction in Operation 'Crossroads', the atomic bomb tests at Bikini. She survived both Test 'Able' on 1 July 1946 and test 'Baker' on 25 July 1946, remaining afloat with structural damage although she was heavily contaminated. She was then towed to Kwajalein, where she was decommissioned from the USN on 29 August 1946. On 21 December 1946 she assumed a 35-degree list due to minor damage at her stern. Salvage crews could not go on board because of the radioactivity but in order to prevent her capsizing she was towed to Enubuj Reef, where she capsized the following day. She remains there to this day, the US Navy having refused persistent requests to break her up. When commissioned into the *Kriegsmarine*, *Prinz Eugen* displaced 16,974 tons, was 654ft long and was armed weith eight 8in guns.

Proximity fuse. Fuse that detonates an anti-aircraft shell at the closest point to the target. The proximity fuse in the shell would transmit a radio signal that would bounce off the aircraft and reflect back to a receiver in the shell. The technical challenge in its production was considerable. The fuse had to fit into the head of 5in shell, be robust enough to withstand shipboard handling and the shock of being fired and be affordable in large numbers. In August 1942 the USS *Cleveland* demonstrated that the challenge had been met when she shot down three target drones with four rounds of proximity-fused 5in ammunition. The first combat use came on 5 January 1943 when the USS *Helena* brought down a Japanese 'Val' with a few rounds of proximity-fused shell. In the Pacific proximity fuses proved especially useful against *Kamikaze*s

PSW. Pro-submarine war. Operations carried out by surface and air forces in order to facilitate the operations of their own submarines. The USSR engaged in extensive PSW in order to support the operations of its own SSBNs.

PT boats. US Navy term for small, fast torpedo craft. Traditionally the US Navy had expressed little interest in such craft but 100 were ordered in 1938 for the defence of the Philippines. Elco Boatyard won a contract for a 77ft, 46-ton boat armed with four torpedo tubes and four .50-cal Browning machine guns. Three Packard petrol engines could drive the boat at a top speed of 41kts. The gun armament was later increased to include 20mm Oerlikon and 40mm Bofors, while the torpedo tubes were replaced by lightweight launchers. Some PT boats were armed with rocket launchers, the US Army 37mm gun and even infantry mortars.

Radar for night operations and smoke generators for smoke-screen-laying completed a formidable armament. A total of 499 PT boats were built for the US Navy, an additional 91 going to Britain and 166 to the USSR. Sixty-nine US PT boats were lost during the war.

Pueblo, **USS.** American intelligence-gathering vessel seized illegally by the North Koreans in international waters off Wonsan on 23 January 1968. One sailor was killed in the seizure. The ship was ill-equipped for her mission and not all the vast number of secret documents and communications equipment on board were destroyed. The intelligence haul for the North Koreans, and by implication the Russians, was probably considerable. The crew were held in primitive conditions and treated with great brutality until they were released in December 1968 after both sides agreed a face-saving diplomatic solution.

Pulse-Doppler. A radar technique for moving-target detection using the Doppler shift of returning echoes.

Q-ship. A British term, but one that now has universal application, for a warship disguised as a merchant ship in order to lure the incautious or unwary submarine to within range of her concealed weapons. The vessel needed to be as inconspicuous as possible and for this reason small coastal tramp steamers or sailing vessels were chosen. A concealed

armament of guns and torpedo tubes was fitted, invisible to the onlooker but which could be brought into action at short notice. An added refinement was the 'panic party', a group of sailors who would pretend to be the 'crew' and would abandon ship in a convincingly terrified fashion, leaving the gunners on board. The idea was developed by the Royal Navy in 1914 and the first success was the sinking of *U36* on 24 July 1915 by the decoy *Prince Charles*. Over eighty such vessels were commissioned in the Royal Navy but they only accounted for eleven U-boats against a loss of twenty-seven of their number. The Germans employed Q-ships in the Baltic in the First World War, and in the Second World War a German Q-ship, *Schiff 40*, sank the British submarine *Tarpon* on 10 April 1940 in the North Sea. In the Second World War Britain once again employed twenty Q-ships with the code-name 'Freighter'. None of them even sighted a U-boat and two were sunk. Early in 1942 the US Navy commissioned five Q-ships and deployed them off the coast of Virginia. *U123* had an encounter with the Q-ship *Atik* on 27 March 1942 and sank her. The US Navy abandoned their Q-ships in 1944. Lastly, the Japanese employed disguised warships off the coast of Java. For Q-ships to be effective they had to rely on the submarine surfacing to establish the identity and cargo of the 'target' in accordance with International Law. The advent of unrestricted submarine warfare meant that submarines shot and sank on sight. Thus, in a sense, Q-ships were self-defeating.

Queen Elizabeth, HMS. Name ship for a class of five battleships (*Queen Elizabeth*, *Warspite*, *Barham*, *Malaya* and *Valiant*) which are generally agreed to be the finest capital ships constructed for the Royal Navy. Their construction represented two considerable steps forward. They were the first capital ships to be completely oil-fired and they introduced the 15in gun into British naval service. Their service careers read like a history of the Royal Navy in the twentieth century. As built they displaced 27,500 tons (normal), were armed with eight 15in guns and fourteen (*Queen Elizabeth* sixteen) 6in guns and had a crew of 950 officers and men. Steam turbines gave a top speed of 23kts. When built they were classed as fast battleships, having the speed to operate with the Battle Cruiser Fleet but having the superior protection and armament of a battleship. *Queen Elizabeth* herself was launched in 1913 and after bombardment duty at the Dardanelles returned to the Grand Fleet, though she was in refit at the time of the Battle of Jutland. On 15 November 1918 the German naval delegation reported on board *Queen Elizabeth* to be told how the naval armistice was to be enforced. The meeting, in Beatty's day cabin, is the subject of a famous painting by Sir John Lavery entitled *The End*. Between the wars she served in the Atlantic and Mediterranean Fleets

before being rebuilt in 1937–41. Badly damaged by Italian *Maiale* at Alexandria on December 1941, she was repaired in the USA and ended the war as flagship of the Eastern Fleet.

Queen Elizabeth, RMS. Liner of 83,673 tons built for the Cunard-White Star Line and launched in 1938. She was incomplete when the Second World War broke out and on 27 February 1940 made a secret dash from the Clyde across the Atlantic to the safety of New York. She was subsequently employed as a troopship. Making three transatlantic crossings per month, she could lift an infantry division in each trip. At the end of the war she returned an equal number of US servicemen to the USA and eventually made her first commercial voyage on 16 October 1946.

Queen Mary, HMS. British battlecruiser launched in 1912 and armed with eight 13.5in guns. Another of the 'Splendid Cats', she was an improved version of *Lion*. She was in action at Heligoland Bight and the Dogger Bank but was sunk at the Battle of Jutland. *Queen Mary* was the crack gunnery ship of the Battle Cruiser Fleet and was the only one fitted with the Pollen director – which may have had something to do with the accuracy of her gunfire. Her guns had just shifted into rapid fire when she was struck on the forecastle by two 12in shells fired by *Derfflinger* which caused the explosion of 'A' and 'B' turret magazines. The forward part of

the ship as far back as the foremast was destroyed and a second explosion sent her remains to the bottom. The photograph showing the pall of smoke which marked her end is one of the most potent images of the First World War. There were only 20 survivors, and 1,266 officers and men lost their lives.

Queen Mary, RMS. Liner of 80,774 tons built for the Cunard-White Star Line and launched in 1936. During the Second World War she brought Australian troops to the Middle East and then was employed on the Atlantic, taking US troops to Europe and German PoWs to the US on the return trip. Her great speed, over 30kts, enabled her to make the voyage without escort, although an anti-aircraft escort was provided when she came within the range of German aircraft. On 2 October 1942 she ran down and sank the light cruiser HMS *Curacoa*, one of her escorts, which was manoeuvring too close to the ship. As with her near-sister ship, *Queen Elizabeth*, she could lift an infantry division in a single voyage, and between them the two 'Queens' carried 24% (425,000 men) of the US troops committed to Britain. The teak rails on her sides were engraved with names of thousands of US soldiers who made the voyage to Europe, many of whom would never return. *Queen Mary* took Churchill to the USA on two occasions: in early 1943 for the Trident Conference in Washington and in September 1944 for the Ottawa Conference. On the first voyage Churchill shared the ship

Above. The liner *Queen Mary* bunkering on the Clyde in 1942 before another fast passage across the Atlantic. (USN)

with 5,000 German PoWs, who travelled in far more spartan conditions! *Queen Mary* was returned to commercial service in August 1947. She is now preserved at Long Beach, California.

Rabaul. Chief town on the island of New Britain in the Bismarck Archipelago in the Bismarck Sea.

Before the First World War it was a German colony and it was captured by an Australian military force on 13 September 1914. It was awarded to Australia in 1919 but was captured by the Japanese in February 1942; they fortified the town, from where they could control the sea and air approaches to New Guinea and Guadalcanal.

Although US Marines landed on New Britain in December 1943 the decision had been taken not to capture the town but to starve the garrison into surrender. More than 29,000 sorties against the town were flown by US aircraft operating from carriers or land airfields. The garrison eventually capitulated on 6 September 1945.

Radar. Radio Direction and Ranging. A means of seeing objects at night, bad weather or smoke and of extending the range of sight in clear weather. It was developed simultaneously in Britain, the USA, France and Germany in the late 1930s.

Radar picket ship. Ship deployed at a distance from the main body of a fleet in order to provide early warning of incoming aircraft, ships and missiles.

RAM. Radar absorbent material. Material draped over ship's superstructures to reduce its radar return. RAM was used extensively by Coalition ships during the 1991 Gulf War.

RAN. Royal Australian Navy.

RAT. Rocket-assisted torpedo. Early American-designed ASW missile. After failure of trials in the USS *Sarsfield* in 1957 it was abandoned in favour of ASROC.

***Rawalpindi*, HMS.** A 16,500 ton P&O passenger liner requisitioned as an armed merchant cruiser at the beginning of World War Two and armed with eight 6in guns. She was sunk in a very uneven, 14 minute gunnery duel with the *Scharnhorst,* south-east of Iceland in November 1939.

'Regenbogen', Operation. German code-word for the attack on convoy JW.51A in December 1942 by the pocket battleship *Lützow* and cruiser *Admiral Hipper. See* Barents Sea, Battle of the. The term *'Regenbogen'* was also used for the scuttling or destruction of all U-boats in the event of a capitulation. Under the terms of the local surrender signed at Lüneberg Heath and the formal capitulation signed at Rheims and Berlin, the destruction of U-boats was expressly forbidden. However, many U-boat commanders argued (with some justification) that the surrender had been signed under duress and that the orders were not applicable. Accordingly 138 U-boat commanders sank or wrecked their boats in the first week of May 1945.

Regulus. A family of jet-propelled American naval land attack cruise missiles. The subsonic Regulus I had a range of 575 miles was operationally deployed in submarines, cruisers and aircraft carriers. A total of 514 missiles were built, but an upgraded Regulus II was cancelled in favour of Polaris.

Renown, HMS. British battlecruiser launched in 1916. She displaced 27,650 tons, was 794ft long and was armed with six 15in guns. She had a top speed of 30kts. Between 1936 and 1939 she underwent a massive reconstruction to serve as a fast carrier escort. During the Second World War she became best known for her operations with Force H in the Mediterranean and Eastern Atlantic. She later served in the Eastern Fleet and was broken up in 1948.

Repulse, HMS. British battlecruiser launched in 1916 and sister ship to *Renown* although not subsequently reconstructed to the same degree. In October 1941 she formed Force Z with HMS *Prince of Wales* and was dispatched to Singapore. On 10 December 1941 she was sunk by Japanese aircraft off the east coast of Malaya after being hit by one 550lb bomb and five torpedoes;. 327 of her crew of 960 were lost.

Rescue ships. Specially adapted merchant ships used by Britain and America during the Second World War to rescue survivors from sunken merchant ships and warships. By 1945 twenty-nine rescue ships were in service in the European theatre. They were manned by Merchant Navy crews, though naval gunners and other specialists were carried. They carried additional lifeboats and rafts, enhanced medical facilities and supplies of clothing and bedding for survivors. British rescue ships rescued 4,190 Allied survivors as well as four German survivors from a U-boat.

Retro-bomb. Anti-submarine weapon developed during the Second World War designed for use with MAD. The accurate position of a submarine detected by MAD could only be determined when the aircraft was directly overhead. Conventional air-dropped weapons, if launched at this point, would have the forward velocity of the aircraft and thus fall some way ahead of the target. The retro-bomb was given reverse velocity, by means of a rocket, equal to the forward velocity of the aircraft, so that it fell in a straight line. The weapon was a modified Mousetrap 7in projectile with a 35lb warhead and a variable firing speed of 174–347kts. In the first half of 1944 retro-bombs were used successfully in the Straits of Gibraltar to sink a couple of U-boats in conjunction with surface forces, but the only sinking directly attributable to the retro-bomb is that of *U1107*, sunk by a US Navy Catalina of VP-63 off Ushant on 30 April 1945.

Reuben James, USS. The first US warship to be sunk during the Second World War. She was hit by a single torpedo fired by *U562* on 31 October 1941, broke in half and sank with the loss of 115 of her 160-man crew. The casualties were exacerbated by her depth charges, which were not set to 'safe', exploding after the ship sank. *Reuben James* was launched in 1920, was 314ft long, displaced 1,190 tons (standard) and was armed with four 4in guns and twelve 21in torpedo tubes.

RFA. Royal Fleet Auxiliary. Civilian organisation which operates the oilers and supply ships of the Royal Navy.

'Rheinübung', Operation. German code-word for the commerce-raiding sortie into the Atlantic made by *Bismarck* and *Prinz Eugen*.

Riga, Gulf of. Strategically important area in the Baltic to the Germans since Russia's control of it and its islands enabled her to threaten the left flank of the German Army. It was finally secured, though at some cost, in Operation 'Albion'.

Riskflotte (Risk Fleet). Doctrine advocated by the German Admiral Tirpitz as a justification for the rapid increase in the German Navy before the First World War. Briefly, it meant that Germany had to have a fleet strong enough that, in a defensive war in the North Sea, the British would fear to challenge it in case they suffered a serious defeat. It was a counter-productive doctrine in that fear of German naval rearmament and the cost of competing directly with Germany forced Britain to enter into a system of European alliances after nearly a century of 'splendid isolation'.

River Plate, Battle of the. The first naval action of the Second World War, taking place on 13 December 1939. The German pocket battleship *Admiral Graf Spee* was brought to action by the cruisers *Exeter*, *Ajax* and *Achilles*. After a brief engagement, in which *Exeter* was badly damaged, *Graf Spee* retired and headed for the Uruguayan port of Montevideo and internment. The 'battle' then turned into a diplomatic offensive. First the British sought to pressurise the Uruguayan authorities into making *Graf Spee* leave. Then, in an abrupt change of plan, they sought to keep the ship in Montevideo until superior forces arrived. This would take some time, but the British wove a web of deceit to convince everyone, including the Germans, that *Ark Royal* and *Renown* were almost over the horizon. However, the Uruguayans insisted that *Graf Spee* leave by 2000 on 17 December. At 1815 that evening *Graf Spee* left the harbour and was then scuttled in Montevideo Roads, her crew seeking internment in Argentina.

RKR. Russian designation for a large- or medium-size ship whose primary armament consists of anti-ship missiles, such as *Kirov*.

Rockets. Unguided missiles used extensively by naval forces in the bombardment role during the Second World War. The ultimate rocket ship was the US Navy's LSMR series, which had twenty automatic-loading, rapid-fire 5in rocket launchers. Carrier-borne aircraft also successfully used rockets to attack ships and submarines and also for ground support. The US 5in aircraft rocket had a 50lb explosive warhead which was lethally effective against ships. Later versions were designated HVAR (High Velocity Aircraft Rocket) but were popularly known as 'Holy Moses'. The US Navy also developed an 11in rocket with a 150lb warhead known as 'Tiny Tim'. An aircraft armed with eight of these packed the same punch as a light cruiser.

Rodney, HMS. British battleship completed September 1929 and scapped in 1948. Sister ship to HMS *Nelson*. Her main armament was nine 16in guns and her top speed was 23 knots. Her most notable action was her involvement with the sinking of the *Bismarck* where she played and important part in the reduction of the German battleship with gunfire.

Roma. Italian *Littorio* class battleship launched in 1940. She had a displacement of 40,992 tons, was 735ft long (pp) and was armed with nine 15in guns. On 9 September 1943 *Roma* was proceeding to Malta and internment in compliance with the terms of the Armistice when she was attacked by a force of eleven Do 217 aircraft of *III./KG 100* carrying FX 1200 radio-controlled bombs. *Roma* was hit twice. The first bomb struck amidships, passing through the ship and exploding under the bottom. The second struck abreast the bridge and went forward, exploding in the forward 15in magazines. The explosions broke the ship in two and she sank. There were 595 survivors from a crew of 1,849.

Room 40. The British naval code-breaking organisation during the First World War. It was named after the room number in the Old Admiralty Building where its workers resided. There was some suspicion between the civilian code-breakers and their naval colleagues, and as a result Room 40 did not become a true intelligence centre until late in the war. Today this historic room has a more prosaic use as part of the Northern Ireland Office's accommodation in Whitehall.

'Rösselsprung', Operation. German code-word for the attack by a surface task group on the British convoy PQ.17 in July 1942.

Rosyth. British base on the southern shore of the Firth of Forth which was much expanded during the First World War. It was the home of the Battle Cruiser Fleet from 1914 and that of the Grand Fleet from April 1918. It was at Rosyth that the German Fleet surrendered in November 1918. During the inter-war period the dockyard was used to break up the German ships scuttled at Scapa Flow. The dockyard was enlarged in the Second World War and in the post-war period, the emphasis on operations in the Arctic gave the port a new importance. With the submarines based at Faslane on the western coast of Scotland and a large proportion of the surface fleet based at Rosyth, some wags referred to the Royal Navy as the 'Scottish Navy'. However in the run-down of British defence bases Rosyth was selected for closure and the yard sold into private ownership.

ROV. Remotely operated vehicle. Small submersibles used in mine-hunting to detect and destroy mines.

Above: Royal Marines raise the Union Flag at the San Carlos beachhead, 21 May 1982, during the Falkland Conflict. (IWM FKD 77)

Royal Navy. The oldest organised fighting service in the world.

Royal Marines. Organised military force under the control of the Royal Navy. Up until the Second World War each ship of cruiser size and above would carry a Royal Marine detachment which would form a fully integrated part of the ship's company but could be deployed as a landing party if required. In 1937 it was proposed to employ Royal Marines as specialised amphibious troops and thus began their metamorphosis into Commandos. During the Second World War Royal Marine Commandos carried out considerable raiding activity on French, Belgian and Dutch coasts. In the Normandy invasion two Marine Commandos, Nos 47 and 48, went ashore with the first wave and suffered heavy losses. Today the Royal Marines are organised into three Commandos, 40, 42 and 45, together with a headquarters and training structure, a Commando Logistics Regiment and support artillery, air squadron and engineer units seconded from the Army who wear their own regimental insignia with the Commandos' green beret. Royal Marine detachments are still carried by individual ships and their special skills are particularly useful in 'stop and search' operations when enforcing UN sanctions. Since the end of the Second World War 1968 has been the only year in which Royal Marines have not been deployed on active service throughout the world. Their most recent hurried deployment was as the spearhead battalion to Kuwait in 1994 in the face of a threatened invasion by Iraq. In a ceremonial role, the bands of the Royal Marines are renowned for their high standards of musicianship and drill.

Royal Oak, **HMS.** British battleship of the *Royal Sovereign* Class completed in November 1914 and sunk by *U47* in Scapa Flow, 14 October 1939. Here main armament was eight 15in guns and her top speed was 21.5 knots. She was present at the Battle of Jutland in the 4th Battle Squadron.

Rubis. French minelaying submarine of the *Saphir* class launched at Toulon in September 1931. During the early part of the Second World War she operated with the Royal Navy in the North Sea but on 3 July 1940, in common with other French warships in UK ports, was seized by the Royal Navy – although the seizure was carried out with a good deal of tact and sensitivity. Her ship's company were offered the choice of remaining in Britain and carrying on the fight or being repatriated to France. With the exception of one officer, one senior rate and three ratings, all decided to stay. *Rubis* carried out a total of twenty-eight patrols under British command and laid 683 mines which claimed fourteen merchant ships sunk, one damaged, seven A/S vessels or minesweepers sunk and one U-boat damaged. *Rubis* had a displacement of 762/923 tons, was 66m long and was armed with three 550mm and two 400mm torpedo tubes, one 75mm gun and thirty-two mines carried in wells in the saddle tanks. She was scuttled off Toulon in 1957 for use as a submerged sonar target.

Rufiji River. River on the east coast of Africa where the German cruiser *Königsberg* took refuge in 1915. There she was located and destroyed by gunfire from British monitors and scuttled by her crew on 11 July 1915. Remnants of her wreck can be seen to this day.

Rules of Engagement (ROE). In post-1945 'peacekeeping' operations it has been quite common for local naval commanders to operate under rules which determine the level of response he may make when faced with a given situation. If coalition or multinational forces are involved then the establishing of ROE becomes a nightmare since the various constituent governments may, and do, have different ideas of how deeply they are prepared to let their forces become involved. Invariably as soon as ROE are established, a situation arises which requires their hurried revision!

Russo-Japanese War. The naval side began with a Japanese torpedo boat attack on the Russian fleet anchorage at Port Arthur on 8 February 1904. The Japanese then blockaded the port. During the first four months of the war two Japanese battleships and two Russian battleships were sunk by mines laid by both sides. On 10 August the Russians attempted a break-out from Port Arthur and this resulted in the Battle of the Yellow Sea, a Japanese success. Four days later the Japanese had another success at the Battle of Ulsan (or the Japanese Sea), a cruiser action. Admiral Togo finally achieved a crushing naval victory over the Russian fleet in the Straits of Tsushima on 27–28 May 1905, which was to lead to the conclusion of the war.

RWR. Rapid-response warning radar. Radar designed to give the quickest possible warning of an incoming threat.

Sabbioncello peninsula. Peninsula on the Dalmatian coast that was the location for a number of Italian and later American schemes for a landing during the First World War with the objective of cutting the coastal shipping traffic between the northern Adriatic and the Austrian port of Cattaro. Numerous schemes were launched but all foundered on the number of forces to be employed and who would provide them. The main difficulty lay in the fact that the peninsula was part of the mainland and therefore would have to be defended against a counter-attack by substantial Austrian forces. The last plan, an American one involving the US Marines, was dropped in March 1918 when the Germans launched their *Kaiserschlacht* offensive on the Western Front. No adventures in the Adriatic could be afforded until the Germans had been contained on the Western Front, and so the plan was quietly abandoned.

SAG. Surface Attack Group. A group of surface ships not accompanied by an aircraft carrier. The introduction of the Tomahawk and Harpoon missiles gave surface ships a considerable punch and this term was coined by the USN in the late 1970s for powerful surface task forces without organic air cover.

Sagarwardene. A 330-ton patrol craft of the Sri Lankan Navy built by Colombo Dockyard in November 1983. On 19 September 1994 she was sunk by Tamil 'Tiger' guerrillas in a suicide attack.

St Nazaire. *See Campbeltown,* HMS.

Saipan. Island in the Marianas chain in the Pacific which was captured by the Americans – though only after fierce resistance which cost the lives of 29,000 of the 30,000 Japanese defenders – in June 1944. From a naval point of view the Saipan landings saw the first use of UDT teams to bring back important information on water depth, channels, tides, currents and beach gradients.

Sakhalin. *See* Kuril Islands.

Salerno. Italian port on the Tyrrhenian Sea, 25 miles south of Naples, chosen for the invasion of Italy in September 1943. Initially successful landings were frustrated by a determined German defence which threatened to drive the invaders back into the sea. Rapidly deployed naval gunfire support from the battleship HMS

Valiant disrupted a German counter-attack and saved the day.

SAM. Surface-to-air missile.

Samar, Battle of. *See* Leyte Gulf, Battle of.

Samuel B. Roberts, **USS.** US Navy destroyer escort, part of Rear-Admiral Sprague's TU.77. 4.3, which was sunk in action with Admiral Kurita's Centre Force during the Battle of Samar, part of the wider action of the Battle of Leyte Gulf. Faced with most of the Japanese surface fleet, including four battleships, Sprague ordered his destroyers and destroyer escorts to make smoke and cover the carriers. Their defence of the carriers was nothing short of epic, but *Samuel B. Roberts* was badly damaged and sank after receiving over twenty hits from heavy-calibre shells. In the post-war period an *Oliver Hazard Perry* class frigate was given the same name. On 14 April 1988 she struck an Iranian contact mine in the Persian Gulf and very nearly broke her back. Repairs were completed in October 1989 and at the time of writing the ship is in commission.

San Diego, **USS.** An armoured cruiser launched in 1904 (ex-*California*) which was mined off Long Island on a mine laid by U156. Only six of her crew were killed, but she was the US Navy's largest single loss during the First World War. The name was also borne by a Second World War *Atlanta* class cruiser (CL53)

Sang-O. The name of a class of an estimated sixteen SSKs built by North Korea and configured largely for special operations, usually the landing of North Korean special forces in South Korea. They have a displacement of 275/330 tons surfaced and are 111ft long with a crew of two officers and twelve ratings. In September 1996 a *Sang-O* ran aground at Kangnung in South Korea while landing a three-man reconnaissance team. The team was to make preparations for a subsequent operation to assassinate South Korean VIPs at the country's national games to be held in October. Of the twenty-six crew and special forces embarked, eleven were shot by their own side, one was captured, one escaped and the remainder were killed in fighting with South Korean troops.

Santa Cruz, Battle of. The critical naval action, on 26 October 1942, in the US campaign to hold the beach-head on Guadalcanal. The Japanese mounted a major effort in which their carrier fleet would co-ordinate operations with land-based aircraft in support of the Army. However, the US Marines held the island and although the Americans lost the carrier *Hornet*, the Japanese were forced to withdraw with two of their carriers damaged and heavy losses in aircrew.

SAR. Synthetic aperture radar. Radar that uses the motion of the platform and computer-processing to assemble a detailed image of the target.

Saratoga, **USS.** Sister ship to the *Lexington*, the 'Sara' served throughout the Second World War and earned seven Battle Stars (q.v,). She recorded no fewer than 98,549 deck landings in the course of operations at Guadalcanal, Makin, the Marshall Islands, Tarawa, Sumatra and Iwo Jima. After the war she operated as a repatriation ship for US troops returning from the Pacific before she was expended in the atomic bomb tests on 25 July 1946. The blast lifted the 36,000-ton ship 143ft clear of the water and moved her horizontally several hundred yards. *Saratoga* was launched in April 1925, had a standard displacement of 36,000 tons, was 888ft long and could operate some ninety aircraft.

Savannah, **USS** (CL42). American cruiser which was struck on 11 September 1943 by a Fritz X missile off Salerno. The missile went through a gun turret and exploded deep in the ship. Only massive flooding of the ship through holes made by the explosion extinguished the fires and prevented a sympathetic detonation of the magazine. 206 men were killed in the attack.

Savo Island, Battle of. Two days after the American landings on Guadalcanal, a powerful Japanese squadron, consisting of five heavy cruisers, two light cruisers and a destroyer, under Rear-Admiral Mikawa was dispatched from Rabaul to attack the beach-head. The Japanese proceeded down 'The Slot' in broad daylight on 8

August and approached Savo Island from the north-west undetected. Reconnaissance aircraft had already told Mikawa where the American-Australian force of five heavy cruisers and six destroyers was deployed but the latter were quite unaware of the approaching Japanese ships. Shortly after 0200 the Japanese opened fire and in very short order the cruisers HMAS *Canberra* and the USS *Astoria*, *Quincy* and *Vincennes* had been sunk or crippled so badly that they foundered later. This remarkable action was achieved at no cost to the Japanese, who then surprisingly withdrew without carrying out the planned bombardment. On the way back to Rabaul the American submarine *S-44* sank the cruiser *Kako* – but it was small consolation. The victory had been made possible by the excellence of Japanese night-fighting tactics, tactics to which the Americans would not find an effective counter until sufficient ships equipped with radar appeared in-theatre.

SBD Dauntless. (see overleaf) US Navy carrier-borne dive-bomber which sank more warship tonnage than any other aircraft. It was the SBD which accounted for the four Japanese carriers at Midway.

SB2C Helldiver. US Navy carrier-borne scout/dive-bomber. It succeeded the SBD but never achieved the popularity or successes of this aircraft.

SBS. Special Boat Section. A specialist section within the British

Above: SB2C Helldivers from a carrier in Task Force 58 on a mission near Saipan. (IWM MH 6873)
Below: SBD Dauntless dive-bombers about to strike Japanese held Eniwetok. (IWM EN 20133)

Above: The German battlecruiser *Scharnhorst* sunk at the Battle of the North Cape on 26 December 1943 with the loss of all but 36 of her complement of 1,800 officers and men. (USN)

commando organisation specialising in waterborne raids behind enemy lines. From 1946 the SBS was a fully integrated part of the Royal Marines and was renamed the Special Boat Service in 1975.

Scapa Flow. Superb natural anchorage in the Orkney Islands which was the base for the British Grand Fleet between 1914 and 1918. The Flow was also the location for the internment of the High Seas Fleet in November 1918 and their subsequent scuttling on 21 June 1919. In the inter-war period extensive salvage operations raised most of the German ships, which were dispatched, upside down, to Rosyth for breaking up. In the Second World War the Flow was the base for the

Home Fleet. Today there are no defence installations at Scapa Flow but there are three war graves: the battleship *Vanguard* which blew up on 9 July 1917 as a result of a magazine explosion; the battleship *Royal Oak*, torpedoed by *U47* on 14 October 1939; and *UB116*, mined while trying to enter the Flow on 28 October 1918.

Scarborough. Town on the East Coast of England which, along with Hartlepool and Whitby, was bombarded by units of the High Seas Fleet on 16 December 1914. There was considerable damage to property and many civilian casualties. Unlike Hartlepool, Scarborough was not a defended town and therefore the bombardment

was illegal under international law. 'The Babykillers of Scarborough' was a taunt that would be hurled at the Germans for the rest of the war.

Scharnhorst. A name that has been used three times for German warships this century. The first was a 12,781-ton armoured cruiser launched in 1906 and sunk at the Battle of the Falkland Islands on 8 December 1914. The second was a 34,841 ton battlecruiser launched in 1936. She took part in the 1940 Norwegian campaign, sinking the British aircraft carrier *Glorious* on 8 June 1940. She participated in Operation 'Berlin' before returning to Germany in the Channel Dash. She was then sent to Norway for operations

Above: The *Schnorkel*, the 'underwater breathing tube' which revolutionised submarine operations before the development of the nuclear submarine. This photograph shows a combined induction/exhaust mast with the characteristic "geffufle" being thrown up by the exhaust. (Author)

against Arctic convoys and was sunk on 26 December 1943 in the Battle of the North Cape. There were 36 survivors from her crew of 1,815. The third *Scharnhorst* was the ex-British *Black Swan* class frigate HMS *Mermaid.* She was acquired in 1959 and broken up in 1990.

Schnellboot. German Second World War term for MTB.

Schnorchel (snorkel). Mechanism designed to allow submarines to use their diesel engines while submerged. It consists of an induction/exhaust mast which can be raised to allow air into the boat. While 'schnorchelling', or 'snorting' in British parlance, confers a number of advantages in that the boat can proceed at a good speed without draining the battery, it has a number of disadvantages.

The noise of the diesels can degrade the submarine's hydrophones and the distinctive 'geffufle' of the exhaust makes the submarine easier to spot from an aircraft or helicopter. The exhaust emissions are also vulnerable to infra-red detection. More importantly, if the battery is charged while the boat is 'snorting', great care must be taken to clear the hydrogen gas given off during the charging process. Lastly, if a submarine is 'snorting' with the wind astern, the exhaust gases can be drawn back into the boat via the induction mast.

SCS (Sea Control Ship). Abortive 1970s US design for a 10,000-ton small carrier operating helicopters and STOVL aircraft. A revised SCS design was built under licence in Spain and commissioned in the Spanish Navy as *Príncipe de*

Asturias. She displaces 16,700 tons, is 187.5m long and can carry an air group of seventeen helicopters or STOVL aircraft. The ship operates the EAV-8B Matador II STOVL aircraft, a US-built variant of the British Harrier.

SDV. Swimmer Delivery Vehicle. The modern successor to the Chariot and *Maiale.* SDVs are used to deliver frogmen/special forces to the beach or on special operations and can carry a variety of stores. They can be launched from ships or carried in containers on the casings of specially adapted submarines. They are widely employed by a number of navies.

Seabees. US Navy construction troops. The first Seabee battalions were authorised on 5 January 1942 and were formed from US personnel who had worked in the building industry. They served in all theatres of war but their most important achievement was the construction of airfields and port facilities on the islands of Guam, Saipan and Tinian from which B-29 bombers could attack Japan.

Seacat. First-generation British shipborne SAM. It was radio command-guided and had a range of 5,000yds and an altitude of 3,300ft. It was incapable of engaging supersonic targets.

Sea Dart. British second-generation long-range shipborne SAM fitted in Type 42 destroyers and *Invincible* class CVSs. It is rocket-boosted with a ramjet sustainer motor and has forty-mile range. Guidance is by semi-active radar homing. The missile performed well in the 1982 Falklands Conflict although Argentine knowledge of its capabilities (the system is fitted in the two Argentine Navy Type 42 destroyers) made most Argentine pilots fly low beneath its Type 901 tracking radar. However, the fact that the missile is limited to a single target per guidance channel means that it easily swamped during multiple attacks. During the Gulf Conflict of 1991 it was credited with shooting down an Iraqi Silkworm anti-ship missile.

Seafire. Naval variant of the famous Spitfire fighter aircraft which served in the RAF. It was employed by the Fleet Air Arm as an interceptor and ground attack aircraft. However, its fragile undercarriage was ill-suited to the rigours of flight-deck landings.

Sea Harrier. Navalised variant of the Hawker-Siddley Harrier VSTOL (Vertical/Short Take Off) combat aircraft. The type is in service the with Royal Navy and the Indian navy. Sea Harriers first saw combat during the

Above: A Sea Harrier FRS 1 seen here while hovering. (IWM FKD 591)

Falklands conflict where they gained over twenty aerial victories for the lose of none to action with enemy aircraft. Ideal for operation from medium and small aircraft carriers with their limited deck space.

SEAL. Acronym for US Navy Special Forces – Sea Air Land teams.

Sea Skua. British air-to-surface missile carried by Lynx helicopters. First used operationally during the 1982 Falklands Conflict when not yet cleared for front-line service, and again during the 1991 Gulf War. *See* Bubyian Channel, Battle of.

***Seawolf,* USS.** Lead unit of a class of very capable SSNs built for the US Navy to replace the *Los Angeles* class. However, the highprice tag per unit has meant that Congress has restricted funding to two vessels.

***Seeadler,* SMS.** A German commerce raider of the First World War, originally the fully rigged ship *Pass of Balmaha*, captured by *U36* and taken as a prize. She was subsequently armed with two 10cm guns. Her disguise, which included Norwegian-speaking German crew members, was such that she fooled the British cruiser which stopped her on her outward passage. Under the command of *Kapitänleutnant* Felix *Graf* von Luckner she sank

Above: A Sea Skua armed Lynx on the flight deck of HMS *Hermes* during the Falklands Conflict. (IWM FKD 591)

or captured sixteen ships. She was wrecked at Mopihaa in the Society Islands on 2 August 1917. Two of her boats survived and in one Luckner and five others set out to capture a schooner but instead were taken as PoWs and transferred to New Zealand. The others set out in the remaining boat and after capturing a small French schooner, which they renamed *Fortune*, reached Easter Island. They were then found by a Chilean cruiser, taken to the mainland and interned. *Seeadler* may not have been the most productive of the German raiders but is certainly the most romantic.

Seehund. Type XXVIIB two-man U-boat which was the most technically advanced of all the German midget craft of the Second World War. The *Seehund* displaced 14.9 tons, was 11.9m long and was powered by a 60bhp diesel and a 25hp electric motor. Top speed on the surface was 7.7kts and submerged speed was 6kts. The armament consisted of two G7e torpedoes or mines. Some 285 craft were built, of which 35 were lost in action. Great care had been taken in the design and the *Seehund* was virtually undetectable. It was too small to give an accurate asdic return while being almost inaudible to the passive hydrophones of the day. The craft were employed from bases in the Netherlands and Heligoland.

'Seelöwe', Operation. Operation 'Sealion' – the projected German naval invasion of Great Britain which was cancelled in October 1940. By the standards of later Anglo-American landings it was a poorly conceived operation.

Seeteufel. German midget submarine developed towards the end of the Second World War which was uniquely fitted with both propeller and a tracked drive for moving overland. The Germans had experienced problems in finding suitable launching sites for *Neger*, *Marder*, *Molch* and *Biber* craft and so *Seeteufel* was fitted with caterpillar tracks so that she could make her own way into the water. Only one such craft was built and she was destroyed after the Second World War. However, the discovery of strange caterpillar-like tracks on the sea bottom off the coast of Sweden suggest that the idea was resurrected by the Soviets.

Seraph, HMS. British 'S' class submarine which participated in a number of unusual special operations, including taking General Mark Clark to North Africa for covert negotiations with the French before the North African landings in October 1942. She then embarked the French General Giraud from occupied France in November 1942 before taking part in Operation 'Mincemeat' in April 1943. *Seraph* was launched in October 1941, displaced 715/842 tons, was 217ft long and was armed with seven 21in torpedo tubes.

Sevastopol. Port on the northern Black Sea coast. In the past it has been the home of the Russian and Soviet Black Sea Fleet. Following the break-up of the USSR, the port is now the major base of the Ukrainian Navy.

Seydlitz, SMS. German battlecruiser 657ft long, displacing 24,594 tons and armed with ten 11in guns. She participated in all the major fleet actions of the First World War. At Dogger Bank she was hit by three 13.5in shells, one of which struck the stern turret and started a massive cordite fire. On 24 April 1916 she was mined and at Jutland she was hit by eight 15in shells, six 13.5in shells, eight 12in shells and a torpedo. She returned to Wilhelmshaven with her forecastle awash and with 5,329 tons of flood water on board. At the end of the war she was interned at Scapa Flow and scuttled on 21 June 1919. Her wreck was subsequently raised and broken up at Rosyth.

Shangri-La, USS. *Essex* class aircraft carrier launched in 1944 and named after the mythical kingdom in James Hilton's novel *Lost Horizon*. When Roosevelt was asked where the bombers had come from which had bombed Tokyo in the Doolittle Raid, he answered 'Shangri-La!' The US Navy promptly gave the name to a carrier then under construction. *Shangri-La* paid off in 1969 and was broken up in 1972.

Shatt-al-Arab. The channel at the northern end of the Persian Gulf by which the Tigris and Euphrates rivers reach the sea after their confluence at Kurnah. During the First World War the waterway was taken by the British, as was the port of Basrah at its northern end, in order to safeguard oil supplies. In the 1980–88 Iran–Iraq War the waterway was the scene of fierce fighting.

Sheffield, HMS. The name selected for one of the eight *Southampton* class cruisers. *Sheffield* was known as the 'Shiny Sheff' as all her metal fittings on the upper deck were bright stainless steel supplied by the steelworks of the city whose name she bore. *Sheffield* was one of those ships never far from the action and her record of service in the Second World War resembles a potted history of the Royal Navy. She served in Norway in 1940, against the Bismarck, at the Battle of the Barents Sea and at the Battle of the North Cape. She had standard displacement of 9,100 tons, was 558ft long and was armed with twelve 6in guns. She was broken up in 1967. The name was given to the first of the Royal Navy's Type 42 destroyers launched in June 1971. She was disabled and set on fire by an Argentine AM.39 Exocet missile on 4 May 1982 and scuttled six days later. The name was given to a Type 22 frigate launched in March 1986 which is still in service.

Shetland Bus. The name given to the clandestine supply line running between Lerwick in the Shetland Islands and occupied Norway during the Second World War. The name had its origins in the regularity with which the service ran.

Shinano. Third of the *Yamato* class super-dreadnoughts, converted to an aircraft carrier while under construction, thus reflecting the nature of naval warfare in the Pacific. She was configured as a support carrier and carried replacement aircraft, fuel and ordnance for other ships. In her day she was the biggest aircraft carrier ever built and she was not superseded in size until the nuclear-powered USS *Enterprise*, which was launched in 1960. *Shinano* was not fully completed when she was torpedoed on 29 November 1944 by the submarine USS *Archerfish*. Even though her crew were not worked up, her watertight subdivision was such that she remained afloat for seven hours after the attack. *Archerfish*'s CO, Lt-Cdr Joseph Enright (who had been previously relieved of submarine command for alleged lack of aggressiveness) claimed a 28,000-ton escort carrier as his target and it was not until after the war that the identity of his victim was known and he was belatedly awarded a Navy Cross. *Shinano* had a displacement of 62,000 tons standard and 71,890 tons full load. She was 800ft long and carried the rather low (for her size) number of 47 aircraft.

Shinyo. Japanese term for a suicide explosive motor boat. These craft were the surface equivalent of the *Kamikaze* aircraft and were built in large numbers from early 1945, total production amounting to some 6,000 units by the end of the war. They had a displacement of between 1.35 and 2.15 tons and were 16ft long. They carried an

explosive charge in the bow or two depth charges. The operator would slink along at slow speed until he had selected a target and then accelerate into the final attack run. Although the operator could abandon the craft at the last moment, most remained with their craft until the end. They were extensively used by the Japanese to attack the invasion fleet off Okinawa in April and May 1945 and plans existed to make even greater use of them should the Anglo-American forces land on the home islands. The threat they posed was successfully countered by radar, intensive patrolling and the illumination of areas where *Shinyo* were thought to be lurking.

Sho-Go. Complex Japanese plan for the destruction of the

American landing force in Leyte Gulf in October 1944. *See* Leyte Gulf, Battle of.

Shoho. The first Japanese aircraft carrier to be lost during the Second World War. She was sunk by US carrier-borne aircraft during the Battle of the Coral Sea after sustaining twelve bomb hits and at least seven torpedo hits. She sank in less than ten minutes with the loss of some 600 lives. *Shoho* was built as a submarine depot ship and converted to a light carrier in 1941–42. She had a displacement of 11,262 tons, was 712ft long and carried thirty aircraft. She had been in commission for less than five months when she was sunk.

Side array. Passive sonar array mounted along the side of a ship or submarine.

SIGINT. Signals Intelligence. A wide term for the intelligence derived from enemy radio communications. It includes analysis of the type of signal – certain signals would suggest a certain type of ship(s) – as well as decoding of signal traffic to reveal the content.

Signature. The distinctive emission – noise, electronic or infrared – of a particular target which can be used for identification or targeting purposes.

Silkworm. Chinese anti-ship tactical cruise missile, a variant of the Russian SS-N-2 Styx.

Simonstown. Naval base in South Africa where the Royal Navy retained facilities after South African independence. In 1967 the agreement whereby Britain used the base was renegotiated in the light of political pressure resulting form opposition to South Africa's apartheid policy. In 1974 the agreement was cancelled by Britain and all base facilities were given up.

Simulation and simulators. The escalating cost of naval training since the end of the Second World War, and in particular the high cost of missiles and other 'smart' ordnance, has led to the development and widespread use of simulators for training purposes. Modern navies use a wide range of simulators to practise high-cost evolutions such as flight deck take-offs and landings and missile firings without having to incur the expense of the real thing.

Singapore. Island at the southern end of the Malayan peninsula

Above: The Japanese aircraft carrier *Shoho*. (IWM MH 6493)

which was selected in 1923 as the site of Britain's main naval base in the Far East after the First World War since the Washington Naval Treaty prohibited the development of Hong Kong. Work progressed extremely slowly and was subject to the financial health of the UK economy. Construction was suspended by the Labour government of 1924 and 1929–31. When war came in 1941 the naval base was complete with adequate defences against attack from the sea. However, land and air defences were inadequate. This weakness, together with the total underestimation of the Japanese Army's jungle fighting capability, caused the swift capture of the base by the Japanese in February 1942. After the war Britain retained base rights at Singapore up to November 1971.

SIOP. Single Integrated Operational Plan. The central nuclear war plan for US strategic forces, including SSBNs and nuclear-capable ships. The first SIOP was drawn up in December 1960 and has been continually updated since then to meet changing threats and requirements.

Sirte, Battle of. The first Battle of Sirte was a brief and indecisive engagement on 17 December 1941 in the Gulf of Sirte between British and Italian ships, all of which were covering the movement of convoys. The Italian force, consisting of two battleships supported by light forces, came into contact with Rear-Admiral Philip Vian's light cruisers and destroyers. Despite the superior odds, the Italians turned away when Vian demonstrated his intention to attack. The second Battle of Sirte, which took place on 22 March 1942, was one of the great convoy defensive actions of the Second World War. A force of four British cruisers and ten destroyers under Rear-Admiral Vian was covering the movement of four fast merchant ships to Malta. The Italians dispatched the battleship *Littorio*, three cruisers and eight destroyers to meet the convoy. The action lasted for approximately four and a half hours in heavy seas. Vian's bold and determined tactics consisted in taking cover behind a smoke-screen laid between him and the Italians and emerging from it periodically to simulate torpedo attacks. Eventually the smoke rolled close enough to the Italians for a torpedo attack to be delivered, at which point the Italians turned away. The British suffered no losses but the cruiser *Euryalus* and the destroyers *Havock*, *Kingston* and *Lively* were damaged by shellfire.

Sirte, Gulf of. Natural bight off the coast of Libya in North Africa. In the early 1980s the Libyan Government claimed the whole of the Gulf, not just the littoral waters, as Libyan territorial waters. This sparked off a major clash with the US Navy, who in 1986 launched operation El Dorado Canyon in which the FAC *Beir Glulud* and an ex-Soviet *Nanuchka* missile corvette, *No 419*, were sunk by A-6 Intruder aircraft. Another *Nanuchka* was damaged.

Skua. British Blackburn-designed monoplane naval fighter and dive-bomber which became the first aircraft to sink a German warship during the Second World War. On 10 April 1940 sixteen Skua aircraft sank the cruiser *Königsberg* in Bergenfjord. On the return trip to Hatston in the Orkney Islands one Skua shot down a Do 18 flying boat – the first aircraft 'kill' for the Fleet Air Arm. The Skua had a maximum speed of 225mph and a range of 760 miles. It was the first

operational monoplane to serve with the Fleet Air Arm but it was withdrawn from service in 1941.

Slapton Sands. A coastal area in South Devon much used by the US Army during the Second World War for amphibious training prior to the Normandy landings. During Exercise 'Tiger' German *S-Boote* intercepted an American landing force, sinking one LST and damaging another with the loss of 638 American lives.

SLC (*Siluro a Lenta Corsa*: lit., slow-running torpedo). One of the most effective weapons of the Second World War, the two-man SLC was used by *Decima Mas* in operations against British shipping in Alexandria and Gibraltar. It could be carried on the casing of a larger submarine or, in respect of the later operations at Gibraltar, released from the specially converted hold in the tanker's hull. It was 6.7m long and had an electric motor giving a

speed of 4.5kts. It was armed with a detachable 200kg explosive charge which the two operators would try to suspend beneath the target's hull, thus increasing the explosive effect. The two operators, wearing rubber suits and breathing pure oxygen, sat astride the craft, but in a later variant, the SSB, they sat in an internal free-flooding compartment. The operation for which the weapon is best remembered is the attack on Alexandria on the night of 19

Above: Skua aircraft on board HMS *Ark Royal*. (IWM A 3782)

December 1941 in which the battleships *Valiant* and *Queen Elizabeth* were damaged together with the destroyer *Jervis* and the tanker *Sagona*.

SLEP. Service Life Extension Program. US-designed refit programme by extending the life of a ship for up to fifty per cent.

Slot, The. Nickname given by the Americans to the body of water between New Georgia, Bougainville, Choiseul and Vella Lavella in the Solomon Islands. It was the route used by the Japanese to reinforce their garrison on Guadalcanal and the scene of a number of notable engagements in 1942–43.

Smyrna. Turkish port in the eastern Mediterranean which was the subject of a British attack from 5 to 15 March 1915 to prevent the Germans using it as a U-boat base. In the event the Turks rendered the port unusable by sinking five blockships at the harbour entrance. The British also had hopes of suborning the loyalty of the Vali of Smyrna – presumably by means of a large bribe – but these plans came to nothing.

SNLE. French Navy classification for an SSBN.

Solomon Islands. The scene of two years of bitter fighting between US and Japanese forces during the Second World War which included no fewer than thirteen separate naval engagements (*see* Guadalacanal for the engagements associated with the possession of that island). As the Americans gradually gained the ascendancy there occurred the actions at Rennell Island, Kula Gulf, Kolombangara, Vella Gulf, Vella Levella, Empress Augusta Bay and Cape St George.

Sonar. The use of sound to detect and track a target. Sonar, called asdic by the British until the post-1945 fusion of terminology, can be either passive, where sounds generated by the target are listened for, or active, where an acoustic pulse is transmitted and reflects back off the target.

Sonobuoy. A buoy dropped into the water from an aircraft or helicopter to search for submarines using either active or passive sonar.

SOSUS. Sound Surveillance System. The deployment of large passive sonar arrays on the sea bottom in the vital choke points – the GIUK gap being one – through which Soviet submarines would have to pass in order to reach the open sea. Deployment began in the 1950s.

***South Dakota*, USS.** US battleship which was awarded a total of thirteen Battle Stars for her service in the Pacific and Arctic during the Second World War. During the Battle of Santa Cruz her gunners shot down an estimated 26 Japanese aircraft – a remarkable achievement which was largely due to her newly fitted 40mm Bofors guns and 5in dual purpose guns firing proximity-fused ammunition. In a later engagement against a Japanese battleship off Guadalcanal on 15 November 1942 she was badly damaged, sustaining 27 hits from large-calibre shells after suffering a series of power failures. After a period of service with the British Home Fleet (the last time US capital ships would come under British operational control during the Second World War) she returned to the Pacific in August 1943 and operated with the fast carrier force. providing AA support and carrying out shore bombardments. Her gunners were credited with a total of sixty-four Japanese aircraft shot down during the war. She was present in Tokyo Bay for the formal surrender of Japan on 2 September 1945 but was subsequently placed in reserve and broken up. *South Dakota* was launched on 7 June 1941. Her standard displacement was 37,970 tons and she was 680ft long. Her armament consisted of nine 16in guns, a secondary armament of sixteen 5in guns and numerous close-range AA weapons.

Spratly Islands. A group of islands in the South China Sea which are little more than barren uninhabited rocks, but under which lie massive deposits of oil and gas. The islands are claimed by China, Malaysia, Indonesia, the Philippines and Vietnam and are thus a potential source for international conflict.

Sprint-and-drift. Technique used by modern ships and submarines to optimise both their speed and the listening capability of passive sonar equipment. Since passive sonar becomes useless at high speeds due to water flow noise, the ship/submarine in question will proceed at high speed for a certain period of time and then slow down to allow the sonar equipment to update the tactical picture. Once the picture is clear then the ship/submarine 'sprints' again until the next time for a 'drift'. It particularly applies to nuclear submarines, since running at speed while at periscope depth creates a noticeable 'hump' in the water, detectable to a sharp-eyed lookout or observer in a helicopter. Submarines dive deep for their 'sprint' and then come slowly to periscope depth for the 'drift'.

Squid. British ahead-throwing anti-submarine weapon developed during the Second World War. It was a three-barrelled 12in mortar with the barrels fixed one behind the other in a frame which could be tilted through 90 degrees to bring the barrels horizontal for loading. The projectiles weighed 390lb with a minol charge weighing 207lb. Sinking speed was 43.5fs and clockwork timer fuses were used set automatically from the depth recorder. Training was possible to 30 degrees either side of the bow although the weapon

Above: Two Squid anti-submarine mortars installed in the frigate HMS *Loch Killin*. Squid was the most deadly ship-borne AS weapon developed during the Second World War.

Above: HMS *Victorious*, the second of Britain's four Trident SSBNs is rolled out of the building shed at Barrow on completion. (VSEL)

was meant to be fired dead ahead. It was automatically fired from the asdic range recorder and threw the three bombs to land in a triangle with 40yd sides 275yds ahead of the ship. The successful installation of Squid depended on the ship having 'Q' attachment and the later Type 147 asdic which gave an estimation of the target's depth. The first successful sinking by Squid was that of *U736* by HMS *Loch Killin* on 6 August 1944. *Korvettenkapitän* Peter Cremer, who commanded *U333*, said that 'Hedgehog [q.v.] was a hand probing for the U-boat with five fingers;, the Squid was a paw which struck out and crushed everything.' In the post-war period the weapon underwent a variety of modifications and emerged as the Mk X mortar, widely fitted in British and Commonwealth ships.

SSBN. Nuclear-powered ballistic missile submarine.

SSCS. Surface Ship Control System. British tactical data system fitted in Type 23 frigates after the failure of CACS.

SSGN. Nuclear-powered submarine armed with guided missiles: a US Navy/NATO classification for

Soviet submarines such as the 'Oscar'.

SSK. Conventional 'diesel-electric' submarine. Whether or not the growth of AIP propulsion systems for non-nuclear submarines will spawn a new submarine classification of SSG – submarine 'green' – is open to question!.

SSN. Nuclear-powered fleet submarine. In US parlance this is known as an attack submarine.

Stark, USS. An *Oliver Hazard Perry* class guided missile frigate which was hit in error by two Exocet missiles fired by an Iraqi aircraft in the Persian Gulf on 17 May 1987. The subsequent inquiry revealed fundamental flaws in the

Above: The British SSN HMS *Torbay*. With her armament of heavyweight torpedoes, anti-ship missiles, mines and cruise missiles, *Torbay* and her sister ships are the capital ships of today. (MoD)

ship's command and control systems.

Starling, HMS. British modified *Black Swan* class sloop launched in October 1942. She was commanded by the redoubtable U-boat hunter Captain F. J. Walker until his death in 1944. *Starling* had a displacement of 1,350 tons, was 292ft 6in long and was armed with six 4in guns. She was broken up in 1965.

START. Strategic Arms Reduction Talks. A two-stage process designed to reduce the total number of strategic nuclear forces. START 1 was signed in July 1991. A post-START agreement was signed in January 1993 as START 2 but cannot take effect until START 1 is ratified by all the signatories. Problems with ratification include the status of nuclear weapons on Ukrainian soil under Russian control and the proposal to enlarge membership of NATO by including former Warsaw Pact countries.

Stealth. The use of a variety of means to disguise a ship's appearance or to reduce the various emissions such as heat and noise emanating from her hull. Stealth 'technology' first made its appearance at sea during the First World War with the use of camouflage to break up a ship's silhouette and make her more difficult to see. The advent of electronic forms of detection such as radar and sonar require more sophisticated means. These include masking systems to reduce propeller noise by passing air bubbles around the hull; radar absorbent material (RAM) to absorb radar transmissions and reflect a reduced or distorted echo; and funnel baffles to disperse exhaust gases and make them less vulnerable to infra-red detection. Submarines have their hulls coated in anechoic tiles to absorb sonar transmissions. Stealth technology is very evident in the appearance of modern warships such as the French frigate *Lafayette*. The ultimate 'stealth' ship is the USS *Sea Shadow*, an experimental craft designed to test new technologies which have been fitted in the *Arleigh Burke* class destroyers. However, stealth technology can do no more than act as a superior form of camouflage. The wake left by a ship in the water will always be visible, even to a satellite, and emissions can only be managed, never eliminated.

'Stonehenge', Operation. British westbound convoy to Malta in November 1942 which arrived without loss. The arrival of this convoy on November 1942, it is commonly agreed, marked the end of the siege of Malta.

STOVL. Short take-off/vertical landing. Aircraft such as the Sea Harrier can carry a much greater payload if they make short take off runs. Hence this is the normal mode of operation, the vertical flight capability being restricted to landing.

Styx. The SS-N-2 anti ship surface-to-surface tactical cruise missile, first deployed in the very early 60s. Most widespread use on board Osa and Komar class missile boats. First missile of its type to have been used operationally, in 1967 by Egypt against Israel and then again in 1971 by Indian vessels against Pakistani ships.

STUFT. Ships Taken Up From Trade. An anronym for merchant ships requistioned for use by the Royal Navy.

Submarine pens. Massive concrete structures constructed by the Germans throughout Europe in order to protect U-boats while in harbour. The pens were constructed of reinforced concrete 15ft or more thick and were essentially invulnerable to conventional bombing. Inside the pens was every facility imaginable for the maintenance of operational U-boats. The German-built submarine pen at Brest in France is still in use by the French Navy as a submarine base.

Subroc. Submarine Rocket. US-designed underwater-to-underwater ASW missile first deployed in 1965. The missile was fired, broke surface and then flew to a point (maximum range was 28.5 miles) above the submerged enemy submarine as indicated on the firing submarine's sonar. It then dropped a 1.5-kiloton W.55 nuclear depth charge. It was withdrawn in 1988.

Suez Canal. Strategically important canal dug between the Mediterranean and the Red Sea, thus saving ships the long passage around the Cape of Good Hope. In both world wars threats against the canal never materialised, but the Germans did mine it intensively with air-laid mines and at one stage planned to drop *Biber* one-man submarines in the Great Bitter Lakes. In the post-war period the canal was nationalised by the Egyptian regime led by Colonel Nasser in 1956. Britain and France reacted by deciding to seize the canal by force in collusion with Israel (*see* 'Musketeer' for details of the assault). In retaliation Nasser sank blockships in the canal, effectively closing it. It remained closed until 1974, when an international naval force, including a British contingent, helped the Eygyptians clear it for traffic. In October 1973 the Egyptian Army crossed the canal in a daring assault to launch the Yom Kippur war against Israel.

Sunda Strait, Battle of. *See* Java Sea, Battle of.

Surcouf. Remarkable French submarine built in 1929. *Surcouf* escaped to Britain just before the fall of France but all efforts to find her satisfactory employment failed largely due to British unfamiliarity with her engineering systems and the lack of suitably qualified French submarine personnel. Rumours abounded about the loyalty of her crew and eventually it was decided to send her off to Tahiti, where she could do no harm and possibly some good. She disappeared in the Caribbean in February 1942. The usual cause given for her loss, that she was rammed by the US freighter *Thompson Lykes* on 18 February

1942, does not stand prolonged examination. Alternative reasons for her loss include accident due to drill or mechanical failure or an attack by USAAC aircraft. *Surcouf* had a displacement of 3,250/4,304 tons, was 360ft long and was armed with eight 21in torpedo tubes, four 15.7in torpedo tubes, two 8in guns, two 37mm guns, four 13mm AA guns and an aircraft.

Suvla. Large bay on the west coast of the Gallipoli peninsula selected for a landing on 8 August 1916 with the object of breaking the stalemate there. The naval part of the landings went very smoothly and was interesting in that it was

the first time that specialist landing craft, Z-lighters, were used.

Swilly, Lough. Anchorage on the north coast of Ireland used by the Royal Navy in 1914–15 until the defences at Scapa Flow were made secure.

Swim-out torpedo tubes. Torpedo tubes which are designed so that the torpedo can swim out under its own power, thus removing the need for complicated and noisy ejection pumps or pistons. Used principally by the Germans in the post-1945 period.

Swordfish. Fairey-designed British carrier borne torpedo-

Above: A Swordfish dropping a torpedo. (IWM MH 23)

bomber and one of the most famous naval aircraft of all time. The aircraft entered service in 1936, by which time it was out-classed by foreign aircraft such as the TBD Devastator and Japanese 'Kate'. Nevertheless, before production ceased in December 1944, a total of 2,391 had been produced. The Swordfish was a biplane of great simplicity, having neither flaps nor a variable-pitch propeller. It had fixed undercarriage and a stalling speed of 60mph. It was highly manoeuvrable and was affectionately known as the 'Stringbag'. The Swordfish participated in almost every single major naval action in European waters – Narvik in 1940, the attack on Taranto, the hunt for *Bismarck* and the 'Channel Dash' – as well as participating in less spectacular but equally important convoy protection duties flying from escort carriers and MAC ships. Maximum speed without a torpedo was 139mph; with a torpedo slung under the aircraft the speed was reduced to 110mph. The aircraft could alternatively carry three 500lb bombs or an air-launched ground mine. The Mk II variant had provision for rockets while the Mk III was fitted with ASV.

Sydney, HMAS. Name used for four warships in the Royal Australian Navy this century. The first was a *Chatham* class light cruiser launched in 1912. She sank the German cruiser *Emden* at Direction Island on 9 November 1914 and was herself broken up in 1929–30. The second was a modified *Leander* class cruiser launched in 1934. While

Above: The last moments of the Austrian battleship *Szent Istvan* torpedoed by an Italian *Mas* boat in the Adriatic on June 1918. The battleship in the background is the *Tegetthoff*. (Author,)

serving in the Mediterranean she sank the Italian cruiser *Bartolomeo Colleoni* on 19 July 1940. On 19 November 1941 she was sunk in a mutually fatal action with the German raider *Kormoran*. The third *Sydney* was an aircraft carrier launched in 1944 as HMS *Terrible* and acquired by the RAN in 1948. She was broken up in 1976. The name is currently borne by a US-built *Oliver Hazard Perry* class frigate built for the RAN and launched in September 1980. She is still in commission.

Szent István, SMS. Austrian *Tegetthoff* class dreadnought battleship launched in January 1914. She was the only one of the four ships in her class to be built by a Hungarian yard, Danubius at Fiume, and her construction took longer than, and was inferior to, that of her sisters. She was torpedoed and sunk on 10 June 1918 by the Italian *MAS.15* while en route for a raid on the Otranto Barrage. She was struck by two torpedoes and took some time to sink, with the result that the majority of her complement were saved. Her loss was filmed by an Austrian cameraman, and the film of her last moments is now wheeled out to represent the loss of almost any capital ship lost in twentieth century warfare.

Taiwan. *See* Formosa.

Talos. US Navy SAM designed to deal with targets at long range, i.e. over 50 miles. It was a large ramjet-powered missile with rocket boost so it could only be carried in ships of cruiser size and above. Beam-riding guidance was used with semi-active and later anti-radar terminal homing. The missile could also be used against surface targets and there was also a variant fitted with a nuclear warhead. Talos was in service from 1957 to 1979 and saw combat service in the Vietnam War.

Tanganyika, Lake. Scene of an ingenious campaign during the First World War. The Germans enjoyed complete command of the lake until the British brought two gunboats overland in sections and assembled them. The journey overcame formidable natural obstacles before the gunboats, named *Mimi* and *Toutou*, could be commissioned. Once in service their effect was immediate. On 26 December 1915 they captured the German gunboat *Kingani*, which was put into British service as *Fifi*. On 9 February 1916 the German steamer *Hedwig von Wissmann* was captured, while the remaining German vessels on the lake scuttled themselves or remained in port.

Taranto. Port on the south coast of Italy that was the main base for the Italian (and Anglo-French) naval forces during the First World War and for the Italian Fleet during the Second World War. It was the location for the first carrier strike in history. The raid was planned by Admiral Sir Andrew Cunningham and would have involved two carriers had not *Eagle* been damaged. On 11 November 1940 twenty-one Swordfish aircraft of 813, 815, 819 and 824 Naval Air Squadrons flying from HMS *Illustrious* attacked the Italian Fleet. In two attacks the Swordfish obtained three torpedo hits on the battleship *Littorio* and one each on *Caio Duilio* and *Cavour*, the last-named sinking to the bottom. The cruiser *Trento* and destroyer *Libeccio* were damaged. *Cavour* was salvaged but never recommissioned; the other two battleships were out of service until the spring of 1941. Two of the aircraft were shot down. The operation made the Italian Fleet withdraw to bases on the west coast of Italy, making it harder for them to intervene in the central Mediterranean. The lessons of the attack were not lost on the Japanese Navy, then in the early stages of planning for Pearl Harbor.

Target motion analysis. The analysis of passive sonar bearing in a submarine to determine the movement of a target.

Tartar. US Navy first-generation SAM designed to engage small and medium-size targets between 2,000 and 11,500yds. It was fitted in the *Charles F. Adams* class destroyers and also as the secondary armament in some cruisers. Like all early systems, it was less than reliable and was replaced from 1968 by the SM-1 (Medium Range).

Task Force. Tactical organisation used by the US Navy and now standard throughout NATO.

Tassafaronga, Battle of. An engagement on 30 November–1 December 1942 between Japanese and American warships in the Guadalcanal campaign which demonstrated the effectiveness of Japanese night-fighting techniques and the potency of the Long Lance torpedo. Six Japanese destroyers under Rear-Admiral 'Tenacious' Tanaka headed for Tassafaronga on the north coast of Guadalcanal with reinforcements. Just before midnight on 30 November they were surprised by a force of five American cruisers and six destroyers. Undeterred, the Japanese launched a volley of Long Lances and four of the American cruisers, *Pensacola*, *Northampton*, *New Orleans* and *Minneapolis*, were hit and damaged; *Northampton* had to be sunk the next day. The sole Japanese loss was the destroyer *Takanami*, sunk by gunfire. Although the battle was a major Japanese tactical success, it did not affect the decision that Guadalcanal be evacuated.

TBD Devastator. US Navy carrier-borne torpedo-bomber which was replaced by the TBF/TBM Avenger. The Devastator is best known for its part in the Battle of Midway, where all forty-one TBDs were shot down without obtaining one torpedo hit. However, their sacrifice allowed the dive-bombers a free rein, which they amply exploited.

TBF/TBM Avenger. The principal US Navy carrier-borne torpedo-bomber of the Second World War. The TBF/TBM was a chunky, single-engine aircraft which was unusual among torpedo-bombers in that the torpedo (and other ordnance) was carried in an internal bomb bay rather than simply suspended from the fuselage. The aircraft could carry one torpedo – either a standard straight-running, anti-ship weapon or a Fido – four depth charges or one 500lb bomb. TBF was the designation for Avengers produced by Grumman, who designed the aircraft, while the designation TBM was given to those Avengers produced under licence by General Motors. At the end of the war a few TBM-3W variants were fitted with the large AN/APS-20 air search radar, while the TBM-3S was a specialised ASW aircraft. Post-war variants included the TBM-3R, a transport aircraft which could deliver mail and crucially needed spares as well as the arming devices for nuclear weapons to task groups at sea. All Avengers had a three-man crew, a maximum speed of 257mph and a range (when armed with a torpedo) of 1,100 miles.

TDC. Torpedo Data Computer. Computer fitted to provide firing solutions for torpedoes. Early models were electro-mechanical and some, like the British 'Fruit Machine', had to be reset after each periscope observation. Modern models are fully computerised.

Tegetthoff. Name ship for a class of four Austro-Hungarian dreadnought battleships. They mounted an armament of twelve 12in guns arranged in four triple turrets all on the centre line of the ship and were the first capital ships to adopt this arrangement. They had a standard displacement of 20,013 tons and were 499ft 3in long. The four ships in the class were *Tegetthoff*, *Viribus Unitis*, *Prinz Eugen* and *Szent István*. *Tegetthoff* was launched in March 1912 and was broken up in Italy between 1924 and 1925.

Ten-Year Rule. A potent means of financial restriction on defence spending originated in Britain in August 1919 which held that the country would not be engaged in a major war for the next ten years. In 1929 the rule was made self-perpetuating but it was abandoned after 1933.

Terrier. First-generation medium-range SAM introduced from 1955. It was a compact two-stage beam-rider although its guidance was later altered to semi-active homing. Its original range was 20 miles but refinement later doubled this. Production ended in 1966 and it was replaced by SM-1 (Extended Range).

Thief. British device developed during the Second World War for taking oil samples from slicks produced by a sunken or damaged U-boat.

Through-deck cruiser. A large cruiser with a flight deck running the entire length of the ship. The term was first coined for the British *Invincible* class CVSs when the use of the term 'aircraft carrier' was politically unacceptable.

'Thursday War'. The weekly exercise at the British naval base at

Portland where ships undergoing work-up were put through a variety of combat situations.

Tigris, River. Scene of a river campaign by the Royal Navy during the First World War in support of the Mesopotamian campaign.

Tinosa, **USS.** American submarine which achieved notoriety on 24 July 1943 by firing fourteen torpedoes at the whale factory ship *Tonan Maru* and observed ten hits. However, problems with the Mk VI Exploder meant that none of the ten torpedoes detonated! *Tinosa*'s commanding officer, Lt-Cdr Dan Daspit, retained his fif-

teenth torpedo for examination by the base staff. What the *Tonan Maru*'s crew thought of the proceedings has not been recorded.

Tirpitz. German battleship of the Second World War which spent her active life securely moored behind the net and mine defences of various Norwegian fjords yet exercised a considerable influence on British operational planning in home waters – a perfect example of the 'Fleet-in-being' After spending a year in the Baltic working-up, she proceeded to Norway in March 1942 where she remained for the rest of her life. She put to sea on but three occasions: she sailed in

March 1942 to attack convoy PQ.12/QP.8 but returned after failing to find the convoys, having survived an attack by Albacore aircraft; she sortied again in July 1942 to attack convoy PQ.17 but was recalled when it became clear that U-boats and aircraft were managing without her assistance; and she put to sea in September 1943 when she and *Scharnhorst* bombarded the island of Spitzbergen (the only occasion when she fired her 15in guns in anger). British planners seemed in awe of the ship and her supposed capabilities – a surprising attitude given that the Royal Navy always enjoyed numerical superiority in

Above: *Tirpitz*. (IWM HU 2627)

home waters – and the ship was almost demonised by Churchill's description of her as 'The Beast'. Nevertheless the British launched what amounted to a campaign to destroy the ship. No fewer than seventeen air attacks by land-based or carrier aircraft were launched, together with a failed attack using Chariots in November 1942 and an attack using X-craft in September 1943. She was finally sunk on 12 November 1944 by Lancaster bombers of the RAF. *Tirpitz* was launched on 1 April 1939 and had a standard displacement of 42,900 tons (52,600 tons deep load). She was 813½ft long and was armed with eight 15in guns.

'Title', Operation. British operation to attack the battleship *Tirpitz* using two Chariots which were to be taken to Trondheim slung beneath the trawler *Arthur*. The operation was abandoned when both Chariots broke free from their slings in bad weather. The *Arthur* was scuttled on 1 November 1942 and the 'Charioteers' escaped to neutral Sweden.

'Tokyo Express'. American term for the nightly Japanese operations to resupply their forces on Guadacanal by sea from August 1942 to early 1943.

Tomahawk. American long-range cruise missile. There are several variants: Tomahawk Land Attack Missile – Nuclear (TLAM-N); Tomahawk Land Attack Missile – Conventional (TLAM-C); and Tomahawk Anti-Ship Missile (TASM). There is also a cluster bomb variant of TLAM-C, sometimes described as TLAM-D. Ranges for each type are 1,350, 675, 250 and 470 miles respectively. The three land-attack types use terrain contour-matching guidance; TASM uses radar homing. Tomahawks can be launched from ships or submarines. With its relatively slow speed, a Tomahawk might take up to half an hour to reach the target area. Since the US Navy was unwilling to accept any guidance link between launching ship/submarine and missile (for fear that such links could be jammed or alert the target) a new form of guidance for these missiles was required. As ships do not move randomly, powerful computers can be used to track and predict a potential target's movements over a period of hours. Powerful data systems supplied with information from the ship's own sensors and supplemented by data from Data Fusion Centers ashore (which would receive data from AWACS, satellites and a host of other sources) could build up a total picture of maritime movements in an area out to well beyond Tomahawk range. No one ship could be aware that she was being targeted, so a Tomahawk would arrive by surprise. The system does of course rely on the opposition giving his position away from time to time.

Tonkin Gulf Incident. On 2 August 1964 three North Vietnamese ex-Soviet P-4 class torpedo boats attacked the American destroyer *Maddox* which was stationed off the North Vietnamese coast. The North Vietnamese claimed that *Maddox* had been violating North Vietnamese territorial waters (North Vietnam claimed twelve miles instead of the more usual three), but the reality was that the destroyer had covered a South Vietnamese attack on the communist-held islands of Hon-Me and Hon-Nieu, which lay only three miles from the Vietnamese mainland, on 31 July. A second attack on *Maddox* and the *Turner Joy* on 4 August precipitated massive US retaliation in the shape of carrier air strikes which resulted in the destruction of twenty-five North Vietnamese naval vessels and fuel bases for the loss of three aircraft and a pilot.

Tonkin Gulf Yacht Club. Irreverent US Navy term for ships and squadrons which had participated in operations off the coast of Vietnam during the 1964–75 war.

Torpedo. A self-propelled underwater missile, launched from a submarine, surface vessel, or aircraft and designed for exploding upon contact with the or close to the hulls of surface vessels and submarines. Propulsion has usually been by compressed air engine or battery-powered electric motors. The submarine has been the naval vessel that used the torpedo most successfully. Torpedoes are also an important element in modern anti-submarine warfare, homing variaties being dropped by helicopters, aircraft and launched from surface warships.

Above: A Mk. VIII** torpedo is loaded onboard the British submarine HMS *Sceptre* in 1943. Introduced before the Second World War the, Mk. VIII remained the mainstay of British submarine armament until the mid-1980s. The Argentine cruiser *Belgrano* was sunk by the British SSN HMS *Conqueror* using Mk. VIIIs during the Falklands conflict in 1982.

Torpedo tube. The cylindrical structure through which torpedoes and missiles can be fired, and mines can be laid. In submarines, torpedo tubes have an outer door, to prevent the aperture being fouled by flotsam, and a rear door, which allows the tube to be reloaded. Interlocks prevent both the outer and rear doors being open at the same time. Ordnance is expelled from the tube means of compressed air or water. Systems exist to prevent the air or water used to fire a torpedo creating a disturbance on the surface and thereby giving the submarine's position away (*see* AIV). Modern German submarines are fitted with 'swim out' torpedo tubes without any ejection system. This is to save weight and avoid the tell-tale noise of a torpedo being fired: the torpedo 'swims' out quietly under its own power before accelerating away to operational speed.

'Total Germany'. Signal sent to all ships of the Royal Navy at 11.15 a.m. on 3 September 1939 to indicate that Britain and Germany were at war.

Toulon. Major naval base on the south coast of France. On 27 November 1942 the bulk of the French fleet still under Vichy control was scuttled there when the Germans decided to occupy the rest of France. Three battleships, one seaplane carrier, five cruisers, thirteen destroyer leaders, five destroyers, one torpedo boat and four corvettes were scuttled and damaged beyond repair. The scuttling was done for purely French reasons rather than out of any desire to join the Allies The real tragedy lay in the French decision not to attempt a break-out by the serviceable units and join the Allied cause.

Towed array. Long array of sonar transducers towed behind surface ships or submarines for the long-range passive detection of submarines.

Treaty Ports. The ports of Cóbh (Queenstown), Berehaven and Lough Swilly in the Irish Republic which were retained by Britain under the 1921 Articles of Agreement. In 1938 the Chamberlain Government returned them to the Irish Government in what must be one of the most short-sighted decisions ever made by a British administration. The Second World War had hardly begun before the British Government requested the use of the ports, a request that the Irish declined each time it was made. Use of the ports would have had a significant effect on the Battle of the Atlantic and the Irish refusal to let the British use the ports was the source of some bitterness. Today the ports lie deserted, their fortifications existing in a state of genteel dilapidation.

Trieste. Important port at the northern end of the Adriatic. Until 1918 it was an Austrian city and the location of STT (Stabilimento Technico Triestino), the shipbuilding company which built nearly all of Austria-Hungary's major warships. In 1918 the port reverted to Italy and the shipbuilding industry was allowed to decline. After the Second World War the city was the scene of considerable tension between Yugoslavia, who claimed the town, and the Italians, supported by Britain and America.

Troika. German-designed minesweeping system which consists of a team of three unmanned craft controlled by a specially adapted coastal minesweeper. The *Bundesmarine* has eighteen such craft, which have been operationally deployed in the Persian Gulf.

Truk. An island group in the Caroline Islands in the Pacific where the Japanese established a major naval base and which became the HQ of the Combined Fleet. It was not invaded by the Americans; rather it was constantly attacked by aircraft and bombarded from the sea and allowed to 'wither on the vine'.

Tsingtao. German colony in China. It was promptly besieged by an Anglo-Japanese naval task force – although the Japanese were in complete control of operations – on the outbreak of the First World War. The German garrison was in a hopeless position but put up a stiff resistance. On the night of 17 October the old torpedo boat *S.90* sank the Japanese cruiser *Takaschio*. However, after the Japanese launched a massive artillery bombardment on 30 October, the garrison surrendered on 7 November. In contrast to their behaviour during the Second World War, the Japanese treated their German and Austrian captives in complete accordance with international law.

Tsushima, Battle of. Crushing victory by the Imperial Japanese Navy over the Russian Fleet, 27–28 May 1905. After an epic 17,000-mile voyage round the world the Russian Fleet was brought to action in the Straits of Tsushima by the Japanese. The Japanese commander, Admiral Togo, boldly crossed the Russians' 'T' and then turned to a parallel course to open a rapid and accurate fire. The battle which followed was one of the most decisive of all time. Of the thirty-eight Russian ships, twenty-nine, including all eight battleships, were either sunk, captured or surrendered. Six reached safety and internment in Shanghai and Manila. Only the cruiser *Almaz* and two destroyers reached Vladivostok. Over 4,800 Russians were killed, against 117 Japanese.

'Tungsten', Operation. Attack on the battleship *Tirpitz*, 3 April 1944, using carrier-borne aircraft.

Turbulent, HMS. Name which has been borne by three ships of the Royal Navy this century. The first was a *Talisman* class destroyer launched in January 1916. She was sunk in the fierce night fighting that followed the Battle of Jutland. On the morning of 1 June she was run down and cut in half by a German capital ship. There were no survivors. An 'S' class destroyer was the next ship to receive the name in 1919, but she was broken up in 1936. The name then went to a 'T' class submarine launched in 1941. She was sunk in March 1943 in the Tyrrhenian Sea, cause unknown. Her commanding officer, Commander J. W. 'Tubby'

Linton, was subsequently awarded the Victoria Cross. The name is now borne by a *Trafalgar* class SSN launched in 1982.

Turret. Armoured structure enclosing the main and secondary armament gun positions on the upper deck of a warship.

Two-Power Standard. British doctrine in the pre-1914 period whereby the size of the Royal Navy should be greater than that of any two prospective opponents plus a margin.

Type VII U-boat. (see overleaf) Mainstay of the German submarine fleet during World War Two. There were many improvements and modifications to the basic design as the War progressed The first design had a surfaced displacement of over 600 tons for the VIIA, to over 1,000 tons for the VIIC, the most common variant. they had a surfaced range of 6,200 to 14,700 miles depending on the variant. Over 700 were built, with 437 being lost in action, many more were lost to Allied bombing of German shipyards and harbours. They represent the most numerous and uniform group of submarines ever to have been built.

'Typhoon'. Western designation for the Soviet Project No 941 *Akula* SSBN. With a displacement of 18,000/25,000 tons and a length of 171m, these are the largest SSBNs in the world. The components of the submarine are so large than when work first began on their assembly at Severodvinsk in 1977 US intelli-

gence analysts thought the Russians were starting work on an aircraft carrier. Armed with twenty SS-N-20 missiles, they are designed to sit out the initial nuclear exchange under the ice and to be available for a reprisal attack on a recovering enemy – hence the extraordinary emphasis placed on habitability for the crew of 50 officers and 100 men (there is even a sauna). The exterior pressure hull conceals five cylinders: two main units running the length of the boat, one forward for the six torpedo tubes and tactical missiles; one for command located under the fin; and one aft for steering. Each of the two main hulls contains a 190mW reactor, a 45,000shp turbine and an 800kW diesel generator. Unusually in SSBN designs, the strategic missiles are placed forward of the fin. Six of the class are in service.

U-boat. *Unterseeboote*, German term for submarine and one that has been corrupted in English as U-boat.

Ultra. The generic term for all intelligence derived from Enigma based decrypted German signal traffic. Before 1941 such intelligence was known as *Boniface*, the implication being that it came from an agent in place. The precise use of the term refers to a security grading, 'Ultra Secret', for signal traffic and documents. The actual decrypts were always referred to as 'Special Intelligence'.

Unrep. Underway replenishment at sea. During the Second World War the Americans pioneered

Above: U52, a Type VII U-boat. (IWM HU 1008)

techniques of refuelling and maintaining their ships while under way by transferring fuel and supplies by means of hose and jackstay. Known in British parlance as RAS (replenishment at sea), these techniques are essential for any navy wishing its ships to acquire operational reach.

UDT. Underwater Demolition Team. US Navy term for frogmen who surveyed beaches before amphibious landings and cleared obstacles and beach defences. The USN's first UDT teams were organised in early 1943, with the first class graduating in July that year. Their first commanding officer was Lt-Cdr Draper Kauffman, who had studied British bomb disposal methods during the German Blitz on London. The frogmen, nearly all USN but with some USMC members, had to be the very best of swimmers. They received training in basic hydrographic techniques as well as how to render mines safe and how to destroy coral reefs and underwater obstacles. First used at Kwajalein in February 1944, they were used in all subsequent landings in the Pacific. By the end of the Second World War there were twelve UDT teams, each with a strength of sixteen officers and eighty enlisted men.

United States Marine Corps (USMC). An organised military force under the jurisdiction of the US Navy Department. As with the Royal Marines, the USMC provided detachments for US ships and embassy guards. However, in the inter-war period the USMC concentrated on developing amphibious warfare techniques, a particular feature of which was close co-ordination of aircraft (the USMC was the only US service with its own air arm) with ground forces.

Above: US Marines storm ashore at Iwo Jima. (IWM NYP 58330)

This subsequently became a feature of USMC operations. It was in the field of amphibious warfare that the Marines won lasting renown. Beginning with the landings on Guadalcanal, they stormed across the Pacific, demonstrating their capabilities and fighting prowess at Makin, Tarawa, New Georgia, Bougainville, Eniwetok, the Marianas, Peleliu, Iwo Jima and Okinawa. Although the US Army conducted a number of amphibious assaults, none came close to the ferocity of some of the USMC assaults. Marine Corps aviators also flew close support missions from escort carriers. In the post-war period the Corps went through a rocky patch when amalgamation with the US Army or wholesale abolition was threatened in the period when integration of all three services was considered. However, the landing of the 1st Marine Division at Inchon on 15 September 1950 and the epic retreat from the Chosin reservoir in the winter of 1950/51 confirmed the Marines' reputation as an élite among the US armed forces.

Unrestricted submarine warfare. The use of submarines to sink enemy merchant ships without warning, contrary to the Hague Convention. During the First World War the Germans resorted to unrestricted submarine warfare as means of breaking the deadlock in the war and of forcing Britain to make peace. The first began in February 1915 and lasted until September. Political pressure from moderate elements in Germany and protests from the United States caused it to be abandoned. The second campaign, from February to April 1916, was even shorter, and, once again, diplomatic pressure from the United States caused it to be called off. The third campaign, begun in January 1917, was started when Germany's overall situation was desperate and fears of offending the USA were ignored. This campaign lasted until the end of the war. In the Second World War Germany, Japan and the United States practised unrestricted submarine warfare from the commencement of hostilities. The British Government insisted that Royal Navy submarines operated in accordance with the Prize Rules, although these restrictions were gradually relaxed.

USN. United States Navy.

VDS. Variable-depth sonar. A sonar with a transducer that can be lowered to an optimum depth to be effective. The effectiveness of hull-mounted sonars can be seriously degraded by different layers of temperature and salinity in the water which act as barriers to long-range sound propagation. VDS is also useful for minehunting since the sonar can be placed close to the sea bottom being examined.

Vella Gulf, Battle of. The fourth of seven naval engagements between US and Japanese forces during the Solomon Islands campaign, taking place on 6–7 August 1943. Four Japanese destroyers attempting to reinforce the garrison on Kolombangara island were surprised by six American destroyers. In a half-hour engagement *Kawakaze*, *Hagikaze* and *Arashi* were sunk and *Shigure* damaged. This American victory was achieved without loss.

Vella Lavella, Battle of. The last action against the 'Tokyo Express', 6–7 October 1943. Six Japanese destroyers were evacuating troops from the island of Vella Lavella in the Solomons when they were engaged by a force of three American destroyers. The Americans received warning of the operation too late to be able to reinforce the three destroyers already on patrol. Despite the Japanese superiority, the three American ships, *Chevalier*, *O'Bannon* and *Selfridge* attacked. They succeeded in sinking the Japanese destroyer *Yugumo*, but *Chevalier* was damaged by a torpedo from *Yugumo* and then rammed by *O'Bannon* and was later scuttled. *Selfridge* was then damaged by a torpedo fired by *Shigure* or *Samidare*. The remaining Japanese ships concentrated on covering the evacuation, which went ahead without loss, even though they had an unrivalled opportunity to finish off the two damaged American destroyers.

Veruchsgleitboot. Experimental air-cushion boat developed by the Austro-Hungarian Navy during the First World War. This was a wooden craft with a spindle-shaped hull with the bottom divided, by a vertical step, into planing and hover sections. A fan positioned at the forward end of the rectangular hull produced an air cushion under the hovering part of the bottom. Skirts on the port and starboard side prevented the air from escaping but there were no skirts at the bow and stern. The main armament consisted of two torpedoes discharged over the stern by compressed air. Launched in September 1915, the *Veruchsgleitboot* underwent extensive trials. However, the design was a little advanced for the technology of the day and was ultimately abandoned. The single *Veruchsgleitboot* was cannibalised for spares.

Victorious, HMS. A British aircraft carrier of the *Illustrious* class completed in May 1941. She had an original complement of 36 aircraft and her top speed was over 30 knots. She was involved in the hunt for the *Bismarck*, her torpedo bombers carrying out attacks on the battleship. Her final wartime operations were in the British Pacific Fleet, where she was hit by a Kamikaze. She was given an extensive reconstruction during the 1950s so that she could operate the contemporary heavyweight jet aircraft, finally being sold for scrap in 1969.

Victory ships. Mass produced fast merchant ships built from 1943 onwards. They were similar to Liberty ships but were a more advanced design and significantly faster.

'Vigorous', Operation. British westbound convoy to Malta in June 1942 which was hampered by too much direction from the shore HQ. The convoy was eventually forced to turn back, not because of the level of opposition but because the numerous alterations of course ordered by the shore-based command caused the escorts to use up nearly all their fuel and fire off nearly all their AA ammunition.

Viribus Unitis. Lead ship of the Austrian *Tegetthoff* class dreadnoughts, her name being the motto of the Habsburg monarchy – 'With Undivided Strength'. She was sunk in an attack by an Italian human torpedo, the *Mignatta*, on the night of 31 October/1 November 1918. Ironically the Austro-Hungarian Navy had been officially 'dissolved' the previous day and

Above: Pre-war diplomacy. In the foreground the Austrian battleships *Viribus Unitis*, *Tegetthoff* and *Zrinyi* fire salutes at Malta during a visit by the Austrian ships in May 1914. The salutes are returned by HMS *Indomitable* in the background.

the ship was now the flagship of the new Yugoslav Navy. Whether the Italian swimmers were aware of this change in circumstances is unclear, but the celebrations had led to chaotic conditions on board. At the time of the attack the ship was fully illuminated and nearly all her watertight doors were open – conditions which contributed to her sinking.

V/STOL. Vertical/short take-off and landing (aircraft). Although the USSR developed the Yak-38 'Forger', the most effective such aircraft at sea is the Harrier/Sea Harrier family in service with the Royal, US, Spanish, Italian and Indian Navies. This aircraft uses vectored thrust for maximum flexibility. More countries are adopting this aircraft, which allows a navy to deploy organic air power at sea in relatively cheap ships.

Vulcan/Phalanx. A US designed CIWS using a 20mm rotary gun for last-ditch defence against missiles and suicide craft.

Walrus. Biplane reconnaissance amphibian carried by British battleships and cruisers during the Second World War. It was an incredibly ugly aircraft and gloried in the unofficial name of 'Shagbat'. Nevertheless the Walrus served in every theatre of operations in which the Royal Navy was to be found.

Walther engine. System of propulsion developed during the Second World War for German submarines. It used the thermal energy produced by the decomposition of hydrogen peroxide (HTP) to produce steam and oxygen at high temperatures (1,765°F) which were fed into a combustion chamber to ignite fuel oil. For submarines this system offered all the benefits of high underwater speed. Initial trials in *U792* and *U794* were successful, the latter achieving an underwater run at 20kts for five and a half hours! However, the nightmare bureaucracy of the Third Reich and scepticism among engineer officers meant that at the end of the war only seven of the Type XVII Walther submarines were completed and none of the Type XVIII long-range or the Type XXVI coastal boats. After the war Britain and America dabbled in Walther turbines. Britain commissioned a Type XVII U-boat as HMS *Meteorite* and then built two experimental HTP submarines, *Explorer* and *Excalibur* (known as *Exploder* and *Excruciator* on account of their volatile performance). Although the Walther propulsion system offered many advantages, it was quickly superseded by nuclear power.

WATU. Western Approaches Tactical Unit. A part of the British Western Approaches Command established at Liverpool during the Second World War by Captain Gilbert Roberts. It had the specific task of subjecting experience gained at sea to rigorous analysis so that results could be disseminated as widely as possible. It played an important role in training officers and men in convoy warfare – using a team of Wrens who became very expert at the

game – but it was also instrumental in developing tactics, often at short notice, to counter new German weapons such as the GNAT.

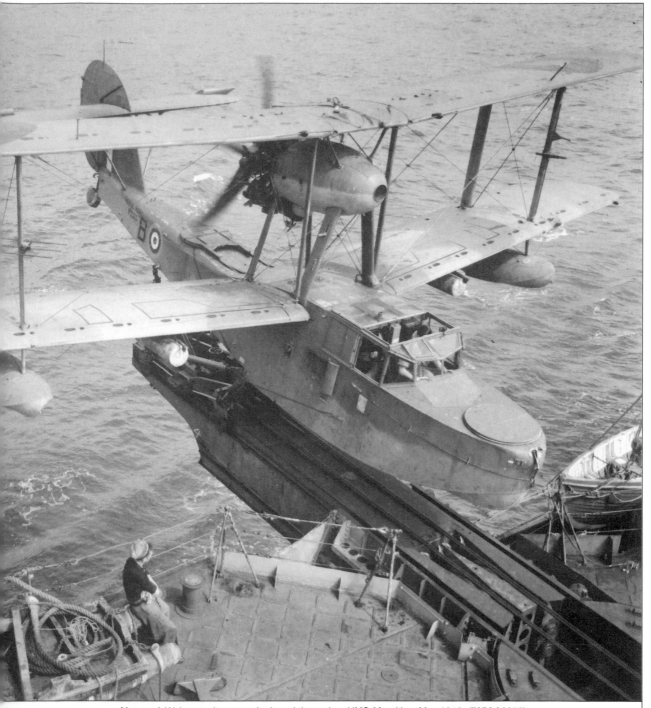

Above: A Walrus on its catapult aboard the cruiser HMS *Mauritius*, May 1942. (IWM A9272)

Welman. A British one-man submarine built by the Special Operations Executive at its experimental establishment at Welwyn Garden City (hence the name – one-man submarine built at Welwyn). It was a hopelessly impractical craft and suffered from poor design and construction. As in all one-man craft the operator had too much to do in order to be effective. Welmans displaced 2.5 tons, were 6.08m long and had a speed of 3kts. They were armed with a detachable

540kg warhead. They were only used once operationally, in an attack on Bergen in November 1943 in which all four craft were lost, one falling intact into German hands. Unbelievably, over 100 were delivered, but the Admiralty could find no employment for them and all were broken up. However, the example captured was the inspiration for the German *Biber* one-man submarine.

Welfreighter. A variant of the Welman designed for cargo-carrying in support of Special Operations personnel.

Wire-guided torpedo. A torpedo guided to the target using information sent down a wire connecting it to the launching platform.

Wolf. Name adopted by the German Navy for two commerce raiders. The first came to an undignified end when she grounded in the Elbe and had to be taken out of service. The second *Wolf* was the Hansa line's *Wachtenfels* armed with seven 15cm guns, four torpedo tubes, 465 mines and a Friedrichshaven seaplane named *Wolfchen.* She sailed on 30 November 1916 and did not return to Germany until February 1918. *Wolf*'s mines, laid as far apart as the Cape of Good Hope and New Zealand, claimed thirteen ships sunk totalling 75,888 tons and a further three damaged together with damage to the Japanese battleship *Haruna.* She sank or captured another seven steamers and seven sailing vessels totalling 114,279 tons.

Wolfpack. The co-ordination of the operations of a number of U-boats so that concerted attacks are made on particular convoys. It was first mooted in the First World War when *Fregattenkapitän* Hermann Bauer, FdU of the High Seas Fleet submarines, suggested that a flotilla commander be embarked in a *U151* class *U-Kreuzer* which would be fitted with additional wireless equipment so that he could act as tactical commander and co-ordinate the attacks of a number of boats at once. Bauer's plan was never implemented but his successor as FdU, *Kapitän zur See* Andreas Michelsen, did try it, though without the control element provided by the command U-boat. Between 10 and 25 May 1918 a dozen U-boats were gathered in the Western Approaches, but the operation was not a success, despite a procession of convoys through the area, and two boats were sunk. In the Mediterranean co-ordinated U-boat attacks were tried but found equally unsuccessful this time owing to poor communications. Wolfpack tactics were refined during the inter-war period and employed by the Germans with considerable success in the Atlantic in the Second World War. U-boats would be formed into scouting lines deployed across the likely track of convoys. As soon as a boat sighted a convoy, it would not attack but would shadow it and broadcast homing signals which would allow other U-boats to concentrate in the area. The system worked very well and was responsible for the early success of the Germans

in the Battle of the Atlantic. However, wolfpack tactics relied on extensive use of wireless in order to set up the patrol lines, broadcast homing signals and redeploy U-boats in response to convoy sightings. HF/DF could pinpoint the position of a U-boat broadcasting a homing signal, while the interception and decryption of German wireless traffic allowed convoys to be easily re-routed and ASW forces, particularly USN 'hunter-killer' carrier groups, to be concentrated in areas where U-boats were known to be operating. In the Pacific the

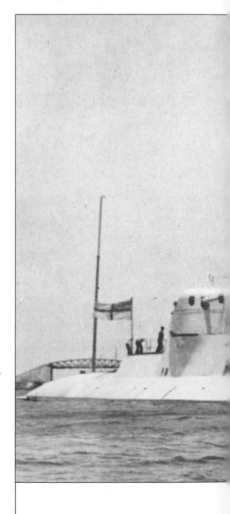

USN initiated wolfpack tactics from September 1943. However, the American command was reluctant to inhibit the operations of individual submarine commanders, while the almost total lack of efficient convoy defences on the part of the Japanese meant that single US submarines were able to operate quite effectively.

Wrens. *See* WRNS.

WRNS. Women's Royal Naval Service, commonly known as 'Wrens'. The organisation was founded in 1917 during the First World War to free manpower for sea service and was disbanded at the end of hostilities. The Wrens proved themselves very adaptable at filling a variety of roles in shore appointments and supplying boat crews for harbour service. Established again at the beginning of the Second World War, the WRNS was retained after the war, with women serving in nearly every capacity of appointment except going to sea. They were a separate service with their own administration and distinguishing badges of rank in distinctive blue cloth. In 1990 the decision was taken to send them to sea. Despite misgivings the system has worked and the Navy has survived the few scandals which have come to the attention of the press. The experiment marked the closer integration of the Wrens into the Royal Navy and in 1994 the decision was taken to abolish the WRNS as a separate service and integrate all personnel into the Royal Navy.

X.1. A radical British Submarine built in 1925. Her main feature was her armament of four 5.2in guns in two turrets. She was also equiped with very powerful

Above: The British submarine *X.1* with her gun armament of four 5.2in guns clearly visible. This submarine was a 'one off' in terms of British submarine design and although she was a success, the experiement was not repeated. (Author)

Above: *Yamato*. (IWM MH 6177)

diesels and for her day she could dive exceptionally deep. She was proclaimed to be a submarine cruiser, a cul-de-sac in submarine development. In fact, apart from her novelty value she achieved little and she was scrapped in 1936.

X-craft. British midget submarine with a crew of four men, built from 1942 for operations against the German battleship *Tirpitz*. The craft displaced 26.9/ 29.7 tons, were 15.7m long and were armed with two 3,750lb Amatex side charges (alternatively, a number of limpet mines could be carried in side compartments). A 'wet and dry' compartment allowed a diver to enter and leave the craft while submerged to deal with net obstructions or plant limpet mines. The top speed was 6.6kts on the surface and 5kts submerged. Fourteen X-craft were built, of which six, *X.5–X.10*, were lost in Operation 'Source' in September 1943 against *Tirpitz*. *X.22* was sunk in February 1944 in a collision and *X.24* is preserved at the Royal Navy Submarine Museum. The remainder were broken up. Six XT-craft were built for

employed by the Royal Navy during the Second World War. A post-war class of four vessels, the *X-51* class, was built but these lacked the manoeuvrability of their wartime predecessors.

***Yamato* Class.** Japanese battleships, comprising two ships, the *Yamato* and the *Musashi*. (A third ship, the *Shinano* was completed as an aircraft carrier). They were the most heavily armed battleships ever built, their main armament being nine 18.1in guns. They were both sunk by bombs and torpedoes from US aircraft, *Musashi* in October 1944 and *Yamato* in April 1945.

Yellow Sea, Battle of the. A decisive victory for the Japanese in the Russo-Japanese War. The Russian Port Arthur squadron (six battleships, four cruisers and eight destroyers under Admiral Vitgeft) broke out of the blockaded Port Arthur on 10 August 1904 and headed for Vladivostok since fire from Japanese shore artillery was making the anchorage untenable. A Japanese fleet under Admiral Togo consisting of four battleships, six cruisers and destroyers intercepted the Russian vessels just after 12.30. In the first engagement the Russians, showing unusual cohesion and determination, outmanoeuvred the Japanese and pressed on to the south-east. Action was resumed at 17.30 north of the Shantung peninsula, and once again the Russians were more than holding their own until a lucky hit struck the Russian flagship *Tsarevich* on the bridge, killing Vitgeft and

training purposes only (all were broken up post-war) and eleven XE-craft were built for service in the Far East (six were broken up in Australia and the remainder in the UK). As well as the attack on *Tirpitz*, X-craft sank merchant shipping and a floating dock in Bergen in Norway and damaged the Japanese cruiser *Takao* in Singapore. However, they proved equally capable in other tasks. In home waters X-craft landed COPP on the Normandy beaches and on the day of the invasion acted as navigational beacons for the invasion fleet. In the Far East XE-craft cut submarine telephone cables between Japanese command centres. Though small and of undistinguished appearance, they were some of the most versatile craft

most of his staff. A second hit disabled the ship's steering, and as she veered out of the line the Russian squadron was thrown into confusion. The Russian fleet separated, some ships returning to Port Arthur (where they were scuttled six months later) and others opting for neutral ports and internment.

York, HMS. Heavy cruiser, half-sister ship to HMS *Exeter*. She was badly damaged by Italian explosive motor boats on the night of 26 March 1941 and attacked subsequently by German aircraft after being beached at Suda Bay, Crete. She was scuttled 22 May 1941.

'Zar', Operation. Minelaying operation in August 1942 by the German minelayer *Ulm* north of Cape Zhelania following the completion of Operation 'Wunderland'. However, *Ulm* was found by the British destroyers *Marne*, *Martin* and *Onslaught* on 25 August and sunk.

'Zarin', Operation. Minelaying operation to the north of Novaya Zemlya by the German heavy cruiser *Admiral Hipper* and five destroyers between 24 and 28 September 1942 to prevent the passage of British convoys around the north of Novaya Zemlya into the Kara Sea.

'Zauberflotte', Operation. Transfer of the German cruiser *Prinz Eugen* from Trondheim to Kiel in May 1942.

Zeebrugge. Port in Belgium used extensively by the Germans during the First World War as a base for destroyers and U-boats. On 23 April 1918 the British attempted to block the harbour by sinking blockships at the entrance to the canal. The cruiser *Vindictive* would land troops on the Mole which covered the harbour entrance, allowing the three blockships to be put in position, while two submarines packed with explosive would blow up the landward end of the mole, thus preventing the Germans from reinforcing the defensive positions there. Although great gallantry was shown in the plan's execution, it was less than successful. Two of the blockships were sunk in the canal, but they only partially blocked it so that it was still possible for destroyers and U-boats to manoeuvre around them, and the port remained usable. Nevertheless, in typical British fashion it was regarded as a great victory.

Zeppelin. Type of airship used extensively by the Germans for aerial reconnaissance over the North Sea during the First World War.

'Zipper', Operation. Allied landing in Malaya in 1945. Despite the Japanese surrender, the landing went ahead on 9 September 1945. The 23rd and 25th Indian Divisions were landed south of Port Swettenham and in the three days following the landing over 100,000 men were put ashore.

'Zitronella', Operation. Bombardment of Spitzbergen on 8 September 1943 by a German naval task force consisting of *Tirpitz* and *Scharnhorst* escorted by nine destroyers. *Scharnhorst* covered the landing of the 349th Grenadier Regiment at Gronfjord while *Tirpitz* bombarded Barentsberg. Coast defence guns were destroyed, coal dumps fired and accommodation and utilities blown up. The squadron returned to Altenfjord on 9 September. It was the only occasion on which *Tirpitz* fired her main armament in anger.

Zonguldak. Port on the Turkish Black Sea coast and an important outlet for coal being sent to Constantinople. It was the object of a series of unsuccessful operations by the Russian Navy during the First World War.

Z Plan. German naval rearmament plan of 1938, which provided for the construction of a substantial surface fleet over a ten-year (later reduced to a six-year) period. The total number of ships aimed for was six large battleships, four aircraft carriers, eight heavy cruisers, seventeen light cruisers, thirty-plus destroyers and 221 U-boats. These units were additional to what was already on order or in service with the *Kriegsmarine*: two battleships (*Bismarck* and *Tirpitz*), two battlecruisers (*Scharnhorst* and *Gneisenau*), three 'pocket battleships' (*Admiral Graf Spee*, *Admiral Scheer*, and *Deutschland*), two heavy cruisers, six light cruisers, thirty-four destroyers and torpedo boats and fifty-six U-boats.

Senior British and US Army and Navy officers meet in Algiers, including Admiral Sir Andrew Cunningham, General Clarke and General Anderson.

NAVAL PERSONALITIES

Abruzzi, Luigi Amadeo Giuseppe Mario Fernando Francesco de Savoia-Aosta, Duca di (1873–1933). Italian admiral and explorer. In 1899 he led an expedition to the North Pole which stopped when only 207 miles short of its destination. In 1913 he was appointed Commander-in-Chief of the Italian Navy and held this position until 1917 when he retired. As a commander he was less than enterprising in prosecuting a war against a numerically inferior enemy and he quarrelled incessantly with his staff.

Akeida, Saburo. Japanese *Ko-Hyoteki* commander who torpedoed the British battleship *Ramillies* with one torpedo at Diego Suarez on 30 May 1942. With his second torpedo Akeida sank the 6,993 ton tanker *British Loyalty*. After the attack he abandoned his craft and with his crewman, Petty Officer Masami Takemoto, made his way overland, but the two were shot when they refused to surrender to a British patrol.

Annaya, Jorge. Argentine naval commander in 1982 at the time of the Falklands War and member of the three-man ruling Junta. Undistinguished by any particular talent, either naval or political.

Arbuthnot, Robert (1864–1916). British destroyer officer renowned for strict discipline and obsession with physical fitness. Arbuthnot was killed at the Battle of Jutland while leading his squadron into place following the deployment of the Grand Fleet. Characteristically, he chose to sail down the engaged side of the Grand Fleet: his ships were engaged by the Germans and his flagship HMS *Defence* blew up and sank with all hands.

Arnauld de la Perriere, Lothar von (1886–1941). The most successful submarine commanding officer in history. Between November 1915 and March 1918, while in command of *U35*, he sank 189 merchant ships totalling 446,708 tons and two warships. His high score was achieved largely by judicious use of his submarine's 88mm gun, although the absence of any coherent anti-submarine policy on the part of the Allies made his task immeasurably easier. On the German capitulation in November 1918 he became a battalion commander with the *Freikorps* and then an instructor at the Turkish naval academy. He re-joined the German Navy in September 1939 but was killed in an air crash in February 1941 at Le Bourget.

Ashworth, Frederick L. (1912–). US Navy weapons officer for the atomic bomb dropped on Nagasaki. He subsequently participated in the Bikini atomic tests in 1946 and commanded the second nuclear-capable US Navy air squadron. He retired in 1968 with the rank of Vice-Admiral.

Assman, Kurt (1883–1962). German naval officer and author. During the First World War he commanded destroyers on the Flanders coast and from April 1933 until June 1943 he headed the historical section at the OKM. After the Second World War he wrote a number of papers and books on German naval policy, some at the behest of the British and American authorities.

Bacon, Reginald Hugh (1863–1947). British Admiral and one of the keen minds behind the technological revolution forced upon the Royal Navy by Fisher in the early years of the century. In 1901 he was responsible for the construction and commissioning of the first submarine to enter British service and was subsequently appointed commanding officer of HMS *Dreadnought*, the first all big-gun battleship. In 1909, after being promoted to Rear-Admiral, he retired to become managing director of the Coventry Ordnance Works. He was recalled in 1915 and appointed Flag Officer Dover in command of forces which were popularly known as the Dover Patrol. This was a multi-faceted command which, by and large, Bacon handled well. However, the apparent ease with which U-boats based in the Flanders ports of Zeebrugge and Ostend slipped through the defences in the Dover Strait led to criticism of his command and was the cause of his eventual relief in January 1918. In retirement Bacon devoted himself to writing, particularly a useful (though strongly partisan) account of the operations of the Dover Patrol. He was also a strong and vocal supporter of Jellicoe in the Jutland controversy. Bacon was a brilliant officer of the *matériel* school and an expert on mines, torpedoes and submarines. However, his arrogant and overbearing manner inspired little in the way of loyalty or affection from his subordinates.

Barbey, Daniel E. (1889–1969). US Navy amphibious specialist who served as amphibious force commander for General Douglas MacArthur in the South-West Pacific Front.

Bass, R. H. American naval officer who tried, unsuccessfully, to develop midget submarines for the US Navy in the late 1940s. His one concrete achievement was the unsuccessful *X-1*, but unknowingly his ideas were to re-emerge as the Deep Submergence Rescue Vehicle (DSRV)

Battenberg, Louis Alexander (1854–1921). British admiral and First Sea Lord on the outbreak of the First World War. Despite his many sterling qualities he was hounded from office in October 1914 by a press campaign focusing on his German origins and connections.

Beatty, David (1871–1936). British admiral. Anglo-Irish by ancestry and the son of a cavalry officer, Beatty determined on a career in the Royal Navy from an early age. He was fortunate to escape the normal round of service in the Victorian Navy and saw active service in the Sudan and in China. He so distinguished himself that by the age of twenty-seven he was a full Captain when the average age for such a rank was forty-three. In 1910 he hoist-

ed his flag as a Rear-Admiral despite lacking the requisite amount of time at sea and thus became the youngest flag officer for over one hundred years. By this time he had two further advantages to add to his formidable ability and thrustfulness: a rich wife and the patronage of the

First Lord of the Admiralty, Winston Churchill. Churchill made him his naval secretary in 1911 and then in 1913 Beatty took the coveted post of Flag Officer Commanding the Battle Cruiser Squadron of the Grand Fleet. He commanded the Battle Cruiser Fleet from 1914 to 1916,

Above: Admiral Sir David Beatty, GCB, KCVO, DSO (IWM)

then was Commander-in-Chief Grand Fleet from 1916 to 1918, although the course of the war gave him no opportunities to show his mettle. He was First Sea Lord from 1919 to 1927, a period in which he fought to retain the Navy's strength. Beatty is often portrayed as possessing more style than substance. However, recent research may show that his reputation is due for reassessment in a more serious and favourable light.

Benson, William Shepherd (1855–1932). US Chief of Naval Operations at the end of the First World War. Benson was an Anglophobe, deeply suspicious of Britain and determined to maintain the American drive for naval supremacy. He put forward a massive construction programme which was only terminated by the Washington Naval Treaty.

Beresford, Lord Charles of Metemmeh and Curraghmore (1846–1919). British Admiral who is best known for the damaging feud he conducted with Fisher while in command of the Channel Fleet in 1907. Though Beresford had been a supporter of Fisher's early reforms, he now felt that the latter had gone too far and was too dictatorial in his methods. The result of the disagreement was that Beresford was ordered to haul down his flag in 1909, and although a subsequent inquiry offered him partial vindication he was not employed again. Beresford was an extremely capable and talented officer who had made a con-

siderable contribution to the Navy in the late nineteenth century, and it is a matter of regret that his career should be best remembered for his clash with Fisher than for its more positive aspects.

Bernotti, Romeo (1877–1974). Italian admiral who served with distinction in the Italo-Turkish War of 1911–12 and the First World War, 1914–18. He is perhaps best known for his writings, which include *Seapower in the Great War* and *The History of the War in the Mediterranean 1940–1943*.

Birindelli, Gino. Italian *Maiale* operator captured by the British at Gibraltar on 30 October 1940. Birindelli's craft had malfunctioned and his Number Two had fallen off but he had physically dragged the craft along the bottom of the harbour toward the battleship *Barham* before exhaustion forced him to give up. He was considered so dangerous by the British that when the Red Cross selected him for repatriation on compassionate grounds, the British refused to release him and spirited him off to Canada. After the war Birindelli enjoyed a distinguished career in the Italian Navy.

Borghese, Junio Valerio. Italian commander of *Decima Mas*, the élite special forces unit responsible for human torpedo and assault swimmer operations. On the Italian Armistice he elected to join the forces of Mussolini's Italian Socialist Republic.

Boue de Lapayrère, Augustin-Emmanuel. French admiral who was the French naval commander at the Dardanelles. An amiable commander, though none too aggressive, he worked well in the Allied command structure in the Mediterranean and when he abruptly resigned in 1916 (largely on account of political pressure from within France for a scapegoat) the British in particular were sad to see him go.

Bucher, Lloyd M. (1934–). American naval officer and commander of the intelligence ship *Pueblo* when she was seized by the North Koreans in January 1968. Throughout his eleven months in captivity, when he was treated with considerable brutality, Bucher behaved with great courage and dignity.

Bulkeley, John D. (1911–). US Navy PT boat commander who carried General MacArthur from the besieged island of Corregidor in the Philippines in March 1942. Subsequently commanded PT boat squadrons in New Guinea and in the English Channel. His exploits are commemorated in the film *They Were Expendable.*

Burke, Arleigh A. (1901–). US Navy destroyer commander who commanded Destroyer Squadron 23, 'The Little Beavers', in operations in the South Pacific in which one Japanese cruiser, nine destroyers, a submarine and a number of smaller craft were sunk. He subsequently became Mitscher's chief of staff and saw action at Saipan, the Philippine Sea, Leyte Gulf, Iwo Jima and

Okinawa. Post-war he held a number of senior appointments, culminating in an unprecedented six-year term as Chief of Navy Operations from 1955 to 1961.

Burnett, Robert Lindsay. Known as 'Bullshit Bob', Burnett was a physical education specialist who nevertheless became one of the Royal Navy's great fighting commanders of the Second World War. Not one of the Navy's intellectuals, Burnett was at his best when on the bridge in the thick of the action. He fought convoy PQ.18 through to Russia in September 1942 and commanded British forces at the Battle of the Barents Sea in December 1942. He later commanded the cruiser squadron at the Battle of the North Cape in December 1943. He was a cheerful, irrepressible man who was dearly loved by all who served with him.

Busch, Fritz Otto. German naval officer and author of a number of popular books on naval history, including *Tragedie am Nordkap* and *Akten des Seekriegs*.

Bush, George (1924–). Reputed to be the youngest US Navy pilot during the Second World War. He was shot down over the Bonin Islands on 2 September 1944 and rescued after an hour and a half in the water by the submarine *Finback*. After the war Bush entered the oil business and then politics, becoming President of the United States in 1989.

Cagni, Umberto (1863–1932). Italian naval officer and explorer.

After the First World War he commanded Italian naval forces occupying the former Austrian ports on the Dalmatian coast and pursued his government's policy ruthlessly in defiance of any inter-Allied agreements. Described by one British officer as 'having more than his fair share of the wisdom of the serpent'.

Callaghan George (1852–1920). British admiral who was abruptly relieved of command of the Grand

Above: Rear Admiral Umberto Cagni, Italian commander in the First World War whose determination to sieze territory for Italy after the war was not matched by his activity during the war. (Museo Storico Navale, Venice)

Fleet on the outbreak of the First World War and replaced by Jellicoe.

Campbell, Gordon (1886–1953). British Q-ship commander during the First World War who sank three U-boats while in command of the *Farnborough* and *Pargust*. He was awarded the Victoria Cross and given accelerated promotion to Captain.

Canaris, Wilhelm (1887–1945). In the First World War Canaris was interned in Chile following the scuttling of the cruiser *Dresden* but made a daring escape over the Andes to return to Germany and subsequently became a submarine commander. After a brief period with the *Freikorps* he rejoined the naval service in 1920 and retired as a Rear-Admiral in 1934, but in 1935 was appointed to head the *Abwehr* (the German armed forces' intelligence service). Canaris was never much enamoured of the Nazi regime and soon joined the circle of those conspiring to assassinate Hitler. The 20 July Bomb Plot was Canaris's undoing. It proved comparatively easy for the security services to discover his complicity and he was hanged at Flossenburg concentration camp on 9 April 1945.

Chatfield, Alfred Ernle Montacute (1873–1967). British Admiral of the Fleet and a gunnery specialist. During the First World War he was flag captain to Vice-Admiral Sir David Beatty in the battlecruiser HMS *Lion*. He commanded this famous ship in the

actions of the Heligoland Bight, Dogger Bank and Jutland. When Beatty became Commander-in-Chief of the Grand Fleet in 1916 Chatfield went with him to command the fleet flagship HMS *Queen Elizabeth*. In the post-war period Chatfield's career followed the classic pattern of command at sea alternating with appointments in the Admiralty. In 1933 he was appointed First Sea Lord, an office he held until 1938. A few months after his 'retirement' he was appointed Minister for the Co-ordination of Defence with, after the outbreak of war in September 1939, a seat in the War Cabinet. The post was abolished in 1940. Chatfield was an austere and aloof personality with an inability to appreciate any ideas but his own. In particular, his belief that the battleship and the big gun would remain the final arbiter of naval power, despite all the experience of the Second World War, brought him a good deal of criticism. Nevertheless, he was respected for his integrity and a strong sense of justice.

Churchill, Winston (1874–1965). British statesman who was twice First Lord of the Admiralty on the occasion of the outbreak of a world war. Appointed first in 1911, Churchill played a considerable role in preparing the Royal Navy for war. Among his reforms were the creation of the naval staff at the Admiralty and his support for developments in aviation, submarines and propulsion (it was Churchill who strongly advocated oil-fired ships). During

the First World War he was dismissed in May 1915 following the failure of the Dardanelles campaign, which was a sound idea but one that was poorly executed. In the inter-war period Churchill's contribution to the Royal Navy was almost entirely negative. While Minister of Munitions he helped dig the grave of the Royal Naval Air Service – which he had done so much to create – and while Chancellor of the Exchequer was responsible for the infamous Ten Year Rule which hamstrung the Defence Estimates between the two wars. It was therefore surprising that his appointment as First Lord of the Admiralty in September 1939 was greeted with such affection throughout the Fleet. When he became Prime Minister in May 1940 Churchill continued to maintain a close interest in naval matters, although his interest often owed more to enthusiasm than to experience. While he frequently made mistakes – the dispatch of Force Z to Singapore in 1941 was one – his influence was generally sound and strong.

Ciliax, Otto. German fleet commander best remembered for his command of German ships involved in the famous 'Channel Dash'.

Corbett, Julian. British naval historian and author of the first three volumes of the official history of the war at sea in 1914–18. Formerly a lawyer, he was appointed professor of history at the Royal Naval College, Greenwich, in 1902. He was a close

Above: Boy 'Jack' Cornwell of the cruiser HMS *Chester*. Cornwell was posthumously awarded the Victoria Cross for his heroism in the Battle of Jutland. (IWM)

his report of the Battle. He was posthumously awarded the Victoria Cross.

Cowan, Walter (1871–1955). British admiral renowned for his length of service and his indomitable spirit. He saw almost uninterrupted active service between 1895 and 1918 and he retired, reluctantly, in 1929. Though too old for sea service during the Second World War, he served with an Indian Brigade and the Commandos in the Western Desert. Taken prisoner in March 1941, he was repatriated on the grounds of his age – he was over seventy. He re-joined the Commandos in Italy and was then actively engaged in the Adriatic in operations in support of the Yugoslav partisans. For these operations he was awarded a bar to the DSO which he had won on the Nile forty-three years earlier. He retired for a second time and was killed in a hunting accident in 1955. Cowan had an insatiable appetite for action, both at sea and on the hunting field. However, he was something of an unbending martinet with no tolerance for those who lacked his dynamic attitude. As a result he was involved in three mutinies in ships or squadrons which he commanded.

Crabbe, Lionel 'Buster'. British diver who founded the Gibraltar Underwater Working Party to counter the activities of the Italian *Decima Mas*. He met his end in mysterious circumstances in 1956 while engaged in a foolhardy operation to examine the hull of the

friend of Fisher's and played an important though unofficial role in amending the drafts of official Admiralty papers which Fisher used to send him for comment.

Cornwell, John Travers (1900–1916). Sixteen-year-old boy seaman in HMS *Chester* whose action

station at Jutland was at the forward 5.5-inch gun as the sightsetter. Although the gun's crew lay dead and wounded all around him, he remained at his post though wounded himself. He subsequently died of his wounds at Immingham and his conduct was given special mention by Beatty in

Above: Admiral Sir Christopher Craddock. (IWM)

Soviet cruiser *Ordzonikidze* at Portsmouth. A small industry has grown up making suggestions as to how Crabbe met his end, most of which border on the farcical. What most likely happened is that he drowned through being unfit for the dive and poorly prepared, and it is probable that his was the body subsequently found in Chichester Harbour.

Craddock, Christopher (1862–1914). British admiral killed at the Battle of Coronel on 1 November 1914. Craddock was an outstanding officer who would undoubtedly have risen to the highest ranks of the Service. His decision to stand and fight the superior German force at Coronel was based on the hope that his ships could inflict enough damage on the Germans that they would have to seek internment. Craddock was determined not to be criticised for failing to engage the enemy (the fate of Admiral Troubridge in the Goeben affair) and thus elected to fight rather than break away. It was a mistaken decision, though brave, and one which cost Craddock his life.

Craig, Christoper. British naval officer who commanded the frigate HMS *Alacrity* with considerable *élan* during the 1982 Falklands War and commanded British naval forces in the 1991 Gulf War. Under his command British warships, particularly the minesweepers, played a vitally important – though barely recognised – role. His very readable book, *Call For Fire: Sea Combat in the Falklands and the Gulf*, is one of the best memoirs by a post-Second World War naval officer.

Cromwell, Richard P. American naval officer who was killed in the submarine *Sculpin* and who was posthumously awarded the Medal of Honor. When the submarine in which he was serving was sunk by a Japanese destroyer, Cromwell was aware that his knowledge of US code-breaking activities and the plans for the forthcoming invasion of the Gilbert Islands would be of immense value to the Japanese. He therefore remained in the control room as *Sculpin* sank to be bottom.

Cunningham, Andrew Browne (1883–1963). First World War destroyer commander who commanded the British Mediterranean Fleet from 1939 to 1943. Cunningham established complete

Above: Admiral Andrew Browne Cunningham. (IWM)

dominance over the numerically superior Italian fleet through his victories at Taranto and Matapan. He kept his nerve and that of his fleet during the costly but successful evacuation of Crete in which many ships were lost but which saved an army. He subsequently oversaw the invasions of North Africa, Sicily and Italy and proved a good coalition commander. In October 1943 he was appointed First Sea Lord, a post he held until 1946. Known as 'ABC', Cunningham was a commander rather than an administrator. He could be intolerant, driving, humorous and supportive as the situation demanded. He was universally beloved by all who served under him and he was respected by his opponents. Unusually, he achieved high command without having attended the Staff Course. He was the outstanding British naval leader of the Second World War.

Cunningham, John D. (1885–1962). British naval commander (no relation to 'ABC') who was CinC Mediterranean from 1943 to the end of the war.

Dau H. Master of the German tanker *Altmark*, one of *Admiral Graf Spee*'s supply ships. After *Graf Spee* was scuttled he brought the *Altmark* as far as Norway through some of the busiest shipping lanes in the world without being detected – a remarkable feat of seamanship.

Darlan, Jean François (1881–1942). French admiral and minister. An officer of exceptional ability who was appointed Commander-in-

Above: Admiral Darlan in Algiers meeting senior Allied military officers. (IWM A 13120)

Chief of the French Navy in 1939 after a long and distinguished career. After the fall of France he became Secretary of State for the Navy and in 1942 was appointed Commander-in-Chief of all military forces of the Vichy regime. However, in November 1942 he relinquished this office in order to become High Commissioner for France in North Africa. When Anglo-American forces landed in North Africa in November 1942 Darlan's decision not to offer any resistance undoubtedly saved many lives. He was assassinated on

Above: Leutnant Lothar von Arnauld de la Perière, second from the left, commander of the German submarine *U35*, the most successful submarine captain in history. (IWM Q 20241)

24 December 1942 in Algiers. Darlan is often regarded as the arch example of the collaborationist French officer. Yet there is no evidence to suggest that he would have allowed the French fleet to fall into the hands of the Germans. Darlan acted wholly in the interests of France and from the summer of 1940 he perceived those interests as the maintenance of French territorial integrity and such armed forces as were allowed her under the terms of the Franco-German Armistice. In defence of those interests he was prepared to fight anyone – including his former allies. Darlan's misfortune was to be cast in a political situation, where he would be vilified whichever side he chose.

De la Perière, Lothar von Arnauld. Germany's supreme U-boat ace. Operating during the First World War his achievements were unequalled by any submarine commander during both world wars. He sank two warships, one auxiliary cruiser, five troopships, 125 steamers and 62 sailing vessels, grossing 453,716 tons.

De la Penne, Luigi Durand. Italian naval officer who disabled the battleship *Valiant* in Alexandria harbour in an SLC operation.

Denham, Harry. British naval officer who was naval attaché in Sweden during the Second World

War. His reports started the hunt for the battleship *Bismarck* which eventually led to her destruction.

De Roebeck, John (1862–1928). British Admiral who commanded naval forces at the Dardanelles in 1915–16. The failure of his ships to force a passage through the Dardanelles convinced him that a landing was required to secure the peninsula. Although he was indefatigable in his support of the military once the troops had been landed, there was nothing that purely naval operations could achieve which would break the land stalemate. After the conclusion of operations in the Dardanelles de Roebeck occupied a number of other appointments before retiring in 1924. Described by a contemporary as 'an exceptionally strong-minded, talented and popular officer of great dignity and charm', de Roebeck was universally admired throughout the Royal Navy by the lower deck as well as the wardroom.

Dixon, Robert E. (1906–). US Navy aviator who on 7 May 1942 led SBD Dauntless dive-bmbers of Scouting Squadron 6 against the Japanese aircraft carrier *Shoho*, sinking her. His radio message 'scratch one flat-top' has gone down in history.

Dönitz, Karl (1891–1980). German naval officer and head of state. A regular officer of the Imperial Navy, Dönitz commanded *UB69* during the First World War and in the inter-war period oversaw the build-up of the U-boat arm of the

Above: Admiral Karl Dönitz.

Kriegsmarine. Promoted to Rear-Admiral in 1939, he commanded U-boat operations with considerable success, thus winning Hitler's confidence, in the early part of the war. On Raeder's resignation he was appointed Commander-in-Chief of the Navy, a post he held until 30 April 1945 when, on Hitler's death, he became head of state, in which capacity he negotiated unconditional surrender with the Allies. Arraigned as a war criminal, he was tried at Nuremberg and sentenced to ten years' imprisonment. Released in 1956, he wrote two volumes of questionable memoirs. Dönitz was a charismatic commander who inspired those who served under him. However, his very personal style of command had limited room for the opinions of others (his staff functioned as little more than a rubber stamp) or the introduction of ideas from outside the service.

Doorman, Karel. Dutch commander of the American, Australian, British and Dutch forces at the Battle of the Java Sea. His dogged determination to attack the vastly superior Japanese fleet earned him the admiration of his opponents at a time when western commanders had not distinguished themselves by their aggressiveness.

Dreyer, Frederick Charles (1878–1956). British admiral and gunnery specialist, known as 'Dreary Dreyer'. His research into the fire control of a battleship's main armament led him to develop the fire control table, a primitive computer. He submitted it to the Admiralty and was instructed to develop it further in competition with other methods of fire control, including those under development by Arthur Pollen. In 1913 the Dreyer Fire Control Table was adopted by the Admiralty; it was used in British ships throughout the First World War and refined thereafter. Dreyer was an officer of some promise who would undoubtedly have risen to the top of the service were it not for the mutiny at Invergordon in 1931. At the time he was Assistant Chief of the Naval Staff and thus shared in the collective responsibility of the

Board for the breakdown in discipline. He was placed on the retired list, but, as with so many retired flag officers, Dreyer returned to duty in the Second World War and served as a convoy commodore, Inspector of Merchant Ship Gunnery and Deputy Director of Air Equipment. He was eloquent in advocating the diversion of more long-range aircraft to the Battle of the Atlantic and events proved him correct in his views. Dreyer was a strange mixture of intellectual power, personal drive and total intolerance for the opinions of others, however valid. Though undoubtedly a brilliant officer, he lacked the gift of leadership and was never popular.

Eck, Heinz. German naval officer and commander of *U852*. On 30 November 1945 Eck was shot by a British firing squad, having been condemned to death by a military court for ordering the massacre of the survivors from the merchant ship *Pelus* which he had sunk on 13 March 1944. Eck was the only U-boat commander to be tried and executed for war crimes in the Second World War.

Above: Kapitanleutnant Heinz Eck at his trial in Hamburg in 1945.

Evan-Thomas, Hugh (1862–1928). British admiral of no particular distinction (but well connected at court) who was given the prize command of the 5th Battle Squadron, composed of the five *Queen Elizabeth* class battleships, which were the fastest and most powerful in the Grand Fleet during the First World War. His handling of his squadron at Jutland has been the subject of considerable debate ever since.

Evans, Edward Radcliff Garth Russell, 1st Baron Mountevans (1880–1957). British admiral who entered the Royal Navy in 1895. He is best known for the period in which he commanded HMS *Broke*, a destroyer serving with the Dover Patrol in the First World War. On the night of 20/21 April 1917, in company with HMS *Swift*, he fought a spirited engagement with six German destroyers in which two of the German ships were sunk. He was therefore known throughout the country as 'Evans of the *Broke*'. During the Second World War, though nominally retired, he held the post of Regional Commissioner for the civil defence of London, an appointment he discharged with great vigour.

Fisher, John Arbuthnot (1841–1920). The dominant figure in the Royal Navy for the first two decades of the century. A gunnery specialist, Fisher had radically overhauled the Royal Navy's personnel and training while Second Sea Lord but when in 1904 he was appointed First Sea Lord he at once embarked on a

Above: Admiral Lord Fisher.

series of reforms which affected every part of the Service. He was responsible for the design and construction of HMS *Dreadnought*, the first 'all-big-gun' ship, while sending dozens of old and obsolete ships to the breakers. He saw the dangers posed by the German naval build-up and concentrated British forces in Home Waters. The Grand Fleet, which dominated the North Sea during the First World War, was essentially Fisher's creation. He was a man of strong passions and arguments – he once advocated a surprise attack on the German fleet to a startled King Edward VII.

He was not an easy man to work with and made as many enemies as converts – the Fisher–Beresford controversy was tremendously divisive in the Service. He resigned in 1910 but was back in office in 1914 on Battenberg's resignation but retired again in May 1915. He retained his intemperate enthusiasm: at the end of his life he advocated the scrapping of all battleships in favour of naval aircraft!

Fleming, Ian (1908–1964). British naval intelligence officer better known as the author of the James Bond spy novels. Fleming's best-known *coup* was Operation 'Mincemeat'.

Fletcher, Frank J. (1885–1973). US admiral who commanded US naval forces at the Battles of the Coral Sea and Midway, at which latter his flagship *Yorktown* was sunk. In August 1942 his early withdrawal of naval forces after the landings on Guadalcanal led to severe criticism by US Marine Corps commanders and, following heavy losses, he was reassigned. He retired in 1947.

Fluckey, Eugene B. (1913–). US submarine commander who sank more Japanese shipping than any other commander. As CO of USS *Barb*, Fluckey sank fourteen Japanese merchant ships (75,000 tons) plus the carrier *Unyo* and an escort. His submarine also carried out shore bombardments of the Japanese islands and is unique for having fired rockets at shore targets. After the war Fluckey held a series of appointments and he

Above: Admiral Frank J. Fletcher. (IWM NYF 12685)

retired in 1972 as a Rear-Admiral and commander of NATO's Iberian Atlantic Command.

Forrestal, James V. (1892-1949). A Wall Street banker who became Secretary of the Navy on 19 May 1944. He had served as Under Secretary of the Navy from 1940, where he had been responsible for ship procurement. After the war he assisted Truman in the creation of the Department of Defense and served as the first Secretary of Defense from September 1947. Psychiatric problems (brought about by overwork) caused his resignation in 1949 and he committed suicide on 22 May that year.

Franz Ferdinand, Archduke. Austrian heir to the Habsburg throne. Used royal influence to promote Austrian naval expansion before the First World War.

Fraser, Bruce. British gunnery specialist who commanded the Home Fleet from 1943 to 1944 and the British Pacific Fleet from 1944 to the end of the Second World War. He served as First Sea Lord from 1948 to 1951. He is perhaps unique among commanders in that while Controller of the Navy he oversaw the design of a ship and her weapons (the 14in gun *King George V* class battleships) which he would later use in action. It was in one of these ships, HMS *Duke of York*, that Fraser flew his flag during the Battle of the North Cape (26 December 1943) in which the German battlecruiser *Scharnhorst* was sunk - the last

capital ship action in European waters. Fraser was a *bon viveur* who, while a hard taskmaster, enjoyed a good rapport with the officers and men under his command.

Friedburg, Hans von. German admiral appointed by Dönitz as Commander-in-Chief of the *Kriegsmarine* on 4 May 1945 and who negotiated the surrender signed on 3 May at Montgomery's headquarters on Lüneberg Heath. He subsequently committed suicide.

Fryatt, Charles. Master of the British merchant ship *Brussels* who was captured on 22/23 June 1916 and shot after being tried by a military court. Fryatt's crime was that he had tried to ram *U33* on 28 March 1916 and therefore the Germans regarded him as a *franc tireur*.

Fuchida, Mitsuo (1902-1976). Japanese naval aviator who led the strike on Pearl Harbor. He was also present at the Battle of Midway (about which he was directed to write a full and frank report) and the Marianas carrier air battles in June 1944. After the war he became a Christian minister and in the late 1960s a US citizen - a strange end for the man who had sent the signal 'Tora, Tora, Tora' over Pearl Harbor on the morning of 7 December 1941.

Gallery, Daniel V. (1901-1977). US Navy aviator and commander of a highly successful US 'hunter killer' group in the Battle of the Atlantic composed of the escort

carrier *Guadalcanal* and five destroyer escorts. Gallery sank *U544*, *U68* and *U515* and captured *U505*. He retired in 1960and became a prolific writer.

Genda, Minoru (1904-1989). Japanese naval aviator who planned the attack on Pearl Harbor. Genda was Air Operations Officer for the Japanese carrier force in 1941-42. After staff duties in Rabaul and Tokyo he directed the naval air defence of the Japanese home islands in the final days of the war. After the war he remained in the new-style Japanese Self-Defence Force and rose to become Chief of Staff of the Japanese Air Defence Force. Following retirement he went into politics.

Ghormley, Robert L. (1883-1958). US naval commander at Guadalcanal. His successful conduct of the landings was followed by hesitation and indecision and in October 1942 he was replaced by Halsey.

Gilmore, Howard W. (1902-1943). US submarine commander awarded the Medal of Honor for giving his life to save his ship. His submarine, USS *Growler*, was rammed and damaged by a Japanese merchant ship. Badly wounded by gunfire, Gilmore remained on the bridge and his last words to the Officer of the Deck were 'Take her down'

Godwin, John. British naval officer engaged in sabotage operations in Norway, captured and sent to Sachsenhausen concentration camp. Godwin was an officer, albeit a temporary and junior one, in the oldest continuing organised fighting service in the world and knew what was expected of him – courage and leadership. He gave both in full measure. On being taken to the execution ground Godwin seized a guard's sidearm and killed him before being shot dead himself.

Goodenough, William (1867–1945). British light cruiser squadron commander during the First World War. At Jutland his ships were the first to sight the German High Seas Fleet.

Gorshkov, Sergei G. (1910–1988). Soviet admiral who served as Commander-in-Chief of the Soviet Fleet for an unprecedented twenty-nine years, during which the Navy was transformed from a rather ramshackle coastal and riverine service to a fully balanced blue-water fleet. He thus increased the strategic 'reach' of the Soviet Union and its visibility in world affairs. Gorshkov argued for, and secured, the construction of aircraft carriers, cruisers, destroyers, missile submarines and large-scale amphibious forces. This was wholly contrary to Soviet practice, but Gorshkov argued that the nature of the USSR's security needs and ideological requirements necessitated a special kind of naval doctrine. In his work he carried the political apparatus of the Soviet Union along with him for practically a generation – and it was only when Mikhail Gorbachev brought a new administration to power that he was dis-

missed in December 1985. To the Americans Gorshkov personified the USSR's claim to superpower parity. However the break-up of the USSR and the economic chaos now raging in Russia and the other CIS states mean that Gorshkov's achievement has barely outlived him.

Hall, William Reginald (1870–1943). British admiral, widely known as 'Blinker' Hall for his habit of rapidly blinking his eyes while talking. Ill-health forced him to resign a sea-going command, but fortunately the post of Director of Naval Intelligence was vacant and he was appointed to it. Hall built up a brilliant organisation which was extremely wide-ranging and included signals intelligence (*see* Room 40) and trade intelligence. After the war Hall retired from the Navy and entered politics. The choice of Hall as Director of Naval Intelligence was one of those inspired decisions which matched the right man to the right job. He was an officer of exceptional intellect and considerable courage, and the victory won over the Germans in 1918 owed much to the sheer brilliance which characterised his activities. For a biography see Admiral Sir William James, *The Eyes of the Navy* (1955).

Halsey, William 'Bull' (1882–1959). A destroyer officer by training, Halsey earned his naval aviator's wings at the age of fifty-three and at the rank of Captain. While in command of the USS *Saratoga* he developed an understanding of the offensive poten-

tial of the aircraft carrier and by the time of the Japanese attack on Pearl Harbor he was in command of the Pacific Fleet's carriers. In the early part of the war the attacks his carriers made on the Gilberts and their role in the Doolittle Raid, won him the status of a national hero. Illness denied him a role in the Battle of Midway, but in October 1942 he was appointed Commander South-West Pacific and promoted to full Admiral in November that year. Halsey and General Douglas C. MacArthur co-ordinated the taking of the Solomon Islands and New Guinea from November 1942 until June 1944, when Halsey was assigned to command the Central Pacific Force. From August 1944 until the end of the war Halsey alternated with Admiral Raymond Spruance as commander of the US Navy's main striking force. However, Halsey's conduct of operations during the Battle of Leyte Gulf in October 1944 are open to question. In December 1944 he was reprimanded after his failure to take precautions against a typhoon in which many of his ships were damaged. A similar lapse in June 1945 nearly led to his relief. At the end of the war Halsey was in command of the Third Fleet, which he led in the final carrier strikes on Japan. In December 1945 he was promoted Fleet Admiral. Halsey aroused tremendous loyalty from those under his command and was known for his willingness to take risks, to delegate and to welcome suggestions from his staff. However, the staffwork of his

Above: Admiral William F. Halsey Jr. (IWM NYP 44734).

command was often mediocre and sloppy. His optimism and aggressiveness were a tonic in the early dark days of the war and it is for this that he will be chiefly remembered.

Hart, Thomas C. (1877–1971). American Admiral who commanded the US Asiatic Fleet on the outbreak of the Second World War and who led a brave but futile attempt to stop the Japanese advance spreading south to Java. Relieved at his own request on 12 February 1942, Hart was subsequently charged with collecting testimony from officers present at Pearl Harbor for use in the forthcoming courts martial of Admiral Husband Kimmel.

Harwood, Henry (1888–1950). British admiral who commanded British forces at the Battle of the River Plate in December 1939 but who showed little promise thereafter.

Haus, Anton. Commander-in-Chief of the Austrian Navy after Montecuccoli. A dour and uninspiring individual.

Hewitt, Henry K. (1887–1972). American admiral who commanded US naval forces at the landings in North Africa, Sicily, Salerno and Southern France.

Heydrich, Reinhard (1904– 1942). German naval officer cashiered from the Navy in 1931 owing to 'conduct unbecoming an officer and a gentleman'. He made a new career in the SD, the intelligence service of the SS, and was assassinated by Czech partisans in Prague, dying on 4 June 1942 of blood poisoning.

Higgins, Andrew J. (1886–1952). American shipbuilder who developed landing craft and motor torpedo boats during the Second World War.

Hipper, Franz Ritter von (1863– 1932). The outstanding German naval commander of the First World War. He commanded the First Scouting Group, the battlecruiser squadron of the High Seas Fleet at Dogger Bank and at Jutland, as well as numerous forays into the North Sea. In August

Above: Admiral Franz Ritter von Hipper. (IWM Q 20352).

1918 he succeeded Scheer as Commander-in-Chief.

Holland, John Phillip (1841–1914). Irish-American inventor and father of the modern submarine.

Holtzendorf, Henning von (1853–1919). German naval officer who became head of the *Admiralstab* in September 1915. Best known for his memorandum of 22 December 1916 in which he argued, using some fairly dubious statistics, for unrestricted submarine warfare to be waged against Britain in order to force her to surrender before Germany starved to death.

Hood, Horace (1870–1916). British admiral and member of the famous naval dynasty. At the Battle of Jutland he handled his squadron, the 3rd Battle Cruiser Squadron, with consummate skill but was killed when his flagship, HMS *Invincible*, blew up. Had he lived he would have undoubtedly risen to the top of the service.

Horthy, Miklos (1868–1957). Austro-Hungarian naval officer who rose to prominence in a service commanded by a gerontocracy by his exploits in command of the light cruiser *Novarra*. He was appointed Commander-in-Chief in 1917 on the grounds that his youth might put the fleet on the offensive, but his handling of the Navy was no more inspired that that of his predecessors. After the First World War he led a right-wing monarchist movement in Hungary and assumed power in

Above: Linienschiffskäpitan Horthy reclining, slightly wounded, in his chair onboard the cruiser *Novarra* after the May 1917 action in the Adriatic. (Author).

1920 as Regent. In the Second World War he sided with the Germans, but when he attempted to switch sides in October 1944 he was captured by the SS and placed in a concentration camp. He went into exile in Portugal, where he died in 1957. In 1994 his remains were returned to Budapest.

Horton, Max Kennedy (1883–1951). British submarine commander of the First World War (the Germans are alleged to have named the Baltic *Hortonsee* on account of his activities), he head-

ed the British submarine service in the Second World War and subsequently succeeded Admiral Noble to become Commander-in-Chief Western Approaches, an appointment from which he directed the Battle of the Atlantic. Horton was a *bon viveur* who combined great charm with total ruthlessness.

Iachino, Angelo. Italian fleet commander at Matapan and the two Battles of Sirte during the Second World War. He is believed to have slept with a biography of Nelson on his bedside table. If this was

Above: Admiral Max Kennedy Horton. (IWM A 20790)

Above: Admiral John Rushworth Jellicoe on board HMS *Iron Duke*, his flagship at the Battle of Jutland. (IWM Q 55499)

the case then it did him very little good for his fleet handling was marked by excessive caution and reluctance to close the enemy.

Ingenohl, Friedrich von (1857–1933). German Commander-in-Chief of the High Seas Fleet for the first eighteen months of the First World War. He was relieved on 2 February 1915 following the Dogger Bank action for not being sufficiently aggressive.

Jellicoe, John Rushworth (1859–1935). A gunnery officer, Jellicoe was groomed by Fisher to take over as Commander-in-Chief of the Grand Fleet on the outbreak of the First World War. He commanded the Grand Fleet at Jutland and won a costly but strategic victory. He became First Sea Lord in 1916 but his tenure of that office was marked by the huge losses suffered in the third German campaign of unrestricted submarine warfare and he was dismissed by Lloyd George in December 1917. He was a man of flawless character and cool judgement.

Kaiser, Henry J. (1882–1967). American industrialist who introduced assembly-line techniques for the construction of shipping during the Second World War.

Kennedy, John F. (1917–1963). American naval officer and son of a US ambassador to Britain, Joseph P. Kennedy. Family connections got him into the Navy despite bad back trouble. He was commanding *PT109* in the Solomons when on the night of 2/3 August 1943 his boat was rammed by a Japanese destroyer.

Kennedy and the survivors swam ashore and, thanks to Coast-watchers, were rescued. The story received considerable publicity in the US and did no harm to Kennedy's subsequent political career. He was elected President in 1960, tieclip replicas of *PT109* being sold to raise funds. He was assassinated in Dallas in 1963.

Keyes, Roger John Brownlow (1872–1945). British admiral who in 1915 planned the naval side of the Dardanelles campaign and managed to emerge from that particular *débâcle* with his career intact. He subsequently commanded the Dover Patrol. He rose to the top of the service although he was baulked of the appointment of First Sea Lord which he ardently desired. He then entered politics as Member of Parliament for Portsmouth and in 1940 became the first Director of Amphibious Warfare. He was sacked in October 1941. Keyes cultivated a glamorous image as the hero of Zeebrugge, but in reality he was an officer of little intelligence and with a poor grasp of technical matters.

Kimmel, Husband E. (1882–1968). American admiral who was in command of the US Pacific Fleet on 7 December 1941, the day of the Japanese attack on Pearl Harbor. The controversy over how much he did or should have done to avert disaster began immediately after the attack and has never ended. Kimmel was an unimaginative man and because he did not expect the Japanese to

Above: Admiral Sir Roger Keyes talking with Professor Lindemann. (IWM H 10481)

attack Pearl Harbor, he took no precautions. He was relieved after the attack and retired from the Navy in 1942. He subsequently joined a shipbuilding firm and did much good, though unrecognised, work in building ocean-going floating dry docks. He pressed for a public hearing into the Pearl Harbor disaster but although he gave his testimony it was not the exoneration he hoped for.

King, Ernest J. (1878–1956). A brilliant officer of broad experience in all branches of the service, King held the unique appointment of Commander in Chief US Fleet and Chief of Naval Operations throughout the war.

On his appointment he allegedly commented, 'When they get into trouble, they send for us sons of bitches'. Although America was politically committed to a 'Germany first' strategy, King argued long, hard and often tactlessly for an offensive strategy in the Pacific. He believed that the US economy was more than capable of supporting a European campaign and a campaign in the Pacific – a belief that was eventually proved correct. He did not neglect the European theatre: on the contrary, he was a strong supporter and advocate for a landing in France. He did believe that in the Pacific it was best for America to seize the offensive immediately. King favoured a thrust up through the Gilbert, Marshall and Marianas chains, but when it proved impossible to appoint a single American commander in the Pacific he approved the development of a two-track campaign which strained Japanese resources to their utmost and probably hastened the end of the war. The sole criticism of King's conduct of operations was his failure to introduce a convoy system on the US East Coast in the first months of 1942 (*see* Happy Time). King's relationship with the Combined Chiefs of Staff was inevitably turbulent. He argued with just about everyone in defence of his conduct of operations. However, he showed a strong grasp of strategic principles – perhaps the most thorough of any of America's wartime leaders. For this he was widely admired and respected, though few claimed to like him. He was promoted to Fleet Admiral in December 1944. When he relinquished his appointments in December 1945 he had turned the United States Navy into the largest, most lavishly endowed and most competent force ever assembled. He remains America's greatest naval officer.

Kinkaid, Thomas Cassin (1888-1972). American admiral who was MacArthur's naval commander in the SW Pacific Front. His was no easy position. The brilliant MacArthur was not easy to work for, while on the other hand Kinkaid had to persuade an often hostile US Navy to release the naval forces he needed for the prosecution of MacArthur's campaigns.

Kirk, Alan G. (1888-1963). Senior US Navy commander in European waters during the Second World War. Prior to that he had been Director of the Office of Naval Intelligence and Naval Attaché in London. He oversaw the American landings in Sicily and Normandy and then all river crossing operations in north-west Europe. At Normandy his decision to launch landing craft as much as eleven miles off the coast was much criticised. He retired from the US Navy in 1946 but continued to serve his country in a number of diplomatic appointments.

Knox, W. Franklin (1874-1944). An officer with a reserve commission in the US Army, Knox served as Roosevelt's Secretary of the Navy from 1940 and thus oversaw the massive US Navy expansion during the Second World War. He died suddenly in April 1944.

Koga, Mineichi (1885-1944). Japanese naval officer who assumed command of the Combined Fleet after Yamamoto's death in April 1943. A cautious and conservative commander, he realised and was not afraid to inform others that US victories at Midway and in the Solomons had to all intents and purposes destroyed the Combined Fleet. He sought to establish 'unsinkable aircraft carriers' on island bases but was continually frustrated by supply difficulties, while the activities of American submarines and US code-breakers allowed US forces to remain one step ahead. He was killed in a plane crash.

Kolchak, Alexander Vasilievich (1875-1920). Russian admiral and monarchist. During the First World War he commanded the Black Sea Fleet, and following the Revolution he assumed a leading role in the White monarchist movement. In November 1918 he was named as the 'Supreme Ruler' of Russia. However, he resigned in January 1920 in the face of a disintegrating military situation. Shortly afterwards he was captured by the Bolsheviks and executed.

Kondouriotis, Paul. Successful commander of the Greek Navy during the 1912-13 Balkan War.

Kretschmer, Otto (1912-). German U-boat commander who

sank forty-four ships totalling 266,629 tons during the Second World War while in command of *U23* and *U99*. Captured on 17 March 1941, Kretschmer proved as much of a handful to the Allies as a prisoner of war as he did at sea. After the war he entered the West German Navy, retiring as a Rear-Admiral.

Kuznetsov, N. G. (1904–1974). Soviet wartime commander of the Navy and architect of Stalin's post-war naval expansion plans. He had first met Stalin in 1932 and became Commander-in-Chief in 1939 having survived the purges. In 1947 he was relieved and charged with treason – he had approved the transfer of a captured German acoustic torpedo to the British. The case was dismissed, but he was demoted and exiled to the Pacific Fleet. In 1950 he was appointed Commander-in-Chief (for a second time) and advised Stalin on the expansion of the Fleet. His relations with Stalin's successors were turbulent and he was sacked by Khrushchev in 1955. His was a remarkable record of survival and he was lucky to die in his bed.

Land, Emory S. (1879–1971). American admiral who was Chairman of the US Maritime Commission during the Second World War charged with overseeing the massive escort carrier, destroyer escort and landing craft construction programmes. His efforts created the largest merchant fleet in history.

Langsdorff, Hans. Commanding Officer of the *Admiral Graf Spee*. After the Battle of the River Plate and the subsequent scuttling of his ship, he took his own life, wrapped in his ship's ensign, on 19 December 1939.

Lapayrere, Boue de. The French Commander-in-Chief in the Mediterranean during the First World War. A competent officer, he fell victim to political intrigue.

Above: Captain Landsdorff with some of his crew at Montevideo.

Above: Admiral Boue de Lapayrere. (IWM Q 19211)

Laurence, Noel. British submarine commander who on 5 November 1916 torpedoed two battleships, the German *Grosser Kurfürst* and *Kronprinz*, with the same salvo – a feat which has never been equalled.

Layton, Edwin T. (1903–1984). Head of US Navy Intelligence in the Pacific during the Second World War and directly responsible for the use of intelligence gleaned from decoded Japanese signals. Nimitz had such a high regard for him that he commanded Layton be present on the *Missouri* to witness the Japanese surrender.

Leahy, William D. (1875–1959). American admiral who was in retirement on the outbreak of the Second World War but was recalled to serve first as US Ambassador to Vichy and from June 1942 as Roosevelt's chief of staff and *de facto* chairman of the Joint Chiefs of Staff. He demonstrated great tact and 'behind the scenes' skill at dealing with strong-minded and argumentative colleagues and won the respect of both his own side and the British. He was one of seven officers to be awarded five-star rank in December 1944. He served under Truman for another four years before retiring for a second time.

Lee, Willis A. (1888–1945). American admiral who spent virtually his entire service career in battleships. He commanded US forces at the second Battle of Guadalcanal, where his ships sank the Japanese battleship *Kirishima* on the night of 14/15 November 1942. Though he never fought the battleship fight with the Japanese that he hoped for, his ships provided essential fire support for shore bombardments and fast carrier operations. Lee died on 25 August 1945 while in the US advising on anti-*Kamikaze* techniques.

Linton, John 'Tubby' (1905–1943). British naval officer who commanded the submarine *Turbulent* in the Mediterranean during the Second World War. He did not sink a massive amount of Axis shipping, but was posthumously awarded the Victoria Cross for his 'constant activity and skill, and his daring which never failed him when there was an enemy to be attacked'. He and his submarine disappeared, cause unknown, in March 1943.

Lockwood, Charles A. Commanded the US Navy's submarine force in the Pacific throughout the Second World War. Though not as flamboyant as some of the carrier commanders, Lockwood was familiar with every aspect of his command and inspired those who served under him.

Luckner, Felix *Graf* von. Commanding officer of the German commerce raider *Seeadler* during the First World War. Thanks to the sympathetic reporting of an American correspondent, Lowell Thomas, Luckner became one of the best known if not most popular German naval officers of the war.

Lüth, Wolfgang (1913–1945). German captain who was the first member of the U-boat service to be awarded the Oak Leaves, Diamonds and Swords to the Knight's Cross of the Iron Cross for his operations in command of *U181*, a U-boat in which he made a record-breaking 220-day patrol in the Indian Ocean. At the end of the war he commanded the naval school in Flensburg which became home to the Dönitz government, and it was while returning to his accommodation on the evening of 14 May 1945 that he was accidentally shot and killed by a sentry. Lüth was author of a set of notes on leadership which, though rather paternalistic and not quite to the Anglo-Saxon taste, are still quoted in contemporary naval circles.

Lutjens, Günther (1889–1941). German admiral and successful (by *Kriegsmarine* standards) fleet commander. In April 1940 he led *Scharnhorst* and *Gneisenau* in support of the German landings at Narvik and sank the British aircraft carrier *Glorious*. In February 1941 he took *Scharnhorst* and *Gneisenau* out into the Atlantic in Operation 'Berlin', a commerce raiding foray against British convoys, and returned successfully, having sunk 116,000 tons of Allied shipping. By this stage Lutjens was probably exhausted and should have been rested but he was named as Fleet Commander to take the new battleship *Bismarck* out into the Atlantic. His conduct during this vessel's brief sortie revealed sev-

Above: Admiral Günther Lutjens. (IWM A 14897)

eral errors of judgement. His continued employment was a sign that the *Kriegsmarine* lacked young and vigorous tactical commanders. He did not survive the sinking of *Bismarck*.

Macintyre, Donald (1904–1981). British naval officer who while in command of HMS *Walker* and *Hesperus* during the Second World War sank five U-boats, including *U99* commanded by Otto

Kretschmer. After the war he wrote the best-selling *U-Boat Killer* and a number of other works of popular naval history.

Mackenzie, Hugh 'Rufus' (1913–1996). British submarine commander – of HMS *Thrasher* in the Mediterranean during the Second World War – who subsequently became Britain's first Chief Polaris Executive, responsible for the procurement, construction, commissioning and deployment of the Royal Navy's nuclear deterrent within strict time and budgetary constraints (which were met).

McCain, John S. (1884–1945). American naval aviator known as 'Slew' or 'Popeye' on account of his appearance. He made a significant contribution to the expansion of the US Navy's carrier forces and their shoreside support while holding appointments in Washington before becoming commander of the Fast Carrier Task Force in July 1944, a post in which he alternated command with Mitscher. He was fearless, aggressive, profane, and hotheaded. He died just after the end of the war from strain brought about by overwork.

McCampbell, David (1910–). US Navy's top scoring fighter pilot, credited with thirty-four Japanese aircraft destroyed. He was awarded the Medal of Honor for air operations during the June 1944 Marianas 'Turkey Shoot'. In a single sortie on 24 October 1944 he shot down nine Japanese aircraft plus two 'probables' – a feat unequalled by any other American pilot in any

war. A feature of McCampbell's attitude was that if there was any doubt (as there often was) between him and his wingman as to who had actually downed an enemy aircraft, he would often insist that credit go to his wingman rather than to himself.

McClusky, Clarence Wade (1902–1976). US Navy pilot who as the commanding officer of VF-6 flying from USS *Enterprise* attacked the Japanese carrier group during the Battle of Midway.

McVay, Charles B. Commanding officer of the American cruiser *Indianapolis*. After the war he stood court martial for the loss of his ship on charges of negligence in that he had not been zig-zagging in an area where Japanese submarines were known to be operating. He was found guilty but was restored to duty without punishment. The chief witness for the prosecution was Lt-Cdr Mochitsura Hashimoto IJN, commanding officer of the submarine *I-58* which had sunk his ship.

Mahan, Alfred Thayer (1840–1914). American admiral, naval historian and theorist. He was the Clausewitz of naval strategy and advocated nothing less than 'command of the sea' by the 'preponderating fleet' as the proper object of naval power; commerce-raiding, coast defence and the idea of the 'fleet in being' he rejected as fruitless and wasteful. His ideas, backed by impressive scholarship, had significant effects on naval policy in Britain, Germany and the United States.

Martin, William. 'The Man Who Never Was'. Major William Martin RM was the creation of Ian Fleming for use in Operation 'Mincemeat'. His role in the operation was relatively brief and afterwards he was given a proper burial in the cemetery at Huelva, where his grave can be found today. His true identity has never been disclosed.

Meurer, Hugo (1869–1943). German admiral of no particular distinction but who in November 1918 had the humiliating task of negotiating the terms of internment for the High Seas Fleet.

Michelsen, Andreas (1869–1932). German naval officer who headed the U-boat fleet at the end of the First World War.

Mitscher, Marc A. (1887–1947). American admiral and naval aviator. Mitscher's record of success in carrier operations is without equal: it was from his *Hornet* that the Doolittle Raid bombers took off and he later commanded the Fast Carrier Task Force of the US Navy in the Pacific and participated in the fighting at Truk, the Philippine Sea, Leyte Gulf, Iwo Jima and Okinawa. His thorough understanding of naval aviation and his relaxed attitude to naval regulations won him the affection of his crews. Like so many commanders, he worked himself to death in his country's service and died of a heart attack.

Montecuccoli, Rudolf. Austrian admiral who oversaw the Austrian dreadnought construction programme before the First World War. Faced with a recalcitrant legislature, reluctant to authorise funds for the programme, Montecuccoli took matters into his own hands. He persuaded the industry to start work on the ships without the promise of official funding and then took a 32 million Crown credit on his own responsibility in order to finance construction.

Morillot, Roland. French naval officer and commanding officer of the submarine *Monge*, rammed and sunk by the Austrian cruiser *Helgoland* on 28 December 1915. Morillot went down with his boat in order to make sure that she did not fall into enemy hands. His name has subsequently been given to three French submarines.

Morison, Samuel Eliot (1887–1976). Naval historian and Turnbull Professor of History at Harvard. On the outbreak of the Second World War he was asked to obtain first-hand experience of naval operations in order to write an operational history of the US Navy at war. The result was his fifteen-volume *History of US Naval Operations in World War II*. An extremely popular and useful work, it suffers from an excess of style in some areas and was written with no knowledge of Allied code-breaking activities.

Mountbatten, Louis Francis Albert Victor Nicholas (1900–1979). British naval officer of royal birth (his father was Prince Louis of Battenberg and his godparents were the Tsar of Russia and Queen of England) whose name was anglicised to Mountbatten in 1917. It must be said that he had little talent as a naval officer or seaman but combined influence and wealth to rise to high command. Political influence won him a spectacular promotion from destroyer commander to director of Combined Operations and then to Supreme Allied Commander South-East Asia. After the war he went still further and was the last Viceroy of India, overseeing the handover of power before returning to the Navy. In 1955 he was appointed First Sea Lord and later became the second holder of the post of Chief of the Defence Staff. It must be said that he had a lively and creative intelligence and sought out unconventional and indirect solutions to problems. As a naval leader Mountbatten has hardly any significance at all: he was no better and probably a good deal worse than the average British destroyer captain in the Second World War. However, as a Supreme Commander, and as Chief of the Defence Staff, he excelled. He was killed by an IRA bomb in 1979.

Müller, Karl von. Commanding officer of the German light cruiser *Emden* who won a reputation for decency and humanity while waging a relentless campaign against shipping in the Indian Ocean during the First World War.

Nagumo, Chiuchi (1887–1944). Japanese admiral who commanded the carrier force which struck at Pearl Harbor and then ventured into the Indian Ocean, attacking Ceylon. Astonishingly, Nagumo, a torpedo specialist, had been given this plum appointment because he was the senior Vice-Admiral on the IJN's active list who was without an appointment at the time. After the Pearl Harbor attack he was criticised for not sending in the second wave of aircraft to attack dockyard installations and the oil depot. Nevertheless, between December 1941 and April 1942 the carriers under Nagumo's command sank more ships and supported the occupation of more territory than any other naval force in history. His fortunes waned with those of his aircraft carriers. He lost four carriers at Midway and after his irresolute conduct at Santa Cruz in October 1943 he was relieved by Vice-Admiral Ozawa and sent to command the Japanese Central Fleet, a headquarters structure with no ships attached, on the island of Saipan. His 6,800 men were among those defeated when the Americans invaded the island in June 1944. On 6 July 1944, when it was clear that all was lost, he committed suicide. Had it not been for the disaster at Midway Nagumo might have been remembered as one of the great naval commanders of all time.

Nasmith, Eric Dunbar. British submarine commander awarded the Victoria Cross for operations in the Sea of Marmara while in command of the submarine *E.11*. A hard-nosed individual, he summarily sentenced his telegraphist to death while on patrol for failing to keep the aerial operational (though the sentence was not applied).

Niemöller, Martin (1892–1984). German U-boat commander of the First World War who subsequently became a Lutheran minister. His opposition to the Nazi regime was conducted with the same vigour with which he had attacked British shipping and he spent eight years in various concentration camps before he was liberated at Dachau in April 1945.

Nimitz, Chester W. (1885–1966). Nimitz commanded the vast US Navy effort in the Pacific during the Second World War with great confidence and ability but little self-promotion. He was an officer of broad experience – he had served in submarines and naval aviation – and was chosen to take command of the Pacific after the relief of Admiral Kummel following Pearl Harbor. Nimitz held the dual post of CinC Pacific Ocean Areas (CinCPOA), responsible for the planning and execution of the advance on Japan through the Gilberts, Marshalls and Marianas, and CinC US Pacific Fleet and thus responsible for providing forces for General MacArthur's South-West Pacific Front. This dual appointment meant that he had to work with the two most powerful personalities on his own side, General MacArthur and Admiral King. Nimitz disposed immense resources: carrier task groups, Marine Corps divisions, amphibious assault groups and a vast logistic tail. From June 1944 onwards he maintained a high tempo of operations by having

Above: Admiral Chester W. Nimitz. (IWM OEM 1979)

two fleet commanders (Halsey and Spruance) who alternated planning the next operation and carrying out the one in hand. Nimitz was known for his self-

control, for his patience and as a keen judge of his subordinates. Many such received a second chance and most did not fail their commander in the trust he placed in them. He was also skilled in his use of intelligence gained from intercepted Japanese radio traffic. His greatest accomplishment was his ability to maintain the broad thrust of his strategic plan while being flexible enough to modify it to suit particular local circumstances. He sped up the timetable for the capture of the Marianas in 1944, supported Halsey in his decision to land earlier than planned on Leyte and abandoned his plan to land on Formosa in favour of offering full support to General MacArthur on the Philippines. In November 1945 he relinquished the Pacific command and then served as Chief of Naval Operations.

Noble, Percy. British admiral who was the first Commander-in-Chief Western Approaches, a command instituted to control the Atlantic convoys. He did sterling work in this appointment before moving to Washington to head the British Naval Mission, and his achievement has been overshadowed by that of Horton, his more ebullient successor.

O'Hare, Edward H. (1914–1943). The US Navy's first fighter ace of the Second World War who was awarded the Medal of Honor for shooting down five G4M1 'Betty' bombers in as many minutes off Bougainville on 20 February 1942. On 26 November 1943 he was killed by 'friendly fire' from a TBF Avenger.

O'Kane, Richard H. (1911–1995). US Navy submarine commander who while in command of USS *Tang* sank twenty-four Japanese ships totalling 93,824 tons. On his last patrol *Tang* was sunk on the night of 24/25 October 1944 by a Mk XVIII electric torpedo which circled back on its track and hit the submarine. O'Kane survived ten months of Japanese captivity and was awarded the Medal of Honor at the end of the war. He retired in 1957.

Onishi, Takajiro (1891–1945). Japanese admiral who was one of the planners of the attack on Pearl Harbor and who later translated the Japanese concept of suicide into a deliberate policy – the *Kamikaze*s. A brilliant and meticulous planner, he had an arrogant and abusive manner which denied him appointments where his talents could be fully exploited. It was only in May 1945, with defeat staring Japan in the face, that he was appointed Vice-Chief of the Naval Staff. He opposed the Japanese surrender and took his own life on August 16 1945.

Paolucci, Raffaele. *See* Rosetti.

Paparrigopoulos. Greek commanding officer of the submarine *Delfin* who made the first submarine torpedo attack in history on 9 December 1913 against the Turkish cruiser *Medjidieh*. Though the torpedo failed to run, Paparrigopoulos' place in history is secure.

Pohl, Hugo von (1855–1916). German admiral who succeeded Ingenohl as Commander-in-Chief of the High Seas Fleet. He fared no better than his predecessor in this appointment and resigned, due to ill-health, on 24 January 1916.

Pollen, Arthur (1866–1937). British inventor who designed a system of fire control which he urged the Royal Navy to adopt but which was rejected in favour of the (inferior) Dreyer system. He subsequently wrote a number of extremely partisan books and articles on naval warfare.

Pound, Dudley (1877–1943). Professional head of the Royal Navy for the first four years of the war and architect of victory in the Atlantic and Mediterranean. Pound was a torpedo specialist who had commanded a battleship at Jutland and whose career alternated between command at sea and staff appointments until in June 1939 he became First Sea Lord and Chief of the Naval Staff. As such Pound was unique among all naval commanders in that not only was he the professional head of his service, but he was also an operational commander. Thus he bore a heavy burden at an age when most men would be thinking of retirement. He was a hard worker and possessed a physical and mental fortitude that stood him in good stead throughout the dark days of the war. He never shirked responsibility and was never dismayed by defeat. His relations with Churchill were by no means as one-sided as they have been portrayed: his view more than usually prevailed in their discussions. Though often seen as remote and aloof, he was capable of gestures that showed he was a kindly man. He died on Trafalgar Day, 21 October 1943. Pound's faults have been well chronicled elsewhere but his achievement has received scant attention. On his death in 1943 the Royal Navy stood on the threshold of victory. The U-boats had been mastered, though not totally defeated, in the Atlantic while the Mediterranean was secure. The victory in the Atlantic owed much to a number of vital factors on which Pound insisted: proper training for escorts and thus resisting the temptation to commit new ships and untrained crews to the battle before they were ready; the bringing of RAF Coastal Command under Admiralty control so that convoys had the maximum air cover (for this he waged a bitter battle with the Air Staff); and the encouragement of research and the development of new weapons. In the Mediterranean the surrender of the Italian Fleet effectively ended hostilities in that theatre. Pound's decision that Malta should be held meant that the island became an important base from which ships, submarines and aircraft sallied forth to attack Axis convoys, compromising the German ability to conduct a land campaign in North Africa. In the Far East, despite early reverses, a new fleet was forming which would eventually take the war to the shores of Japan. It was no mean legacy.

Prien, Günther. German U-boat commander whose outstanding success was the sinking of the battleship HMS *Royal Oak* on 14 October 1939. He sank twenty-eight ships totalling 164,953 tons while in command of *U47* and was lost, cause unknown, in March 1941.

Raborn, William F. US naval officer who oversaw the development, construction and commissioning of the US Navy's Polaris missile

Above: U-boat Captain Prien after sinking HMS *Royal Oak,* shaking hands with Admiral Raeder. (IWM HU 2226)

Above: Admiral Erich Raeder. (IWM A 14906)

Ramage, Lawson P. (1909–). US submarine commander who was awarded the Medal of Honor for an attack on a Japanese convoy in July 1944 while in command of the USS *Parche* in which two ships were sunk and a third damaged.

Ramsay, Bertram Home (1883–1945). British admiral who, to all intents and purposes, had abruptly terminated his career by resigning in 1938. Recalled in 1940, he was in charge of the naval evacuation at Dunkirk and from April 1942 onwards planned the naval side of every major Allied amphibious operation, culminating in the invasion of Normandy in June 1944. He was killed in an air crash in January 1945. He was the Royal Navy's supreme practitioner of amphibious warfare during the Second World War.

Reuter, Ludwig von (1862–1943). German Commander-in-Chief of the High Seas Fleet who authorised the scuttling of the Fleet at Scapa Flow on 21 June 1919.

Richardson, James O. (1878–1974). US admiral dismissed by President Roosevelt in February 1941 for his opposition to basing the US Fleet at Pearl Harbor. Richardson argued that the repair facilities at Pearl Harbor were inadequate, that there was insufficient fuel and that the Fleet was dangerously exposed to a surprise attack. He further protested at the deployment into the Atlantic of ships from his command and in February 1941 was dismissed and replaced by Admiral Husband E. Kimmel.

system. Although he was not a technician he was selected for the role because of his leadership and management skills.

Raeder, Erich (1876–1960). German admiral who was Commander-in-Chief of the German Navy from 1928 to 1943. As such he tried to build up a large surface fleet, but the declaration of war in September 1939 ruined his plans. He never enjoyed Hitler's confidence and after the Barents Sea fiasco was replaced by Dönitz in January 1943. He was arraigned on war crimes charges at Nuremberg and sentenced to life imprisonment but was released in 1955 on grounds of ill-health.

fast motor boats armed with torpedoes. On 10 December 1917 he torpedoed and sank the old Austrian battleship *Wien* at Trieste and on 10 June 1918 he torpedoed the Austrian dreadnought *Szent István*.

Rochefort, Joseph I. (1899–1976). US Navy cryptanalyst who played a vital role in the decoding of Japanese signal traffic prior to the Battles of Coral Sea and Midway. However, disputes between intelligence staffs at Washington and Pearl Harbor resulted in Rochefort being sidelined, and he was appointed in command of a non-propelled floating dock. His work was denied any official recognition until 1986, when President Reagan presented his family with the Distinguished Service Medal.

Rosetti, Raffaele. Italian pioneer of human torpedo operations. He played an important part in the development of the *Mignatta* and participated in the operation which resulted in the sinking of the Austrian battleship *Viribus Unitis* on the night of 31 October/ 1 November 1918.

Ruge, Friedrich (1894–1961). German naval officer and historian who after service in torpedo boats during the First World War specialised in mine warfare. From 1943 he was Rommel's naval adviser charged with protecting the coast of France against Allied invasion. After a brief incarceration as a PoW Ruge wrote a number of studies for the US Navy before becoming the first head of

Above: Admiral Bertram Home Ramsey. (IWM A 23438)

Rickover, Hyman G. American naval officer who controlled the US Navy's nuclear propulsion programme (and much else) from 1948 until 1981. His unique command style won him few friends and he relished provoking the conservative naval establishment. His achievement needs no advertisement, bringing nuclear power to the US

Navy's carriers, surface ships and submarines with safety standards of exceptional rigour. There can be few men who have done so much for their country and who have received so little by way of recognition.

Rizzo, Luigi. Italian naval officer who was a pioneer in the use of

the *Bundesmarine.* He retired in 1961 and became a prolific writer and lecturer.

Sakaibara, Shigematsu. Japanese naval commander on Wake Island who ordered the execution of ninety-eight US civilians on the grounds that they had been in communication with the enemy. On his surrender in September 1945 Sakaibara was tried for war crimes and found guilty. He was hanged on the island of Guam on 18 June 1947.

Sakamaki, Kazuo. Japanese *Ko-Hyoteki* commander who participated in the midget submarine attack on Pearl Harbor on 7 December 1941 and was the only one to survive. Sakamaki was washed ashore near Kanoehe naval air station after he and his crewman, Petty Officer Kiyoshi Inagaki, abandoned their craft after a series of technical problems and thus became America's first prisoner of war in the Second World War. He was refused, despite repeated requests, permission to end his own life honourably. When news of his capture reached Japan, his face was removed from commemorative postcards showing the ten officers and men who had died in the midget submarine attack on Pearl Harbor.

Sauro, Nazario. Italian naval officer captured when the submarine *Giacinto Pullino* grounded in July 1916. Sauro was a native of Trieste and therefore an Austrian subject. He was tried by court martial, where his alias of Niccolo

Above: Nazario Sauro. (Kriegsarchiv, Vienna)

Sambo collapsed when his mother was brought into court. He was hanged on 10 August 1916 and was Italy's first naval hero of the First World War.

Scheer, Reinhard Karl (1863–1929). German commander of the High Seas Fleet during the First World War. He advocated an offensive strategy, seeking to draw out units of the Grand Fleet and destroy them piecemeal. However after Jutland, where he successfully extricated his fleet from annihilation, he realised that the key to a German victory at sea lay in the U-boat and he became a firm advocate of unrestricted submarine warfare. In August 1918 he

Above: Admiral Reinhard Karl Scheer. (IWM Q 20348)

the First World War. He was responsible for the German defence of Zeebrugge and Ostend against British landing operations in 1918.

Schwieger, Walther. German U-boat commander who incurred international opprobrium for the sinking of the liner *Lusitania* on 7 May 1915. He was killed on 5 September 1917 when his submarine, *U88*, was mined off the Horns Reef.

Sherman, Frederick 'Fightin' Freddie'. American naval aviator who succeeded Mitscher in command of the Fast Carrier Task Force in the Pacific. He was an extrovert character and a superb tactician.

Sims, William Sowden (1858–1936). American admiral who commanded US Navy forces in Europe during the First World War. He did not share the anglophobe tendencies of Benson and was respected and trusted by his British colleagues.

Somerville, James Fownes (1882–1949). British commander of Force H who operated with distinction in the western Mediterranean and eastern Atlantic. He subsequently commanded the Eastern Fleet. He was one of the most active and successful of British naval commanders of the Second World War.

Souchon, Wilhelm (1864–1933). German admiral and commander of the German squadron in the Mediterranean on the outbreak of

was promoted to command the naval staff and organised a wholesale mobilisation of labour and shipbuilding assets to build as many U-boats as possible.

Schepke, Joachim. A German U-boat ace, who commanded *U3*, *U19* and *U100*. He sank 39 ships totalling 159,130 tons. He was lost when *U100* was depth charged and rammed by destroyers HMS *Vanoc* and HMS *Walker*, northwest of the Hebrides in March 1941.

Schroder, Ludwig von (1854–1933). German admiral and commander of the coast defence forces on the Belgian coast during

Above: Admiral James Fownes Somerville (see previous page). (IWM A 23479)

the First World War. His decision to take his two ships, the battle-cruiser *Goeben* and cruiser *Breslau*, to Turkey had a major influence on that country entering the war on the German side. He was subsequently appointed CinC of the Turkish Navy.

Spee, Maximilien Graf von (1861-1914). Commanded the German East Asia Squadron and won a notable victory at Coronel. However, he was killed and his squadron was destroyed at the Battle of the Falkland Islands.

Spruance, Raymond A. (1886–1969). Spruance was unusual among great commanders in that he was an exceptionally private man. His reticence concealed a powerful intellect which was recognised within the US Navy although his name was barely known outside that service. A gunnery specialist and a believer in the battleship as the final arbiter of naval power, Spruance commanded, as a Rear-Admiral, under Halsey in the opening days of the Second World War. When Halsey was stricken with severe dermatitis in May 1942 he chose Spruance to replace him in command of the Pacific Fleet's aircraft carriers. Nimitz concurred even though Spruance was a non-aviator. Spruance was not found wanting in his new appointment. Even though he had a reputation for cautious and meticulous planning, he did not hesitate to launch his aircraft against the Japanese carriers at the Battle of Midway in June 1942. The resulting action saw four of Japan's aircraft carriers

sunk and their irreplaceable air groups decimated. Victory did not go to his head for he prudently withdrew his carriers before night-fall, thus avoiding a potentially disastrous night engagement with the superior, and intact, Japanese surface fleet. After Midway Spruance served as Nimitz's chief of staff until August 1943, when he assumed command of the Fifth Fleet. His first operations were the seizure of the Gilbert Islands in November 1943 followed by the taking of Kwajalein and Eniwetok in the Marshall Islands in February 1944. It was then decided that Spruance – by now promoted to full Admiral – go to sea in order that one admiral and his staff would be planning the next operation while the other was at sea. Spruance's decisions during the June 1944 invasion of the Marianas and the subsequent Battle of the Philippine Sea have aroused much debate among naval officers and historians. Critics accuse him of losing opportunities to destroy the Japanese Mobile Fleet by tying his carriers too closely to supporting the landing force. His adherents point to the Japanese habit of dividing their forces in order to confuse the opposition, making the focal point for a strike harder to identify, and the reluctance of his battleship commander to risk a night action with the Japanese fleet. Above all, the results of Spruance's decision speak for themselves – 400 Japanese aircraft shot down and three carriers sunk. Although he was cautious, Spruance's tactics are defensible in that he successfully covered the landings while

inflicting a significant defeat on Japanese air power. After the Marianas Spruance turned over to Halsey but resumed command in January 1945 to command operations for the capture of Iwo Jima and Okinawa. At the latter he was criticised for complaining about the slowness of the Army and Marine forces ashore, but his complaints were properly motivated by the fact that his fleet was taking a real beating from Japanese *Kamikaze*s. In May 1945 he turned over to Halsey and returned to Pearl Harbor to plan for the invasion of Japan, but this was cancelled by the Japanese capitulation in August 1945. He succeeded Nimitz as Commander-in-Chief Pacific and retired in 1948. Although both Spruance and Halsey were considered for promotion to five-star rank in late 1944, the award was given to Halsey who was senior to Spruance. However, the latter did receive special compensation and benefits from a grateful Congress. Spruance is remembered as a meticulous planner whose operations had an uncanny habit of turning out exactly as he had foreseen them. Although he lacked many of the characteristics which made some commanders, like Halsey, a house-hold name, he must be remembered for being skilful, coolly competent and highly successful.

Stark, Harold R. (1880-1972). American admiral who was Chief of Naval Operations from August 1939 to March 1942 and who was responsible for recommending and commencing the dramatic expansion of the US Navy to meet the threat of war and also for recommending the 'Germany first' strategy to Roosevelt (a strategy which was ultimately adopted). From March 1942 to August 1945 he served as Commander US Naval Forces in Europe.

Sturdee, Frederick Charles Doveton (1859-1925). British admiral who destroyed von Spee's squadron at the Battle of the Falkland Islands. A brilliantly intelligent officer, he did not suffer fools gladly but was able to get the best out of those working for him.

Sullivan brothers, The. The five Sullivan brothers, George, Francis, Joseph, Madison and Albert, were born between 1914 and 1920. All five served in the cruiser *Juneau* which was sunk by the Japanese submarine *I-26* on the night of 12/13 November 1942 off Guadalcanal. All were killed, and US Navy regulations were subsequently changed to prevent close relatives serving in the same ship. In memory of the brothers, a destroyer was named *The Sullivans* and launched on 4 April 1943.

Takagi, Takeo (1892-1944). Japanese commander of the carrier force in the Battle of the Coral Sea.

Tennant, William (1890-1963). British naval officer who directed the evacuation of British and French troops from the beaches at Dunkirk in 1940 and commanded the battlecruiser HMS *Repulse* when she was sunk on 10 December 1941. He subsequently commanded a cruiser squadron and directed the construction and deployment of the Mulberry harbours for the invasion of Normandy.

Tirpitz, Alfred von (1849-1930). One of the earliest entrants to the Prussian Navy, Tirpitz transformed it from a coast defence force into a 'blue water' fleet, presenting a challenge to the Royal Navy. A keen student of Mahan, he was appointed Naval Secretary in 1898 and he successfully harnessed royal patronage to secure political support and funding for ships and shore facilities. However, during the First World War he failed to persuade the *Kaiser* to use the fleet more offensively and he resigned in 1916.

Above: Admiral Frederick Charles Doveton Sturdee. (IWM Q 18063)

Togo, Heichahiro (1849–1934). Joined the Imperial Japanese Navy in 1863 and studied in England between 1871 and 1878. During the Russo-Japanese War his ships annihilated the Russian Fleet at the Battle of Tsushima.

Topp, Erich (1916–). German U-boat commander who sank thirty-four ships totalling 193,684 tons while in command of *U57* and *U552*, making him the third-ranking U-boat commander in terms of tonnage sunk. After the war Topp enjoyed careers as a fisherman and an architect before re-entering the German Navy. He retired in 1969 as a Vice-Admiral. His memoirs, *The Odyssey of a U-Boat Commander*, are the frankest written by any German combatant and deal with the dilemma of how German servicemen who fought bravely and correctly for their country place their deeds in the overall context of the Nazi period.

Tovey, John Cronyn (1885–1971). British admiral who commanded the destroyer *Onslow* at the Battle of Jutland. From 1940 to 1943 he commanded the Home Fleet and was responsible in May 1941 for the pursuit and destruction of the German battleship *Bismarck*. He was a highly principled man, possessed of strong opinions, great optimism and a deep religious faith. He was not afraid to cross swords with anyone – even Churchill, with whom he enjoyed an ambivalent relationship.

Trapp, Georg von. Austrian U-boat commander in the First

Above: Admiral John Cronyn Tovey. (IWM A 14845)

World War. While in command of *UV* he sank the French cruiser *Léon Gambetta* on 27 April 1915 – a strategic victory, for it forced the French to withdraw their capital ships from the Adriatic. After the war he founded the Trapp Family Singers and emigrated to America.

Troubridge, Ernest Charles (1862–1926). British naval officer from a distinguished naval family who enjoyed a career before the First World War which promised much. However, his failure to bring the *Goeben* to book and the court martial which followed ruined him, even though he was acquitted. Described as a 'danger to the State', he was exiled to Serbia as Head of the British Naval Mission. He never held another naval appointment and died, a bitter and broken man, in exile.

Turner, Richmond Kelly (1885–1961). The premier US Navy amphibious commander of the Second World War. After a less than successful period as head of the Office of Naval Intelligence, he was dispatched to the Pacific in July 1942 as Commander Amphibious Forces. He oversaw the landings in the Solomons, Gilberts, Marshalls, Marianas, Iwo Jima and Okinawa.

Tyrwhitt, Reginald Yorke (1870–1951). The outstanding British naval officer of the First World War, throughout which he commanded the Harwich Force.

Valentiner, Max. German U-boat commander of the First World War

who sank 299,326 tons of shipping. After the war he became an instructor in submarine warfare for the Turkish Navy.

Vian, Philip. British destroyer commander who rose, by virtue of his offensive spirit, to command the carrier forces of the British Pacific Fleet at the end of the Second World War. He commanded the destroyer *Cossack* in the Norwegian campaign and led the destroyer attack on the *Bismarck*. He subsequently commanded a cruiser squadron in the Mediterranean, where he successfully defended a Malta-bound convoy from a superior Italian force in the Battle of Sirte, one of the great convoy battles of history. Vian was brave, intolerant and profane, but he was one of Britain's great fighting admirals of the Second World War.

Above: Vian with the Right Hon R. F. Casey, Minister of State for the Middle East, while the latter was visiting the British Eastern Mediterranean Fleet, Alexandria, 23 May 1942. (IWM A 10462)

Above: Captain F. J. Walker on board HMS *Starling*, with the 2nd Escort Group. The sloop HMS *Woodpecker* goes into attack and Captain Walker shouts encouragement to her through the loud hailer. (IWM A 21988)

Vinson, Carl (1883–1981). US Congressman who served from November 1914 until January 1965 and who became the principal supporter of the US Navy in Congress during the Second World War.

Visintini, Licio. Italian naval officer who was responsible for the conversion of the tanker *Olterra* (conveniently interned in Algeciras) into a covert base from where *Maiale* attacks could be launched on Gibraltar. He was killed in an attack on Gibraltar on 8 December 1942. His body was recovered from the harbour and he was buried at sea with full naval honours.

Walker, Frederick John (1896–1944). British naval officer whose peacetime career was, frankly, a failure but who was extremely successful as a U-boat hunter in the Second World War. Walker commanded the 36th Escort Group and the 2nd Escort Group, the latter accounting for fourteen U-boats while Walker was in command. He developed the 'creeping attack'.

Walther, Helmuth. German engineer and scientist who developed the closed-cycle propulsion system for submarines.

Wanklyn David (1911–1942). British submariner who commanded HMS *Upholder* in the Mediterranean in the Second World War. Despite a shaky start – at one time he was seriously considered for relief – Wanklyn sank two submarines, a destroyer and over 100,000 tons of Axis shipping and was awarded the Victoria Cross. His loss in April 1942 was

Above: Lieutenant Commander Wanklyn, VC, DSO, RN, with members of the cew of HMS *Upholder*. (IWM A 7274)

marked by the Admiralty by the issue of a special signal – something which has never been done before or since for a single vessel – which concluded: 'The ship and her company are gone but the example and the inspiration remain.'

Weddigen, Otto. German U-boat commander who achieved the remarkable feat of sinking the British cruisers *Aboukir*, *Hogue* and *Cresy* in the space of a single attack on 22 September 1914 while in command of *U9*. He was killed on 10 March 1915 when his submarine, *U29*, was rammed by the battleship *Dreadnought*. In his brief career Weddigen was dubbed the 'Polite Pirate' by the British

press for his courtesy towards the crews of the ships he sank.

Wilkinson, Theodore S. (1888–1946). Leading US amphibious forces commander in the Pacific. He directed amphibious landings in the Solomons and New Guinea before commencing the planning for the invasion of Japan.

Woodward, John 'Sandy' (1932–). British submariner who commanded the naval forces in the 1982 Falklands War. His appointment was received with some surprise since it was assumed by many that another, more senior flag officer with more experience of amphibious operations, would be selected. Seldom can a British

naval commander have set out to fight a war with so many restrictions on his conduct of operations. Woodward's ships were operating at the sharp end of an 8,000-mile supply line and with no friendly harbour with docking facilities within hundreds of miles. Another pressure was the coming of the austral winter. The war started in April 1982 but by June the winter would make operations impossible. These two factors imposed a tight timetable on Woodward: the war had to be over before the inevitable mechanical problems associated with prolonged periods of operations made themselves felt and before winter made operations impossible. A third factor was that the forces at Woodward's disposal were, literally, all that were available. If either of his two carriers or two assault ships were damaged, there were no replacements in the UK which could be dispatched south. These constraints were always appreciated by Woodward's fellow commanders and he was alternately accused of overconfidence and excessive caution. Despite these difficulties Woodward conducted the campaign with as much vigour as his meagre assets allowed. He showed his determination in the circumstances attending the sinking of the Argentine cruiser *General Belgrano*: it was his urgings that persuaded London to get off the fence and alter the Rules of Engagement so that the cruiser could be sunk.

Wright, Jerauld (1898–). American naval officer who participated in a number of clandestine operations to enlist the support of the French before the Allied landings in North Africa in November 1942. On one occasion he was even given nominal command of the British submarine *Seraph* in order to allay the anglophobe feelings of a particular French general.

Wulff, Olaff Richard (1877–1955). Austrian naval officer who commanded the *KuK Kriegsmarine*'s Danube Flotilla with considerable success during the First World War. In the confused political situation in central Europe following the dissolution of the Austrian Empire, Wulff managed to serve the almost royalist Hungarian government led by Karolyi, followed by the communist government led by Bela Kun and finally the ultra-nationalist regime of Admiral Horthy with the same equanimity and without being dismissed by any of them.

Only the close of the Second World War brought his appointment to an end and he died in exile in Costa Rica.

Yamamoto, Isoroku (1884–1943). Commander-in-Chief of the Japanese Fleet on the outbreak of the war and architect of their early successes. Yamamoto was an advocate of air power and worked tirelessly as commander of the Kasumigaura naval air base and as director of naval aviation to improve flying standards and doctrine. He was unusual among his contemporaries in that he was aware of America's industrial might and Japan's inability to match it. He had travelled widely, had been a language officer at Harvard and the Naval Attaché in Washington and had attended the 1936 Naval Conference as Japan's senior naval delegate. As such he supported naval disarmament, believing that Japan could not afford a naval race with the United States. He was acutely aware of Japan's economic weakness and how this would affect her ability to prosecute a war with America, and this attitude brought him into conflict with groups in the Army at a time when assassination was the principal means of determining Japanese policy. Consequently he was packed off to sea and safety as Commander-in-Chief of the Combined Fleet in August 1939. Throughout 1940, as relations between Japan and the US deteriorated, Yamamoto believed that war was inevitable and so planned to strike the first blow on the Americans by means of a carrier assault on the American base at Pearl Harbor. In doing so he aban-

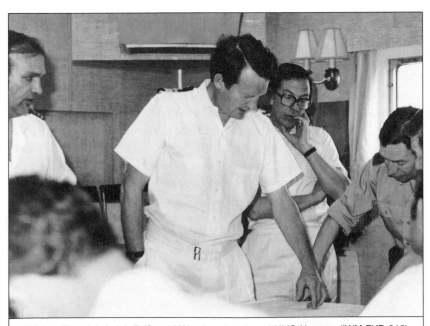

Above: Rear Admiral J. F. 'Sandy' Woodward on board HMS *Hermes*. (IWM FKD 212)

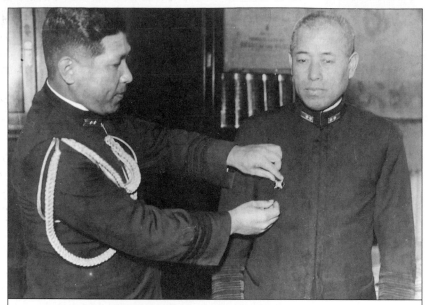

Above: Vice Admiral Yamamoto recieving the Medal for War Wounds, 2 October 1938. (IWM HU 31025)

doned the Japanese plan for a decisive engagement between the two fleets. The attack caused much damage but the American aircraft carriers and the huge oil stores at Pearl Harbor were unscathed because of the cautious handling of the operation by Vice-Admiral Chuichi Nagumo, the task force commander. Moreover, Yamamoto was dismayed that the attack had gone in before the formal declaration of war. He knew of nothing which would enrage the Americans more and said, 'I fear all we have done is to rouse a sleeping giant and fill it with a terrible resolve.' 'In the first six months I shall run wild,' said Yamamoto. He was right: in three days following Pearl Harbor the Japanese Navy seized control of seas and oceans equivalent to a quarter of the world's circumference. For his officers and men it was period of sublime exhilaration: for his opponents it was a terrifying prospect. Yet Yamamoto

still sought a decisive battle with the Americans which would complete the work done at Pearl Harbor. However the fact that his codes were being read by the Americans meant that he could never achieve the essential ingredient of surprise and his policy collapsed with the Japanese defeat at Midway in June 1942 in which the Japanese naval air arm was decimated. By January 1943 Yamamoto was enough of a realist to appreciate that Japan had shot its bolt and it was now time for retrenchment, and he advocated a strategic withdrawal from the Solomons to better defensive positions. It was while he was on a tour of forward bases that his aircraft was intercepted by USAAC P-38 Lightning fighters – the Americans having had advance warning of his route through intercepted radio signals – and shot down. He was killed when the plane crashed in the jungle. It is a tribute to his reputation that the

operation was the only occasion on which the Americans deliberately set out to kill an opposing commander. Yamamoto was a moderate who felt that war was not in the best interests of his country. Once war was inevitable, he did his job as well as any professional naval officer would have done. He was a fair man, fighting hard but cleanly, and while he lived the Imperial Navy was the same. He was not a genius and made mistakes. Once war was declared there was no going back, and, although under certain circumstances events might have taken a different course. Yamamoto had the dubious privilege of being proved a true prophet. Nevertheless his reputation as the first practitioner of carrier war is secure.

Yohai Bin-Nun. Israeli commander who sank the Egyptian warship *El Amir Farouk* off Gaza on 22 November 1948 using three surplus Italian one-man explosive motor boats.

Zumwalt, Elmo. Youngest CNO in the history of the US Navy. He was appointed at a time when the USN was grappling with the problem of maintaining the right combination of quality and quantity. Ruinously expensive ships such as the nuclear powered CGNs could only be built in small numbers. Zumwalt argued for a high/low mix to the US fleet with not all vessels built to the same level of capability. At the 'high' end of his spectrum were the *Spruance* and *Ticonderoga* classes while at the 'low' end were the *Oliver Hazard Perry* class frigates.